AF774943

The Corporate Forms of Antebellum US Literature

LAW AND LITERATURE

The Law and Literature series publishes work that connects legal ideas to literary and cultural history, texts, and artefacts. The series encompasses a wide range of historical periods, literary genres, legal fields and theories, and transnational subjects, focusing on interdisciplinary books that engage with legal and literary forms, methods, concepts, dispositions, and media. It seeks innovative studies of every kind, including but not limited to work that examines race, ethnicity, gender, national identity, criminal and civil law, legal institutions and actors, digital media, intellectual property, economic markets, and corporate power, while also foregrounding current interpretive methods in the humanities, using these methods as dynamic tools that are themselves subject to scrutiny.

Series Editors

Robert Spoo, Princeton University
Simon Stern, University of Toronto

The Corporate Forms of Antebellum US Literature

PETER JAROS

OXFORD
UNIVERSITY PRESS

OXFORD
UNIVERSITY PRESS

Great Clarendon Street, Oxford, OX2 6DP,
United Kingdom

Oxford University Press is a department of the University of Oxford.
It furthers the University's objective of excellence in research, scholarship,
and education by publishing worldwide. Oxford is a registered trade mark of
Oxford University Press in the UK and in certain other countries.

© Peter Jaros 2026

The moral rights of the author have been asserted.

All rights reserved. No part of this publication may be reproduced, stored in a retrieval system, transmitted, used for text and data mining, or used for training artificial intelligence, in any form or by any means, without the prior permission in writing of Oxford University Press, or as expressly permitted by law, by licence or under terms agreed with the appropriate reprographics rights organization. Enquiries concerning reproduction outside the scope of the above should be sent to the Rights Department, Oxford University Press, at the address above.

You must not circulate this work in any other form
and you must impose this same condition on any acquirer.

Links to third party websites are provided by Oxford in good faith and
for information only. Oxford disclaims any responsibility for the materials
contained in any third party website referenced in this work.

Published in the United States of America by Oxford University Press
546 Fifth Avenue, New York, NY 10036, United States of America

British Library Cataloguing in Publication Data
Data available

Library of Congress Control Number: 2025948348

ISBN 9780198996514

DOI: 10.1093/9780198996491.001.0001

Printed and bound by
CPI Group (UK) Ltd., Croydon, CR0 4YY

MIX
Paper | Supporting responsible forestry
FSC® C013604
FSC www.fsc.org

The manufacturer's authorized representative in the EU for product safety is
Oxford University Press España S.A. of Parque Empresarial San Fernando de Henares,
Avenida de Castilla, 2 – 28830 Madrid (www.oup.es/en or product.safety@oup.com).
OUP España S.A. also acts as importer into Spain of products made by the manufacturer.

Cover image: Edward W. Clay, On the Way to Araby! (Detail). New York: H.R. Robinson,
48 Courtlandt Street, C [signed on stone, E.W. Clay], 1836. Courtesy, American Antiquarian Society.

For Brenna, Aurie, and Theo

Acknowledgments

Writing this book has taken me well over a decade, and the shape it has taken owes a great deal to the assembled company of people and organizations who have helped me along the way. I offer my thanks to this wide-ranging collective, with apologies to those I have neglected to name here, for their insight, encouragement, and support.

This book did not grow from my dissertation, but I trace its earliest seeds back to conversations with Julia Stern toward the end of my studies at Northwestern University as I was wrapping up a project on physiognomic, theatrical, and republican conceptions of the person and *Citizens United* was barreling toward the Supreme Court. "What about artificial persons?" I asked idly. Julia pushed me to pursue that question and I'm glad that she did. I'm indebted to my transformative mentors and teachers at Northwestern, including Julia Stern, Jay Grossman, Sam Weber, Helen Thompson, Betsy Erkkila, Larry Lipking, Jeffrey Masten, Peter Fenves, Susanna Gottlieb, Kevin Bell, Laurie Shannon, and Vivasvan Soni. They, along with the friends and interlocutors I got to know there, shaped my thought, my taste, and my prose in ways that I will always carry; I am enduringly grateful to the generous, buoyant, and challenging spirits of Sarah Blackwood, Katy Chiles, Sarah Mesle, Marcy Dinius, Rob Ryder, and Bishupal Limbu, and to the American Cultures Colloquium and the Paris Program in Critical Theory. I also want to thank the earlier teachers whose inspiration and encouragement let me imagine that studying and teaching literature was something I could do: Tim Farrell, Ian Baucom, Elizabeth Fowler, I am grateful.

Since arriving at Franklin & Marshall College in 2010, I've received generous support, both institutional and personal, from many individuals and organizations. I'm grateful for the College's support, particularly the opportunities for sustained research afforded by a junior faculty leave in 2013–14 and a sabbatical in 2018–19, which were crucial to developing this project, as well as its conscientious parental policy, which allowed me to balance my roles as scholar, teacher, partner, and father. My colleagues in the English department and beyond at F&M have constituted a generous company and made this place a joy to work at even during challenging times. As a small liberal arts college, F&M has asked a lot of me in the classroom and rewarded me in turn. I am grateful to my talented and thoughtful colleagues in the English department and beyond, and to my students, particularly those in my courses on American literature and law, literature, and the person, who shared my sense of the strangeness of personhood and demanded clear accounts of thorny concepts. The College's recognition of the individualized trajectory of faculty work has allowed this study to blossom at its own pace rather than at a forced march. I'd particularly like to thank colleagues at F&M and beyond who have read and responded to drafts of my work along the way from their many angles of expertise, including Judith Mueller, Erik Anderson, Shari Goldberg, Kostis Kourelis, John Modern, and Jeffrey Nesteruk at F&M, and Benjy Kahan, Marcy Dinius, and John Garcia further afield. I'm also grateful to Patrick Bernard, Jeff Steinbrink, Doug Anthony, Maria Mitchell, Emily Huber, Jon Stone, and Cristina Pérez for mentorship, friendship, and solidarity, and to Deb Saporetti and Cynthia Jones for indispensable support. During my years in Lancaster I have been nourished by sustaining friendships; Jeremy Moss and Leigh Hickman Moss, Susan Knoll and Erik Anderson, Melissa Markley and Chris Pratt, thank you for being my village. A. J. Shue, Walt Miller, Michael Ellinger, and Michael Pressel have fed my soul with music and camaraderie.

I'm thankful for support from scholarly organizations and research collections, which provided capacious and generative environments for research. The McNeil Center for Early American Studies at the University of Pennsylvania has provided a generous and provocative intellectual community and concrete support including a Consortium Faculty grant that supported some of my earliest work on this project. I'm particularly grateful to the National Endowment for the Humanities and the Library Company of Philadelphia for a year-long Post-Doctoral Fellowship at the Library Company, which was crucial in enabling me to dig into a broad base of nineteenth-century treatises, periodicals, and visual culture; I'm especially grateful for the vast knowledge and gentle nudges of Jim Green and Connie King, who supplemented my guesswork with encyclopedic knowledge and kind support, and for the Early American Literature and Material Texts Seminar at the Library Company, one of the best ongoing parties I ever crashed, where I gleaned as much book history as I could. I'm grateful to the Huntington Library and the American Antiquarian Society for short-term fellowships during my 2018–19 sabbatical year, where I encountered the bulk of the material that would become chapters 2 and 5 respectively, and to the Kislak Center for Special Collections, Rare Books, and Manuscripts at the University of Pennsylvania, which was essential for my research on Robert Montgomery Bird. I'm thankful for the support and camaraderie of library staff and the community of fellow researchers at all of these research collections.

As a scholar of collectives, I'd also like to acknowledge the societies and conferences—the assembled companies and the unpredictable formations to which they give rise—particularly C19, the Society of Early Americanists, the Melville Society, and the Association for the Study of Law, Culture, and Humanities—where I have encountered generous, demanding, and creative co-panelists, interlocutors, and friends, too many to name. And I would like to thank the American Association of University Professors, both nationally and at F&M, for tirelessly undertaking the unforgiving work of advocating for academic freedom and the working conditions of teachers and scholars.

I am deeply grateful to the readers and editors who helped shape and focus this work along the way in earlier iterations. Jana Argersinger and anonymous readers for *Poe Studies*, Dana Nelson and anonymous readers for *J19*; Gordon Hutner and anonymous readers for *American Literary History*; and Sharif Youssef and Jody Greene. More broadly, I am grateful for conversations with and feedback from colleagues working at the intersections of law, literature, and culture, particularly Lisa Siraganian, Sharif Youssef, Christine Wooley, Stefanie Mueller, and Bob Weisberg, as well as the interlocutors in the University of Toronto Law and Literature seminar, where I presented an early version of chapter 2, particularly Simon Stern, its indefatigable and broad-minded organizer.

I gratefully acknowledge *Poe Studies*, which published an early version of chapter 1; *J19*, which published an early version of chapter 3; and *American Literary History*, which published an early version of chapter 4. I gratefully acknowledge Johns Hopkins University Press and Oxford University Press for permission to reprint material that first appeared in those publications. I gratefully acknowledge University of Toronto Press for permission to republish a condensed version of material that appeared in *Human Rights After Corporate Personhood: An Uneasy Merger*, edited by Jody Greene and Sharif Youssef.

Simon Stern approached me a number of years ago with interest in this project; since then, he and Bob Spoo, as series editors, have offered tremendous generosity and insightful feedback as I have developed it. I'm thankful for their faith in this oddball book and all of the support and guidance they have offered along the way. The three anonymous readers of my manuscript offered patient, thorough, and incisive contributions that enabled me to shape and sharpen a sprawling project. I would also like to thank Jack McNichol, Jo Spillane, and the editorial staff at Oxford University Press, as well as Dolarine Fonceca at Straive, who have shepherded this book's final stages.

Jo and John Jaros have believed in me forever, even as they've also known that I tend to take my time. My gratitude to them is beyond measure. Kyle Jaros has gamely crossed disciplinary and state lines, pushing me to clarity and showing love in writing, music, argument, and more. Brenna Stuart has schemed and adventured with me; she knows when to push me and when to give me space; she nourishes and grounds and inspires me in turn. Where would I be without her patience, her impatience, her honesty, her integrity, her kindness, and her wit? Aurie and Theo Jaros are both younger than this book project. As it has slowly taken shape, they have grown into complementary and inspiring forces of nature. Every day they astonish me and teach me how to live.

Contents

Introduction

Incorporate Things

"Society everywhere is in conspiracy against the manhood of every one of its members. Society is a joint-stock company, in which the members agree, for the better securing of his bread to each shareholder, to surrender the liberty and culture of the eater."

Ralph Waldo Emerson, "Self-Reliance" (1841)[1]

"So strongly and metaphysically did I conceive of my situation then, that while earnestly watching his motions, I seemed distinctly to perceive that my own individuality was now merged in a joint stock company of two; that my free will had received a mortal wound; and that another's mistake or misfortune might plunge innocent me into unmerited disaster and death."

Herman Melville, *Moby-Dick* (1851)[2]

From the Supreme Court's expansions of corporate power in *Citizens United v. FEC* (2010) and *Burwell v. Hobby Lobby* (2014) to Mitt Romney's 2011 assertion that "Corporations are people, my friend" and the angry rejoinder "No, they're not!," debates about corporations—particularly over the doctrine of corporate personality—have marked American political discourse in the early twenty-first century.[3] Cases including *Citizens United* and *Hobby Lobby* have increased the power of corporations through ever-broader recognition of their constitutional rights. *Citizens United* removed barriers to corporations' (and unions') election spending in the name of free speech and *Hobby Lobby* permitted closely held corporations to limit their employees' access to contraception in the name of free exercise of religion. The strong reactions engendered by these cases stem in part from the corporation's status as a legal person and the corresponding sense that

[1] Ralph Waldo Emerson, "Self-Reliance," in *Essays and Lectures*, ed. Joel Porte (New York: Library of America, 1983), 261.

[2] Herman Melville, *Moby-Dick*, ed. Hershel Parker and Harrison Hayford (New York: Norton, 2002), 255. Subsequent references in parentheses.

[3] Ashley Parker, "'Corporations Are People,' Romney Tells Iowa Hecklers Angry Over His Tax Policy," *New York Times*, August 11, 2011, http://www.nytimes.com/2011/08/12/us/politics/12romney.html.

corporate personhood and rights impinge on or threaten the personhood and rights of human beings.

This book examines the prehistory of these controversies. It investigates the surprisingly varied ways that writers, both within and beyond the legal profession, described and imagined the corporation. From Hobbes's description of the state as an "artificial man" to Blackstone's classification of corporations as artificial persons to contemporary critiques of corporate personhood, these figurations have often centered on the person and personification. This study thus attends to theories of corporate personhood and the rhetoric and debate surrounding them, but it also offers insight into other, less obvious, manifestations of the corporate form, ranging from imperial states to intentional communities to temporarily assembled companies of strangers. Corporations abounded in the antebellum United States, although they rarely conformed either to the colloquial sense of the corporate—faceless, staid, hegemonic, for-profit—or to the contemporary understanding of the corporation as a business grounded in fungible shares, limited shareholder liability, and centralized management. Rather, American corporations in the first half of the nineteenth century constituted a surprisingly varied landscape. The two companies described above can help us get our bearings.

It's difficult to contemplate Emerson's joint-stock company—an emblem of emasculation and dehumanization—without the resonance that the corporation and the corporate have accrued since his time.[4] He presents the company of "society" as a bad political and spiritual bargain, an unfair trade of "liberty and culture" for the material security promised to shareholders. In doing so, he echoes the venerable trope of the social contract but reframes social contract theory in starkly individualist terms. Rather than reconstruct the fiction of an originary contract that might justly ground political authority and collectivity, Emerson portrays both joint-stock and social belonging as explicit economic contracts to which individuals may assent and from which they may withdraw.[5]

His metaphor echoes changes, recent in Emerson's time, in the conception of corporate belonging. As Kevin Butterfield has shown, during the first three decades of the nineteenth century, a substantive conception of membership prevailed, emphasizing individual consent and the reciprocal responsibilities of members and associations.[6] By the 1830s, however, the "business corporation was

[4] Christopher Newfield sees the root of this sense of the corporate in Emerson. Newfield defines "corporate individualism," the "desired outcome of Emerson's liberalism,' as "the enhancement of freedom through the loss of both private and public control," in Christopher Newfield, *The Emerson Effect* (Chicago: University of Chicago Press, 1996), 5.

[5] Emerson explicitly rejects the indiscriminate collectives gathered by the "foolish philanthropist" in favor of company grounded in "spiritual affinity" (Emerson, "Self-Reliance," 262).

[6] Kevin Butterfield, *The Making of Tocqueville's America: Law and Association in the Early United States* (Chicago: University of Chicago Press, 2015), 129. I follow Butterfield's account in emphasizing a broad conception of technologies of association, according to which the similarities between the corporation, the joint-stock company, and other formal associations outweigh technical legal distinctions among them.

coming to be understood, in an important way, as something wholly different from the other voluntary associations of the American social landscape," grounded not in mutual responsibility but in a conception of shareholding as the pursuit of profit through the mechanism of the corporation. In 1822, Pennsylvania Supreme Court Justice William Tilghman had asserted that "there never has been, or certainly never ought to have been, a corporation created with a view solely to the private interest of the corporators," a view echoed by Chief Justice John Bannister Gibson in 1831. Yet the dominant conception of the corporation as an association of members was challenged by the emergent understanding of the corporation—or in any case one kind of corporation—that framed shareholding precisely as a means to private gain.[7] Political theorist David Ciepley aptly distinguishes "member corporations," associations that foreground belonging and democratic decision-making, from "property corporations," in which belonging is reframed as the ownership of alienable, fungible, and commodified shares (and which gives rise to the notion of shareholder primacy that Tilghman found unthinkable).[8] Emerson's joint-stock company, with its implicit suggestion that we might sell off our stock in society, rests on the conception of the property corporation. By describing participants first as "members," then as "shareholders," he recapitulates the shift underway in his day in the dominant conception of corporate belonging.

In contrast to the emergent understanding of the corporation as an economic abstraction, Herman Melville's "joint stock company of two" suggests an older sense of corporate belonging as a bond between bodies or a body constituted by such bonds. In our moment, in which the expansion of corporate power, the ascendancy of the property company, and neoliberal ideology go hand in hand, it can be difficult to bring his vision of the corporation—messy, intimate, predicated on mutual exposure—into focus. While Emerson urges the self-reliant man to withdraw from joint-stock arrangements into manly liberty, Melville suggests that, for better or worse, joint-stock investments are inescapable.[9] Sometimes, they offer gratuitous salvation, as when Ishmael, early in *Moby-Dick*, imagines the reasoning that drives Queequeg to save a drowning bumpkin: "It's a mutual, joint-stock world in all meridians. We cannibals must help these Christians" (*MD*, 64). As Ishmael notes, however, such belonging can also threaten exposure to "unmerited disaster and death." These words appear in chapter 72 of *Moby-Dick*,

[7] Butterfield, *The Making of Tocqueville's America*, 154. In this light, Newfield's claim that Emerson's liberalism "appear[ed] well before the familiar mode of business organization" is surprising (Newfield, *Emerson Effect*, 5).

[8] David Ciepley, "Member Corporations, Property Corporations, and Constitutional Rights," *Law & Ethics of Human Rights* 11 (2017): 31–60.

[9] Of course, even Emerson embraces belonging to "a class of persons to whom by all spiritual affinity I am bought and sold" (Emerson, "Self-Reliance" 262).

"The Monkey-Rope," in which Ishmael describes the device linking him to Queequeg as at once precaution and vulnerability:

> It was a humorously perilous business for both of us. For, before we proceed further, it must be said that the monkey-rope was fast at both ends; fast to Queequeg's broad canvas belt, and fast to my narrow leather one. So that for better or for worse, we two, for the time, were wedded; and should poor Queequeg sink to rise no more, then both usage and honour demanded, that instead of cutting the cord, it should drag me down in his wake. So, then, an elongated Siamese ligature united us. Queequeg was my own inseparable twin brother; nor could I anyway get rid of the dangerous liabilities which the hempen bond entailed. (*MD*, 255)

Ishmael and Queequeg's predicament—the lifesaving but compromising "bond" by which they are "merged in a joint stock company of two"—reveals that Emerson's metaphor is more unstable than we might realize: the joint-stock form could threaten material security as well as ensure it. As Michael Rogin has pointed out, Melville knew this hard truth too well. His father Allan Melvill had been ruined financially by investment in joint-stock ventures with unlimited shareholder liability.[10] His misfortune illustrates how crucial the emerging principle of limited liability was for conceiving of shareholding as ownership rather than belonging. Protecting shareholders from individual liability for corporate debts allowed company shares to look more like individually-held commodities than stakes in a collective compact. Nonetheless, Melville insists on the ways that corporate entanglements underscore radical forms of embodied, affective, and political belonging. Stefanie Mueller has recently underscored how the nineteenth-century "transformation of the corporation from a political actor to an economic actor" was framed by "literature and culture" as well as law and business.[11] As Melville's words reveal, however, a sense of the corporate form as inescapably political persisted in mid-century literary texts.

The modern business corporation is marked by four features: "limited liability for investors, free transferability of shares, perpetual life, and centralized management."[12] In 1800, however, only one of these traits—perpetual succession—was securely in place. Limited liability emerged unevenly: beginning in Massachusetts in 1805, courts increasingly found that members of associations were not liable for corporate debts; in other words, they interpreted limited liability as a feature of

[10] *Subversive Genealogy: The Politics and Art of Herman Melville* (Berkeley, CA: University of California Press, 1985), 249–50. Rogin convincingly argues that Alan Melvill is the model for the story of China Aster in *The Confidence-Man.*

[11] *The Corporation in the Nineteenth-Century American Imagination* (Edinburgh: Edinburgh University Press, 2023), 2.

[12] Roberta Romano, *Foundations of Corporate Law* (New York: Oxford University Press, 1993), 63.

associational form even when it was not expressly guaranteed by statute or by-law.[13] (This gradual change challenges the hard-and-fast distinction scholars have sometimes drawn between joint-stock company and corporation on the basis of limited or unlimited liability.[14]) From today's perspective, the corporate form without limited liability looks bracingly strange, marked by dangerous mutual exposure. Ishmael's metaphors of increasing intimacy illustrate this entanglement: the rope is first a marriage bond, then the "Siamese ligature" that joined the celebrated Chang and Eng Bunker. His climactic figure—"a joint stock company of two"—seems a bathetic swerve until we recognize that such a company, for Ishmael, constitutes an almost unbearably intense connection—a far cry from the impersonality and flat affect that "corporate" invokes today.

The company engendered by the monkey rope is less a business alliance than something like Jean-Luc Nancy's notion of community: "the sharing that divides and that puts in communication bodies, voices, and writings," an originary exposure that constitutes its communicants as something more and something less than individuals.[15] Yet while Ishmael initially laments, in Emersonian terms, the surrender of autonomous "individuality" and "free will" forced on an "innocent me," he comes to acknowledge the link—and exposure—of "every mortal that breathes" to "a plurality of other mortals": "If your banker breaks, you snap; if your apothecary by mistake sends you poison in your pills, you die" (*MD*, 255–56). From this perspective, no me is innocent, much less autonomous. As happens frequently in *Moby-Dick*, the trajectory of Ishmael's moralizing swoops back to reverse the premise that occasioned it. The monkey-rope dialectically corrects the liberal, Emersonian picture by dramatizing two features ascribed to joint-stock belonging—interdependence and mutual liability—as fundamental to the human condition. These inescapable enmeshments are constitutive of, rather than impediments to, Ishmael's and Queequeg's manhood and liberty. In this light, the company is less a newfangled technology of association or a constraining facet of modernity than an originary—and not altogether undesirable—predicament of human plurality. Rather than sweeping risk out of sight behind fungible commodities (like the notorious credit-default swaps that triggered the 2008 financial crisis)[16], Melville's monkey-rope foregrounds risk as what constitutes

[13] Butterfield, *The Making of Tocqueville's America*, 120, 127.

[14] Rogin, for instance, insists on unlimited liability as central to the joint-stock form (*Subversive Genealogy* 137–38). As Margaret M. Blair and Elizabeth Pollman note, however, the joint-stock form was "designed to mimic the benefits" of the corporation, even though it was generally treated as a partnership for legal purposes. Margaret M. Blair and Elizabeth Pollman, "The Supreme Court's View of Corporate Rights: Two Centuries of Evolution and Controversy," in *Corporations and American Democracy*, ed. Naomi R. Lamoreaux and William J. Novak (Cambridge, MA: Harvard University Press, 2017), 258.

[15] Jean-Luc Nancy, *The Inoperative Community*, ed. Peter Connor, trans. Peter Connor, Lisa Garbus, Michael Holland, and Simona Sawhney (Minneapolis: University of Minnesota Press, 1991), 6.

[16] On the subjectivities instantiated by such financial entities, see Anna Kornbluh, *Realizing Capital: Financial and Psychic Economies in Victorian Form* (New York: Fordham University Press, 2013).

shared connections that enliven, expose, and endanger us beyond the efforts of "exceeding caution": "[D]o what I would," Ishmael says, "I only had the management of one end of it" (*MD*, 256). This web of disindividuating corporate entanglements surely adumbrates the downward spiral of that seafaring company, the *Pequod*, but it also prefigures Queequeg's coffin, the buoyant embodiment of the joint-stock company of two, which carries Ishmael free of the wreck. Joint-stock exposure may have ruined Allan Melvill, but it saves Ishmael.

Ishamel's—and Melville's—investment in the corporate form recalls Sir William Blackstone's description of corporations as bodies politic and his reciprocal framing of "the great corporation or body politic of the kingdom."[17] Far more novel, in this light, is Emerson's insistence that such a body politic consisted merely of contractual bonds, a position that both adumbrates the libertarian nexus-of-contracts theory of the corporation and, as Emerson's contemporary Francis Lieber understood, erroneously equates economic contracts and political bonds. The fact that the same legal instrument could metaphorically ground both Emerson's conception of radical individualism and Melville's image of radical interdependence indicates the breadth and complexity of the corporation's imaginative resonance in the antebellum United States. Nineteenth-century writers—along with lawyers, politicians, caricaturists, and others—devoted intense attention to corporations not only as worldly entities but as figures of individuality and collectivity, representation and belonging, humanity and inhumanity. The conceptions of the corporation they entertained—including the models of voluntary but constraining associations and collectivities that both sustain and compromise the individual—enter into conversation with the well-documented legal history of the corporation but are not reducible to it. By drawing their work together, this book shows how American writers confronted the possibilities and dangers of the corporate form long before *Citizens United*. Gathering the threads of writing around the corporate form—imaginative and theoretical, legal and literary, conventional and radical—*The Corporate Forms of Antebellum US Literature* shows how seemingly conservative legal conceptions of the corporation provided the vocabulary for a nineteenth-century corporate imaginary that afforded the bold reimagining of both personhood and collectivity. Thus, while this study draws on the accounts of the corporation identified by legal scholars—the artificial entity, aggregate, and real entity theories—it also pursues the ways that literary accounts of the corporation have departed from and exceeded these theories.

As a growing body of work by literary scholars including John O'Brien, Henry Turner, Daniel Stout, Lisa Siraganian, and Stefanie Mueller has demonstrated,

[17] Sir William Blackstone, *Commentaries on the Laws of England: Book I: Of the Rights of Persons*, ed. David Lemmings (Oxford: Oxford University Press, 2016), 149. Subsequent reference in parentheses.

the corporate form has long played an important if sometimes underappreciated role in questions of literary representation, political theory, and form, and has been central to framing issues ranging from empire to epistemology. This scholarship highlights the interplay between literary and cultural history and the corporation and frequently aligns a traditional literary historical period and its questions—early modern framings of political theory, romantic interrogation of the self, modernist investigations of personality and impersonality—with key developments in the legal, political, and cultural history of the corporation.[18] Each of these studies identifies a particular moment in legal and literary history as central to its account of the corporation; on the aggregate, they reveal not a single watershed for the literary-corporate nexus but a rich succession of problems, configurations, and articulations.

[18] John O'Brien, in *Literature Incorporated*, updates and revises the project of the New Economic Criticism—and its insistence on the shared metaphorical work of literary and economic writing—to examine the "cultural unconscious of the business corporation." His focus centers on economic forms—and the ways they can be read into phenomena such as Locke's psychological and political theory, the great British imperial companies, the economic speculations of eighteenth-century investors and literary speculations of writers like Addison and Steele. He contends that "[t]he ascendancy of the business corporation... has shaped possibilities for thought and feeling throughout that period [since the seventeenth century] while offering itself as an inevitable, unavoidable *fact* that asks we understand it, rather than the other way around" (O'Brien, *Literature Incorporated*, 27). O'Brien is rightly suspicious of "creating a new 'framework' for understanding the business corporation," which he calls "a fool's errand" because "the corporation can never be comprehensively *understood*, because it is bound up in larger systems of sovereignty, affect, and figuration that change over time" (O'Brien, *Literature Incorporated*, 27). Yet part of the argument of the present book is that attending to the legal and ontological *form* of the corporation is worth our while can afford more understanding than his pessimistic formula suggests. In contrast to O'Brien, Henry Turner's *The Corporate Commonwealth* argues that the corporate form needs to be understood *as* a form—and principally as a political form. Turner aptly reminds us that the best way to understand the fictionality of the corporation is as material artifice: "the corporation is always in the process of being assembled and decomposed"—a process that "is never simply material or intellectual but takes pace through a constant translation between the two" (Turner, *The Corporate Commonwealth*, 30). Turner illuminates a genealogy that stretches from early modern political theory—notably, Hobbes's characterization of the state as at once a "mortall god" and a corporate body—to the legal pluralists of the early twentieth century—Gierke, Laski, Maitland. Turner's work also aptly captures the ways that political theory of the corporation and actor-network theory, centered on describing assemblages and the relations that constitute them, can inform each other. Because the unity of the corporation is inevitably figurative and narrative, these assemblages embrace the stories corporations tell about themselves in their self-constitution: "The corporate person's 'action' and its self-narration are thus never fully distinct: they run alongside one another, sometimes overlapping, sometimes lagging, as the corporate agent shuttles back and forth between material and linguistic assemblages" (Turner, *The Corporate Commonwealth*, 106). Most recently, Stefanie Mueller has tracked with particular acuity the emergence of the corporation as economic actor in nineteenth-century US law and the broader literary and cultural imaginary. Turner, *The Corporate Commonwealth*; John O'Brien, *Literature Incorporated* (Chicago: University of Chicago Press, 2015); Daniel Stout, *Corporate Romanticism: Liberalism, Justice, and the Novel* (New York: Fordham University Press, 2016); Lisa Siraganian, *Modernism and the Meaning of Corporate Persons* (Oxford: Oxford University Press, 2020); Stefanie Mueller, *The Corporation in the Nineteenth-Century American Imagination* (Edinburgh: Edinburgh University Press, 2024); Walter Benn Michaels, *The Gold Standard and the Logic of Naturalism: American Literature at the Turn of the Century* (Berkeley, CA: University of California Press, 1987); and Newfield, *The Emerson Effect* made important earlier investigations of literary history and the corporation.

Joining this conversation, this study emphasizes the ways that writers wrote about, thought through, and worked with the corporate form to ask fundamental questions about persons and polities, mortality and immortality, statecraft and empire. It shows how they reached far beyond the contemporary antithesis "Corporations are people"/"No they aren't" and its implication that the central issue raised by the corporation is its equivalence to or difference from the human being. While recent controversies have centered on the extent to which corporations ought to be considered persons in law, Emerson and Melville's examples show how different conceptions of corporate belonging can engender dramatically different visions of personhood and collectivity.

American political and national identity—from colonial company charters to New England covenant theology, from Enlightenment social contract thought to the Tocquevillean conception of democratic individualism moderated by the tendency to association—has repeatedly been articulated in terms of the constitution and legitimacy of collective entities and their anchoring in discourses ranging from theology to political theory to jurisprudence. Nineteenth-century writers drew on these notions of corporateness as they witnessed phenomena including the emergence of modern business corporations and the simultaneous ascendancy and vulnerability of corporate power in the Bank War. For them, the corporation was many things at once: a body politic, a variety of person, and a paradigm for collectivity. The corporate form provided a focus for perennial questions about the one and the many—questions that writers variously phrased in metaphysical, poetic, and narrative registers as well as explicitly legal or political ones. Corporations thus constituted laboratories, not only for lawyers, judges, institution-builders, and entrepreneurs, but also for imaginative projects of understanding and reconfiguring collective existence.

The Corporate Form in the Antebellum United States

The powerful corporations we know today have a long prehistory. The corporate form stretches back to Roman law, features prominently in early modern political theory, and undergirds the transformative and devastating imperial companies of the seventeenth and eighteenth centuries.[19] In the antebellum United States, the corporation rose from an infrequently granted privilege to the dominant structure of business organization. Early American businesses and other associations took a variety of forms, including partnerships and unchartered joint-stock companies as well as corporations. Jurists, legislators, and corporators created and

[19] Oscar Handlin and Mary F. Handlin, "Origins of the American Business Corporation," *Journal of Economic History* 5 (1945):1–23; Philip J. Stern, *Empire Incorporated: The Corporations That Built British Colonialism* (Cambridge, MA: Harvard University Press, 2023).

critiqued different varieties of the corporate form: from unlimited liability to limited liability, and from bridges and turnpikes to banks to intentional communities, from special charters to general incorporation statutes. Writers both within and beyond the legal profession variously portrayed corporations as exotic creatures, malign infestations, complex machines, and quasi-sovereigns, even as others drew on the corporate form as a paradigm for new political imaginaries and even for plural and divided conceptions of human subjectivity. This interchange between legal and literary idioms, conceptions, and genres emerged from a literary discourse of civic letters whose "authors and editors... were typically lawyers."[20] The familiar treatment of legal concepts and categories in a wide variety of literary texts attests to the network of elite institutions and publications through which both legal and literary writing circulated.

This study centers on the United States between two watersheds. In 1819, the Marshall Court's decision in *Dartmouth College* articulated a theory of the corporation and granted it powerful Constitutional protections even as a contemporaneous financial panic showed the vulnerability of banking and business corporations. And in 1868, the Reconstruction Amendments wrote citizenship and legal personhood into Federal law. As Howard Jay Graham and Morton Horwitz have noted, the Fourteenth Amendment, designed to ensure equality before the law to formerly enslaved people, ultimately cleared the way for increased corporate rights and the more familiar rise of the postbellum corporation. And as scholars including Walter Benn Michaels and Lisa Siraganian have detailed, this new constitutional basis for corporate rights gave literary representations of the corporation particular urgency.[21] Between these landmarks, however, both the corporation and the person were powerful but legally contested forms. As the Bank War and *Charles River Bridge* case revealed in the 1830s, corporations were formidable but vulnerable entities, nominally immortal but practically subject to limited lifespans and strategic dismantling. And as *Dred Scott v. Sandford* (1857) starkly emphasized, the legal standing of human beings—particularly Black Americans—could be dismantled as well.

At the same time, as noted above, corporations also supplied a field for articulating collectivity and membership bound by constitution-like documents that both mirrored the early republic and could offer alternatives to it. In their classic study of early American corporations, Oscar and Mary Handlin argue that early Americans were attracted to the corporate form less for economic advantage

[20] Guyora Binder and Robert Weisberg, *Literary Criticisms of Law* (Princeton, NJ: Princeton University Press, 2000), 14, 39. See also Robert Ferguson, *Law and Letters in American Culture* (Cambridge, MA: Harvard University Press, 1984); Robert A. Ferguson, *The American Enlightenment, 1750–1820* (Cambridge, MA: Harvard University Press, 1997).

[21] Howard Jay Graham, *Everyman's Constitution: Historical Essays on the Fourteenth Amendment, the "Conspiracy Theory," and American Constitutionalism* (Madison, WI: Wisconsin Historical Society Press, 1968); Morton Horwitz, *The Transformation of American Law, 1870–1960* (Cambridge, MA: Harvard University Press, 1977), 65–107; Michaels, *The Gold Standard*; Siraganian, *Modernism*.

(it did not yet guarantee "unusual economic efficiency,...limited liability,...[or] freedom from state interference") than for participatory governance: "the corporation was conceived as an agency of government, endowed with public attributes, exclusive privileges, and political power, and designed to serve a social function for the state."[22] The political aspect of the corporation was two-sided. On the one hand, state constitutions had grown from the royal charters of colonial companies, and the US constitution echoed this tradition of authorizing documents. On the other, incorporated groups—from mutual insurance companies to Black churches to socialist intentional communities—afforded forms of collectivity and belonging in ways that recalled these constitutions but supplemented the early republic's failure to conceive of the inclusion and flourishing of all Americans.[23] As a contrast category—and sometimes an uncanny reflection—for both the individual and the state, the corporation thus offered a resource for reimaging both personal and national identity. At the same time, corporations also impinged on both individual persons and the republic itself, in ways that contemporaneous observers often found monstrous.

As Naomi Lamoreaux and William Novak emphasize, Americans have long regarded corporations ambivalently "as both a bulwark of democracy and its persistent menace."[24] Such ambivalence has produced strange bedfellows, as when entrenched banking interests and anti-bank Locofocos joined forces in the 1830s to oppose the rechartering of the Bank of the United States, yet it has not always centered on corporations' status as persons.[25] Like contemporary critics, nineteenth-century writers recognized and played on the uncanniness of the corporate person. Yet it would be inaccurate to reduce either the corporation's nineteenth-century history or its currently contested status to the question of personhood. Even *Citizens United* did not derive corporations' First Amendment rights from corporate personhood but rather treated corporations as pass-through entities for the individual rights of an "associations of citizens."[26] Yet this language of associations fits the nineteenth-century corporate landscape far more

[22] Handlin and Handlin, "Origins of the American Business Corporation," 22–23.

[23] Butterfield, *The Making of Tocqueville's America*; Carl J. Guarneri, *The Utopian Alternative: Fourierism in Nineteenth-Century America* (Ithaca, NY: Cornell University Press, 1991); Sarah Gordon, "The African Supplement: Religion, Race, and Corporate Law in Early National America," *William and Mary Quarterly* 72 (2015):385–422.

[24] Naomi Lamoreaux and William Novak, "Corporations and American Democracy: An Introduction," in Naomi Lamoreaux and William Novak, *Corporations and American Democracy*, 32.

[25] Eric Hilt, "Early American Corporations and the State," in Lamoreaux and Novak, *Corporations and American Democracy*, 61.

[26] Adam Winkler, "*Citizens United*, Personhood, and the Corporation in Politics," in Lamoreaux and Novak, *Corporations and American Democracy*, 382. For this reason, Winkler is pessimistic about reform on the basis of "personhood": "While 'corporations are not people' has broad public resonance, that was not the basis of *Citizens United*. Eliminating corporate personhood might not succeed in overturning the Court's ruling and could have the unwelcome effect of undermining the free speech rights of media corporations like the New York Times Company and Fox Entertainment Group" (386).

aptly than it does our own: as Margaret Blair and Elizabeth Pollman point out, "the actual population of corporations in the [nineteenth-century] United States" consisted principally of "associations of individuals acting through a legal entity."[27]

The antebellum corporate landscape—populated by charities and public works companies as well as business associations—looks quite different from our own. Early nineteenth-century Americans drew on a well-established tradition of formally organized associations, with the armature of constitutions and by-laws, to meet a wide variety of ends, as Tocqueville famously described: "Americans group together to hold fêtes, found seminaries, build inns, construct churches, distribute books, dispatch missionaries to the antipodes. They establish hospitals, prisons, schools by the same method. Finally, if they wish to highlight a truth or develop an opinion by the encouragement of a great example, they form an association."[28]

Henry David Thoreau offers a disillusioned view of this culture of association when he complains, "The American has dwindled into an Odd Fellow, . . . whose first and chief concern, on coming into the world, is to see that the Almshouses are in good repair; and, before yet he has lawfully donned the virile garb, to collect a fund for the support of the widows and orphans that may be; who, in short, ventures to live only by the aid of the Mutual Insurance company, which has promised to bury him decently."[29] Thoreau's account, like Tocqueville's, illustrates how antebellum Americans theorized and practiced what Butterfield calls "the technology of how to associate" with both talent and zeal. Unlike Tocqueville, though, Thoreau suggests that the culture of association reduces the man to the mere member.[30]

As Tocqueville and Thoreau demonstrate, writers both within and outside the legal profession saw novelty, promise, and menace in the variety of forms and purposes such associations could take. It's worth remembering, as Blair and Pollman note, that nineteenth-century jurists' accounts of corporations as persons are not "ontological assertion[s] about the nature of corporations."[31] Nonetheless, the tropes by which lawyers and lay writers represented corporations demand our attention. Although judges could insist that corporate personhood remained a legal convenience, they could hardly prevent the overflow of corporate personhood into literary personification—and into literary culture more broadly. Edgar Allan Poe's fictional business man Peter Pendulum recognizes the quandaries of agency and ethics that corporations raised: "corporations,

[27] Blair and Pollman, "The Supreme Court's View," 246.

[28] Alexis de Tocqueville, *Democracy in America* and *Two Essays on America*, ed. Isaac Kramnick, trans. Gerald Bevan (London: Penguin, 2003), 596.

[29] Henry David Thoreau, "Resistance to Civil Government" (1849), in *Walden and Civil Disobedience*, ed. Michael Meyer (New York: Penguin, 1983), 393.

[30] Butterfield, *The Making of Tocqueville's America*, 103.

[31] Blair and Pollman, "The Supreme Court's View," 246.

it is very well known, have neither posteriors to be kicked, nor souls to be damned."[32] As I discuss in more detail below, the difficulty of pinning down the corporation's ontological status derives in part from its tropological status: its grounding in representation—or gathering a dispersed group into a figurative body—rather than essence. Canonical definitions of the corporation in the common law detail just these traits—frequently with flurries of metaphor and catachresis. Blackstone, in the *Commentaries*, explains that when "the advantage of the public" requires "any particular rights kept on foot and continued," "it has been found necessary...to constitute artificial persons, who may maintain a perpetual succession, and enjoy a kind of legal immortality" (*CLE*, 455). Chief Justice John Marshall echoes Blackstone in his well-known account of the corporation in *Trustees of Dartmouth College v. Woodward* (1819): "A corporation is an artificial being, invisible, intangible, and existing only in contemplation of law. Being the mere creature of law, it possesses only those properties which the charter of its creation confers upon it either expressly or as incidental to its very existence. These are such as are supposed best calculated to effect the object for which it was created. Among the most important are immortality, and, if the expression may be allowed, individuality—properties by which a perpetual succession of many persons are considered as the same, and may act as a single individual."[33]

Marshall's words are so familiar to scholars of the corporation that it's worth highlighting their strangeness and their stutters. While Marshall derives the form of a corporation from two sources—the explicit stipulations of its charter and the practical properties "incidental to its very existence"—he does not specify from which source the attributes of immortality and individuality proceed. Further, while he takes care to minimize the corporation's ontological footprint—"only those properties"—the very properties he describes as fundamental to the corporate form grant it superhuman duration and coherence. Finally, as he ascribes "individuality" to the corporation, he hedges—"if the expression may be allowed"—though it's unclear whether it is the word itself, unusual in the eighteen-teens, or its implied definitions of both indivisibility and particularity, that might trouble a scrupulous reader.

By foregrounding the properties of immortality and individuality, Marshall's words remind us that personhood is only one facet of the corporation's form. His wide-ranging but hesitant account of the corporation is emblematic of the varied idioms nineteenth-century jurists regularly applied when discussing the corporation. As Blair and Pollman note, "references to corporations as either 'artificial entities' or 'associations'" were hardly "opposing views"; rather, "the Court used both phrases in the nineteenth century to describe different aspects of the

[32] Edgar Allan Poe, "The Business Man," in *Collected Works of Edgar Allan Poe*, ed. Thomas Ollive Mabbott (Cambridge, MA: Harvard University Press, 1969–78), 2: 489.

[33] *Trustees of Dartmouth College v. Woodward*, 636.

corporate form."[34] While Marshall's *Dartmouth College* ruling foregrounds the corporation as an "artificial being" in itself, it also recognizes Dartmouth College's charter as granting rights to the college's founder and successors: an association of citizens. In contrast to subsequent scholars' neat differentiation among corporate theories, nineteenth-century jurists drew on various conceptions of the corporation, sometimes simultaneously and rarely comprehensively.

From Corporation Theory to Corporate Form

As noted above, the deleterious results of decisions like *Citizens United* and *Hobby Lobby* have lent urgency to journalists' and scholars' investigations into the nature and evolution of the corporation. Legal scholars have illuminated the history by which the twenty-first-century corporation has come to enjoy the First and Fourteenth Amendment rights traditionally accorded to individuals.[35] They have also shown the convoluted and deceptive process through which the Supreme Court first came to recognize corporations as persons entitled to Fourteenth Amendment due process protections.[36] Historians and theorists of governance and empire have highlighted the ways corporations behave more like sovereign states (i.e., the kinds of bodies the First and Fourteenth Amendments limit) than individual persons (those they protect).[37] If we can better understand what corporations are, the hope goes, perhaps we can find a way to make the law recognize their rights and duties—and to confront the kinds of power and danger they embody—more fairly and effectively.

What corporations really are, however, has long been a contentious matter. Legal historians and theorists generally recognize three competing theories of the corporation in American law: artificial entity (or concession), aggregate, and real entity. Artificial entity theory treats the corporation as a special grant of rights conceded by the government and thus centers charters as central to corporations' being. It is captured in Marshall's description of a corporation as "an artificial

[34] Blair and Pollman, "The Supreme Court's View," 256.

[35] See particularly Mark, "The Personification of the Business Corporation in American Law"; Lamoreaux and Novak, eds., *Corporations and American Democracy*; Jody Greene and Sharif Youssef, eds., *Human Rights after Corporate Personhood: An Uneasy Merger* (Toronto: University of Toronto Press, 2020).

[36] Graham, *Everyman's Constitution*; Adam Winkler, *We the Corporations: How American Businesses Won Their Civil Rights* (New York: Liveright, 2018), 113–60.

[37] Joshua Barkan, *Corporate Sovereignty: Law and Government under Capitalism* (Minneapolis, MN: University of Minnesota Press, 2013); Elizabeth Anderson, *Private Government: How Employers Rule Our Lives (and Why We Don't Talk about It)* (Princeton, NJ: Princeton University Press, 2017); Philip J. Stern, *The Company-State: Corporate Sovereignty and the Early Modern Foundations of the British Empire in India* (Oxford: Oxford University Press, 2012); Nick Robins, *The Corporation that Changed the World: How the East India Company Shaped the Modern Multinational*, 2nd ed. (London: Pluto Press, 2012).

being, invisible, intangible, and existing only in contemplation of law" that "possesses only those properties which the charter of its creation confers upon it either expressly or as incidental to its very existence."[38] Aggregate (or association) theory, in contrast, minimizes the importance of state authority by recognizing corporations as reducible to the "aggregation of natural persons" who make up the corporation. The proliferation of general incorporation statutes in the nineteenth century, which permitted incorporation for any purpose and without legislative action, weakened the conception of a corporate charter as a government concession. Increasingly, courts identified the identity and interests of a corporation with those of its members, to the point that "the corporation is seen as a collection or aggregate, of individuals who contract with each other to utilize the corporation for their mutual benefit."[39] This view led the late-nineteenth-century jurist Victor Morawetz to insist that "the rights and duties of an incorporated association are in reality the rights and duties of the persons who compose it, and not of an imaginary being."[40] This view would be eagerly embraced by late-twentieth century nexus-of-contracts theorists, who minimized the ontological footprint of the corporation, which they identified as merely a shorthand for bundle of contracts among owners, managers, and employees, in the name of maximizing the economic liberty of shareholders.[41]

In contrast to both the artificial entity and aggregate theories, real entity theory recognizes the corporation as a separate being whose existence is reducible neither to its aggregated members nor to the governmental grant of a charter. Promulgated by the German political theorist Otto von Gierke and his English-language popularizers including Frederic Maitland and Ernst Freund, real entity theory essentially asserts that "if *n* men unite themselves in an organized body, jurisprudence, unless it wishes to pulverize the group, must see $n + 1$ persons."[42] On the one hand, real entity theory empowers the corporation as a juridical entity; on the other, it offers the clearest framework for enforcing corporations' responsibilities beyond maximizing profits.[43] Legal historians have broadly acknowledged these three models of the corporation and presented them as successive developments in the history of American jurisprudence (while also acknowledging their earlier sources in Roman law and common law).[44] In *Bank of the United States v. Deveaux* (1809), the Marshall Court relied explicitly on an

[38] *Trustees of Dartmouth College v. Woodward*, 17 US (4 Wheat.) 518 (1819), 636.

[39] Susanna Kim Ripken, *Corporate Personhood* (Cambridge: Cambridge University Press, 2019), 29.

[40] Victor Morawetz, *A Treatise on the Law of Private Corporations Other than Charitable* (Boston: Little, Brown, 1882), Volume 1, 2.

[41] Ripken, *Corporate Personhood*, 32.

[42] F. W. Maitland, "Moral Personality and Legal Personality" (1904), in *State, Trust, and Corporation*, ed. David Runciman and Magnus Ryan (Cambridge: Cambridge University Press, 2003), 69.

[43] Ripken, *Corporate Personality*, 37.

[44] Horwitz, *The Transformation of American Law, 1780–1860*, 109–39; Horwitz, *The Transformation of American Law, 1870–1960*, 65–107; Mark, "Personification"; Ripken, *Corporate Personality*, 21–57.

aggregate view of the corporation, reckoning that the effective citizenship of a corporation (for jurisdictional purposes) could only be understood as reflecting the citizenship of its members. In *Louisville, Cincinnati & Charleston Railroad Co. v. Letson* (1844), in contrast, the Taney court would favor the artificial entity view, ruling that a corporation's quasi-citizenship was determined by the state where it was chartered.[45] And in the *Railroad Tax Cases* (1882), Justice Stephen Field succinctly foregrounded the corporation as real entity: "the lives and liberties of the individual corporators are not the life and liberty of the corporation."[46] At the same time, elements of all three theories predate their explicit formulation. As Reuven Avi-Yonah has convincingly shown, the three theories have come to ascendancy in a cyclical fashion—yet one that favors the real entity theory, which he argues is best suited to balance the rights of corporations and the regulatory powers of the state.[47]

While the debate among models of the corporation preoccupied legal scholars in the early twentieth century, courts thereafter increasingly "sidestep[ed] discussions of corporate persons' existential features."[48] Legal historians regularly identify John Dewey's widely cited essay on corporate personality as a watershed. Dewey turns down the heat on questions of corporate personality when he writes that "for the purposes of law the conception of 'person' is a legal conception; put roughly, 'person' signifies what law makes it signify."[49] Recasting the question of corporate personality as instrumental—a method for bundling rights and duties—rather than ontological, Dewey emphasizes practical consequences over theoretical ones. Subsequently, courts have rarely theorized the nature of corporation explicitly, even as aspects of the three theories continue implicitly to animate their rulings.[50] Both the majority and the dissent in *Citizens United*, to take a prominent example, avoid "the issue of corporate personality theory."[51]

Of course, Supreme Court decisions and prevailing legal theories capture only one facet of corporations' existence. Corporations are creatures of law, but they

[45] *Bank of the United States v. Deveaux*, 9 U.S. 61 (1809); *Louisville, Cincinnati & Charleston R. Co. v. Letson*, 43 U.S. 497 (1844); Winkler, *We the Corporations*, 35–70; Austin Allen, *Origins of the Dred Scott Case: Jacksonian Jurisprudence and the Supreme Court, 1837–1857* (Athens, GA: University of Georgia Press, 2006), 127–28.

[46] *The Railroad Tax Cases. County of San Mateo v. Southern Pacific R. Co.*, 13 F. 722 (9th Cir. 1882), 746–47; Lamoreaux and Novak, "Introduction," 28.

[47] Reuven Avi-Yonah, "The Cyclical Transformations of the Corporate Form: A Historical Perspective on Corporate Social Responsibility," *Delaware Journal of Corporate Law* 30 (2005):767–818.

[48] Siraganian, *Modernism*, 28.

[49] John Dewey, "The Historic Background of Corporate Legal Personality," *Yale Law Journal* 35 (1926):655.

[50] Michael J. Phillips, "Reappraising the Real Entity Theory of the Corporation," *Florida State University Law Review* 21 (1994):1123; Blair and Pollman, "The Supreme Court's View"; Ripken, *Corporate Personality*.

[51] Stefan Padfield, "Killing Corporations to Save Humans: How Corporate Personhood, Human Rights, and the Corporate Death Penalty Intersect," in *Human Rights after Corporate Personhood: An Uneasy Merger*, ed. Greene and Youssef, 194.

are also entities entangled with everyday experience, representation, and power. While Dewey helped turn jurisprudence away from questions of corporate ontology per se, theories of the corporation nonetheless contribute to the repertoire of conceptions and images of the corporation on which people have drawn to confront corporate entities and their power. Thus, while indebted to and in conversation with legal and historical scholarship, this book foregrounds the genealogy of the corporation as viewed from the side of literary texts and other cultural productions. It attends to what I call the corporate imaginary: representations of the corporate form in the overlapping material and discursive worlds of nineteenth-century literary and legal culture, as well as the corporate ontologies they describe, imply, and project.[52] To consider the corporate imaginary as such is to recognize the interpenetration of legal, theoretical, and literary discourses that are too often treated separately. In attending particularly to the corporation's figurative status, I seek to recover a view of the corporation's history as a history of tropes: both the rhetorical figures that the writers of literary and legal texts have used to represent corporations and the legal and political forms that corporations have been understood to be. By looking beyond the work of legal theorists and practitioners, this tropological history can illuminate our understanding of the corporation in surprising ways. For instance, we can recognize the widely expressed sentiment "corporations are not people" at once as imprecise legal reasoning and as evidence of the ascendancy of personhood as the dominant, contested trope of the corporation in the early twenty-first century imaginary. Attending to this wider corporate imaginary can clarify both how corporations are constituted and the means by which laypeople (as well as lawyers) encounter, understand, resist, and reshape them.

The ungraspability of corporations is proverbial. As Lord Thurlow—Peter Pendulum's precursor—wrote, "they have neither bodies to be punished, nor souls to be condemned."[53] As his famous words suggest, it is difficult to punish corporations directly because the corporate form resists the categories of body and soul, which grant the law power over natural persons. By the same token, the ontological status of the corporation deserves our attention not only as a matter of abstract theory but because conceptions of corporate ontology have always

[52] Stefanie Mueller also uses the term "imaginary" in relation to nineteenth-century corporations, particularly in the sense of a "cultural imaginary" as a "site of new meanings that seek to become socially recognized" and "a repertoire of images, affects, and desires." Mueller, *The Corporation in the Nineteenth-Century American Imagination*, 9.

[53] Edward, First Baron Thurlow, qtd. John Poynder, *Literary Extracts from English and Other Works* (London: Hatchard, 1844), Vol. 1, 268. The quotation often appears as "Did you ever expect a corporation to have a conscience, when it has no soul to be damned, and no body to be kicked?" *Oxford Essential Quotations*, 4th ed., ed. Susan Ratcliffe. Thurlow is regularly cited in the legal literature on corporate civil and criminal liability. See John Coffee, "'No Soul to Damn, No Body to Kick': An Unscandalized Inquiry into the Problem of Corporate Punishment," 79 *Michigan Law Review* 386 (1981); C. M. V. Clarkson, "Kicking Corporate Bodies and Damning Their Souls," *Modern Law Review* 59 (1996): 4.

provided the vocabulary by which laypeople come to grips, both conceptually and strategically, with the corporation. The corporate imaginary, in other words, is entangled with the affordances—"the potential uses or actions latent in materials or designs," the "actions or thoughts ... made possible or impossible by the fact of a form"—of the corporate form.[54] The corporation's affordances include the familiar legal points of access identified by Blackstone: the corporation's name and seal, its capacity to sue and be sued, the agents who speak on its behalf. I would argue that they also include the tropes of personification, metaphor, and catachresis, as when Blackstone efficiently defines corporations as "artificial persons, who may maintain a perpetual succession, and enjoy a kind of legal immortality" (*CLE*, 455). Enmeshed with the law and its tropes, the corporation is accessible through them rather than despite them. (And while these tropes intersect with legal theories of the corporation—artificial entity, aggregate, real entity—they are not reducible to them.) Put differently, the history of tropes of the corporation embraces both the legal figures that constitute corporations and the literary and visual figures that writers and artists have employed to depict them. Of course, the distinction between the tropes that *represent* corporations and the tropes that *constitute* corporations is a slippery one, in part because the nature of the corporation makes it hard to draw the line between the object represented and the act of representation.

In attending to the affordances of the corporate form and its modes of engagement with other (literary, aesthetic, political, social) forms, this book resonates with a methodological intuition articulated by Caroline Levine. "Instead of assuming that social forms are the grounds or causes of literary forms, and instead of imagining that a literary text has *a* form," she writes, "what does each form afford, and what happens when forms meet?"[55] Literary observers, theorists, and exploiters of the corporation, I contend, have been asking these questions for centuries. This study thus resists the temptation to treat the legal (or for that matter the literary, the political, or the economic) as a fundamental register to which other phenomena are to be reduced; rather, it strives to articulate their interconnection and interdependence, in the hopes that a pluralistic mode of description can offer unfamiliar approaches to familiar assumptions and impasses.

Whereas "corporate personhood" evokes the uncanny and contested nature of nonhuman persons, "corporate form" may seem neutral, as if "form" were self-explanatory, or as if corporations took a single and self-evident form. Yet as recent

[54] Caroline Levine, *Forms: Whole, Rhythm, Hierarchy, Network* (Princeton, NJ: Princeton University Press, 2015), 6, 152. Levine adapts the term from the psychologist James J. Gibson. See James J. Gibson, "The Theory of Affordances" in James J. Gibson, *The Ecological Approach to Visual Perception* (Boston: Houghton, 1979). Samuel Weber's analysis of Walter Benjamin's use of the suffix *-barkeit* (-ability) demonstrates a similar insight in a different theoretical tradition. Samuel Weber, *Benjamin's -Abilities* (Cambridge, MA: Harvard University Press, 2010).

[55] Levine, *Forms*, 16.

literary scholarship has emphasized, form is anything but a self-evident term. This study wagers that attending to the corporation *as* a form—or collection of forms—at the intersection of antebellum US law, literature, and culture can both shed light on the prehistory of our current entanglement with the corporation and bring an unfamiliar perspective to contemporary debates about form. By examining the ways writers theorized, figured, and deployed the corporate form both within and beyond the law, it looks beyond the history of nineteenth-century corporations as they existed in order to illuminate a multitude of paths not taken. Attending to this multiplicity reveals that the hegemonic status of contemporary multinational business corporations—deterritorialized but quasi-sovereign entities with liberty and property rights, dedicated to maximizing profit and generally lacking meaningful democratic accountability—is not the inevitable and immutable terminus of a historical trajectory but one contingent possibility among many.[56]

Corporate Bodies and Souls

Corporations are often understood as a kind of legal fiction even as they constitute undeniable and intrusive facts of our lives—in the words of Arthur Machen, "a fiction, yet . . . a fiction founded upon fact."[57] It might be more accurate, however, to say that the corporation is a fact constituted by fictions. Stewart Kyd observed this paradox in his 1793 treatise on the corporation: "That a body framed by the policy of man, a body whose parts and members are mortal, should in its own nature be immortal, or that a body composed of many bulky, visible bodies, should be invisible, in the common acceptation of the words, seems beyond the reach of common understandings. A corporation is as visible a body as an army; for though the commission or authority be not seen by every one, yet the body, united by that authority, is seen by all but the blind."[58]

In contrast to typical legal fictions—conditions that the law treats, for convenience, as if they were true despite their obvious falsity—the corporation is, as Kyd points out, an undeniable and formidable fact: "as visible a body as an army."[59]

[56] Studies that emphasize the potential of other iterations of the corporate form include Gerald Frug, *City Making: Building Communities without Building Walls* (Princeton, NJ: Princeton University Press, 1999); Timothy V. Kaufman-Osborn, *The Autocratic Academy: Reenvisioning Rule within America's Universities* (Durham, NC: Duke University Press, 2023).

[57] Arthur Machen, "Corporate Personality," *Harvard Law Review* 24 (1911), 266. On legal fictions as both like and unlike literary fictions, see Simon Stern, "Legal and Literary Fictions," in *New Directions in Law and Literature*, ed. Elizabeth Anker and Bernadette Meyler (Oxford: Oxford University Press, 2017), 313–26.

[58] Stewart Kyd, *A Treatise on the Law of Corporations* (London: Printed for J. Butterworth, 1793), Vol. 1, 15–16).

[59] As Guyora Binder and Robert Weisberg write, paraphrasing Walter Benn Michaels, "A corporation, however artificial and different from a natural person, can be as 'real' as an artificial lake", Binder and Weisberg, *Literary Criticisms of Law*, 529.

And in this sense Romney is right: corporations, like armies, are (composed of) people. The aggregate theory, which holds that corporations are constituted by "free contract among individual shareholders," asserts so much.[60]

But we cannot stop here because, as Kyd continues, corporations only exist *as* corporations because of the legal powers that constitute a collective right or capacity distinct from individual rights and capacities: "When, therefore, a corporation is said to be invisible, that expression must be understood, of the *right* in many persons, collectively, to act as a corporation, and then it is as visible in the eye of the law, as any other right whatever, of which natural persons are capable."[61] Thus, in contrast to the legal fiction (an as-if that contravenes physical fact), a corporation comprises a physical fact (an assembled body), "seen by all but the blind," *bound by a legal fact* (a right) that is "visible in the eye of the law." This mixed structure demands a kind of ontological double vision that refuses to recognize either nature or law as fundamental—and which recognizes legal fictionality as irreducible to specific fictions.[62] (Despite their differences, the three conventional theories of the corporation—artificial entity, aggregate, and real entity—all attempt to ground the corporation's status in either nature—i.e., fact—*or* law.) Some recent scholarship has underscored this hybridity in various idioms: David Ciepley argues that the corporation, created by means of "government interference," is "a messy public/private offshoot of public government and cannot be separated from it historically, analytically, or normatively."[63] And Henry Turner has aptly described corporations as "relatively durable assemblages of human persons and nonhuman things; of technologies, economic practices, and information gathering procedures; of places, ports, and trading sites; of archival structures and legal systems; of diverging interests, representatives, and spokespersons—all held together by many different points of translation."[64] For nineteenth-century observers, a corporation like the Bank of the United States, which gathered shareholders, managers, and employees as well as architectural, financial, and legal and organizational structures, and exercised power that spread beyond itself, this expansive heterogeneity was palpable.

What Ciepley and Turner, like Kyd, articulate in varied ways is the corporation's fundamentally hybrid form, an assemblage that entangles the legal *and* the physical just as it does the public *and* the private, the human *and* the nonhuman, without asserting the ontological primacy of one or the other. To see such hybrid

[60] Horwitz, *The Transformation of American Law, 1870–1960*, 75.

[61] Kyd, *A Treatise on the Law of Corporations*, Vol. 1, 16.

[62] As Stern argues, the traditional understanding of legal fictions as exceptional obscures the prevalence of legal contrivances and the stories adduced to support them, a situation he terms *legal fictionality*. Corporate personhood is thus less an isolated legal fiction, than an instance of meaning-making in a legal system characterized by artifice. Stern, "Legal and Literary Fictions," 322.

[63] David Ciepley, "Beyond Public and Private: Toward a Political Theory of the Corporation," *American Political Science Review* 107 (2013), no. 1:141.

[64] Turner, *The Corporate Commonwealth*, 104.

beings accurately means seeing with our own eyes *and* the eye of the law, even when they offer conflicting information. That means understanding the law's tropes of metaphor and personification as not merely decorative but constitutive. A personified law confers personality on a hitherto unincorporated body (an oxymoron, as Maitland pointed out).[65] The panoptic eye of the law surveys the army-like assembly of the corporation and sees a person.

At the heart of Kyd's concept of the corporation is the double vision of the human eye and the eye of the law—and the overlapping realms to which they grant access. A strikingly similar account of doubleness and incorporation appears in what might seem a surprising place: the enigmatic opening lines of Poe's "Sonnet—Silence":

> There are some qualities—some incorporate things,
> That have a double life—life aptly made,
> The type of that twin entity which springs
> From matter and light, evinced in solid and shade.[66]

Poe's speaker reasons gingerly as he addresses the "double life" of "some qualities—some incorporate things." Despite this metaphysical preamble, he begins with a doubling that proceeds merely from the physical: from the bare facts of "matter and light" we can derive the phenomena of opaque solidity and shadow. If physical bodies have a double life, the speaker suggests, then it should follow that some nonphysical ones do as well. Poe's very diction creates a double vision of its own: "incorporate things" ambiguously suggests both incorporeal things *without* a body and incorporated things *gathered into* a body. This resonant phrase not only puns on the corporation but also felicitously captures the twin aspects—incorporation and incorporeality—that Kyd's account of the corporation struggles to reconcile.

I expand on Poe's conception of "double life" in chapter 1. In the meantime, I'll suggest that the ontological questions Poe raises recur stubbornly when dealing with corporations. As the poet Jena Osman has recently argued, the "separation of the corporation from the individuals that make it up reanimates age-old ideas of a mind-body split."[67] "Industrial Palace," the final poem in her remarkable book on the corporate form, depicts this Cartesian separation of material body and immaterial mind as inevitably clunky by imagining the human body as a business corporation:

[65] Frederic Maitland, "The Unincorporate Body," in *State, Trust, and Corporation*, ed. David Runciman and Magnus Ryan (Cambridge: Cambridge University Press, 2003).
[66] Edgar Allan Poe, "Silence. A Sonnet," *Burton's Gentleman's Magazine* 6 (1840):166.
[67] Jena Osman, *Corporate Relations* (Providence, RI: Burning Deck/Aynart, 2014), 73.

a suited one reads alone in the office of sensation
three argue around a table in the office of reason
a lab-coated one checks the dials in the gland center
two work the switchboard of the muscle center
three suited ones discuss the will[68]

With its juxtaposition of early modern faculty psychology and retro-futuristic industrial bureaucracy, Osman's image of "an army of homunculi" demystifies the mind by playfully turning the notion of organizational psychology inside out.[69] At the same time, the poem's final line insists upon the mystery of the body, whether human or corporate: "look at the body: it moves."[70] Osman suggests that we can frame the problem of the corporation as the problem of animation: the relation between—or mutual constitution and coordination of—bodies and souls.

In doing so she echoes an early modern conception of corporations, bodies, and souls that predates even Descartes's *cogito*. The case of *Tipling v. Pexall* (1614) records Chief Baron Manwood's concise and surprisingly durable theory: "The opinion of Manwood Chief Baron was this, as touching corporations, that they were invisible, immortall, and that they had no soule; and therefore no subpoena lieth against them, because they have no conscience nor soule; a corporation, is a body aggregate, none can create soules but God, but the King creates them, and therefore they have no soules: they cannot speak, nor appear in person, but by attorney."[71]

The metaphysical status of the corporation, by this often-invoked standard, follows from the analogy between the divine creation of (ensouled) natural persons and the royal creation of (soulless) artificial persons. This doctrine of artificial persons would be reiterated in various forms by Sir Edward Coke, Blackstone, and Kyd, and in Chief Justice Marshall's characterization of the corporation as "an artificial being...existing only in contemplation of law."[72] Although Marshall dispenses with Manwood's explicit metaphysics, he similarly reduces the ontological—and with it, it would seem, the ethical—footprint of the corporation. Emphasizing the artificiality of the corporation often serves to minimize its liability. (Nonetheless, as Lisa Siraganian has argued, corporate intention—for the purposes of civil or criminal liability—need not depend on the presence of a soul.)[73]

[68] Jena Osman, "Industrial Palace," in *Corporate Relations*, 71–2, ll. 3–7.
[69] Osman, "Industrial Palace," l. 52. [70] Osman, "Industrial Palace," l. 55.
[71] *Tipling v. Pexall*, 2 Bulstrode 233, 80 English Reports (1614):1085.
[72] *Trustees of Dartmouth College v. Woodward*, 636.
[73] *Modernism and the Meaning of Corporate Persons* (Oxford: Oxford University Press, 2020), esp. 80–140.

The American lawyer Amasa Mason Eaton observed in 1903 that Manwood's "curious scholastic reasoning" might be applied to bodies as well as souls, leading the way to a *reductio ad absurdum*:

> It would be equally correct (and equally childish) to reason that none can create bodies but God, but the King creates corporations, therefore they have no bodies. Therefore a corporation has no soul nor body. Having no soul nor mind, it can do nothing requiring the exercise of mental powers; having no body it can have no members and can do nothing requiring the exercise of physical powers. It has no arms, no hands, etc. It cannot sign a deed nor affix the corporate seal; nor can it express intention to have these things done for it. It cannot do anything.[74]

Eaton rejects this "childish" vision of the incapacitated corporation in favor of a reversal of Manwood's logic that anticipates Osman's play with bodies and souls: "If any force is to be given to such reasoning…instead of coming to the conclusion that a corporation has no soul, it would be more correct to conclude that a corporation is nothing but a soul, it being an immaterial entity, a persona ficta."[75] For all its playfulness, Eaton's logic can help explain why it is so difficult to purge the theory of the corporation of metaphysical language. A corporation is an artificial soul, an animation with visible consequences. It moves.

Natural and Artificial Persons

Ultimately, these disputes about bodies and souls are questions about where to locate the essence of corporation, which inheres not in a mysterious substance but in a group of capacities. Blackstone identifies a bundle of "powers, rights, capacities, and incapacities" that are "necessarily and inescapably incident to every corporation": "1. To have perpetual succession.…2. To sue or be sued, implead or be impleaded, grant or receive, by its corporate name, and do all other acts as natural persons may. 3. To purchase lands, and hold them…. 4. To have a common seal. For a corporation, being an invisible body cannot manifest its intentions by any personal act or oral discourse: it therefore acts and speaks only by its common seal.…5. To make by-laws or private statutes for the better government of the corporation." (*CLE*, 463)

[74] Amasa Mason Eaton, *The First Book in English on the Law of Incorporation* (New Haven, CT: Ryder's Printing House 1903) (reprinted from the *Yale Law Journal*, March–April 1903), 10.

[75] Eaton, *The First Book in English*, 11. Eaton echoes Boethius's definition of the person as "an individual substance of a rational nature." Boethius's definition of the person as "an individual substance of a rational nature." See Bartosz Brożek, "The Troublesome 'Person'," in *Legal Personhood: Animals, Artificial Intelligence, and the Unborn*, ed. Visa A. J. Kurki and Tomasz Pietrzykowski, (New York: Springer, 2017), 4.

Blackstone's framing of the corporation's capacity to "do all other acts as natural persons may" recalls his efficient—if circular—distinction between natural and artificial persons: "Natural persons are such as the God of nature formed us: artificial are such as created and devised by human laws for the purposes of society and government; which are called corporations or bodies politic" (*CLE*, 119) Like Manwood, Blackstone initially derives the features of the natural person from the creative act of "the God of nature"; like his Enlightenment contemporaries he grounds "the absolute *rights* of individuals...which every man is intitled to enjoy whether out of society or in it," in the "immutable laws of nature" (*CLE*,119–20). In contrast, he derives the rights of artificial persons not from the nature of corporate bodies themselves but from the practical considerations that give rise to them. Although his discussion of corporations opens with a nod to the "natural capacities" and "rights and duties" of natural persons, he acknowledges the "inconvenient, if not impracticable" problem of "investing a series of individuals, one after another, with the same identical rights" (*CLE*, 455). The canonical corporate properties of individuality and immortality arise as a pragmatic solution to this problem. As a vehicle for consolidating "privileges and immunities" and "estates and possession," the corporation is "but one person in law, a person that never dies" (*CLE*, 456).

Thus, while he initially presents the artificial person as parasitic upon the natural person, Blackstone's theory of the corporation ultimately clarifies the affordances of personhood *tout court*. As Maitland notes, "Like the man, the corporation is...a right-and-duty bearing unit."[76] And as noted above, Dewey generalizes this formula: for the purposes of law "'person' might be used simply as a synonym for a right-and-duty-bearing unit."[77] To recognize the corporation's personhood is to recognize that the enumerated affordances of the corporate form coincide (roughly, in any case) with the affordances of all persons under the law—a fact that often elicits uneasiness.

Barbara Johnson's "Anthropomorphism in Lyric and Law," aptly diagnoses the discomfort that personified corporations can provoke. Johnson argues, following Gregory Mark, that the features of the corporation—and particularly the for-profit business corporation—have been read back into human nature in the form of *homo oeconomicus*, "the quintessential economic man." More broadly, she suggests that "theories of rationality, naturalness, and the 'good,' presumed to be grounded in the nature of 'man,' may in reality be taking their notions of human essence not from 'natural man' but from business corporations." This insight can be disturbing, because "the mingling of personifications on the same footing as 'real' agents threatens to make the lack of certainty about what humanness is

[76] Maitland, "Moral Personality," 63.

[77] Dewey, "The Historic Background," 656.

come to consciousness."[78] The legal homology between artificial and natural persons, she argues, recapitulates the relationship between personification (the poetic attribution of a *persona*) and anthropomorphism (the poetic attribution of human features, and thus the implicit assertion of a human essence beyond the relational structure of tropes). By this logic, the legal category of natural person is not, as it might initially appear, a simple recognition of the human in law, but itself a form of personification, no less artificial than the artificial personhood to which it is contrasted.

The through-line of Johnson's argument, which links Paul de Man's poetics to the law of corporations, is the deconstruction of the anthropomorphism—the positing of human essence—that lies at the heart of the common law account of the person. Anthropomorphism, in de Man's sense of identification, captures what both sides of "Corporations are/not people" share: a theory that takes the human for granted.[79] The Corporations-Are-People view asserts that corporations are ontologically insignificant because they are reducible to the people who compose them (or, in a familiar variation, the nexus of contracts among them), while the Corporations-Are-Not-People position argues that rights are grounded in human nature and thus that nonhuman corporate persons cannot and should not possess them. Both positions anchor the nature of the corporation in an implicit theory of the human; both express a desire to frame the person without the mediation of legal tropes. What de Man and Johnson help us see is the way attempts to distinguish between natural and artificial persons rest on an untenable, if often unspoken, anthropomorphism—a version of the same metaphysics that Osman and Eaton target in their critiques of Cartesian body/soul conceptions of the corporation.

Yet the person need not coincide with or transparently represent the human being, as the common law theory of the natural person would have it. Another perspective suggests that the uncanniness of corporate personhood arises less from the introduction of mysterious entities than from the reconceptualization of the person as "a purely technical device."[80] As a technical entity that allows the law to recognize groupings of rights and duties, the person loses its presumptive role as the transcendent source of value, rights, and duties—what Bartosz Brożek calls the "axiological" conception of the person. As Brożek writes: "Instead of asking, what is the proper definition of the person,...one should concentrate on a different kind of questions, such as 'Should comatose patients be protected by the law and in what way?' or 'Should non-human primates be objects of ownership?'

[78] Barbara Johnson, "Anthropomorphism in Lyric and Law," *Persons and Things* (Cambridge, MA: Harvard University Press, 2008), 206–7.

[79] Paul de Man, "Anthropomorphism and Trope in the Lyric," *The Rhetoric of Romanticism* (New York: Columbia University Press, 1984), 241.

[80] Yann Thomas, "The Subject of Right, the Person, Nature: Remarks on the Current Criticism of the Legal Subject," in *Legal Artifices: Ten Essays on Roman Law in the Present Tense*, ed. Thanos Zartaloudis and Cooper Francis (Edinburgh: Edinburgh University Press, 2021), 119.

The important insight is that the answer to those questions cannot be 'Yes/No, because they are persons/nonpersons.'"[81]

As Brożek implies, the contemporary anxiety over corporate personhood is, in an important sense, misplaced: it confuses technical questions about legal capacities of persons with ethical questions about human identity. In any case, the claim of humanity is rarely an effective ground for the assertion of rights. As Jeannine DeLombard has pointed out, the "assault on black dignity"—whether legal or pseudoscientific—has "operated primarily through the exploitative recognition, rather than denial, of black humanity." After all, proslavery writers freely acknowledged that "the very idea of a *slave* is a human being in bondage."[82]

The Romanist legal historian Yann Thomas and his readers have shown how the Civil Law tradition, in contrast to Blackstone's derivation of the natural rights of persons from the nature of man, sidesteps questions about humanity. As Edward Mussawir and Connor Parlsey write, Roman law foregrounds the "discrete and self-conscious techniques of shaping the legal person." They clarify what Blackstone's account of the person obscures: "It is as though there were a split, within the modern law of persons, between the technical and the natural registers: on the one hand, such law embraces its technical virtuosity, and on the other, seemingly in response, law seeks to reassure us of its basis in 'natural' human life." Framing the person as a legal category rather than an extralegal essence enables "a return to a casuistic, concrete and immanent conception of the jurisprudential art of crafting the person."[83] Roman law, Thomas argues, conceives of the person first and foremost as a legal entity, not a natural being. He offers the personhood of municipalities as exemplary: "The personification of communities was a purely technical device, one that obeyed only the imputation of obligations and rights." In order to avoid confusion over property rights, jurists relied on a patently obvious artifice and used "the traditional legal category of the person in order to find solutions to newly emerging legal problems."[84] Civil law thus foregrounds what common law hides: that legally speaking the artificial person precedes the natural person—because the law itself is an artifice. The consequence is not simply a deconstruction of the *human* (as Johnson stresses) but a revealing account of the *person*, which appears with greatest clarity in its artificial forms.

Johnson's deconstructive account and Thomas's historicist account thus point to a shared conclusion: to read the corporation as an unnatural encroachment on the human person ("Corporations aren't people!") is to misrecognize personhood

[81] Bartosz Brożek, "The Troublesome 'Person,' V.A.J. Kurki, T. Pietrzykowski (eds.), *Legal Personhood: Animals, Artificial Intelligence and the Unborn*, Law and Philosophy Library 119, 7, 13.

[82] Jeannine Marie DeLombard, "Debunking Dehumanization," *American Literary History* 30 (2018):800, 804.

[83] Edward Mussawir and Connal Parsley, "The Law of Persons Today: At the Margins of Jurisprudence," *Law and Humanities* 11 (2017):45–46.

[84] Yann Thomas, "The Subject of Right, the Person, Nature," 119.

as something natural. Rather—and counterintuitively—both Johnson and Thomas suggest we might better understand the person and its affordances in the context of the corporation, where it is comparatively disentangled from the question of the human. In this way, the very facets of personhood that seem inherent to the natural person come to the fore as pragmatic and artificial when we foreground the corporate person. Beginning an account of personhood with the corporation foregrounds personhood itself as a set of techniques, capacities, or affordances rather than a natural or metaphysical essence.

If we abandon a metaphysical opposition between natural and artificial persons, what remains is the task of describing corporate forms and corporate tropes. Like the ultimately untenable distinction between form and structure (which relies on the assumption of a dichotomy between the aesthetic and the social), the difference between form (as macrocosm) and trope (as microcosm) is a matter of scale rather than substance. Insofar as corporations are creatures of law and of representation, tropology *is* their ontology. Recognizing it as such affords an unfamiliar—and, I hope, revealing—perspective on the law's apparently metaphysical categories that can circumvent the reflexive moral intuitions evoked by bodies, souls, and personhood. Stripped of their metaphysical trappings, these categories emerge as rhetorical or legal affordances that offer a grasp on the elusive corporation. Thus, attention to the legal and rhetorical forms that constitute corporations—and the representational forms that make them knowable to members, managers, lawyers, and judges—has also afforded observers, whether playful satirists, earnest theorists, or activists, material for critique and strategic resistance.

Corporate Tropes

The corporate form has invited a long list of analogies, including the human being, the army, the township, the nation. While these comparisons often emerge from the legal doctrine of the corporation, they also indicate a broader figurative field. Although they may lack legal force, these figures shape intuitive conceptions of the corporation and reveal fundamental facets of the corporation's way of being; they thus afford means by which contemporaries could encounter (and counter) the corporate form—and the way that the figure of the corporation could offer new purchase on problems of individuality and collectivity, freedom and servitude.

Blackstone, as noted above, derives the rights of natural persons from the "laws of nature" but derives corporate rights from practical considerations. That is not to say, however, that associations might not have their own laws of nature. For political observers in the 1830s, there was no contradiction in describing artificial persons as natural phenomena. As I discuss in chapter 2, the Prussian-American polymath and political theorist Francis Lieber devoted particular attention to the complexity and power of associations—and to the political properties that spontaneously emerge from them. Tocqueville reveals Lieber's influence when he describes the township as a spontaneous corporate form: "the grouping so close to man's nature that wherever men gather together township automatically comes into being."[85] In doing so, he stakes a position that would subsequently be elaborated by late-nineteenth and early-twentieth-century real entity theorists. Lieber himself goes a step further, describing the nation as "the great corporation, comprehending all the others."[86]

More skeptical writers would echo both Lieber's vision of the corporate nation and Kyd's description of the corporation: "as visible a body as an army." Much like Kyd, Thoreau imagines the corporation as neither a spontaneous association nor a ghostly threat but rather as a concrete, militarized collectivity. He quips that "a corporation of conscientious men is a corporation *with* a conscience," yet frames the nation as a corporation without conscience, cynically dependent on the deference that turns citizens into "the agents of injustice."[87] An "undue respect for the law," he writes, reduces morally autonomous men to "a file of soldiers, colonel, captain, corporal, privates, powder-monkeys and all, marching in admirable order over hill and dale to the wars, against their wills, aye, against their common sense and consciences, which makes it very steep marching indeed, and produces a palpitation of the heart.... Now, what are they? Men at all? or small movable forts and magazines, at the service of some unscrupulous man in power?"[88]

In language that anticipates Nietzsche's well-known depiction of truth itself as figuration—"a mobile army of metaphors, metonymies, and anthropomorphisms"—Thoreau insists that ingrained obedience transforms men into a mobile army of military technologies in service of a personified nation. His account of the dehumanizing potential of ordered collectivity culminates in a surprising image of artificial personhood: "The mass of men serve the State thus, not as men mainly, but as machines, with their bodies. They are the standing army, and the militia, jailers, constables, *posse comitatus*, &c. In most cases there is no free exercise whatever of the judgment or of the moral sense; but they put themselves on a level with wood and earth and stones; and wooden men can perhaps be manufactured that will serve the purpose as well."[89]

[85] Tocqueville, *Democracy in America*, 72.

[86] Francis Lieber, "Corporation," in *Encyclopaedia Americana*, Vol. 3, ed. Francis Lieber and Edward Wigglesworth (Philadelphia, PA: Carey and Lea, 1830), 547–48.

[87] Thoreau, "Resistance to Civil Government," 387. As Siraganian has pointed out, Thoreau's quip—attributing the conscience of members to the corporation—implies the aggregate theory. Siraganian, *Modernism*, 24–25.

[88] Thoreau, "Resistance to Civil Government," 387.

[89] Thoreau, "Resistance to Civil Government," 388.

By distinguishing between men and machines on the basis of "the exercise of the judgment or the moral sense," Thoreau offers his own account of natural and artificial persons. Although he makes no reference to Blackstone's legal categories, he relies on the "as if" logic of legal fiction as he develops the metaphor of men as "small movable forts and magazines" into an explicit comparison: "as machines," "on a level with wood and earth and stones." The unquestioningly obedient are transformed by their "undue respect for the law" into artificial persons. Thoreau implicitly invokes Hobbes's account of the artificial person as agent: "he whose words and actions...are considered as representing the words and actions of an other."[90] Thoreau frames such artificial persons—"at the service of some unscrupulous man," "serv[ing] the purpose well"—as servants who yield moral judgment to an absent principal. Ironically, in Thoreau's essay, that principal is "the State," no longer the representative of a republican populace but a rogue actor in its own right (or a "tool" in the service of "comparatively a few individuals") cynically committed to perpetuating and expanding Black servitude.[91] Thoreau thus reframes the law of agency—the nucleus of corporate law, as Mueller notes—as the law of slavery.[92]

Both slavery and the modern corporation demonstrate how legal conceptions of personhood and property overlap. As Stephen Best has argued, the doctrine of slaves as both property and persons set the stage for the personified property corporation.[93] Thoreau, likewise, indicates a connection between servitude and corporateness, yet does so without invoking property: he shows how unquestioning obedience can reverse the relations of principal (republican citizen) and agent (state), rendering the so-called natural person artificial. His account thus provides a revealing complement to Harriet Jacobs's description of enslaved people as "God-breathing machines" reduced to "no more, in the sight of their masters" and slaveholding law "than the cotton they plant, or the horses they tend."[94] Whereas Jacobs shows how slaveowners forcibly "reduce" human beings to chattel, Thoreau's obedient soldiers willingly "put themselves" on the plane of "wood and earth and stones." Echoing Wordsworth's image of a lifeless body "Rolled

[90] Thomas Hobbes, *Leviathan* (1651), ed. Richard E. Flathman and David Johnston (New York: Norton, 1997), 88.

[91] Thoreau, "Resistance to Civil Government," 385.

[92] Mueller, *The Corporation in the Nineteenth-Century American Imagination*, 27–28.

[93] The law of slavery and corporations, Best contends, gives rise to a virtualized form of property, no longer "tangible" but "abstract, intangible, or...a mere 'bundle of rights.'" A similar change affects the form of the person, increasingly understood as accessible through and as intangible, even "fugitive" property. Best characterizes the historical arc from the precapitalist to the capitalist as a movement from concreteness to abstraction. Yet early modern theorists of the corporation were already quite comfortable treating it as the abstract "bundle of rights" that he presents as a function of high capitalism. Stephen Best, *The Fugitive's Properties: Law and the Poetics of Possession* (Chicago: University of Chicago Press, 2004), 14. See also DeLombard, "Debunking Dehumanization."

[94] Harriet Jacobs, *Incidents in the Life of a Slave Girl, Written by Herself* (1861), ed. Nell Irvin Painter (New York: Penguin, 2000), 10.

round in earth's diurnal course / With rocks and stones and trees," Thoreau's words suggest that uncritical subservience to the incorporated state amounts to and self-annihilation.[95] Here, incorporation into an orderly body grants neither immortality (à la Blackstone) nor vitality (à la Tocqueville) but unfreedom, inertness, and death.

Thoreau's final image of "wooden men" who might "be manufactured" to "serve the purpose" provocatively rearranges the building blocks of the law of corporations: person, corporation, agency. Here, the mystery is not how (as for Blackstone) an incorporated body can be said to have an individual and immortal personality, nor how (as for Hobbes) the political consent of natural persons can create an artificial sovereign. Rather, it lies in the way some incorporated bodies (companies, states, armies) operate by reducing their constituent members (putatively natural persons) to subjects, artificial persons, or amoral machines. While the corporation figures as an immortal person in the eye of the law, it also imposes its own law upon the persons it commands. Thoreau's conception of the state thus adumbrates the dynamic Elizabeth Anderson has recently highlighted in her account of business corporations as private governments.[96] (One ghastly mirror image of Anderson's insight is the claim that the US government ought to be run like a private corporation, the consequences of which are emerging as I put the finishing touches on this text.) Thoreau's biting description of corporate authoritarianism occupies one extreme of the wide spectrum of antebellum views of the corporation—and dramatizes how corporations gave rise to a constellation of tropes that exceed legal doctrine and provoke questions about assembly and animation, consciousness and conscience, sovereignty and subjection.

* * *

As this introduction's preliminary tour of the corporate imaginary suggests, the project of describing the corporation—in the nineteenth century or the twenty-first—is irreducible either to legal theories of the corporation or a literary vocabulary of tropes. Rather, it takes place at the intersection of disciplinary vocabularies, and thus raises the difficulties that Jonathan Kramnick and Anahid Nersessian have identified for literary and interdisciplinary accounts of form. Formal explanation in literary studies, they argue, "requires a working vocabulary proper to the literary before form can be welcomed into analogy with other things." At the same time, they recognize that "a truly interdisciplinary practice will accept that notions of form vary meaningfully across disciplines, that the differences among them are sometimes irreducible, and that no single discipline or

[95] William Wordsworth, "A Slumber Did My Spirit Seal," in *Wordsworth's Poetry and Prose*, ed. Nicholas Halmi (New York: Norton, 2014), 115 ll. 7–8.

[96] Anderson, *Private Government*.

field-specific concept need obtain absolute explanatory priority over others."[97] As a literary scholar studying the intersection of nineteenth-century legal and literary worlds—and participating in the interdisciplinary discourse of law and literature—I am acutely aware of the risk of conceptual incommensurability between fields. Yet as I have tried to show, the law's dependence on literary tropes reveals that law and literature have never been clearly separable disciplinary or ontic domains; nor are they separable historically, particularly in a period of pervasive interpenetration between law and letters.[98] My own disciplinary formation means that my account of form proceeds from a "vocabulary proper to the literary" even as I grapple with a plurality of approaches to form, both legal and literary, historical and contemporary.

The Corporate Forms of Antebellum US Literature seeks first and foremost to recover the surprising views of corporate form that antebellum texts make manifest. In doing so it attends, to borrow Anna Kornbluh's apt language, to antebellum accounts of "composed relationality." By proliferating possibilities for forms of relationality ranging from aesthetic abstractions to social ties, she writes, literature constitutes a powerful reserve of "the political imagining that can issue from studying forms." Aesthetic attention to form can thus enable a kind of political epistemology and pragmatics because "forms inscribe, thereby making relations among abstractions fathomable and reconfigurable."[99] This study does not posit a unified theory of form—or of politics, for that matter. Rather, it tracks the intersecting forms—legal, political, social, narrative, poetic—that animate and traverse nineteenth-century texts. As I have argued, canonical accounts of the corporation's legal form rely on complex knots of literary form—metaphors, analogies, and personifications—as well as chains of allusion by which these tropes invoke literary precursors as well as legal precedents. My goal, then, is not to subsume legal language under the umbrella of literary language (or vice versa) but rather to show how the project of describing the corporation takes us to the borderlands where these two notions of form cohabitate. When literary figure and legal doctrine interpenetrate, the disciplinary autonomy invoked by Kramnick and Nersessian becomes (appropriately and fruitfully, I would argue) unstable. Antebellum US law and literature overlapped both figuratively—the law incorporates and relies on literary tropes; literature borrows and reimagines legal categories—and in their material production and circulation—legal and literary writers and writing regularly traveled in the same social circles, often in the same bodies and published volumes.

[97] Jonathan Kramnick and Anahid Nersessian, "Form and Explanation," *Critical Inquiry* 43 (2017):652.

[98] Binder and Weisberg describe the post-Civil War reframing of the legal profession "as scientific experts rather than exemplars of civic literacy," marked by the ascendancy of Harvard Law School Dean Christopher Langdell's case method. Binder and Weisberg, *Literary Criticisms of Law*, 57.

[99] Anna Kornbluh, *The Order of Forms: Realism, Formalism, and Social Space* (Chicago: University of Chicago Press, 2019), 4, 8.

Chapter Summaries

The Corporate Forms of Antebellum US Literature examines the corporation's history as a history of tropes, forms, and affordances: the figures that writers, in literary, legal, and other sorts of texts, used to represent corporations and the figures that corporations have been understood to be. These figures include (im)mortality, association, personhood, empire, and aesthetic and social arrangement. Each chapter centers on a text or group of texts that highlights one facet of the corporate form and its literary genealogy. Chapter 1, "A Double Life: Personifying the Corporation from *Dartmouth College* to Poe," pursues the early nineteenth-century prehistory of contemporary debates over corporate personhood, with a particular emphasis on the attribute of immortality. It demonstrates how early nineteenth-century corporations confronted both jurists and lay writers with an idea of personhood irreducible to the human being. *Trustees of Dartmouth College v. Woodward* (1819) enshrined the common-law definition of the corporation—an artificial person, immortal and invisible—in American jurisprudence. In contrast, contemporaneous satirical poems on failing banks personified corporations as strikingly visible and mortal. Less than two decades later, the Bank War would give rise to rhetorical and visual critiques of banking corporations that drew on a metaphysical register that both echoed and exceeded legal doctrine. Poe's poetry and tales, in particular, drew on the legal doctrine of artificial personhood and juxtaposed it unsettlingly with the seemingly natural personhood of human beings, articulating the challenges posed by the corporation to the logic of human identity. Like anonymous versifiers responding to the Panic of 1819, Poe found analogs for the legal theory of corporate immortality in registers beyond the law, including the materiality of bodies and the metaphysics of haunting. Their vivid poetic and satirical fictions offer revealing conceptions of the uncanny possibilities of corporate personhood.

Chapter 2, "The Corporation and the Encyclopedia: Theorizing and Practicing Assemblage in the Age of Association," situates the theory of the corporation as a form of association amid the network of legal and lay theorists of the corporation among whom it circulated. In particular, it investigates the ways the Prussian-American émigré, editor, and political theorist Francis Lieber both framed the corporation and situated himself in associative networks. It contends that Lieber's *Encyclopaedia Americana* article on the corporation both articulates of a theory of association and occupies an important node in a practice of association. Lieber draws on jurisprudence of the corporation and liberal political theory, yet also theorizes of the political consequences of association in a way that exceeds both legal theory of the corporation and liberal contract theory. Attending to his accounts of the varied forms that assembly took—and of the ontological questions raised by the corporate form—both illuminates the prehistory of the corporation as we know it and suggests paths not taken. By investigating the possibilities and quandaries of assembling companies and groups as political phenomena, Lieber and his contemporaries anticipate both the real entity theory of the corporation and subsequent theories of assemblage. Lieber's work thus opens paths between the law of corporations and more open-ended ontologies of political and textual plurality.

Chapter 3, "The Faculties of Law: Constituting Persons in Robert Montgomery Bird's *Sheppard Lee*," centers on the constitution of the corporation via succession. It argues that Robert Montgomery Bird's supernatural picaresque novel, *Sheppard Lee, Written by Himself*, comes into focus when we recognize it as a foray into the law of persons. I situate *Sheppard Lee* and its play with personhood-as-succession amid two 1830s debates over the law of persons. In and around Pennsylvania's 1837–38 constitutional convention, both the corporate personality of the Bank of the United States—could its charter be revoked?—and the political personhood of Black Pennsylvanians—was the franchise limited to whites?—engendered contentious debate. Bird's novel, which represents a single protagonist successively embodied in a variety of social roles, experiments with the very facets of personhood whose recognition was at stake in the convention. Its play with embodiment, disembodiment, and succession, I argue, explores the crossing of racialized and corporate personhood in revealing ways that contemporaneous political discourse did not. *Sheppard Lee* offers an idiom of personhood that can speak both to the embodied politics of race and the apparently spectral power of corporations, even as it ironically reveals the limitations of Bird's own politics.

Chapter 4, "Irving's *Astoria* and the Forms of Enterprise," foregrounds the corporation as a form of empire—and the ways that literary form makes it manifest. Centered on antebellum America's most notable corporate biography, this chapter contends that Washington Irving frames the literary problem of narrating the corporation as analogous to and intertwined with the governance of imperial corporations. In *Astoria, or Anecdotes of an Enterprize beyond the Rocky Mountains*, Irving both personifies a corporate protagonist and sketches its operations as an imperial form. I argue that *Astoria* inherits its apparent disorder—and its resulting obscurity in critical discourse—from its subject, John Jacob Astor's American Fur Company. The world *Astoria* frames can appear formless and lawless from the perspective of territorial sovereignty, yet it follows the patterns of nomadic corporate capitalism, not least its attempt to lay claim to an ungovernable energy that it attributes both to the company and to the Indigenous people it disrupts and displaces. While scholars in recent decades have given ample attention to the interplay of nation and empire—and framed nineteenth-century US nationalism as fundamentally imperial—I insist that we recognize the corporation as a crucial third term that mediates the familiar dyad of nation and empire. Attending to the literature of commercial empire can help us understand the narrative and rhetorical affordances of the corporate form and better recognize the virtual sovereignty exercised by multinational corporations in our own time.

Whereas the narrative failures of *Astoria* reveal the odd fit between the corporation's narrative role as person (protagonist) and its imperial role as networked form, the final two chapters examine convoluted intersections of literary and organizational form even as they show how nineteenth-century theories of corporate form reached beyond the domain of law. Chapter 5, "A Company of Socialists: The Corporate Imaginary in Associationist Print," turns to the possibilities and pitfalls that emerged in the conjoined histories of Associationism (Fourierist socialism) and the corporate form in nineteenth-century America, and to show how these histories took a particularly literary turn as Fourierist periodicals became important venues for poetry and fiction as well as social theory. Like chapter 2, it draws on the methods of book history to trace the practices through which theories of association were formulated and promulgated. It particularly tracks the *Phalanx* and its successor the *Harbinger*, which was published at the Brook Farm Community, where Hawthorne set *The Blithedale Romance*. By reading Associationism as a milieu of print, aesthetic, and social production, not just an object of satire, this chapter explores the ramifications of what F. O. Matthiessen described long ago as the "age of Fourier."[100] As Matthiessen's phrase suggests, scholars have long recognized the connections between romantic aesthetics and utopian and anti-utopian critiques of nineteenth-century capitalism. But by situating Associationism among the corporate investments and strategies of reformist print culture and Fourierist social theory, we can gain a clearer view of the interpenetration of aesthetic form and social form—and how these strategies underpinned a secular millennialism.

Whereas Associationists strove to craft an aesthetically and politically perfect form of association, Melville's final novel catalogued—and satirized—a dizzying range of such forms. Chapter 6, "Assembled Companies: The Corporate Forms of *The Confidence-Man*," turns to the compound protagonist and seemingly arbitrary episodic form of *The Confidence-Man*, which have longed challenged critics. In contrast to accounts of the novel centered on its titular figure(s), this chapter approaches the novel's play with unity and multiplicity by examining the various "companies" that Melville's fiction depicts in passing. *The Confidence-Man* devotes sustained attention to the corporate attributes of assembly and succession and sketches a number of corporate forms and practices, including the exchange of shares of the Black Rapids Coal Corporation, the vision of an eleemosynary empire under the auspices of the World's Charity, and the choreography by which the company aboard the riverboat *Fidèle* assembles, disassembles, and reassembles itself. While the novel is often read as casting uniform suspicion on mid-nineteenth-century America's simultaneous love affairs with confidence and skepticism, I show how it catalogues and anatomizes the possibilities,

[100] F. O. Matthiessen, *American Renaissance: Art and Expression in the Age of Emerson and Whitman* (New York: Oxford University Press, 1941), viii.

both optimistic and horrific, of the corporate form and the entities to which it gives rise. Melville's framing of these varied forms of collectivity suggests that thinking through the corporation can offer a more supple idea of human plurality than traditional political, natural, or religious conceptions. I attend particularly to the way *The Confidence-Man* imagines a corporate entity generated by perpetual succession but without persistent identity. In doing so, it draws on familiar legal, political, and religious conceptions of plurality but also points beyond them.

As *The Confidence-Man* suggests, it might be more accurate to speak not of the corporate form but of corporate *forms*: forms of association and collectivity engendered by the law but productive of potentialities that reach beyond it. Informed by but not confined to legal conceptions of the corporation, the writers at the heart of this study produced a surprisingly broad and sophisticated repertoire of images, tropes, and theories as they depicted and investigated collective entities. Foregrounding this prolific corporate imaginary—from Poe's and Bird's accounts of the forms that persons can take to Lieber's, Brisbane's, and Melville's ontologies of collectivity—*The Corporate Forms of Antebellum US Literature* insists that neither business nor law has a monopoly on the corporate form. In a moment when corporations appear principally as instruments of economic accumulation, unaccountable power, and private governance, this study transmits an untimely repository of ways the corporation has been—and can be—imagined differently. Like Roman law's conception of the person as "a purely technical device" and Ishmael and Queequeg's device of the monkey rope, the corporation is a surprisingly flexible technology whose uses, both practical and imaginative, have not yet been exhausted.

The Corporate Forms of Antebellum US Literature. Peter Jaros, Oxford University Press. © Peter Jaros 2026.
DOI: 10.1093/9780198996491.003.0001

1
A Double Life
Personifying the Corporation from *Dartmouth College* to Poe

Edgar Allan Poe's satirical sketch "Peter Pendulum, the Business Man" (1840) clearly belongs to its time—the aftermath of the Panic of 1837—but its closing is equally at home in ours: "The frauds of the banks I can't, of course, help.... These, however, are not individuals, but corporations; and corporations, it is very well known, have neither posteriors to be kicked, nor souls to be damned."[1] For readers who have lived through the age of bank bailouts and *Citizens United*, Poe's key notes—fraudulent banks that shift their losses to small-time customers, the exasperating disembodiment of artificial persons, and the prominence of the corporate form in a moment of economic crisis—are all too familiar.

During the early decades of the nineteenth century, American corporations gained visibility and elicited controversy through a confluence of events: the legal watershed of *Trustees of Dartmouth College v. Woodward* (1819) and its foregrounding of the law of artificial persons, the role of banking corporations in the imperial economic and territorial expansion of the US after the War of 1812 and in subsequent financial panics, the unprecedented proliferation of business corporations, and the publication of important legal works on the corporate form. Grappling with corporations, however, was hardly the sole province of jurists. Rather, this chapter argues, the antebellum corporate imaginary emerges most clearly when we read legal texts alongside and in conversation with contemporaneous literary forays into the mechanics of personification. This chapter investigates a number of the legal and literary texts that confronted the problems of imagining and personifying the corporation: jurists' accounts of the corporate form; verse and visual satire that anthropomorphized corporations during the Panic of 1819 and the Bank War; and finally, a number of works by Poe, with particular attention to "Silence. A Sonnet" (1839–40), a poem that uses the structure of the corporation to trouble the ontology of personhood. These texts converge on a group of questions raised by the legal doctrine of corporate personality. What does it mean to call a corporation immortal and individual, bodiless and soulless? How might the attributes of the corporation unsettle its status as a

[1] Edgar Allan Poe, "Peter Pendulum, the Business Man," *Burton's Gentleman's Magazine* 6, no. 2 (1840): 89. Subsequent references in parentheses.

person, and how do they demand a reconsideration of so-called natural persons and their mortality, individuality, and corporeality? What effects proceed from accounts of the corporation that maximize or minimize its ontological footprint? These texts, that is, reveal the connections antebellum writers drew between two questions: *what is a corporation* and *what is a person*?

By tracking the corporate attributes of immortality, individuality, and intangibility in the transformative decades after *Dartmouth College*, this chapter sketches some of the lineaments of the corporate imaginary that emerged at the intersection of legal theory and practice, literary and visual representation, and political commentary on corporations. Corporate immortality drew particular attention from jurists and lay writers alike. The doctrine of corporate immortality was at once familiar, because it derived from longstanding common law tradition; disconcerting, because it conjured ghostly entities; and perverse, because corporate dissolution was a regular occurrence, due both to limited-term charters and to company failures, particularly in the Panics of 1819 and 1837.[2] While jurists developed a theory of the corporation that would undergird the rapid growth of American businesses, satirists and commentators unfolded the disorienting consequences of corporations' immortality and individuality. The light these writers cast on the corporate form sometimes reflected back on so-called natural persons, bringing, in Barbara Johnson's words, "the lack of certainty about what humanness is...to consciousness."[3] In 1839–40, Poe crystallized this uncertainty in a number of investigations of personhood, by turns cryptic, haunting, and playful. In idioms that evince consideration of the corporate form yet do not simply repeat legal theories of the corporation, they explore the consequences of maximizing the field of persons (as when corporations are treated as real entities) or minimizing it (as when they are treated as associations without substantive existence).

Corporations and Personhood

The early United States inherited what English legal historian Frederic W. Maitland efficiently distills as the "English Law of Persons...since the days of Sir Edward

[2] Limited-term charters—such as the twenty-year charters granted to manufacturing corporations in Pennsylvania—were common. Moreover, as reported in "A Digest of the Cases Contained in the 19th Vol. of Johnson's Reports," *United States Law Journal* 1 (1822–23): 461–510, a corporation could dissolve by surrendering its corporate rights, by committing or suffering "acts which destroy the end and object for which it was instituted," or by "ceas[ing] to own any property, real or personal, and...ceas[ing], for two or three years, to do any one act manifesting an intention to resume its corporate functions" (465). *Slee v. Bloom*, (NY Sup. Ct. 1822) 19 Johnson 456. For a contemporaneous discussion of corporate dissolution, see James Kent, *Commentaries on American Law* (New York: O. Halsted, 1826–30), Vol. 2, 245–53. On bank failures in the wake of the Panic of 1819, see Murray N. Rothbard, *The Panic of 1819: Reactions and Policies* (New York: Columbia University Press, 1962).

[3] Barbara Johnson, "Anthropomorphism in Lyric and Law," in *Persons and Things* (Cambridge, MA: Harvard University Press, 2008), 188–207, 207.

Coke": "Persons are either natural or artificial. The only natural persons are men. The only artificial persons are corporations. Corporations are either aggregate or sole."[4] Sir William Blackstone's *Commentaries on the Laws of England* (1765–69), the foundational compendium of early modern English law and the most important source for nineteenth-century legal discussions, both reiterates and contributes to this tradition. Blackstone frames the law of corporations as a means of reconciling personal rights with human mortality: "As all personal rights die with the person; and, as the necessary forms of investing a series of individuals, one after another, with the same identical rights, would be very inconvenient, if not impracticable; it has been found necessary, when it is for the advantage of the public to have any particular rights kept on foot and continued, to constitute artificial persons, who may maintain a perpetual succession, and enjoy a kind of legal immortality."[5]

By solving the problem of natural mortality with "legal immortality," the doctrine of artificial persons disrupts the seemingly natural binary of life and death. The doctrine also gives rise to ambiguity regarding number, providing for both corporations sole—offices like bishop or king whose identities are legally distinct from the individual persons who successively fill them—and corporations aggregate—incorporated associations. An individual in the role of a corporation sole is legally doubled (the king, as Ernst Kantorowicz famously points out, has two bodies).[6] A corporation aggregate, although "kept up by a perpetual succession of members," is legally an individual.[7]

These ambiguities drew the attention of Stewart Kyd, author of the frequently-cited *Treatise on the Law of Corporations* (1793). Rather than treat the attributes of the corporation as axioms from which to proceed, Kyd approaches them as linguistic problems to be solved: "That a body framed by the policy of man, a body whose parts and members are mortal, should in its own nature be immortal, or that a body composed of many bulky, visible bodies, should be invisible, in the common acceptation of the words, seems beyond reach of common understandings." He reasons that *invisible* has a particular meaning in this context: that "the *right* in many persons, collectively, to act as a corporation, and then it is as visible in the eye of the law, as any other right whatever, of which natural persons are capable." What is distinctive about corporations aggregate, Kyd argues, is neither the physicality of the persons that constitute them nor the metaphysical attributes attributed to them, but rather the very capacity—physically invisible but legally visible—of incorporation. He likewise explains corporate immortality in

[4] Frederic W. Maitland, *State, Trust, and Corporation*, ed. David Runciman and Magnus Ryan (Cambridge: Cambridge University Press, 2003), 9.

[5] William Blackstone, Sir William Blackstone, *Commentaries on the Laws of England: Book I: Of the Rights of Persons*, ed. David Lemmings (Oxford: Oxford University Press, 2016), 455.

[6] Ernst Kantorowicz, *The King's Two Bodies: A Study in Medieval Political Theology* (Princeton, NJ: Princeton University Press, 1957).

[7] Blackstone, *Commentaries*, 457.

terms of capacity: "When it is said that a corporation is immortal, we are to understand nothing more than that it is *capable* of an indefinite duration."[8] At the same time, he refuses to reduce the corporation itself as a capacity: "A corporation has been called 'a mere capacity to sue and be sued, and to take and to grant'; which is as ridiculous as is [*sic*] would be to say 'that a man is a mere capacity to walk with two feet.' It is not a capacity, but a political person, in which many capacities reside."[9] As an artificial person, Kyd argues, a corporation is the *subject* to which qualities and capacities appertain: "In this sense a corporation cannot be called a franchise; the latter is a privilege, or liberty, which can have no existence without reference to some person to whom it may belong; the former is a political person, capable, like a natural person, of enjoying a variety of franchises; it is to a franchise, as the substance to its attribute; it is something to which many attributes belong, but is itself something distinct from those attributes."[10] In identifying the corporation as a "political person," Kyd articulates an entity theory of the corporation without belaboring the question of the corporate entity's naturalness or artificiality. When we focus on the association of persons granted a corporate charter, incorporation may look like a "mere capacity," but when we recognize the "many capacities" of the corporate form, it appears as a being in its own right, a "political person."

This language of capacities—and the accompanying debates about the substantiality or insubstantiality of corporate entities—had attended the chartering of the First Bank of the United States. Thomas Jefferson and James Madison had argued that Congress could not charter corporations, not having explicitly been granted that power in the Constitution.[11] Alexander Hamilton, as the bank's champion, strategically minimized both the power to charter and the ontological status of the corporation itself. In a 1791 defense of the bank, Hamilton uses this language to dematerialize corporations as mere associations or aggregates: "An incorporation seems to have been regarded as some great, independent, substantive thing—as a political end of peculiar magnitude & moment; whereas it is truly to be considered as a *quality*, *capacity*, or *mean* to an end." He gives the example of a company founded by a group of merchants: "Suppose that an incorporation were added to this; it would only be to add a new *quality* to that association; to give it an artificial capacity by which it would be enabled to prosecute the business with more safety & convenience."[12] Hamilton's language of qualities and capacities,

[8] Stewart Kyd, *A Treatise on the Law of Corporations* (London: printed for J. Butterworth, 1793), Vol. 1, 15–17.

[9] Kyd distinguishes corporation ("a political institution") from incorporation ("the act by which that institution is created"). See *Treatise*, Vol. 1, 13–14.

[10] Kyd, *Treatise*, Vol. 1, 15.

[11] Adam Winkler, *We the Corporations: How American Businesses Won Their Civil Rights* (New York: Liveright, 2018), 39.

[12] Alexander Hamilton, "Final Version of an Opinion on the Constitutionality of the Bank" (1791), in *The Papers of Alexander Hamilton Digital Edition*, ed. Harold C. Spratt (Charlottesville, VA: University of Virginia Press, Rotunda, 2011), http://rotunda.upress.virginia.edu/founders/ARHN-01-08-02-0060-0003.

which articulates a version of the aggregate theory, identifies incorporation as an attribute of a preexisting "association" rather than an entity in itself, and thus rhetorically minimizes the corporation while arguing for fewer restrictions on corporate charters.

The first major Supreme Court case concerning the rights of corporations—notably including those of the Bank—turned on the question of whether corporations were entities or mere associations. In *Bank of the United States v. Deveaux* (1809) and its companion case *Hope Insurance Company v. Boardman* (1809), a central question was whether the Bank had standing to bring a lawsuit in Federal court, which depended in turn on whether the bank was regarded as a "citizen" of a particular jurisdiction. As Adam Winkler has detailed, lawyers arguing on behalf of the Bank and an insurance company minimized the corporate form by foregrounding, like Hamilton, the theory of corporation as association. It was the citizenship of members (i.e., shareholders) of the corporation, rather than that of the corporation itself, that should settle jurisdictional questions. Their opponents, in contrast, argued that corporations were "independent entities with legal rights and obligations separate and apart from the people who made them up." Foregrounding the entity status—the personhood—of the corporation afforded a mechanism to limit corporate rights; minimizing this entity status, in contrast, was a mechanism to bolster them. In a seeming paradox, the less substantial the corporation was in legal terms, the more powerful it became.[13]

Legal theorists, polemicists, verse writers, and visual artists addressed the same problem: how to represent and comprehend unprecedented forms of personality. They struggled to reconcile the seemingly paradoxical features of corporations and sometimes found—as did Poe—their power to unsettle persons and personifications alike. Reasoning about the life and death, singularity and plurality, or embodiment and disembodiment of corporations might seem an abstract exercise in philosophy, rhetoric, or even theology. Yet in the early decades of the nineteenth century, as the corporate form became central to American economic life and withstood legal scrutiny, such reasoning carried legal, political, and ideological consequences.

Dartmouth College: Theorizing the Corporation

The foundational nineteenth-century decision on corporations had a surprising source. In 1816, New Hampshire's legislature passed an act that reconfigured Dartmouth College as Dartmouth University, changing the institution's principal charge from seminary training to secular education and altering the composition

[13] Winkler, *We the Corporations*, 61.

of its board of trustees "to make the governance of the college more public and less self-perpetuating."[14] The majority of the Trustees of Dartmouth College sued to reinstate the college's original charter but were defeated when New Hampshire's Superior Court ruled in 1817 that the college's charge of education concerned the public interest and thus fell within the bounds of state legislative action.[15] Subsequently, the trustees appealed the case and prevailed in the US Supreme Court in *Trustees of Dartmouth College v. Woodward* (1819). (In the interim, Dartmouth operated messily as "two institutions, competing both legally and often ludicrously for students, keys, books, possession of buildings, commencement dates, and public favor"; both "held commencements and... conferred honorary degrees on President James Monroe when he visited New England in 1817.")[16] One central question concerned the meaning of private and public. Whereas the New Hampshire ruling had turned on the substantive judgment about the college's public purpose, viewing education as a public good and therefore within the legislature's scope, the US Supreme Court ruling turned on a novel analysis of the college's charter, the US Constitution, and the public/private distinction.[17] Because the charter had been granted to particular individuals, and not the colonial legislature, the court reasoned, the college was a private corporation. Moreover, the court read the charter as subject to the Contract Clause of the US Constitution, under which no state may "pass any... Law Impairing the Obligation of Contracts."[18] Ignoring New Hampshire Governor William Plumer's prescient concern that "legislatures were incautiously passing acts of incorporation, often 'in the nature of grants,' without reserving legislative power of repeal or modification 'when they cease to answer the end for which they were made, or prove injurious to the public interest,'" the Marshall Court set a precedent of vigorously protecting corporate charters.[19]

14 Eldon L. Johnson, "The Dartmouth College Case: The Neglected Educational Meaning," *Journal of the Early Republic* 3, no. 1 (1983): 47.

15 Timothy Farrar, *Report of the Case of the Trustees of Dartmouth College against William H. Woodward. Argued and Determined in the Superior Court of Judicature of the State of New-Hampshire, November 1817. And on Error in the Supreme Court of the United States, February 1819* (Portsmouth: John W. Foster, 1819), 213–15.

16 Johnson, "The Dartmouth College Case," 55–56.

17 The *Dartmouth College* case is widely recognized as introducing a strong private/public division. While New Hampshire Governor William Plumer and the New Hampshire court considered Dartmouth "already a public institution," Chief Justice Marshall defined it as a private institution, driving "a giant wedge into a small fissure." Marshall's language—which differentiated private Dartmouth College from public Dartmouth University—depicted Dartmouth's status in terms far more black and white than the college itself had employed: "Dartmouth unofficially had called itself a 'university' as early as 1782 and through the catalogs of the entire 1801–1814 period" but possibly abandoned the term due to "the fact that in English law 'university' meant a public corporation, whereas 'college' meant a private charity." See Eldon Johnson, "Dartmouth College Case," 55. As Gerald E. Frug notes, neither Blackstone nor Kyd "mentioned the idea of public and private corporations"; *Dartmouth College* articulated this division in terms of property rights (*City Making: Building Communities without Building Walls* (Princeton, NJ: Princeton University Press, 1999), 36, 41).

18 US Constitution, art. I, sec. 10.

19 Eldon Johnson, "Dartmouth College Case," 50. Johnson notes that "Farrar, Webster's former partner, immediately rushed the decision... into print in 1819 to reach the public in addition to the

Chief Justice Marshall's majority opinion in *Dartmouth College* elaborates a doctrine of the corporation that would have lasting resonance. By establishing a firm constitutional basis for the sanctity of corporate charters, *Dartmouth College* would underwrite the proliferation of American business corporations in the 1820s and 1830s. Even so, the decision itself hardly mentions business corporations. Rather, it closely parses the legal ontology of corporations more generally: their properties, their means of creation, and the conditions necessary to establishing their identity. "A corporation," writes Marshall, "is an artificial being, invisible, intangible, and existing only in contemplation of law. Being the mere creature of law, it possesses only those properties, which the charter of its creation confers upon it, either expressly, or as incidental to its very existence."[20] Marshall's language simultaneously portrays corporations in two antithetical ways. On the one hand, repeated negative adjectives—invisible, intangible—and restrictive descriptions—"only in contemplation of law," "only those properties"—minimize the ontological footprint of the corporate form. On the other, the very accretion of descriptors of this "being" or "creature" rhetorically substantiates the "very existence" that Marshall's adjectives render so shadowy.

Marshall elaborates of the corporation's properties with language borrowed—reluctantly, it seems—from metaphysics and theology:

> Among the most important are immortality, and, if the expression may be allowed, individuality; properties, by which a perpetual succession of many persons are considered as the same, and may act as a single individual. They enable a corporation to manage its own affairs, and to hold property without the perplexing intricacies, the hazardous and endless necessity of perpetual conveyances for the purpose of transmitting it from hand to hand. It is chiefly for the purpose of clothing bodies of men, in succession, with these qualities and capacities, that corporations were invented, and are in use. By these means, a perpetual succession of individuals are capable of acting for the promotion of the particular object, like one immortal being.[21]

In this description, the corporation is a "single individual" in its actions and at the same time a metaphorical garment that "cloth[es]" the "bodies of men" with certain "qualities and capacities"; its pursuit of a "particular object" enables "a perpetual succession of individuals" to act as "one immortal being." Marshall's tone is cautious—"if the expression may be allowed"—yet his account of the corporation

professional audience of the official Wheaton report" (61). Governor Plumer, under the name "Cincinnatus," argued the New Hampshire position with anti-corporate flair in an 1820–21 series of essays in the *New-Hampshire Patriot* (Concord) (51). Contemporary accounts of the case include Henry Wheaton's official report, *Trustees of Dartmouth College v. Woodward*, 17 US (4 Wheat.) 518 (1819); Farrar, *Report of the Case*; "Constitutional Law," *North American Review* 10 (1820): 83–115.

20 *Dartmouth College*, 636.

21 *Dartmouth College*, 636.

presents a striking paradox: legally powerful but insubstantial, individual but multiple, immortal but composed of mortals.

If Marshall's rhetoric is ambiguous—sometimes presenting the corporation as a substantial being, sometimes as a mere figment—so is his account of the corporation. *Dartmouth College* is often read as presenting the artificial entity (or concession) theory of the corporation: the corporation is a creation of the state, so its existence derives from the circumstances of its chartering and is distinct from its members. (As noted in the introduction, this theory contrasts with both the aggregate theory—that a corporation is fundamentally an association of persons—and the real entity theory—that a corporation has an existence distinct from its members and prior to its legal recognition.) Nonetheless, as legal scholars have observed, Marshall's decision relies on the assumptions of aggregate theory: although Marshall describes the artificial personhood of the corporation, he invokes the Contract Clause on behalf of the rights of the associated trustees—not the corporation of the college itself.[22] By presenting the corporation as a pass-through entity for the rights of its founders and their successors, he relies not on the entity status of Dartmouth College but on the persons whose interests—private interests, he emphasizes—are at stake. As Adam Winkler points out, "Piercing the veil, and allowing a corporation to claim the rights of its members, would be the conceptual tool the court would use to justify the extension of a wide variety of constitutional rights to corporations."[23]

While Marshall's opinion is consequential, its rhetoric is restrained. In contrast, Associate Justice Joseph Story's concurrence is broad and axiomatic. Story's opinion supplements Blackstone's taxonomy of corporations—spiritual and lay, civil and eleemosynary—with a distinction that is only implicit in Blackstone: public and private. Whereas only eleemosynary (charitable) corporations had been treated traditionally as private, Story argues that any corporation founded and administered privately, "however extensive the uses may be to which it is devoted," constitutes a private corporation.[24] Countering the State of New Hampshire's claim that the public significance and benefit of Dartmouth College's educational charge allowed the state to reorganize it as a public institution, Story determines its status as private because it was founded by—and its royal charter was granted to—particular individuals, not government entities.

Story's opinion is also rhetorically bolder than Marshall's. He defines the aggregate corporation as "a collection of individuals united into one collective body under a special name and possessing certain immunities, privileges and capacities in its collective character, which do not belong to the natural persons composing it." In this figuration, the act of incorporation creates not a garment

[22] Reuven Avi-Yonah, "The Cyclical Transformations of the Corporate Form: A Historical Perspective on Corporate Social Responsibility," *Delaware Journal of Corporate Law* 30 (2005): 767–818.

[23] Winkler, *We the Corporations*, 68.

[24] *Dartmouth College*, 669.

but rather, in a more substantial metaphor, "one collective body." Story frames the corporation as "an artificial person, existing in contemplation of law, and endowed with certain powers and franchises which, though they must be exercised through the medium of its natural members, are yet considered as subsisting in the corporation itself, as distinctly, as if it were a real personage." For Marshall, the corporation exists "*only* in contemplation of law"; for Story it simply "exist[s] in contemplation of law." Likewise, while Marshall describes the corporation as "*like* one immortal being," Story flatly proclaims it "an artificial person."[25] Concurring in their conclusions but differing in their rhetorical personification of the corporation, Marshall and Story thus enshrine a double vision in American jurisprudence: the corporation aggregate appears at once as a theoretical being (Marshall) and as a forceful artificial person (Story), the flimsiest legal fiction and the most solid legal fact. *Dartmouth College* thus captures two ambiguities about the corporation: legal ambiguity between entity and aggregate theories, and rhetorical ambiguity around the substantial or insubstantial character of the corporate person.

Story's opinion also departs from Marshall's in explicitly including business corporations within the scope of the *Dartmouth College* ruling.[26] As legal historian R. Kent Newmyer writes, Story's "broad approach," and particularly his "doctrine of public and private corporations" constituted "the crucial bridge from private eleemosynary educational institutions to the American business corporation."[27] When discussing the distinction between public and private corporations, he contrasts "an hospital created and endowed by the government for general charity" with "a bank whose stock is owned by a private person." By conjuring a paradigmatic eleemosynary corporation—a hospital—as public, and an acknowledged civil corporation—a bank—as private, he implies that the private/public distinction supersedes the traditional civil/eleemosynary divide. "The same doctrine," he continues, "may be affirmed of insurance, canal, bridge, and turnpike companies"; he later brings up banking and insurance companies, with their directors and stockholders, as examples of private corporations.[28] Such moments seem particularly prescient in light of the role *Dartmouth College* would play in subsequent decades as the cornerstone of the law of business corporations and a spur to their growth. Where Marshall's opinion looks backward to the common law tradition, Story's looks forward to the future of corporate America. Far more than Marshall's opinion, Story's offers a clear view of the corporate form's

[25] *Dartmouth College*, 667; emphasis added.

[26] The *Dartmouth College* ruling "emerged in the context of education, not of commerce—of the small college, not, as later, the big corporation" (Johnson, "Dartmouth College Case," 67). Yet Story's mention of business corporations presciently—or ominously—aligns his opinion with his own later positions on corporations.

[27] R. Kent Newmyer, *Supreme Court Justice Joseph Story: Statesman of the Old Republic* (Chapel Hill, NC: University of North Carolina Press, 1985), 131.

[28] *Dartmouth College*, 669, 711.

legal affordances: the Contract Clause protects corporate charters from governmental interference; the expansive definition of private corporations extends the domain of this constitutional protection.

The Supreme Court's ruling was thus at once conservative and innovative. It yoked the common law doctrine of corporate personality to the Contract Clause of the US Constitution, and recognized corporations as both entities and associations, as artificial persons and as contracts (governmental concessions) immune to legislative action. For the Marshall Court as for Kyd, who could only dismiss metaphysical language by invoking the "eye of the law," corporate jurisprudence provided for entities whose power was bolstered by their uncertain ontological footprint.

When Banks Die

The Marshall Court was tacit on the question of how putatively immortal corporations might cease to exist. Contemporaries, however, vividly imagined the death of corporations in verse and prose satire. While the *Dartmouth College* case attracted some readers' attention, many more eyes were focused on the contemporaneous Panic of 1819, the crisis that brought a period of economic growth and confidence to an abrupt halt.[29] A rapidly expanding banking industry had fueled western settlement by generously issuing credit and paper, with the support of state legislatures' generous chartering of new banks. In 1814, for instance, Pennsylvania's legislature chartered forty-two new banks in a single act.[30] Most "were established in the interior where people were anxious for an increased supply of currency and credit."[31] An April 1819 item in the *Port Folio*, likewise, counts "no less than 375 chartered banks in the United States," including seventy-one in the western states of Ohio and Kentucky.[32] Although banks were nominally required to yield specie on demand to their depositors, such payments were rare and banknotes circulated as currency. During the War of 1812, specie payments had been suspended in order to prevent catastrophic bank runs, but even after the war banks were reluctant to resume payments.[33] Because bank paper circulated far in excess of specie, the postwar economic boom depended on banks maintaining their creditors' confidence. Historian Charles Sellers explains that "both banks and borrowers were gambling on the indefinite continuance of high

[29] See, for instance, "Constitutional Law" (*North American Review*), which discusses the *Dartmouth College* case, as well as the numerous items on banks and banking in *Niles' Weekly Register* 16 (1819).

[30] Charles Sellers, *The Market Revolution: Jacksonian America, 1815–1846* (Oxford: Oxford University Press, 1991), 123.

[31] Robert M. Blackson, "Pennsylvania Banks and the Panic of 1819: A Reinterpretation," *Journal of the Early Republic* 9 (1989): 346.

[32] "American Banks," *Port Folio*, 4th ser., 7 (1819): 352.

[33] Blackson, "Pennsylvania Banks," 339–41; Sellers, *Market Revolution*, 131–36.

commodity prices and speculative profits"; according to one contemporary writer, he notes, "anyone who demanded specie from the banks... 'would have been persecuted as an enemy of society.'" In late 1818, the Bank of the United States began to demand payment for loans, starting a chain reaction that "saved the national Bank by sacrificing not only its debtors but the state banks and their hordes of debtors as well, which is to say, most of the market economy."[34]

As bank paper lost value, borrowers defaulted on loans and banks folded—or, frequently, lingered in a twilight state: they might suspend specie payment while formally continuing operations, only to dwindle away before officially liquidating. The complexity of such situations is best illustrated by the fate of banks in Kentucky during and after the Panic: the state legislature allowed banks to operate even after suspending payments but set a limit on the quantity of banknotes that could be circulated, violation of which would cause a bank to lose its charter.[35] A brief notice in an August 1819 issue of *Niles' Register*, for instance, reported critically, "The friends of the paper system are getting up some meetings... to encourage the bank of Kentucky to 'suspend specie payments,' as the term is for the bankruptcy of banks."[36] As fewer and fewer Kentuckians accepted banknotes, banks first ceased operations and later had their charters repealed; in mid-1820 the sole operating bank was the Bank of Kentucky, which itself soon halted active business, though it maintained a formal existence for decades.[37] This pattern of rapid expansion and equally rapid failure echoed Kyd's insistence that corporations are merely "*capable* of an indefinite duration." While banks could persist for some time after their practical operations ceased, their immortality was merely nominal. A brief item in the April 1819 *Port Folio* played on this fact: "The establishment of a new bank in Kentucky, was lately announced, by posting bills to the following effect: 'A new bank will be opened in a few days.' Some wag was at the pains of altering the word *in* to *for*. The projectors taking the hint, the bank was not opened."[38]

In March 1819, the *Port Folio* printed a series of three poems titled "The Banks; or Western Melodies" that portrayed banks as both embodied and vulnerable. Set to tunes popularized by the Irish poet and balladeer Thomas Moore, creator of such songs as "Believe Me If All Those Endearing Young Charms," the verses depict insolvent banks anthropomorphically as mortals.[39] The trajectory of

[34] Sellers, *Market Revolution*, 135–36. See Condy Raguet to David Ricardo, April 19, 1821, in David Ricardo, *Minor Papers on the Currency Question, 1809–1823*, ed. Jacob H. Hollander, (Baltimore, MD: Johns Hopkins Press, 1932), 201–3.

[35] Rothbard, *Panic of 1819*, 99.

[36] "Banks and Banking," *Niles' Weekly Register* 16 (1819): 421.

[37] Rothbard, *Panic of 1819*, 102, 109.

[38] *The Port-Folio,* 4th ser., 7 (April 1819): 352.

[39] The poems also appear, in slightly different form, in the *Niles' Weekly Register*, supplement to 16 (1819): 18–19. The *Register* indicates that the first two poems initially appeared in the *Lexington (KY) Reporter* and the third in the *Pittsburg Gazette.* "The Banks—No. 1" is set to the tune of "Oh! blame not the bard"; nos. 2 and 3 are set to "Oh! think not my spirits are always as light." Moore's originals were widely published; see, for instance, Thomas Moore, *Irish Melodies* (Philadelphia, PA: Mathew Carey, 1815).

western bank paper contrasts with that of the poems' book paper: whereas the currency of ephemeral, locally circulating banknotes quickly and irreversibly declined, that of ephemeral, locally circulating newspaper verse was renewed by reprinting in stately periodicals with national pretensions.[40] "The Banks—No. 1," credited to an "Ohio Bard," addresses suspension of payment: banks' refusal to pay specie to depositors, a tactic that could halt a bank run but also devalued banknotes.[41] The Ohio Bard begins with mock sympathy for the failing banks:

> Oh! blame not the banks if they fly to suspension,
> Where *Av'rice* lies carelessly smiling at *Shame*;
> They would have done better, and 'twas their intention
> T' have paid the last dollar, and died in a flame.

Legal doctrine notwithstanding, the Bard has no trouble imagining corporate mortality. As he explains, in order to defer their own demise, the banks defer payments indefinitely, with the predictable consequence of deflation:

> Unpriz'd are their notes, or at *ten per cent* selling,
> Unhonour'd at home, unredeem'd on demand:
> But still they've a merit—I joy in the telling,
> They're taken for *pork*, though rejected for land.[42]

The uselessness of discredited banknotes in real estate transactions—and their subsequent rejection by a host of businesses—was calamitous at a moment when the sudden restriction of capital was ruining many Americans, particularly recent western settlers. Nonetheless, the Bard archly suggests that these depreciated notes maintained just enough value to buy material necessities—and perhaps political favor—to delay the banks' "d[ying] in a flame." By 1822, however, banknotes themselves would fuel bonfires, and bank charters would outlive the institutions they had authorized.[43]

[40] While Meredith McGill has noted that 1830s and 1840s literary periodicals were themselves "regional and ephemeral" by modern standards, they still contrasted with newspapers, whose circulation was geographically circumscribed and whose contents, including "fugitive verse," were "considered public property by law." Reprinting, McGill argues, gave rise to a "stutter of locally interrupted circulation" that was "crucial to the imagination of the federal form of the nation" in Jacksonian America (*American Literature and the Culture of Reprinting, 1834–1853* (Philadelphia: University of Pennsylvania Press, 2003), 17, 106–8). On Thomas Carlyle's commonplaces of book paper, bank paper, and the paper age, see Kevin McLaughlin, *Paperwork: Fiction and Mass Mediacy in the Paper Age* (Philadelphia, PA: University of Pennsylvania Press, 2005), 1.

[41] Ohio had twenty-four banks before the Panic, of which just six or seven were redeeming notes by 1819 (Rothbard, *Panic of 1819*, 77).

[42] "The Banks; or Western Melodies," *Port Folio*, 4th ser., 7 (1819): 248.

[43] The italics suggest the metaphorical sense of "pork"—a benefit from the public "pork barrel" in a political quid pro quo—though the verse predates the *OED*'s earliest recorded use of this sense in 1862. Commercial groups such as merchants, tavern keepers, and butchers decided collectively to

The infernal undertone of flames lights the next stanza, in which the putative immortality of banking corporations takes on a theological cast. The banks have "cease[d] to redeem" banknotes, not souls, but the language of redemption evokes Christian doctrine. The banks' passing identification with the redeemer—the granter of everlasting life—collapses into their irredeemability and the unlikelihood of their rising again. The speaker closes with a proleptic elegy that paints a landscape dotted with doomed banks:

> The stranger in passing each village shall say,
> (As he eyes the sad spot with his hand on his breast)
> THERE ONCE STOOD A BANK! but unable to pay,
> It *suspended itself*, and has now gone to rest!![44]

This tongue-in-cheek lament depends on a double entendre: the departed bank, practiced at suspending payment, either suspends its actions in perpetuity or, like a desperate human debtor, hangs itself. The ambiguity of "suspension"—endless deferral or the end of life—captures the paradox of chartered banks, theoretically immortal but practically mortal. Both law and light verse personify corporations, but whereas *Dartmouth College* emphasizes the fictionality and immortality of artificial persons, the Ohio Bard anthropomorphizes banks through a sequence of actions: standing, suspending, and dying. The sequence hinges on "suspension," which slips from a financial term of art into a figure of embodiment. By blurring the distinction between endless deferral and the finality of death, it aptly captures the status of banks that had practically ceased operations but not formally dissolved.

While "The Banks—No. 1" hints at the lethal (if ambiguous) consequences of suspension, the grisly conclusion of "The Banks—No. 2" (by the "Laureate to the Banks") pushes for a decisive end:

> But send round the bowl—while a relic of hope
> Is in banks or in bankers, this toast shall be mine,
> May they cease to *suspend*, and escape from the rope,
> Or, *suspending*, be stretch'd at the end of the line.[45]

If the banks won't cease suspensions of payment, the depositor-poet proposes, let's suspend *them* once and for all. In the Laureate's satirical imaginary, the corpses of banks hang from every tree—melancholy suicides or the victims of mob violence. As in "The Banks—No. 1," the legal personification of corporations gives way to

cease honoring banknotes; the general population soon followed. Eventually, recalled banknotes were burned in public bonfires (Rothbard, *Panic of 1819*, 101–2, 109).

44 "The Banks," 248. 45 "The Banks," 249.

anthropomorphism, granting not merely a legal *persona* but rather a mortal body to frustratingly incorporeal entities. More ominously, "The Banks—No. 2" identifies the imagined bodies of "banks" with the concrete bodies of "bankers," pushing its depiction of a bank at the end of its rope toward a threat to stretch bankers "at the end of the line." This slippage mirrors the ambiguity of the *Dartmouth College* decision, which conjured the doctrine of corporate personality while effectively endorsing the notion of corporation as association, a pass-through mechanism for the private rights of members. The doctrine of corporate invisibility gives way to Kyd's reminder that "a corporation is as visible a body as an army," with the visible bodies of corporators serving as targets for the wrath of those ruined by the corporation. At the same time, the slippage from "banks" to "bankers"—from the incorporated to the corporeal—reveals the difficulty of depicting a chartered entity's death, which becomes visible only when it ceases to limit the liability, or the lynchability, of corporators. Corporations are people, indeed.[46]

As these playful if menacing verses suggest, while the shameless "av'rice" of the banks made them easy targets of resentment, their bodilessness posed an obstacle to retribution. By locating the limit of corporate immortality in corporeal mortality, they figuratively reverse the vulnerability that banks imposed on their human clients.

"The Errors in Grammar Are Very Abundant"

The rapid expansion of business corporations—and the implications of the doctrines of corporate immortality and individuality—would trouble legal writers as well.[47] By the beginning of the nineteenth century, as James Willard Hurst has shown, chartered corporations in the United States already "represented the main type of the most ambitious and sophisticated business associations," and "by 1830 . . . the corporation would emerge as the preferred style of structured business organization."[48] In the first three decades of the nineteenth century, incorporation proceeded at an unprecedented pace: nearly 1900 corporations received charters in New England alone. As legal historian E. Merrick Dodd observes, "American case law of corporations was, to a much larger extent than is true of

[46] The dissolution of a corporation could make individual stockholders liable. The question of liability was hotly debated, particularly after Massachusetts passed statutes holding the stockholders of manufacturing corporations personally liable for losses. See "Digest of the Cases" *United States Law Journal*, 464; "Manufacturing Corporations," *American Jurist and Law Magazine* 2 (1829): 92–118, esp. 94–95.

[47] "Angell and Ames on Corporations," *American Jurist and Law Magazine* 8 (1832): 7.

[48] James Willard Hurst, *The Legitimacy of the Business Corporation in the Law of the United States, 1780–1970* (Charlottesville, VA: University of Virginia Press, 1970), 14. From 1781 to 1800, 315 business corporations were chartered by the states and two by the federal government. Joseph S. Davis, *Essays in the Earlier History of American Corporations* (Cambridge, MA: Harvard University Press, 1917), 2:27.

most branches of our judge-made law, an indigenous product," because English cases generally "dealt with nonprofit corporations" and thus "were of limited value for the solution of business corporation problems."[49] Yet as the editors of the *United States Law Journal* noted in 1822: "The Law of Corporations has not been much studied in the United States. The great number of our corporate bod ies, and the rapid manner in which they are increased by the State Legislatures, will yet render this branch of jurisprudence of great importance, and open a wide and fertile region of research."[50]

Until 1832, when the Rhode Island lawyers Joseph K. Angell and Samuel Ames published *A Treatise on the Law of Private Corporations Aggregate*, this legal region was inhabited principally by Marshall's and Story's *Dartmouth College* opinions. Angell and Ames, like the *Law Journal* editors before them, emphasized the case's centrality.[51] Their *Treatise* was recognized upon its publication as both necessary and authoritative; its triumphs and its failures reveal both how ubiquitous and how vexed the corporate form was in Jacksonian America.[52] A reviewer for *American Jurist* noted that "the urgent want of a treatise on corporations adapted to the United States, ha[d] long been felt by the profession," given that corporations had "multiplied" over the previous thirty years "to an extent without parallel in any other country."[53] A few years later, the same periodical claimed that the *Treatise* was "in the hands of the greatest part of the profession."[54] By 1882 it would appear in eleven editions with frequent revisions and expansions, paralleling the concurrent growth of the corporate form in the United States.[55] Beyond its practical application, the *Treatise* had the rhetorical task of normalizing the business corporation.

Describing a being that is singular in some contexts but plural in others bedeviled the treatise's writers and readers alike. The *American Jurist*'s review of the *Treatise*, after noting the book's importance, turns to a critique of its style: "The composition is often loose and slovenly in the extreme, and in many places sets

[49] E. Merrick Dodd, *American Business Corporations until 1860 with Special Reference to Massachusetts* (Cambridge, MA: Harvard University Press, 1954), 11, 13.

[50] "Law of Corporations," *United States Law Journal* 1 (1822): 294–95.

[51] The most extensive treatment was Chancellor James Kent's "Of Corporations," in *Commentaries on American Law*, Vol. 2, 215–53. Angell and Ames also mention the English barrister John William Willcock's 1827 treatise on municipal corporations; its scope does not extend to private corporations. See Joseph K. Angell and Samuel Ames, *A Treatise on the Law of Private Corporations Aggregate* (Boston: Hilliard, 1832), 2.

[52] Angell also edited the *United States Law Intelligencer and Review*; he is the likely author of an article warning that the privilege of limited liability means that "the legislative power of creating corporations is therefore a prerogative, which should be exercised with the utmost caution, and in such a manner, as to afford as little opportunity as possible for dishonesty and fraud" ("Personal Responsibility of the Members of an Incorporated Company for the Debts of the Company," *United States Law Intelligencer and Review* 2 (1830): 212).

[53] "Angell and Ames on Corporations," 105.

[54] "Erratum in Angell and Ames on Corporations," *American Jurist and Law Magazine* 11 (1834): 263.

[55] The Library of Congress lists eleven editions, reaching into the 1880s.

all the rules of grammar at defiance." The reviewer offers a "sample out of a much larger number" of errors, including these:

> 'But still that seminary, like others, *were* usually called schools.' p. 29.
> 'A school-house and land *was* vested in trustees.' p. 89.
> 'That the corporation named as *plaintiffs* was created.' p. 226.
> 'When the interests and good government of the corporate body *requires* it.' p. 246.[56]

Although attributed to haste, these errors suggest a more fundamental problem: what is the appropriate grammar for describing entities that are at once singular and plural? In two cases, a singular verb is erroneously applied to a compound subject; in another, a grammatically singular but semantically plural or ambiguous subject—"the corporation"—is reconstituted as a grammatically plural subject—"plaintiffs." Echoing the numerical ambiguity of the corporation aggregate, at once singular and plural, these apparent mistakes register the effects of the corporate form's rapid expansion on the grammar—and perhaps the ontology—of persons. Some of the most attentive responses to these unsettling consequences, however, came from outside the legal profession.

Visualizing the Bank

Another versifier offered a view of banking corporations that contrasts with both the gallows humor of "The Banks" and the accidental poetics of Angel and Ames's *Treatise*. In 1823, shortly after beginning his tenure as President of the Second Bank of the United States, Nicholas Biddle wrote a piece of light verse for his friend Sarah Lukens Keene narrating his transition from man of letters to man of finance.[57] Biddle playfully recounts his own willingness to "exchange…[f]or one sheet of bank notes, the whole quire celestial" (13). Even as he mocks his descent from solitary poetry to incorporated finance, his verse insists on the similarity of these two callings. Punning on "choir"/"quire" and musical "notes"/bank "notes," he playfully revises the conventional trope of poetry as song to stress the shared material reality of poets and financiers as consumers of paper. But unlike contemporaries who denigrated a speculative literary marketplace by highlighting the similarities between bank-paper and book-paper, Biddle insists, with playful

[56] "Angell and Ames on Corporations," 107.
[57] Nicholas Biddle, (Untitled verse epistle to Sarah Lukens Keene, 1823), *An Ode to Bogle* (Philadelphia, 1889), 11–14. Subsequent references in parentheses.

self-deprecation, on the aesthetics of banking.[58] The philhellene—and later director of the Bank's building committee—imagines "a *bank* on Parnassus" (12)—and suggests, despite his promised retreat from poetry, that banking and poetry share more than might be imagined.[59] Despite complaining that his enclosure in the bank's neoclassical edifice—"my vast marble tomb"—could "quell all the fancy of Shakespeare or Byron," he proclaims his preference for "my last letter from Barings or Hope / To the finest epistles of Pliny or Pope" and "two lines of plain prose with a good name upon it / To the tenderest fourteen ever squeezed in a sonnet" (13). The pleasures of banking neatly compensate for those of poetry.

Ironically, many of the tropes Biddle employs would become familiar in anti-Bank discourse a decade later. As an enthusiastic scholar of classical antiquity, Biddle would have known that the Athenian Parthenon housed large stores of money and served as a public treasury: a temple for which lucre was no profanation. Thus, rather than defend the celestial purity of the arts from worldly gain, Biddle playfully insists that banks ought to be kept safe from poets:

> Alas! had the ancients, who so much surpass us,
> In their pure golden age, fixed a *bank* on Parnassus,
> What a model of wisdom and pleasure to follow!
> Only think now—to sign one's bank-notes like Apollo!
> But that rake of Olympus—too happy to rove—
> Would have scorned to make money and cease to make love;
> And the Muses whose sex condescends to protectors
> Have a true female scorn for all sorts of directors.
> 'Tis fiercely avenged though, for Banks, where they know it,
> Feel a horror that warns them to shun every poet;
> And since the first rhyme, the Muses' fond votary
> If ever he's trusted soon goes to the notary. (13)

Biddle briefly imagines Apollo, the god of poetry, as a banker, but recognizes the risk in the god's contempt for money—and the Muses' resistance to (a board of) "directors." In place of these inherited deities, Biddle animates "Banks" themselves via personification: they "know" and "feel a horror" for poets and poetry. He returns to classical personification returns late in the poem, deploying poetics as he disavows poetry: "While the Bank is my goddess, its desks are my altars, / And all my 'fine phrenzy' is spent on defaulters."[60] Biddle's poem is ultimately an

[58] For a sustained analysis of the figures of book-paper and bank-paper and their interplay, see McLaughlin, *Paperwork*.

[59] Jeffrey Sklansky, "A Bank on Parnassus." *Common-Place* 6.3, 2006.

[60] Biddle, *An Ode to Bogle*, 14. "Fine phrenzy," of course, alludes to Theseus's image of "The poet's eye, in a fine frenzy rolling." *A Midsummer Night's Dream* 5.1.12. *The Norton Shakespeare Based on the Oxford Edition*," ed. Stephen Greenblatt (New York: W. W. Norton & Company, 1997). Biddle's

argument about succession: the true heir to antique divinity is not the poet but the banker. Thus, despite his professed abandonment of Olympian gods and Parnassian aesthetics, Biddle apotheosizes the Bank and boldly takes his place as its high priest. By putting the poetic tropes of personification and allusion in service of his new role as banker, he reclaims the power of the gods, manifest as financial might and legal personality.

Biddle's antagonists shared his penchant for figuratively rendering the Bank as a classical temple—and his confidence that these tropes could afford a grasp on the elusive corporation. In contrast to Biddle's smug allusions, their work underscores the fearsome power of the Second Bank of the United States and lionizes President Andrew Jackson's so-called war against it. With the Bank's federal charter set to expire in 1836, Congress voted in 1832 to recharter it, but Jackson, in a bold election-year move, vetoed the charter. He went on to undermine the Bank by redistributing the federal government's deposits, a significant proportion of the Bank's capital, to so-called pet banks. After the veto, so-called wildcat banks proliferated: far-flung, insecure institutions whose paper money issues were risky propositions. (While Jackson had struck a blow against centralized banking, his 1836 Specie Circular, which stipulated that payments to the government could only be made in hard money, was ironically most disastrous for the youngest, smallest banks, many of which folded in the ensuing Panic of 1837.) Prints and pamphlets from the Bank War reveal how the popular corporate imaginary framed corporate ontology and improvised tools for shaping, grappling with—and in this case, dismantling—what might seem ungraspable entities. These rhetorical and visual representations reveal how a tactical confrontation with the corporate form depends on recognizing and reconfiguring its tropes.

Whereas Blackstone contrasts natural (human) persons to artificial (corporate) persons, critics of the Bank availed themselves of the broader resonance of "natural," a word with antonyms including artificial, unnatural, supernatural, and divine. Some early anti-bank pamphleteers invoked the *unnatural* in the sense of natural processes that yielded abnormal or deviant results. Depicting society as a natural body threatened by parasitic growths, these writers transform the legal distinction between natural and artificial persons into a normative distinction between natural and unnatural reproduction. Thus the Boston businessman and politician David Henshaw contrasts good "business corporations," the "natural offspring" of a society, to "monopolies and perpetuities," which he terms

argument thus resonates with Kornbluh's contention (quoting the same speech) that "Bankers *are* poets because their techniques 'body forth the form of things unknown,'—effectuate in present material form things heretofore unembodied and unknown." Anna Kornbluh, *Realizing Capital: Financial and Psychic Economies in Victorian Form* (New York: Fordham University Press, 2014), 26.

"alarming excrescences upon the body politic."[61] Similarly, the Philadelphia lawyer and legislator Charles Jared Ingersoll decries a rising corporate aristocracy as "a vast fungus grown upon government, upon property, upon liberty and equality."[62] This conceit of natural growth and its malevolent or parasitic aberrations is particularly pervasive in Theodore Sedgwick's pamphlet *What Is a Monopoly?* Sedgwick describes the "increase" and "multiplication of corporations in the United States" and identifies banks as the "most mischievous offspring of our vicious legislation."[63] All these cases posit a "natural" collectivity—the body politic—to which an unnatural entity is parasitically attached.

Visual representations of the Bank addressed the challenges of making the corporation both visible and readily recognizable. Two iconographic tropes anchor these images: William Strickland's Second Bank building, modeled on the Parthenon; and the likeness of Bank president Nicholas Biddle himself. Both strategies relied on synecdoche, but pulled in different directions. The Bank's building could emphasize permanence, both through the edifice's monumentality and the continuity it presented with classical canons of architectural taste, yet was frequently portrayed in destruction or disarray (Figs. 1.1, 1.2). Like Stuart and Revett's contrasting images in *The Antiquities of Athens*, the eternal temple and the belated ruin were always co-present (Figs. 1.3, 1.4). Anti-bank prints used the same iconography but reversed the philhellenes' visual rhetoric: rather than conjure the eternal, Parnassian Bank from the Parthenon's ruins, they put the accent on the ruinability of the too-powerful Bank of the United States (BUS).

If the BUS building framed the Bank's corporate persistence amid the alternatives of classical immortality and outdated ruin, caricatures of Biddle himself did something quite different. By reducing the Bank to a single human countenance, they figuratively insisted on piercing the corporate veil. And by frequently identifying Biddle as "Old Nick," they closed the circle linking devilish bankers to plutocratic wealth and the lord of the underworld. Sometimes the devil himself (as in "The Downfall of Mother Bank"), and sometimes only the devil's high priest or high chancellor, Biddle's face nearly always appeared when iconography demanded that the bank assume a human figure. His centrally placed face anchors the widely-circulated image of the Bank as "The Many Headed Monster" (Fig. 1.5). Particularly intriguing is a cartoon in which Biddle presents the Pennsylvania charter of the BUS after Jackson's veto. In "On the Way to Araby" (Fig. 1.6),

[61] David Henshaw, *Remarks upon the Rights and Powers of Corporations, and the Rights, Powers, and Duties of the Legislature toward Them. Embracing a Review of the Opinion of the Supreme Court of the United States, in the Case of Dartmouth College, in New Hampshire, Given in 1819* (Boston: Beals and Greene, 1837), 9.

[62] Charles J. Ingersoll, "Speech of Charles J. Ingersoll, Esq., in the Convention of Pennsylvania, on Legislative and Judicial Control over Charters of Incorporation," *Democratic Review* 5, no. 13 (1839): 111.

[63] Theodore Sedgwick, *What Is a Monopoly? Or, Some Considerations upon the Subject of Corporations and Currency* (New York: Printed by G. P. Scott, 1835), 4, 12, 37.

Fig. 1.1 William Strickland (architect) and Samuel H. Kneass (delineator), Front Elevation of the Bank of the United States (1824). The Library Company of Philadelphia.

Fig. 1.2 Edward Williams Clay, *The Downfall of Mother Bank: Draw'd off from Natur by Zek, Downing, Neffu to Major Jack Downing.* New York: E.W. Clay, 1833. Courtesy, American Antiquarian Society.

Fig. 1.3 Measured Drawing of the Parthenon, from Stuart and Revett, *Antiquities of Athens*, Vol. 2 (1787), ch. 1, plate 3. Archive.org. Getty Research Institute, Los Angeles (85-B3279).

Fig. 1.4 A View of the Eastern Portico of the Parthenon, from Stuart and Revett, *Antiquities of Athens*, Vol. 2 (1787), ch. 1, plate 1. Archive.org. Getty Research Institute, Los Angeles (85-B3279).

Fig. 1.5 *General Jackson Slaying the Many Headed Monster*. [New York] : Printed & pubd. by H.R. Robinson, 52 Courtdt. St. N.Y., [1836]. Courtesy, American Antiquarian Society.

Fig. 1.6 Edward W. Clay, *On the Way to Araby!* New York: H.R. Robinson, 48 Courtlandt Street, C [signed on stone, E.W. Clay], 1836. Courtesy, American Antiquarian Society.

Jackson appears to make good on his promises "never [to] recharter that monster of corruption" and "Sooner than live in a country where such a power prevailed, [to] seek an asylum in the wilds of Arabia."[64] His "veto stick" broken, Jackson flees, while Martin Van Buren awkwardly attempts to inherit the General's mantle. Most interesting, though, is the image's presentation of the bank, which conjoins four elements: Biddle himself, the Doric architecture of the BUS building, an unfurled scroll representing the Pennsylvania charter (which replaced the federal charter), and a double-faced devil mask. Biddle exclaims, "General allow me to introduce an old friend with a new face!" The image suggests not only that the Pennsylvania-chartered bank retains the identity of the federal Bank but also that the new charter proves what anti-Bank propagandists had claimed all along: the supernatural quality of the Bank, its devilish excess of the formalities of law. In these caricatures, the monstrous threat of an endlessly-regenerating persona—whether a hydra's head or a Janus face—dramatize the sinister side of what for Blackstone is the corporation's raison d'etre: the maintenance of identity and privileges beyond the span of individual human life.

Whereas images of Biddle as the devil or the devil's attendant typically toy with metaphysics in playful or propagandistic ways, their religious overtones are amplified in the writing and prints of the Rhode Island labor advocate Seth Luther (1795–1863), who invokes theology in earnest. A prolific anti-bank polemicist across visual media, oratory, and print culture, Luther was best known in the 1830s for his stirring addresses delivered to working-class audiences in various northeastern cities. Framing labor struggles in the language of Christian morality, his oratory recalls the imagery of anti-Bank prints like "A Confederacy Against the Constitution" (Fig. 1.7), likely published by Luther himself, and heightens their religious implications. In his *Address to the Working Men of New England* (1833), Luther characterizes avarice in diabolical terms as "the father of *all crime* from the days of Adam until the present time. This *fiend* induced Judas to betray his master, and Benedict Arnold to make an attempt to sell his country."[65] Personifying greed as a "fiend," Luther insists on the metaphysical unity of historically dispersed phenomena. He amplifies this strategy in his *Address on the Origin and Progress of Avarice* (1834), which repeats the examples of Judas and Arnold and explicitly links them to idolatry and devil worship. In a litany that reads as an ekphrasis of "A Confederacy Against the Constitution," Luther weaves together the figures of biblical idolatry and Greek polytheism with the

[64] Bray Hammond, *Banks and Politics in America from the Revolution to the Civil War* (Princeton, NJ: Princeton University Press, 1957), 430.

[65] Seth Luther, *An Address to the Working Men of New England, on the State of Education, and on the Condition of the Producing Classes in Europe and America. With Particular Reference to the Effect of Manufacturing (as Now Conducted) on the Health and Happiness of the Poor, and on the Safety of Our Republic. Delivered in Boston, Charlestown, Cambridgeport, Waltham, Dorchester, Mass., Portland, Saco, Me., and Dover, N.H.* (New York: Published at the Office of the Working Man's Advocate, by George H. Evans, 1833), 6.

Fig. 1.7 [Seth Luther], *A Confederacy Against the Constitution and the Rights of the People, with an Historical View of the Component Parts of this Diabolical Transaction* (1833). The Library Company of Philadelphia.

commonplaces of bank as temple, banker as priest, and money—particularly paper money—as idol:

> [W]e have been required to bow our necks to the image these modern Nebuchadnezzars have set up, or the calf, that some of their Aarons or Biddles have made, with the fruits of our labor. We are *worse* than the Israelites; they fell down and worshipped a golden calf, made of materials furnished by themselves; we are called upon to worship a paper calf. These modern shrine makers are worse than those who made silver images for Diana, the goddess of the Ephesians. For they have taken away the golden calf, and put a paper calf in its room, gilded with gold leaf, ten thousand times thiner [*sic*] than that used for looking glasses. We are made to believe, that it is the real Simon Pure, the veritable golden calf. While we are thus worshipping, we ought to have an inscription on the altars of Mammon,—the banks—'To THE UNKNOWN GOD,' and may it well be said of us, 'Ye know not what ye worship.'[66]

[66] Seth Luther, *An Address on the Origin and Progress of Avarice, and Its Deleterious Effects on Human Happiness, with a Proposed Remedy for the Countless Evils Resulting from an Inordinate Desire*

Luther's treatment of bank-dependence as idolatry is confoundingly dense. His allusion to the story of the golden calf and his description, by analogy, of the "paper calf" of paper money frame idolatry as error—the mistaken worship of an empty thing. Yet his references to Mammon and the Unknown God invoke a contrasting understanding of idolatry as disloyalty: the worship of a competing but real god.[67]

Luther's final flourish, a parody of Acts 17:23, deserves particular attention. In this verse, the Apostle Paul preaches on the Areopagus that those who revere its altar to the Unknown God unknowingly worship Christ: "Whom therefore ye ignorantly worship, him declare I unto you." Luther, fashioning himself as a new Paul, reveals the Bank to be the inverted image of the altar of the unknown God—an unintended, if frighteningly real, object of veneration. Luther's religious register allows him to route his central conceit of avarice as idolatry from Exodus and Exile to New Testament Greece. Playing on the same architectural and ideological tropes to which Nicholas Biddle and William Strickland had appealed to cast banking as divinely inspired, the Bank as a temple, and Philadelphia as Athens, Luther invokes the Athens of Paul rather than Pericles. He recasts neoclassical bank buildings as secret temples of Mammon. Our everyday financial practices, he warns, make bankolaters of us all.

In the wake of Jackson's triumph, the Bank's defeat, and the ensuing Panic of 1837, however, Luther would abandon this systematic theology of Mammon in favor of structural explanations. His *Bank-ometer* (1840), produced together with the lithographer Stephen Lawton, promises "TRUTHS FOR THE PRODUCERS OF WEALTH THE BANKING SYSTEM UNMASKED OR THE TRUE CAUSES OF PANIC PRESSURE AND DISTRESS." (Fig. 1.8). Centered on a precise rendering of the BUS building, the print is plastered with quotations on the dangers of banking and paper money (from figures including Washington and Jefferson and even bank proponents like Hamilton and Clay), data on the rapid growth of American banking, and a streetscape-like grouping of charts: a Paperometer and Stockometer tracking the quantities of various assets in circulation, and a Flourometer and a Wageometer tracking workers' buying power. The image presents these charts as nodes in an interconnected system of tubes centered on the Currency Reservoir. Hidden in the Bank's foundation, this Reservoir is linked to various conduits that control the money supply: the State Bank Tube, the Bank of England Tube, and, largest of all, the Expansion and Contraction Tube.

for Wealth. Delivered before the Union Association of Working Men, in the Town Hall, Charlestown, Mass., January 30, 1834 (Boston: Published by the Author, 1834), 14.

[67] Moshe Halbertal and Avishai Margalit identify four different conceptions of idolatry: as disloyalty, as error, as the worship of an intermediary, as foreignness or strangeness of worship. See *Idolatry* (Cambridge, MA: Harvard University Press, 1992), esp. 237. See also Josh Ellenbogen and Aaron Tugendhaft, *Idol Anxiety* (Stanford: Stanford University Press, 2011), particularly Marc Fumaroli, "The Christian Critique of Idolatry," trans. Benjamin Storey, 32–40.

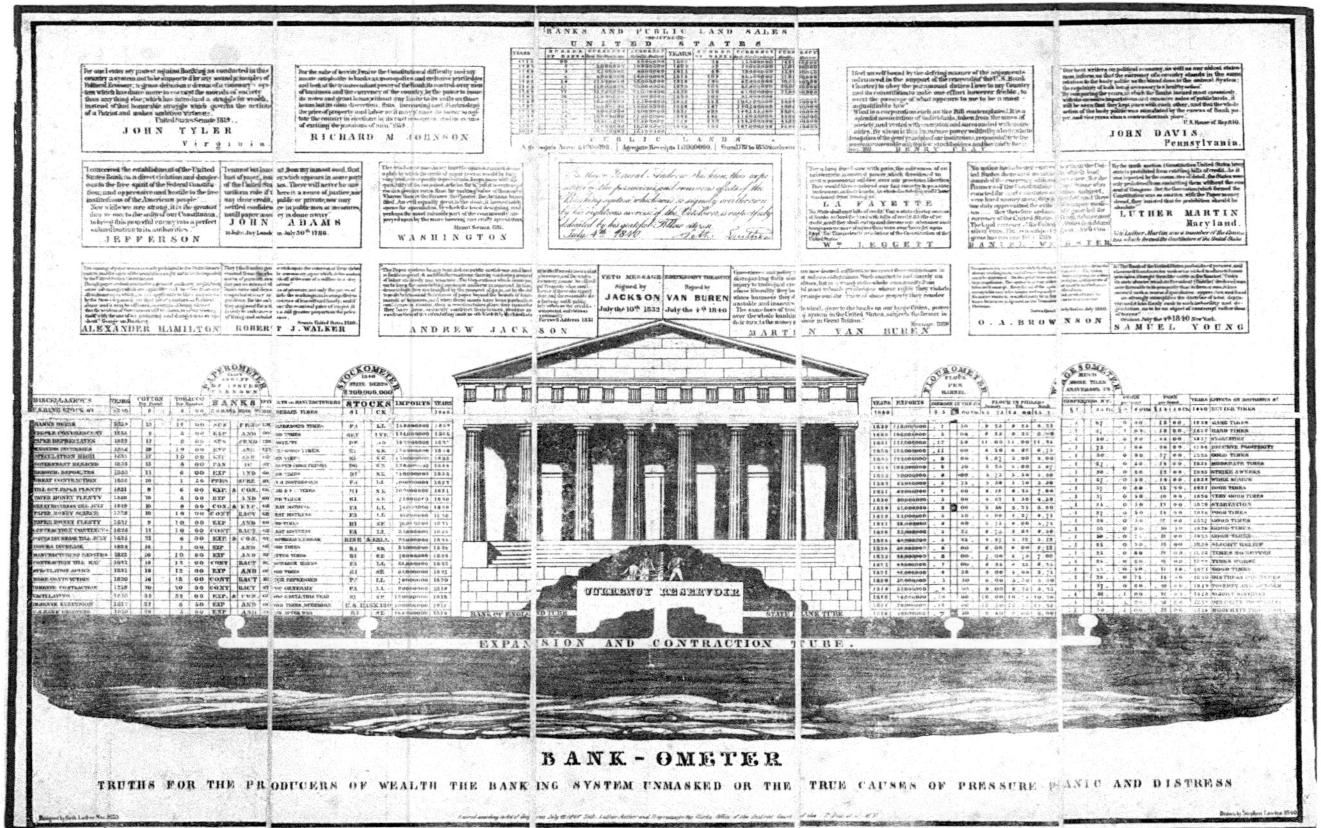

Fig. 1.8 Seth Luther and Stephen Lawton, *Bank-ometer: Truths for the Producers of Wealth the Banking System Unmasked or the True Causes of Pressure Panic and Distress* (1840). The Library Company of Philadelphia.

In stark contrast to Luther's earlier images and accounts of the bank, the subterranean expanses beneath the bank are free of devils or other supernatural agents. Instead of conjuring metaphysical figures of corporate personhood and financial abstractions, this image offers a vision of a material—perhaps pneumatic—system situated in a physical underworld conveniently situated beneath the Bank's edifice. The only figures in this complex image are the tiny ones, in the attitude of laborers and the elegant dress of bankers, who turn the screw press that pressurizes the Currency Reservoir. The *Bank-ometer* is notable for more than its absences: its system of tubes links diverse entities—from the quotidian materiality of flour and wages to complex banking institutions and the financial abstractions of monetary expansion and contraction—and situates the whole amid the discursive surround of quotations theorizing and critiquing banking. The Bank's facade is no longer a mask behind which a devilish spirit hides but rather, like the charts echo its architectural form, a schematic grid of epistemological access.

In one sense, the networked ontology of the *Bank-ometer* and the religious imagery of Luther's *Confederacy* and *Address* present different facets of a coherent picture: the *Bank-ometer* anatomizes—and depersonifies—the artificial god against which the address on idolatry makes its prophetic case. Yet the *Bank-ometer* also suggests that the problem with worshiping idols, whether paper calves or marble banks, is not the veneration of empty representations but rather the fact that the entities to which they refer are all too real, yet can only be apprehended indirectly. We can understand Luther's religious and materialist representations as approaching from different angles the mysterious growth of greed and the money supply, as well as the mysteries, at once theological and legal, of animation and incorporation. What has changed, in other words, are the means by which Luther gets a handle on the bank. The *Bank-ometer* refigures what had seemed a malevolent deity as an entity that allows measurement and thus, potentially, reconfiguration. Their representation captures the bank's epistemological, tropological, and economic affordances in a way a legal account of the corporation alone cannot. By capturing the Bank as both ghost *and* machine, person *and* form, entity *and* network, Luther shows how different ways of imagining corporateness can engender different forms of critique and resistance.

Luther and Lawton show how the elusive corporation can be apprehended through quotidian entities: wages, flour, and savings. In a sense, they echo the medical register of anti-Bank pamphlets that described corporations as parasitic "excrescences" on the body politic. But rather than figure an ailing body politic, their figure of financial interconnectedness exposes the innards of the United States' most powerful artificial person, rendering "an artificial being, invisible, intangible, and existing only in contemplation of law" in visible, tangible terms that subject it to the laws of observation. Rather than an inert body awaiting direction from a sovereign soul, the *Bank-ometer* depicts the corporation's artificial soul as an assemblage in its own right. This artificial person, in any case, would prove mortal after all. After hobbling along briefly under its Pennsylvania charter, the Second Bank folded in 1841. While the ensuing ascendancy of the corporation would prove unstoppable, its paradigmatic example was dead on the table.

Incorporate Silence

In 1839, Poe began working for William Burton as assistant editor of *Burton's Gentleman's Magazine*, in an office a short stroll from Strickland's Second Bank building and directly across Dock Street from the Philadelphia Merchants' Exchange, also designed by Strickland (Figs. 1.9, 1.10). Like the Bank building, the imposing edifice, erected only six years earlier, vested Philadelphia's financial nerve center with the architectural idiom of classical Athens, lending marmoreal permanence to capitalist modernity.[68] In the wake of the Panic of 1837, the brokers who traded stocks there, as well as the printers and publishers concentrated nearby, were confronted with the mismatch between the building's monumental physicality and apparent timelessness and the volatility and vulnerability of the institutions that it could only tenuously anchor.[69]

In contrast to Strickland's monumental embodiment of capitalist abstraction, a number of Poe's works of 1839–40 evoke the paradoxes of materiality and immateriality that mark the corporate form. In "Peter Pendulum, the Business Man," "William Wilson," and particularly "Silence. A Sonnet," the numerical ambiguity of corporations converges with their putative immortality and intangibility.[70]

PHILADELPHIA.
PUBLISHED BY WILLIAM E. BURTON,
DOCK STREET, OPPOSITE THE EXCHANGE.
1839.

Fig. 1.9 *Burton's Gentleman's Magazine* 5 (1839), detail of title page. The Library Company of Philadelphia.

[68] Strickland's design references the Choragic Monument of Lysicrates, the subject of a chapter in James Stuart and Nicholas Revett, *Antiquities of Athens* (London: printed by John Haberkorn, 1762), Vol. 1, 27–36, chap. 4, plate 3.

[69] On the effect of the Panic of 1837 on American publishing, see James N. Green, "The Rise of Book Publishing," in *A History of the Book in America*, Vol. 2, *An Extensive Republic: Print, Culture, and Society in the New Nation, 1790–1840,* ed. Robert A. Gross and Mary Kelley (Chapel Hill, NC: University of North Carolina Press, 2010), 119, 126.

[70] All three works appeared in *Burton's Gentleman's Magazine* during Poe's tenure with Burton: "William Wilson" in October 1839 (5: 205–12); "Silence. A Sonnet" in April 1840 (6: 166);

Fig. 1.10 William Strickland and John Sartain, *The Philadelphia Exchange*, mezzotint (Philadelphia: [printed by D. Stevens], ca. 1835). The Library Company of Philadelphia.

As noted above, "Peter Pendulum" registers with frustration that "corporations... have neither posteriors to be kicked, nor souls to be damned"; the narrator complains that banks' "infamous suspension has put [him] to ruinous inconvenience" (89). In contrast to the bodiless, soulless banks, the eccentric, grotesquely embodied narrator ascribes his character to a childhood accident: "a good-hearted old Irish nurse...knocked my head into a cocked hat against the bed-post," and the resulting bump "turned out to be as pretty an organ of *order* as one shall see on a summer's day" (87). That the remainder of the tale satirically undercuts the narrator's claim to phrenologically grounded "order" and "method" suggests that the best business men might be not individuals like Peter Pendulum (renamed "Peter Proffit" in Poe's 1845 revision) but the incorporeal, inanimate corporations that bedevil him. Whereas the Business Man's schemes are continually undermined by violence and abuse, corporate fraud carries on unmolested because the artificial persons that perpetrate it are unmolestable. For Poe's narrator, as for the aggregate

"Peter Pendulum, the Business Man" in February 1840 (6: 87–89). I cite the *Burton's* texts except in the case of "William Wilson"; Poe's later revisions reflected in T. O. Mabbott's copy-text (principally carried out in 1845) underline issues I stress here. See *Collected Works of Edgar Allan Poe*, ed. T. O. Mabbott (Cambridge, MA: Harvard University Press, 1969–78), Vol. 2, 426. I use the *Burton's* titles to emphasize the circumstances of their publication in the magazine.

theory of the corporation, the power of corporations flows from their very insubstantiality.

More troubling quandaries around body, soul, and number arise in "William Wilson" and "Silence" (both 1839), which address the problem of "double life."[71] Reading these texts' play with doubleness in light of the corporate form allows us to revise a dominant topos in recent treatments of Poe's work: the hauntings of racial, economic, and legal specters. Teresa A. Goddu has insisted that we read antebellum gothic texts and tropes not as escapes from history, but rather as crucial sites at which "the horrors of history are…articulated."[72] Scholarship in recent decades has centered on race as the animating source of the American gothic and Poe's gothic in particular.[73] At the same time, these texts, as critics from Marc Shell to David Anthony and Gavin Jones have demonstrated, are pervaded by gold bugs and paper money men—and by the uncanny economics of language and semiotics of money more broadly.[74] Terence Whalen has shown how financial crises resonated in Poe's life and work,[75] and scholars including Margaret

[71] Nicholas Canady has pointed out that the two texts share a concern with "'double life' or 'twin entity' (twin aspects of one entity)." Reading "William Wilson" as a moral allegory, Canady argues that the narrator William Wilson, initially horrified by "physical degeneration," brings upon himself "the ultimate spiritual death," which Canady equates with the poem's enigmatic phrase "incorporate silence." See Canady, "Poe's 'William Wilson,'" *Explicator* 40, no. 2 (1982): 28–29.

[72] Goddu, *Gothic America: Narrative, History, and Nation* (New York: Columbia University Press, 1997), 2.

[73] Goddu and others have read Poe profitably in light of Toni Morrison's insistence that "the American gothic's blackness needs to be historicized not only in terms of slavery but also, more important, in terms of the racial fantasies that haunt it" (*Gothic America*, 75). Attending to the racial resonance of the shadows in Poe's texts, such works as Goddu's *Gothic America* and J. Gerald Kennedy and Liliane Weissberg's edited collection *Romancing the Shadow: Poe and Race* have explored what Goddu calls, in the context of *The Narrative of Arthur Gordon Pym*, "'visitant[s] from the world of shadows'—the ghost[s] of race" that appear in the "schism between the scientific and the supernatural" (88).

[74] See Marc Shell, *Money, Language, and Thought: Literary and Philosophic Economies from the Medieval to the Modern Era* (Berkeley and Los Angeles, CA: University of California Press, 1982), 5-23; David Anthony, *Paper Money Men: Commerce, Manhood, and the Sensational Public Sphere in Antebellum America* (Columbus, OH: Ohio State University Press, 2009); Gavin Jones, "Poor Poe: On the Literature of Revulsion," *American Literary History* 23, no. 1 (2011).

[75] Terence Whalen argues that Poe was distinguished by "his ability to imagine the literary implications of an emerging capitalist order and his willingness to manipulate, albeit unsuccessfully, the peculiar logic that this new order was insinuating into the culture at large" (Terence Whalen, *Edgar Allan Poe and the Masses: The Political Economy of Literature in Antebellum America* (Princeton, NJ: Princeton University Press, 1999], 75). Poe likely acquired knowledge of banking and monetary policy, as Whalen suggests, through his foster father, Richmond merchant John Allan; Poe would also attempt to solicit the support of Second Bank president Nicholas Biddle for his *Penn Magazine* in the wake of the Bank War (196). As Poe—and his correspondent Biddle—knew well, the Panic of 1837 was precipitated in large part by a political and legal crisis. Whalen shows how financial crisis permeates Poe's sketches and reviews of the 1830s and 1840s (27). Jill Lepore, likewise, frames Poe's career with "the Panic of 1819 and the Panic of 1837, the pit and pendulum of the antebellum economy." (Jill Lepore, "The Humbug: Edgar Allan Poe and the Economy of Horror," *New Yorker*, 27 April 2009, http://www.newyorker.com/arts/critics/atlarge/2009/04/27/090427crat_atlarge_lepore). Gavin Jones sees Poe generating "an aesthetic of *revulsion*"—a nineteenth-century term that embraced economic depression as well as distaste ("Poor Poe," 2–3).

Alterton and Colin Dayan have tracked Poe's engagement with legal thought.[76] It should thus come as no surprise that Poe's tales and poems of the 1830s and 1840s grappled not only with psychological and racial specters but also with entities conjured by legal and economic theory. As "Peter Pendulum" makes clear, to grasp capitalism and crisis in Jacksonian America involved confronting their political and legal underpinnings. Due to the successive shocks of the dismantling of the BUS and the rapid failure of smaller banks in the Panic of 1837, the mortality of putatively immortal beings was, as it had been two decades earlier, a topic of practical and not merely philosophical interest. Poe's tales and verse contend with the lives, deaths, and afterlives of inhuman and intangible yet consequential things.

In a virtuoso reading of "William Wilson" as legal allegory, Dayan foregrounds the legal fiction of civil death and its close proximity to slavery: "William Wilson dies not once but twice, as if Poe felt compelled to redouble this fiction of law, to make a fiction twice over"; the tale's "use of this unusual fiction of law to produce the juridical nonexistence of the person raised the specter of natural versus artificial."[77] Poe's readers, however, would have been equally familiar with another legal artifice: the corporation. Wilson's seemingly endless reserves of cash, the crooked gambling in which he engages, and the disastrous loans in which he involves his poorer classmates echo the actions of the incorporated banks that brought "ruinous inconvenience" to Peter Pendulum. Additionally, the doubling that structures "William Wilson" echoes a key trope in the language of corporations. Wilson's well-known description of a parvenu who shares his name, appearance, and even clothing paradoxically aligns multiplicity with identity: "Not a thread in all his raiment—not a line in all the marked and singular lineaments of his face which was not, even in the most absolute identity, *mine own*!"[78] By making a claim of identity rather than resemblance, Wilson both invokes the Lockean notion of personal identity and gestures toward its ramifications for the law of corporations, the means by which diverse individuals can be considered identical.[79] Calling to mind Chief Justice Marshall's description of the corporation as simultaneously a "single individual" and a garment that "cloth[es]" the "bodies of men," the narrator William Wilson describes himself as at once "exposed" and doubly clothed in his own garment and that of his alter ego: "The singular being

[76] Margaret Alterton, *Origins of Poe's Critical Theory* (1925; New York: Russell and Russell, 1965), 46–67; Dayan, *Fables of Mind: An Inquiry into Poe's Fiction* (Oxford: Oxford University Press, 1987); Dayan, "Poe, Persons, and Property, in *Romancing the Shadow: Poe and Race*, ed. J. Gerald Kennedy and Lilliane Weissberg (Oxford: Oxford University Press, 2001). David K. Jackson observes that Poe's knowledge of the law was likely not as broad as Alterton asserts. Yet Jackson concedes that Poe's acquaintances and collaborators on the *Southern Literary Messenger* included a number of lawyers. "Poe's Knowledge of Law During the *Messenger* Period: Some Comments on Chapter II of Margaret Alterton's *Origins of Poe's Critical Theory*," *American Literature* 10 (1938): 331–39.

[77] Dayan, "Poe, Persons, and Property," 115.

[78] Poe, *Works*, Vol. 2, 448.

[79] On Poe's indebtedness to the Lockean problematic of personal identity, see Dayan, *Fables of Mind*, 133–92.

who had so disastrously exposed me, had been muffled, I remembered, in a cloak; and none had been worn at all by any of the members of our party, with the exception of myself.... I took the one offered me by Preston; placed it, unnoticed, over my own."[80] Like the legal fiction of the king's two bodies, Poe's fiction posits the protagonist's two bodies as simultaneously identical and distinct. It manifests this paradox in a play of layers analogous to the law of corporations by blurring the distinction between person and garment, entity and association, piercing the corporate veil and stabbing the human body, death and "the agonies of dissolution."[81]

"Silence," like "William Wilson," registers a "double life" that can be understood as both metaphysical and legal. The poem's seemingly abstruse speculation on corporeality and incorporeality corresponds to a longstanding debate about the nature of corporations: are they mere legal abstractions—as defenders like Alexander Hamilton had alleged—or substantial entities—as their critics insisted? (As noted above, Marshall's and Story's *Dartmouth College* opinions implicitly differed on this question.) Thomas Jefferson, late in his life, stressed the political danger posed by such political persons, predicting "government of an aristocracy, founded on banking institutions, and moneyed incorporations under the guise and cloak of their favored branches of manufactures, commerce, and navigation, riding and ruling over the plundered ploughman and beggared yeomanry."[82] Charles Jared Ingersoll situated himself as Jefferson's anti-aristocratic heir in a speech arguing for the revocability of bank charters, printed in the Jacksonian *Democratic Review* in 1839: "We have lived to feel corporations—all that [Hamilton] treated as absurd creations of imagination—great independent substantive things, political engines of peculiar magnitude and moment. And it is as curious as it is instructive, that what Jefferson foretold and Hamilton treated as preposterous, is the reality of our present government by corporate supremacy."[83]

Ingersoll's remark reveals the political stakes at play in "Silence." With its mention of "incorporate things" and "corporate Silence," the poem's relation to corporations may seem to be punning at best.[84] But like "Peter Pendulum" and "William Wilson," "Silence" foregrounds the contested corporate attributes of individuality, intangibility, and immortality. It opens, "There are some qualities—some incorporate things / That have a double life." Beginning in the decidedly abstract terrain of "qualities" or "incorporate things," the poem echoes Hamilton's rhetoric of "qualities" and "capacities." But unlike Hamilton, who minimizes the corporation

[80] Poe, *Works*, Vol. 2, 444. [81] Poe, *Works*, Vol. 2, 448.

[82] Thomas Jefferson, letter to William B. Giles, 26 December 1825, in *The Writings of Thomas Jefferson*, ed. Paul Leicester Ford (New York: Putnam, 1892–99), Vol. 10, 356.

[83] "Speech of Charles J. Ingersoll, Esq., in the Convention of Pennsylvania, on Legislative and Judicial Control over Charters of Incorporation," *United States Magazine and Democratic Review* 5, no. 13 (1839): 111.

[84] Edgar Allan Poe, "Silence. A Sonnet," *Burton's Gentleman's Magazine* 6 (1840): 166.

through the rhetoric of insubstantiality, and also unlike Hamilton's critics Jefferson and Ingersoll, who stress the corporation's substantiality, Poe identifies the power and the terror of "incorporate things" with their very intangibility. Moving to the graveyard, his speaker identifies "a two-fold *Silence*": both the "corporate Silence" of graveside mourning and its inchoate "*shadow*." Whereas "The Banks" had presented corporate mortality as a way to contain banking companies, "Silence," attuned to corporations' uncertain status (living, dead, or undead), is more ambiguous and less sanguine. Unlike "The Banks" or even "Peter Pendulum," which flirt with the anthropomorphic embodiment of corporations, "Silence" moves from questions of corporate (in)tangibility and (im)mortality to broader questions about what persons are.

As Poe's editor T. O. Mabbott has shown, "Silence" both echoes and departs from two sonnets by Thomas Hood, "Silence" and "Sonnet: — Death," one of which Poe included in *Burton's Gentleman's Magazine* in 1839, a few months before his own poem appeared there. Hood's "Silence" contrasts the physical silence "where hath been no sound" and "where no sound may be" with "the true Silence...self-conscious and alone" that occupies the "ruins...where Man hath been." In contrast to the mere silence of human absence, where "No voice is hush'd—no life treads silently," the silence of ruins carries the melancholy trace of a departed human voice. As if searching for this voice, the speaker anthropomorphizes inhuman sounds as evidence of human mourning: "the dun fox, or wild hyena, calls, / And owls, that flit continually between, / Shriek to the echo, and the low winds moan." In a similar vein, "Sonnet: — Death" valorizes mourning and its centrality to human subjectivity: "It is not death," the speaker says, that "This eloquent breath shall take its speechless flight" and "this warm conscious flesh shall perish quite." True death "is not...to know this, but to know / That pious thoughts, which visit at new graves, / In tender pilgrimage will cease to go / So duly and so oft." The death that Hood's poem mourns is the demise of mourning itself, of the rich and pious subjectivity whose intimations of immortality allow it to remember and to hope. The sonnet's final lines depict this mourning of mourning as the cessation of spiritual rebirth: "there may be then / No resurrections in the minds of men!"[85]

Like Hood's sonnets, Poe's contemplates human presence and absence, silence and death, and the possibility of transcendence. But in "Silence," unlike its precursors, immortality registers not as comforting "resurrections in the minds of men" but as an excessive, alien presence. Poe's sonnet is fifteen lines long, with an "extra" line in the second quatrain. An extra entity occupies the world Poe depicts as well: while Hood's sonnets explore the layered plenitude of subjectivity that

[85] Poe, *Works*, Vol. 1, 320–22.

Poe will call "human memories and tearful lore," "Silence" grapples with the "double life" of the inhuman.

> Silence. A Sonnet
>
> There are some qualities—some incorporate things,
> That have a double life—life aptly made,
> The type of that twin entity which springs
> From matter and light, evinced in solid and shade.
>
> There is a two-fold *Silence*—sea and shore—
> Body and Soul. One dwells in lonely places,
> Newly with grass o'ergrown. Some solemn graces
> Some human memories and tearful lore,
> Render him terrorless—his name's "*No More*."
>
> He is the corporate Silence: dread him not!
> No power hath he of evil in himself;
> But should some urgent fate—untimely lot!
> Bring thee to meet his *shadow* (nameless elf,
> Who haunteth the dim regions where hath trod
> No foot of man)—commend thyself to God![86]

In contrast to Hood's poems, Poe's sonnet rejects as "terrorless" the mourning of a lost loved one—the "*No More*" or "Nevermore" that carries such haunting force in his own poems "Lenore" and "The Raven."[87] Nor is it the end of mourning itself that Poe's speaker fears. Critics Richard Wilbur and Nicholas Canady have suggested that the second silence indicates a second death—that of the soul rather than the body—which inspires terror and commends us to God.[88] Such a reading rightly attends to Poe's "two-fold *Silence*... Body and Soul" but skips over the more ambiguous and less anthropomorphic "sea and shore" that comes in the midst of the unfolding of "two-fold *Silence*" into, at the least, a two-fold of two-folds. Terror, this dynamic suggests, is latent in the very "double life" with which the poem opens—the ontology shared by the legal mechanism of incorporation and the "twin entit[ies]" of which "incorporate things" are the "type." Paradigmatic among these twin entities are "corporate Silence" and its "nameless" shadow,

[86] Poe, "Silence," 166.

[87] Adam Bradford has argued that, in such poems of mourning as "Annabel Lee" and "The Raven," Poe "fostered both a sense of communion and a 'prescience of the glories beyond the grave' through, rather than in spite of, the most extreme feelings of grief." Extravagant though they seem, these poems were "perceived by many [contemporaneous readers] in much the same way as contemporary consolation literature" (93). See "Inspiring Death: Poe's Poetic Aesthetics, 'Annabel Lee,' and the Communities of Mourning in Nineteenth-Century America," *Edgar Allan Poe Review* 12, no. 1 (2011): 72–100.

[88] Wilbur cited in Poe, *Collected Works*, 1:320; Canady, "Poe's 'William Wilson,'" 29.

a pairing that gestures back to the antithetical glosses of the phrase "incorporate things": "things gathered into a body" and "bodiless things." With this doubleness, "incorporate things" at once registers and troubles the opposition between body and soul, corporeality and incorporeality. Incorporeal things can have corporeal effects; incorporated things can cast haunting shadows.[89]

It is in this metaphysical murkiness that Poe's doubled Silence, which belongs to two different ontological registers, recalls the legal doctrine of natural and artificial persons. In contrast to the king, that celebrated corporation sole, Poe's Silence has a double *life*, but has a body only by analogy or catachresis. Or we might say that its body, like a corporation, lacks the visibility and mortality that characterize natural bodies. The poem thus resonates with the conception of the corporation aggregate as an "incorporate thing" instantiated by law, with a double life of its own—at once an entity and an association; at once a person and a contract. Poe's knowledge of the law and his contemporaneous attention to corporate ontology in "Peter Pendulum" suggest that this resonance is no coincidence. Personifying Silence as a doubled being with paradoxical attributes, and even anthropomorphizing it as a "he," the sonnet dramatizes the poetics of a corporate charter.[90]

Yet if the corporation lurks in the background of Poe's "incorporate things," it remains implicit. In contrast to his well-known satires of contemporary institutions—capitalist "method" in "Peter Pendulum," technological hype and military heroism in "The Man That Was Used Up," magazine culture in "The Folio Club" and "How to Write a Blackwood Article"—"Silence" recasts the structure of a legal and economic institution as the structure of lyrical solitude, moving from the ontology of law to the experiential and aesthetic possibilities it affords. Whereas "The Banks" attributes natural mortality to artificial persons as an antidote to the unsettling status of corporations, "Silence" transposes the structure of incorporation into the sphere of personal identity, consciousness, and memory, where it resonates uncannily. The earlier poems constrain the proliferation of artificial persons by likening them to natural persons; "Silence," in contrast, depicts the artificial person as a presence that destabilizes the "natural" speaker.[91] In a world shaped by powerful but intangible "incorporate things," human personhood itself is revealed to be doubled, shadowed, and framed by contrasting silences. The imaginative payoff of the corporate form, in Poe's hands, is a powerful

[89] Dayan has also noted Poe's treatment of souls as things. *Fables of Mind*, 204.

[90] On Poe, personification, and the similarities of poetic and legal personification, see Dayan, "Poe, Persons, and Property"; Barbara Johnson, "Anthropomorphism" and "Strange Fits: Poe and Wordsworth on the Nature of Poetic Language" in *The American Face of Edgar Allan Poe*, ed. Shawn Rosenheim and Stephen Rachman (Baltimore, MD: Johns Hopkins University Press, 1995), 37–48.

[91] In Paul de Man's terms, the former poems rest on the ontological assumptions of anthropomorphism, while "Silence" reveals the natural person to be structured by the trope of prosopopoeia. See de Man, "Anthropomorphism and Trope in the Lyric," in *The Rhetoric of Romanticism* (New York: Columbia University Press, 1984); Barbara Johnson, "Anthropomorphism."

capacity for exploring, even undermining, the subjectivity of so-called natural persons, a new way to complicate human identity on the pattern of the corporation's ghostly legal paradoxes of mortality and immortality, singularity and plurality. The speaker tells us that the silence of bodily mortality leaves a "*shadow* (nameless elf, / Who haunteth the dim regions where hath trod / No foot of man)." Blackstone's explanation of the artificial person as a convenient instrument that outlives the human individual allows for a troubling possibility: an inaccessible realm from which artificial beings can exert their force on mere mortals. In these "dim regions," Poe frames something like "exist[ence] only in contemplation of law," befitting a "nameless elf" but inaccessible to human feet.

What is so terrifying about Poe's "elf"—a nightmare vision or a supernatural being, to take two of the word's senses? And why does he imply that a "power…of evil" lurks in it? The "urgent fate" adumbrated in the poem recalls the Business Man's "ruinous inconvenience" at the hands of banks, beings with worldly consequences but without punishable bodies and souls. This complaint, echoed by politicians like Henshaw and Ingersoll, certainly indexes the asymmetry between the tangible effects of incorporated banks' power and the difficulty of pinning them down.[92] As I have tried to show, the metaphysics of Poe's poem were never far from such legal and economic concerns. His texts afford a glimpse of 1830s corporate America as a mysterious region populated by beings conjured by the legal magic of charters, and likely to disappear, just as magically, into the ether. Thus, if the corporate form granted early nineteenth-century bankers unprecedented tools for exercising power, it afforded Poe both an idiom to characterize these new forms of power and the capacity to recognize new wrinkles in human personhood.

By pursuing the consequences of the corporate form for the lyric subject, "Silence" thus prefigures the counterintuitive but insightful conclusion reached by the early twentieth-century jurist Amasa Mason Eaton. The corporation, Eaton reasons, does not *lack* a soul; rather, as a virtual entity that exists on an immaterial plane and unites disparate persons and things, "a corporation is nothing but a soul."[93] A corporate charter, to follow Poe's logic, conjures the virtual source of corporate speech or the impossible source of corporate silence—an artificial soul—whose effects do not require tangible existence.[94] Even after it "suspend[s] itself," as the Laureate of the Banks imagines, a corporation can continue to damn

[92] David Henshaw, *Remarks Upon the Rights and Powers of Corporations, and the Rights, Powers, and Duties of the Legislature toward Them. Embracing a Review of the Opinion of the Supreme Court of the United States, in the Case of Dartmouth College, in New Hampshire, Given in 1819* (Boston: Beals and Greene, 1837); *Opinion of Charles J. Ingersoll, Esq. "with Reference to the United States Bank and the Question of Vested Rights"* (Philadelphia, 1836); Ingersoll, "Speech."

[93] Amasa Mason Eaton, *The First Book in English on the Law of Incorporation* (New Haven, CT: Ryder's Printing House, 1903), 11; repr. from *Yale Law Journal* 12 (March–April 1903).

[94] On the problem of understanding the source and intentions of corporate speech, see Lisa Siraganian, *Modernism and the Meaning of Corporate Persons* (Oxford: Oxford University Press, 2020).

borrowers like Poe's Business Man, particularly if its liabilities disappear with it. The problem, from this perspective, is not that corporations lack morals because they lack "souls to be damned" but rather that the law of corporations provides for virtual souls with real, potentially devastating consequences.

By amplifying the metaphysical strangeness of "incorporate things," Poe departs from the more familiar identification of the menace posed by corporations as "great independent substantive things." As I've suggested, his account of corporate ontology can offer us insights that 1830s critics like Ingersoll and their present-day heirs miss. What kinds of critical resources might we gather today from Poe's investigation of the constitution of artificial souls? The familiar twenty-first-century assertion that corporations are *not* persons can have the unintended consequence of shuffling the corporate form—and corporate responsibility—offstage. Indeed, as association theorists from Hamilton to "nexus of contracts" theorists have recognized, defining corporations as nothing but bundles of contracts between individuals can hamper efforts to identify corporate malfeasance and enforce corporate liability.[95] As Winkler has stressed, treating corporations as associations or aggregates—pass-through vehicles for the rights of members—was a powerful early nineteenth-century strategy to expand their power, whereas treating them as entities—as persons in law—served as a strategy to limit corporate rights.[96] Poe's work, which acknowledges the complex ontology and genealogy of the corporation and refuses to reduce legal personhood to the logic of human identity, gestures toward more effective means of characterizing and countering business corporations' power.

While Poe devoted attention to the corporation's legal metaphysics, his contemporaries focused more often on another facet of the corporation: its potential as a form of associated collectivity. As the next chapter shows, Francis Lieber and other early theorists of the corporation would come to understand it both as a revealing foil for other associated bodies and a surprisingly flexible political form in its own right.

The Corporate Forms of Antebellum US Literature. Peter Jaros, Oxford University Press. © Peter Jaros 2026.
DOI: 10.1093/9780198996491.003.0002

[95] Richard Posner has argued, for instance, that "a corporation is not a rich person, natural or artificial; it is a network of relationships among people (shareholders, workers, customers, suppliers, executives), some wealthy, some not" (*The Problems of Jurisprudence* (Cambridge, MA: Harvard University Press, 1993), 186). See also Frank H. Easterbrook and Daniel R. Fischel, "The Corporate Contract," *Columbia Law Review* 89 (1989): 1416–48; Lewis A. Kornhauser, "The Nexus of Contracts Approach to Corporations: A Comment on Easterbrook and Fischel," *Columbia Law Review* 89 (1989): 1449–60.

[96] Winkler, *We, The Corporations*, xx.

2

The Corporation and the Encyclopedia

Theorizing and Practicing Assemblage in the Age of Association

"A nation itself is the great corporation, comprehending all the others."[1]
"Corporation," *Encyclopaedia Americana* (1830)

One of the clearest and most widely circulated—if idiosyncratic and infrequently remembered—nineteenth-century accounts of the corporation comes from the Prussian-American encyclopedist, educator, and publicist Francis Lieber, in the midst of the vast collective project that was the *Encyclopaedia Americana* (*Americana*).[2] Lieber's article "Corporation" appears in Volume 3 of the *Americana* (1830), a decade after the *Dartmouth College* decision (1819) but before the publication of Joseph K. Angell and Samuel Ames's *Treatise on the Law of Private Corporations Aggregate* (1832).[3] Admittedly, an unsigned reference article might seem a strange anchor for a theory of the corporation, yet "Corporation" both consolidates existing jurisprudence and departs boldly from received understanding. Notwithstanding his close personal and intellectual ties to Associate Justice Joseph Story, Lieber presents an understanding of the corporation beyond the legal doctrine of *Dartmouth College*. By framing corporations as both entities and aggregates, and both persons and property, *Dartmouth College* gives rise to conundrums around corporate rights, familiar in our day from *Citizens United* and *Hobby Lobby*. Lieber in contrast, presents the corporation less as a legal convenience than as a body politic: "a political or civil institution, comprehending

[1] Francis Lieber, "Corporation," in *Encyclopaedia Americana*, ed. Francis Lieber and Edward Wigglesworth (Philadelphia: Carey and Lea, 1830), Vol. 3, 547–48.

[2] Publicist was Lieber's preferred term of art. The *Oxford English Dictionary* notes that "publicist" derives from the German and French term for a theorist of law of nations, expands to signify a commenter on public affairs generally (1833 ref.), and only later develops the sense of the proponent of a particular cause.

[3] I follow Kevin Butterfield in attributing the article to Lieber. It expands greatly on the corresponding article in the *Conversations-Lexicon* and is not among the articles written by Story, Lieber's chief writer on legal subjects. See Kevin Butterfield, *The Making of Tocqueville's America: Law and Association in the Early United States* (Chicago: University of Chicago Press, 2015), 66; Valerie Horowitz, ed., *Joseph Story and the Encyclopaedia Americana* (Clark, NJ: The Lawbook Exchange, 2006), iii–iv; Joseph K. Angell and Samuel Ames, *A Treatise on the Law of Private Corporations Aggregate* (Boston: Hilliard, 1832). Not only do concepts from the article reappear in Lieber's subsequent work, he uses the distinctive phrase "the whole political system" in *Legal and Political Hermeneutics* (Boston: Little and Brown, 1839), vi.

one or more persons, by whom it is conducted according to the laws of its constitution." He thus anticipates the German jurist Otto von Gierke's insight that "there seems to be a genus of which State and Corporation are species."[4] By framing the nation as "the great corporation, comprehending all the others," Lieber highlights aspects of the corporation that escape our usual attention to its legal form and economic power: as a form of association and a political entity. Lieber's account of associations at all scales emphasizes the properties that emerge from plurality and de-emphasizes formal charters and contracts. His account of the corporation thus emerges as a key strand in an evolving theory of association. While his focus shifts over time—from a singularly expansive view of the corporation in the *Americana* to later, nuanced theoretical distinctions between different kinds of associated bodies—his focus on the nature of these bodies remains a consistent thread.

Further, the context of the *Americana* situates Lieber's discussion of associated bodies amidst the editorial and authorial practices that assembled the encyclopedia, the social and publication networks through which it reached a broad readership, and the contemporaneous enthusiasm for voluntary associations. "Corporation" thus constitutes a revealing node in a fascinating feedback loop: a focused theory of associations produced amidst and promulgated by a culture self-consciously devoted to what Kevin Butterfield has termed "the technology of how to associate."[5] As I will argue with reference to Lieber's writing—from the *Americana* to his works of political theory—he and his contemporaries offered far-reaching theories of associated bodies, formal and informal, of their deliberate or spontaneous assembly and reorganization, and of the relations from which they were built. Thanks particularly to Tocqueville's widely read discussion of voluntary associations in *Democracy in America*, this culture of association can seem quintessentially, even tautologically a product of nineteenth-century America. Yet attending to Lieber and his German-American contemporaries reveals its transnational context. The first encyclopedia published in the United States, the *Americana* itself was at once a translation of a German encyclopedia and an ambitious collective project carried out by Lieber and his American associates. Like the *Americana*, contemporaneous American theory and practice of association drew on German models, particularly those pioneered by the radical German student movements of the early nineteenth century.

I thus situate Lieber in the self-conscious American culture of associations in which he participated as well as the less familiar milieu of German voluntary associations that shaped his early life and ultimately propelled him to the US. Because Lieber was so skilled at gathering others around himself—the likes

[4] Frederic Maitland, "Translator's Introduction," in Otto Gierke, *Political Theories of the Middle Age*, trans. Frederic Maitland (Boston: Beacon, 1958), ix.
[5] Butterfield, *The Making of Tocqueville's America*, 103.

of Story and Nicholas Biddle, Charles Sumner and George S. Hillard, Alexis de Tocqueville and Gustave de Beaumont—and because he compiled others' ideas both professionally (as encyclopedia editor) and temperamentally (thanks to his magpie sensibility)—it can be difficult to discern where his thought ends and others' begins. It's thus as a self-conscious "principle of thrift in the proliferation of meaning," in Foucault's famous words, that I invoke his name as an author-function that inevitably gathers an assemblage—the German university system in which he was educated and radicalized, the elite social worlds and print culture institutions of 1820s and 1830s America (particularly Boston and Philadelphia) in which he ingratiated himself while nonetheless failing to achieve insider status or the northern university position he sought.[6] As the editor of the *Americana* and a well-connected man of letters, Lieber was many things: a stunningly quick study, a brilliant synthesizer, an ambitious if occasionally clumsy political thinker, and a consummate networker—a "Forrest Gump with brains, a real-life Zelig."[7] He merits our attention both as a theorist and as a representative of the processes and habits of incorporation, encyclopedic compilation, and informal association that could generate a powerful company or a patchwork author.

Lieber and his contemporaries developed a vocabulary that not only classified and explained existing forms of social organization but also pointed to the uncertain territory beyond them. As I will argue, his accounts of the relationship among the members of different kinds of collectives—from insurance companies to proto-states to national governments to fortuitously assembled crowds—come into focus when we see the way they draw on and put into play overlapping intellectual and legal traditions. By gathering Lieber's work on various forms under the rubric of assemblage, this chapter argues for a through-line in his work that is hard to see if we only consider him as, say, a political theorist, an educational theorist, or a popularizer of encyclopedic knowledge. Throughout his work, Lieber is attentive to connections—strong or weak, firm or shifting—and the entities and ontologies they constitute. Rather than treat legal and theoretical entities—the corporation, the state—abstractly, he traces how the properties of assemblages—the despotic power of associations, the quasi-governmental status of vigilantes—emerge from the particular relations that constitute them. He examines, at an unusually granular level, the way plurality gives rise to state and corporate power.

[6] The most comprehensive biographies of Lieber are Frank Freidel, *Francis Lieber: Nineteenth-Century Liberal* (Baton Rouge, LA: Louisiana State University Press, 1947) and the early, somewhat hagiographic Thomas Sergeant Perry, *Life and Letters of Francis Lieber* (Boston: James R. Osgood, 1882). See also Gerhard Weiss, "The Americanization of Franz Lieber," in *German Culture in Nineteenth-Century America: Reception, Adaptation, Transformation*, ed. Lynne Tatlock and Matt Erlin (Rochester, NY: Camden House, 2005), 273–87.

[7] Aviam Soifer, "Facts, Things, and the Orphans of Girard College: Francis Lieber, Protopragmatist," *Cardozo Law Review* 16 (1995): 2305–2319, 2306.

This sustained and shifting theorization of associated bodies, as well as the practical traversal of networks, offers an unfamiliar perspective on more recent theories of assemblage associated with Gilles Deleuze, Felix Guattari, and Bruno Latour. For Deleuze, Guattari, and Latour, the notion of assemblage demonstrates the way that mundane connections among heterogeneous elements can give rise to radically different kinds of collective entities and collective power, and thus emphasizes the contingency of seemingly fundamental social structures like the family, class, or state. On the one hand, Lieber anticipates key facets of these theorists' work, such as Latour's attention to the forms that networks take and Deleuze and Guattari's interest in the forces that traverse them. On the other, by distinguishing among various kinds of associations, Lieber offers clarity where later assemblage theorists often remain vague. By highlighting the continuities between conventional forms of plurality—student associations, corporations, states—and techniques of association ranging from the casual to the revolutionary, his work avoids both the Dionysian antihumanism of Deleuze and Guattari and the Latourian tendency to frame the description of networks as an end in itself.

I frame the work of Lieber and his contemporaries with the term *assemblage* for a few reasons. First, I acknowledge to its use by scholars to grapple attentively and flexibly with entities in all their collectivity and interconnection on what Deleuze and Guattari call "a single plane of consistency."[8] Second, it serves as an umbrella that gathers terms—association, society, assembly—used by the writers I examine without privileging any particular one of them. Finally, it enables shifts between scales—the theories Lieber and his contemporaries developed, the configurations of institutions and practices—including the law, print culture, the state, and charitable institutions—in which they participated. One might object that while "assemblage" might be appropriate to describe configurations of persons and institutions, it is anachronistic as a characterization of the early nineteenth-century theoretical perspectives I treat here. Yet such anachronism underscores the kinship between nineteenth century and more recent theories of assemblage (without drawing a straight line of influence between them). Further, and more importantly for my purposes, it underscores the flexibility with which Lieber and his contemporaries—jurists like James Kent and Story and publicists like Tocqueville—thought through collectivity and the various forms it could take. Not only did they discuss corporations, states, and informal bodies in similar terms; they also raised the question of the extent of those similarities, what they mean, and where they give out. In this light, Lieber's interest in the law, politics, and corporate and related forms of association makes his work a crucial but understudied site for reconstructing a broad view of the corporation before it

[8] Gilles Deleuze and Felix Guattari, *A Thousand Plateaus*, trans. Brian Massumi (Minneapolis, MN: University of Minnesota Press, 1987), 90.

became recognizably "corporate"—which is to say, before it was understood as an economic rather than a political formation. Reading Lieber as a theorist of association and assemblage allows us to trace the threads of his corporate imaginary beyond the *Americana* and through his subsequent writing on legal and political theory. Doing so reveals how fundamentally his theory of the corporation is tied to his understanding of the political and the human—in particular, to a theory of political belonging that exceeds the liberal notion of voluntary contract.

The Great Corporation

Lieber's article "Corporation" opens with an apparently straightforward definition that hews close to Blackstone and Marshall's descriptions of the corporation as legal entity: "A corporation is a political or civil institution, comprehending one or more persons, by whom it is conducted according to the laws of its constitution. It is a conventional and artificial organ, of an integral or individual character, whether it embraces one or more members, and is invested with certain powers and rights, varying according to the objects of its establishment. Its acts, when done in pursuance of its powers, are considered those of the body, or organ, and not those of the member or members composing the corporation."[9]

With its emphasis of the artificiality of corporations and the distinction between corporation (as entity) and members (as aggregate), the introduction reiterates common law doctrine. Yet Lieber goes on to present a view of the corporation from the vantage point of political theory, articulating a taxonomy of corporations which culminates in a political order: "The whole political system is made up of a concatenation of various corporations, political, civil, religious, social and economical. A nation itself is the great corporation, comprehending all the others, the powers of which are exerted in legislative, executive, and judicial acts, which, when confined within the scope, and done according to the forms, prescribed by the constitution, are considered to be the acts of the nation, and not merely those of the official organs."[10]

The culminating example of the nation hammers home Lieber's central point: the hallmark of the corporate is its "integral . . . character," manifested in its acts. While composed of various members or organs—or even other corporations—it operates as a dynamic unit. In short, the corporation is a legal and political technology for crafting unity from multiplicity by means of law.[11] His striking formulation preserves Thomas Hobbes's recognition of the likeness of state and corporation, yet it rejects Hobbes's image of corporations as "lesser

[9] Lieber, "Corporation," 547. [10] Lieber, "Corporation," 547.

[11] On corporations as a characteristic example of nineteenth-century "law-mindedness," see Butterfield, *The Making of Tocqueville's America*.

Common-wealths in the bowels of a greater, like wormes in the entrayles of a naturall man."[12] Hobbes finds the corporate form threatening because its uncanny statelikeness threatens to undermine the authority and ontological priority of the state. Lieber, in contrast, recognizes corporations as crucial constituents of a political order because his political ontology does not take the sovereign state as its point of origin.

It's surprising that the *Americana* article on the corporation was not written by Story, one of the architects of the American law of corporations and Lieber's most crucial American ally, advocate, and mentor. An Associate Justice of the US Supreme Court, Dane Professor of Law at Harvard, and a prolific legal theorist, Story connected Lieber to elite legal and intellectual circles in Boston and beyond, writing letters of introduction and trying to secure him a professorship. When his protégé came to edit the *Americana*, Story provided a significant number of legal articles; he would eventually advise Lieber about the possibility of studying and practicing law.[13] (Lieber finally found long-term employment in 1835 as a professor at the College (now University) of South Carolina, where he lectured on history and political theory and remained for two decades, despite his distaste for the South and quiet ambivalence about slavery.[14] Although he never became a lawyer, in his later life he would have a profound impact on international law and the law of war.)

As discussed in chapter 1, Story and Chief Justice John Marshall had framed the prevailing view of the corporation in American jurisprudence in *Dartmouth College*. The Supreme Court construed corporate charters to be protected by the Contract Clause of the US Constitution, thus significantly strengthening both the corporate form and the rights of corporations' members and directors. Marshall's opinion emphasizes the priority of charters, enshrining the artificial entity theory of the corporation in American jurisprudence, even as it implicitly endorses the aggregate theory by highlighting the rights of the trustees rather than those of the college itself, echoing his earlier judgment in *Deveaux*.[15] Story's concurrence frames a doctrine of private and public corporations; centered on members and

[12] Thomas Hobbes, *Leviathan* (1651), ed. Richard E. Flathman and David Johnston (New York: Norton, 1997), 230.

[13] William Wetmore Story lists Story's contributions in his biography of his father: William Wetmore Story, *Life and Letters of Joseph Story* (Boston: Little & Brown, 1851), Vol. 2, 27. See also Morris L. Cohen's "Introduction" in Joseph Story, *Joseph Story and the Encyclopaedia Americana* (Clark, NJ: Lawbook Exchange, 2006).

[14] Lieber kept a careful and ambiguous position on slavery during his time in South Carolina: although he opposed slavery in principle he carefully refused the title of abolitionist, espoused white racial superiority, and even owned slaves. He did not openly express antislavery views until he left the South for New York in 1857. Samara Trilling, "A Tale of Two Columbias: Francis Lieber, Columbia University, and Slavery." https://samaratrilling.com/project/francis-lieber.

[15] Ruth H. Bloch and Naomi R. Lamoreaux, "Corporations and the Fourteenth Amendment," in *Corporations and American Democracy*, ed. Naomi R. Lamoreaux and William J. Novak (Cambridge, MA: Harvard University Press, 2017); Adam Winkler, *We the Corporations: How American Businesses Won Their Civil Rights* (New York: Liveright, 2018), 35–70.

their interests, it conceived of the corporation less as person than as property. In the words of legal historian R. Kent Newmyer, Story's theory of the corporation "ignored the mixture of private and public in the corporation and hypostasized each into a symmetrical and self-contained category."[16] Story's broad construction of the sanctity of corporate charters, along with his equally broad definition of private corporations, enabled the rise of private business corporations and all but foreclosed a theory of the corporation's public or political life.[17]

In this respect, Lieber departs dramatically from his mentor. Whereas Marshall and Story emphasize the legal forms of charter, contract, and Constitution and foreground the private/public distinction, Lieber stresses a different kind of form: not the legal qualities of the corporation but the emergent properties of associations of all sorts, from charitable institutions to ad hoc regimes of justice to the state itself. "Corporation" goes beyond Lieber's American legal contemporaries in drawing on the brief *Conversations-Lexicon* article on "Körperschaften."[18] This earlier article foregrounds municipal corporations and their historical importance in creating political rights and tempering monarchical sovereignty, themes that resurface in the *Americana* article "Community."[19] By conjoining this continental focus on municipal rights with American jurisprudence on corporations, "Corporation" bears witness to the *Americana*'s heterogeneous origins. Thanks to this pluralistic perspective, Lieber frames the similarities and distinctions among various sorts of associations—states, voluntary associations, business corporations—more clearly than any of his contemporaries.

Lieber's attention to the variety of associations and their powerful effects makes him an unacknowledged precursor both to later theorists of the corporation and to twentieth and twenty-first century theorists of the ontologies of networks and assemblages. As I will show, his distance from both the artificial entity and aggregate theories of the corporation foreshadows his later rejection of social contract theory. Whereas Story emphasizes the distinction between private and public bodies and emphasizes the corporation's status as property, Lieber stresses the difference between voluntary *associations* and more integral *societies*, thus highlighting their status as collective political bodies. In his suspicion of the centrality of charters and concessions to the corporate form and his anti-contractarian theory of the state, Lieber emphasizes the composition and persistence of pluralistic bodies over the performative compacts (whether corporate charters or social

[16] R. Kent Newmyer, *Supreme Court Justice Joseph Story: Statesman of the Old Republic* (Chapel Hill, NC: University of North Caroline Press, 2010), 136.

[17] A competing view would rise to power in *Charles River Bridge v. Warren Bridge*, 36 US 420 (1837), in which Story found himself in the minority on the Taney court. See Stanley I. Kutler, *Privilege and Creative Destruction: The Charles River Bridge Case* (Baltimore, MD: Johns Hopkins University Press, 1989). On Story's pro-corporation jurisprudence, see Newmyer, *Supreme Court Justice Joseph Story*, 125–37.

[18] *Conversations-Lexicon*, 7. Aufl. (Leipzig: Brockhaus, 1827), Vol. 6, 262–64.

[19] *Encyclopaedia Americana*, Vol. 3, 395–98.

contracts) understood to inaugurate and legitimize them. His work thus anticipates Gierke's real entity theory of the corporation, itself rooted in the world of German associations that Lieber knew well, which frames the sovereign conferral of corporate charters as secondary to the existence of corporate plurality and, further, underscores the resemblance between state and corporation.[20] Ironically, the protégé of the great exponent of the Contract Clause as the basis of corporate identity and stability would come to minimize both corporate charter and social contract in favor of the fundamental plurality underlying both corporations and states.

Although Lieber's description of the corporate state—characterized by constitutionality, rights and duties, and unified action—departs from Story's corporation theory, it harmonizes with Story's *Americana* article on the Law of Nations: "Nations are considered as moral persons, having duties to perform, as well as rights to enforce, and are bound to the observation of the great principles of justice, which are applicable to the relations which subsist between each nation and its own subjects, and between each nation and every other nation."[21] This conception of moral personhood as both embracing a specific bundle of rights and duties and implying a more general "observation of the great principles of justice" prefigures what Lieber will later theorize as "jural relations," relations founded on right.[22] For Lieber, human individuals, corporations, and nations belong essentially to an order based on justice—legible in microcosm in his notion of the "political system." His language of "concatenation" and his crowning figure of the nation as "the great corporation, comprehending all the others" come into focus when we consider a "political system" constituted by interlocking rights and duties.

The Age of Association

In recognizing the underlying similarity of voluntary associations, business corporations, and states, Lieber made a crucial contribution to his era's loquacious theorizing of association. One of the first to identify an age of association was the renowned jurist James Kent, Chancellor of New York, who in his *Commentaries on American Law* (1826) points out the unprecedented multiplication of corporate charters: "The propensity, in modern times, has...been to multiply civil

[20] Gierke, *Political Theories of the Middle Age*. See also Frederic William Maitland, *State, Trust, and Corporation*, ed. David Runciman and Magnus Ryan (Cambridge: Cambridge University Press, 2003).

[21] Joseph Story, "Law of Nations," in *Encyclopedia Americana*, ed. Lieber and Wigglesworth, Vol. 9, 141. Freidel ascribes a number of Lieber's legal and political conceptions to Story. Freidel, *Francis Lieber.*

[22] Francis Lieber, *Manual of Political Ethics: Designed Chiefly for the Use of Colleges and Students at Law* (Boston: Little and Brown, 1838–39), Vol. 1, 176. Lieber anticipates Dewey's often-cited notion of the corporation as a bundle of rights and duties. John Dewey, "The Historic Background of Corporate Legal Personality," *Yale Law Journal* 35 (1926): 655–73.

corporations, especially in these United States, where they have increased in a rapid manner, and to a most astonishing extent. The demand for charters of incorporation is not merely for municipal purposes, but usually for the more private and special object of assisting individuals in their joint stock operations and enterprising efforts directed to the business of commerce, manufactures, and the various details of internal improvement."[23]

Kent emphasizes not only corporations' multiplication but their multifariousness: "We are multiplying, in this country, to an unparalleled extent, the institution of corporations, and giving them a flexibility and variety of purpose, unknown to the Roman or the English law. The study of this title is becoming every year more and more interesting and important."[24] Throughout the 1820s, 1830s, and 1840s, theorists of law, institutions, and society would offer accounts of associations and corporations that said nearly the same thing over and over again.

Lieber's *Americana* article echoes Kent in pointing out that "Charters of incorporation for mere economical purposes, as the construction of roads and canals, and carrying on of banking, insurance, manufactures, &c., are more frequent in the U[nited] States than in any other country."[25] By the time of Angell and Ames's *Treatise*, this trope was well-worn. Angell and Ames frame corporations as institutions of belonging that confer status on their members—with a nod to Kent's account of corporations' "astonishing" spread:

> In no country have corporations been multiplied to so great an extent, as in our own; and the extent, to which their institution here has been carried, may very properly be pronounced 'astonishing.' There is scarcely an individual of respectable character in our community, who is not a member of, at least, one private company or society which is incorporated. The number of Banking Companies, Insurance Companies, Canal Companies, Turnpike Companies, Manufacturing Companies, &c., and the number of literary, religious, and charitable associations, that are diffused throughout these United States, and fully invested with corporate privileges, must excite the surprise of Europeans, especially when they call to mind, that not much more than two centuries have elapsed since civilized man first found the country a wilderness, wherein the unlettered savage roamed in unmolested freedom.[26]

In Angell and Ames's description, membership of "individual[s] of respectable character" has become key—and indeed, membership and shareholding became increasingly widespread in the early republic as charters multiplied.[27] What

[23] James Kent, *Commentaries on American Law* (New York: O. Halsted, 1826), Vol. 2, 271.
[24] Kent, *Commentaries*, Vol. 2, 281. [25] Lieber, "Corporations," 548.
[26] Angell and Ames, *A Treatise on the Law of Private Coporations Aggregate.*
[27] By the 1820s, "Shareholders and directors remained atypical of the population, but became less so over time as larger numbers of corporations were created." Eric Hilt, "Early American Corporations and the State," in *Corporations and American Democracy*, ed. Lamoreaux and Novak, 51.

Angell and Ames make clear is both the proliferation of corporations and their variety—some connected to infrastructural improvements (canals and turnpikes), others to the lucrative foundations of the financial system, and still others with the voluntary "literary, religious, and charitable associations" that are grouped together here but still (in the spirit of *Dartmouth College*) included under the heading of private corporations. Moreover, their closing explicitly frames associations as a force of settler colonialism that displaces the "unlettered savage," thus identifying Indigenous people as both a displaced ideal of Lockean liberty and outsiders to a Lockean theory of property. In this gesture, they suggest (as will Tocqueville and Irving, among others) that the romantic solitude attributed to Indigenous people must necessarily fall before the organized sociality of corporate forms.

Angell and Ames's apparently offhand remark belies a wealth of recent jurisprudence concerning Indigenous people. Their treatise appeared shortly after the Marshall Court's landmark opinion *Cherokee Nation v. Georgia* (1831), which identified Native American tribes as "domestic dependent nations" and, along with *Johnson v. McIntosh* (1823) and *Worcester v. Georgia* (1832), laid the groundwork for relations among Indigenous nations, the federal government, and the states.[28] Marshall's "realistic and ambiguous" doctrine, in Newmyer's words, recognized the sovereignty and treaty-making power of Indigenous nations while denying them standing as foreign nations (which would grant them access to the Supreme Court via original jurisdiction).[29] (As my discussion of Washington Irving's *Astoria* in chapter 4 shows, Native Americans and the trope of wilderness would come to play a more complicated and ambivalent role in the 1830s corporate and imperial imaginary.) By rhetorically distancing Indigenous people from legally-recognized collectivity, Angell and Ames departed from the Marshall court's rulings and ironically echoed Justice William Johnson's disparagement of the Cherokees as "a people so low in the grade of organized society" in his virulently racist *Cherokee Nation* concurrence.[30] The increasing identification of corporations as business entities rather than bodies politic was thus linked to a misapprehension of Native people as both savage and unincorporated.

As the preceding examples indicate, the most celebrated commentator on American associations (and the Americanness of association) was less a lone genius than a reader informed by the *Americana* and the increasingly conventional wisdom it promulgated. Tocqueville echoes Kent, Lieber, and Angell and Ames when he writes, "In no country in the world has greater advantage been

[28] *Cherokee Nation v. Georgia*, 30 US 5 Pet. 1 (1831); *Johnson & Graham's Lessee v. McIntosh*, 21 US 8 Wheat. 543 (1823); *Worcester v. Georgia* 31 US (6 Pet.) 515 (1832).

[29] R. Kent Newmyer, *John Marshall and the Heroic Age of the Supreme Court* (Baton Rouge, LA: Louisiana State University Press, 2001), 450.

[30] *Cherokee Nation*, 21.

derived from association nor has this powerful instrument of action been applied to a wider variety of objectives than in America."[31] He later elaborates:

> Americans of all ages, conditions, and all dispositions constantly unite together. Not only do they have commercial and industrial associations to which all belong but also a thousand other kinds, religious, moral, serious, futile, very general and very specialized, large and small. Americans group together to hold fêtes, found seminaries, build inns, construct churches, distribute books, dispatch missionaries to the antipodes. They establish hospitals, prisons, schools by the same method. Finally, if they wish to highlight a truth or develop an opinion by the encouragement of a great example, they form an association. Where you see in France the government and in England a noble lord at the head of a great new initiative, in the United States you can count on finding an association.[32]

Tocqueville's innovation is not, as most readers have supposed, his recognition of the importance of associated (i.e. corporate) form, but rather his three-way comparison between the state, the aristocracy, and associations. Tellingly, his account features two of the commonplaces for understanding the corporation: (artificial) person and (miniature) commonwealth. By the same token, the article "Societies," in the supplemental Fourteenth Volume of the *Americana* (1846), edited by Henry Vethake, distills the formula in diction that recalls Tocqueville: "There is no circumstance more characteristic of the present age, as contrasted with the times which preceded it, than the disposition of individuals to associate together for the accomplishment of a common object."[33] Thus, while Butterfield is correct to identify techniques of association and membership as central to "Tocqueville's America," Tocqueville was only one of a distinguished club of commentators to remark on them.

What do we make of all this repetition? And of the jurists and publicists, to use their preferred terms, who promulgated it? Rather than take these theorists' unanimity as evidence of unoriginality or conformity, I'd like to consider both the commonplace they repeat—that they live in a time and place unprecedented for its wealth of examples of and techniques of association—and this view's tendency to repetition or repeatability as itself a function of association—the assemblage comprising lawyers, publicists, and the texts, like the *Americana* and Angell and Ames's *Treatise*, to which they made common reference. Their redundant

[31] Alexis de Tocqueville, *Democracy in America* and *Two Essays on America*, ed. Isaac Kramnick, trans. Gerald Bevan (London: Penguin, 2003), 220.

[32] Tocqueville, *Democracy in America*, 596.

[33] "Societies," *Encyclopaedia Americana*, Vol. 14, 553.

extravagance can become audible not merely as bluster but rather as a manifestation of the age of association it trumpets.

These writers come into focus as a network: Lieber had read and corresponded with the learned Chancellor Kent and cherished the endorsement of his mentor Story; Tocqueville cribbed all he could—too much, Lieber and Story complained—from the *Americana*, which Lieber had presented to the man he saw as his peer, even as Tocqueville's formulations found broader purchase than Story's or Lieber's own.[34] Thus, if this cohort can sometimes seem a self-parodying echo chamber, it also embodies the power of association—and the way that an "association of citizens," whether an incorporated body or an informal network, constitutes an entity irreducible to the individuals who make it up. Turning our attention to the practice of encyclopedic assemblage can situate their theories amid the networks of print and sociability that gave rise to them.

Assembling General Knowledge

The *Americana* had begun as—and in large part remained—a translation of the seventh edition of the Brockhaus *Conversations-Lexicon* (1827–29). Lieber's familiarity with the German reference work, supplied with articles on an astonishing variety of topics, convinced him of a niche ripe for development in the world of American publishing. The eminent Philadelphia publisher Mathew Carey agreed, and offered Lieber the sum of $20,000 to cover the considerable cost of translation and adaptation as well as Lieber's own compensation. The *Americana* strove for a uniform editorial voice even as it acknowledged the necessary plurality of contributors. Gathered under Lieber's editorial command, it stitched together the anonymous work of translators and contributors (paid fifty cents and one dollar per page, respectively).[35] By concatenating specialized bodies of knowledges, and by disaggregating and recombining topics, it aimed at a composite knowledge. The encyclopedic understanding it promised inevitably emerged from a collective and fragmented process, its unity reliant on the fiction of editorial authority, at once as commanding as Hobbes's *Leviathan* (1651) and as obviously patched together as a scarecrow. In short, the network that created the *Americana*—Brockhaus and the writers of the *Conversations-Lexicon*, Lieber's contributors, and his many translators and copyists (including Matilda Lieber,

[34] As Freidel notes, an older Lieber would boast "that the most prominent three of a certain class of politico-philosophers were Montesquieu, Tocqueville, and Lieber" (Freidel, *Francis Lieber*, 89). On Tocqueville's debt to Lieber and Story, see Freidel, *Francis Lieber*, 91; Joseph Story to Francis Lieber, MSS LI 3277, Francis Lieber Papers, Huntington Library.

[35] Drake De Kay, "Encyclopedia Americana, First Edition," *The Journal of Library History* 3.3 (1968): 205–6, 201–20; David Kaser, *Messrs. Carey & Lea of Philadelphia: A Study in the History of the Booktrade* (Philadelphia, PA: University of Pennsylvania Press, 1957), 133.

his polyglot Anglo-German wife, and the assistant editors Edward Wigglesworth and Thomas Gamaliel Bradford)—constituted another informal body on a continuum with the associations Lieber and his contemporaries theorized.

The encyclopedia's centralizing authority and the body of "general readers" it could gather were at the heart of Lieber's proposal to Carey to translate the *Conversations-Lexicon* from German, with suitable additions and alterations for American and English readers.[36] In a circular letter that garnered the endorsements of many members of Boston's literary elite, Lieber explained the need for a reference work that would both embrace specialized professional domains and open them to a broader readership: "The work embraces a large amount of information on a great variety of topics, including the useful and elegant arts, commerce, law, theology, medicine, navigation, biographical accounts of the distinguished men of all nations and all ages, in fact every branch of knowledge and all sciences, *in so far as the different objects are interesting to general readers.* For this reason it is found in the hands not merely of the learned but of every merchant, trader and mechanic, who makes any pretensions to intellectual culture."[37]

The undertaking had not yet taken on the title *Encyclopaedia Americana*, and Lieber's endorsers in the circular letter follow his awkward lead, translating or transliterating the German title as "Lexicon for Conversation" (Edward Everett) or "Dictionary for Conversation" (Charles Follen). If the *Americana*, from one angle, supplied general readers with general information, from another it met a public need for a "Dictionary for Conversation." While Lieber momentarily segments his readership—the learned, merchants, traders, mechanics—the appeal of the project was its promise to assemble "general readers" into both a civic public and a paying body by supplying the intellectual equivalent of bank paper: a circulating medium of exchange, and thus of value. Lieber and Carey astutely identified both a tremendous marketing opportunity (Lieber's *Americana* would go through numerous reprintings from 1829 to 1858, most of them by publishers who paid to rent Carey's stereotype plates[38]) and an as yet unrealized public with "pretensions to intellectual culture" that exceeded its grasp.

The project of the *Americana*, in short, was twofold: the concatenation of knowledge and the assembly of a public in relation to it. In this sense, it anticipates Latour's conception of the social in terms of the connections among entities rather than a particular "domain of reality" distinct "from other domains such as economics, geography, biology, psychology, law, science, and politics."[39] Latour conceives of social theory not as the study of acknowledged social phenomena

[36] De Kay, "Encyclopedia Americana."
[37] Circular Letter, MSS LI 88, Francis Lieber Papers, Huntington Library. Emphasis in original.
[38] De Kay, "Encyclopedia Americana," 212.
[39] Bruno Latour, *Reassembling the Social: An Introduction to Actor-Network Theory* (Oxford: Oxford University Press, 2005), 3.

but "the *tracing of associations*," embracing "any type of aggregate from chemical bonds to legal ties, from atomic forces to corporate bodies, from physiological to political assemblies," a project he describes as potentially, if faintly, utopian: "all those heterogeneous elements *might be* assembled anew in some given state of affairs."[40] Lieber's project for the *Americana* hoped to do just that: to consolidate a public of readers around and with reference to a novel assembly of knowledge by means of his ambitious print culture project.[41]

That something so mundane as a reference work could reassemble the social—gather a public, animate conversation, and supply its lexicon—might seem naïve or ludicrous. But a contemporaneous illustration of this process appears in a surprising place: Edgar Allan Poe's tale "The Man That Was Used Up." Echoing Lieber's proposal to consolidate encyclopedic knowledge and promulgate conversation among the literate classes, Poe's tale mordantly depicts the way social networks form themselves as they collect, repackage, and distribute general knowledge as a form of social power. The emblem of this process is the tale's would-be war hero Brevet Brigadier General John A. B. C. Smith. Poe's narrator is uncannily entranced by General Smith, who gamely rattles off war stories but "invariably c[omes] back" to singing the praises of "the rapid march of mechanical invention":

> 'There is nothing at all like it,' he would say; 'we are a wonderful people, and live in a wonderful age. Parachutes and rail-roads—man-traps and spring-guns! Our steam-boats are upon every sea, and the Nassau balloon packet is about to run regular trips (fare either way only twenty pounds sterling) between London and Timbuctoo. And who shall calculate the immense influence upon social life—upon arts—upon commerce—upon literature—which will be the immediate result of the great principles of electro magnetics! Nor, is this all, let me assure you! There is really no end to the march of invention. The most wonderful—the

[40] Latour, *Reassembling*, 5. Although Anna Kornbluh has recently criticized Latour as a "destituent" theorist opposed to the potential of form- and institution-building, Caroline Levine's and Henry Turner's work demonstrates the potential of Latourian language for thinking political, legal, and literary form. Anna Kornbluh, *The Order of Forms: Realism, Formalism, and Social Space* (Chicago: University of Chicago Press, 2019); Caroline Levine, *Forms: Whole, Rhythm, Hierarchy, Network* (Princeton: Princeton University Press, 2015); Henry S. Turner, *The Corporate Commonwealth: Pluralism and Political Fictions in England, 1516–1561* (Chicago: University of Chicago Press, 2016).

[41] Although the *Americana* was grounded in a culture of reprinting that minimized authorial identity in favor of networks, Lieber would become an ardent proponent of intellectual property and international copyright, and would argue that literary property "exist[s] by spontaneous right, and…requires only to be acknowledged by way of protection on the part of government." Lieber, On International Copyright, in a Letter to the Hon. William C. Preston (New York, 1840), reprinted in Lieber, *Miscellaneous Writings*, ed. Daniel C. Gilman (Philadelphia, PA: Lippincot, 1881) Vol. II, 337–38. See Frank Freidel, "Lieber's Contribution to the International Copyright Movement," *Huntington Library Quarterly* 8, no. 2 (1945): 200–6. On the culture of reprinting, see Meredith L. McGill, *American Literature and the Culture of Reprinting, 1834–1853* (Philadelphia, PA: University of Pennsylvania Press, 2003).

> most ingenious—and let me add, Mr. —Mr.—Thompson, I believe, is your name—let me add, I say the most *useful*—the most truly *useful* mechanical contrivances are daily springing up like mushrooms, if I may so express myself, or, more figuratively, like—ah—grasshoppers—like grasshoppers, Mr. Thompson—about us and ah—ah—ah—around us!'[42]

The General's pitch is packed with platitudes and misrecognizes its addressee, but it follows a discernible thread: wonderful people, wonderful age; mechanical invention and its "immense influence" on every sphere of human life; technical novelty "springing up" with the nonhuman vitality of grasshoppers and mushrooms. As technical knowledge transforms the world, it demands to be transmuted into and circulated as general knowledge through the spheres of "social life," "arts," "commerce," "literature"—spheres that the tale goes on to dramatize as the narrator inquires after General Smith in various milieus of polite civil society: the church of Doctor Drummummupp, the Rantipole Theatre and the Mistresses Cognoscenti who number among its audience, the salon of Mrs. Kathleen O'Trump, populated by the likes of Mrs. Pirouette and Miss Bas-Bleu, and the elite homosocial intimacy of a visit to Mr. Theodore Sinivate. However hollow the hype may be, it pulls Poe's narrator—and reader—powerfully along.

Poe's burlesque, subtitled "A Tale of the Late Bugaboo and Kickapoo Campaign," gestures to the Black Hawk War and Second Seminole War and more broadly to the violence of Indian Removal. Like Angell and Ames, who posit a "wilderness" traversed by "savage[s]" as the prehistory of a miraculous age of association, Poe's Indian-fighting General Smith presents the bloody work of genocide as the precondition of his wonderful age. In tracing the circulation of both Smith's war stories and his theory of modernity, the tale offers the rudiments of a theory of assemblage: the way that new things, and people's relationships with and accounts of those things, both traverse existing networks and transform them. As we learn at the tale's climax, Smith himself is the assemblage par excellence: a cybernetic collection of high-tech prostheses crafted by renowned artisans and painstakingly affixed by his Black servant Pompey to the unrecognizable remnant of his body. Smith is "used up" as an individual, reduced, in the narrator's words, to a "bundle" or "nondescript," yet as a cybernetic construction embedded in a broader social and technological assemblage he is arrestingly fascinating. And while the General's view of the networks that constitute his body and his reputation is admittedly blinkered, it reveals more than most readers have recognized. The story's impact, in large part, is in the irony that emerges when we connect the dots between the content of Smith's pronouncements and the circumstance of their utterance: from the artificial mouth of an artificial man, at

[42] Edgar Allan Poe, *Collected Works*, ed. Thomas Ollive Mabbott (Cambridge, MA: Harvard University Press, 1969–78), Vol. 2, 381–82.

once a figure for wars exerting racialized national sovereignty over Indigenous people (those "domestic dependent nations" in yet another list) and African Americans and a mutilated victim of those wars. As assemblage and prophet of assemblage, the figure of the General aligns brutality and depletion on an imperial scale with the glorious, if stiff, beauty conjured by a long roster of artisans whose technological wizardry parallels the technologies, for conquering space and conquering subject peoples, that the General lauds.[43]

The juxtaposition of Smith's sunny theory of progress and his ghoulish war stories is jarring, but it also offers a glimpse of the mechanical-rhetorical assemblage centered on and constitutive of the General. The prospect of drawing links among these discordant parts both disorients readers and offers them the pleasure of reassembling the familiar materials of the present in a new, indelible guise—giving the date its physiognomy, to borrow Walter Benjamin's phrase. In the tale of his reassembly, what becomes particularly visible is not just the truth or untruth, or the significance or vacuity of the General's pronouncements but also the way they traverse the networks, conduits of circulation, and operations of power that undergird his "wonderful age." His biography and pet theories circulate through the varied institutions of that comprehensive, if mostly elite, public that Lieber addresses as "general readers."[44] Despite his rank, General Smith appears less as a figure of command than an example of the power of circulation, broadcasting commonplaces as an expertly—if also violently—constructed body that at once forms a polished and beautiful whole and, in its excessive perfection, is awkwardly and obviously artificial. Despite his apparent singularity, General Smith succeeds in propagating "general" information and opinions through the tale's many speakers, institutions, and social situations and making them speak in unison.[45] Notwithstanding his oddly mechanical voice, nothing could seem more natural than the circulation of his platitudes as public opinion. (The mechanistic unanimity that animates conversation about the general ominously suggests that conversation itself, however affectively charged, is superfluous for formulating and propagating public opinion.)[46] The tale thus casts a satirical light on the the-

[43] See Mabbott's introductory note in Poe, *Collected Works* as well as Colin (Joan) Dayan, *Fables of Mind* (Oxford: Oxford University Press, 1987), 158; Jonathan Elmer, *Reading at the Social Limit: Affect, Mass Culture, & Edgar Allan Poe* (Stanford, CA: Stanford University Press, 1995), 49–50; Robert Beuka, "The Jacksonian Man of Parts: Dismemberment, Manhood, and Race in 'The Man That Was Used Up,'" *Edgar Allan Poe Review* 3 (2002), no. 1: 27–44; John Carlos Rowe, "Edgar Allan Poe's Imperial Fantasy and the American Frontier," in *Romancing the Shadow: Poe and Race*, ed. J. Gerald Kennedy and Liliane Weissberg (Oxford: Oxford University Press, 2001), 75–105.

[44] See also Elmer's account of Smith's "generality" in Elmer, *Reading at the Social Limit*, 49–50.

[45] It's worth mentioning that Poe published Lieber's own war-hero reminiscences of the Napoleonic wars, in which the nationalistic teenaged Lieber fought and was wounded, in the *Southern Literary Messenger*. Francis Lieber, "A Reminiscence," *Southern Literary Messenger* 2, no. 9 (August 1836): 535–38.

[46] Lieber writes that public opinion, "in its most comprehensive sense, not only meaning the opinion of the community as far as it has been made public, especially with regard to some specific measures, pending or adopted, but as the opinion of the public, of civil society, as we are apt to term

orists of the age of association discussed above: Kent, Lieber, Angell and Ames, Tocqueville, and the anonymous author of "Societies." These writers—jurists writing for the legal profession and publicists writing for a broader readership—make an eminent list. Yet like Poe's image of the redounding, self-aggrandizing platitudes of a manufactured man, their breathlessly unanimous heralding of a new age soon begins to sound weary, automated, "used up."

For all its parodic excess, the tale thus undertakes an analysis of ideology via the descriptive practice that Latour calls tracing associations: assiduously following the connections between human and inhuman nodes in a network. If Poe's tale patiently sketches a social assemblage in all its flatness, it also helps to focus the issue that occupied Lieber in his diverse projects as encyclopedist, memoirist, and political theorist: the way assemblages constitute authority. As I have been trying to suggest, the hastily assembled and conveniently alphabetized Brevet Brigadier General John A. B. C. Smith—at once commanding and vulnerable, put-together and fragmented—shares a great deal with the encyclopedia's odd juxtaposition of patchwork construction and nexus of authority. (The general's brevet rank follows this pattern: brevet appointments conferred honor with a temporarily elevated rank, and thus served the practical purpose of allowing officers to fill vacant positions of authority for which they would otherwise be ineligible.) As both Poe and Lieber understood, the ramshackle construction of such virtual authorities can be strategic: the encyclopedia's lack of structure beyond mere alphabetization allows it to propagate epistemological authority without the framework of systematic doctrine.

A few years after completing his editorial work, Lieber celebrated the artificial juxtapositions of alphabetical order, which both denaturalizes the normally perceived connections between things and suggests playful new linkages. Perhaps paradoxically, he identified arbitrary alphabetization as the facet of the encyclopedia that brought it closest to lived experience: "Life, you know well, does not select and classify, does not present things by gradual transitions, but seems to delight in contrasts, and is much like the index of an encyclopedia, where *Locke* follows *Lobster*, where *Lace* precedes *Lacedæmon*, and *Shakers* is the neighboring article to *Shakespeare*."[47]

The encyclopedia is like life, Lieber suggests, in both its comprehensiveness and the bittersweet absurdities that emerge from its juxtaposition. His observation anticipates Deleuze's penchant for compiling lexicons: "the arbitrary

public, anything connected with the state, for instance, public life, public character. *I understand by public opinion the sense and sentiment of the community, necessarily irresistible, showing its sovereign power everywhere. It is this public opinion which gives sense to the letter, and life to the law: without it the written law is a mere husk* [emphasis added]." Lieber, *Political Ethics*, Vol. 1, 255–56. We might thus read his account alongside Tocqueville's understanding of public opinion as the vehicle of the tyrannical majority and Dickens's scathing critique in *American Notes* of "public opinion" as glib justification for American slavery.

[47] Francis Lieber, *Letters to a Gentleman in Germany, Written after a Trip from Philadelphia to Niagara* (Philadelphia: Carey, Lea & Blanchard, 1834), 98.

character of the alphabetical order is the most certain way of not superimposing upon the multiple relations of imbrication between concepts as an artificial order of reasons."[48] While Lieber's playful comparison uses the arbitrariness of alphabetization to dramatize life's juxtapositions, it also sheds oblique light on the project of an encyclopedia: the incongruities introduced by a project of totalizing inclusion and the inevitable gaps and leaps that mark its impossibility—and the connections unmade and remade by the process of ordering. Yet Lieber had long been deeply interested in the political possibilities of organization.

Student Societies and Shadow States

Lieber, as I have argued, demands our attention at once as a theorist of association, studying the pluralistic power exercised by corporations and states, and as a practitioner of assemblage, who deployed the circulatory power of the encyclopedia and occupied a crucial node in the network of luminaries involved with it. Lieber had arrived in Boston in 1827 as an erudite and well-connected Prussian emigré, and his unorthodox account of associated bodies comes into clearer focus in the context of his German background. Lieber was born in Berlin to a merchant family and grew up during Napoleon's domination of Europe. From his youth, he was involved in the liberal-nationalist gymnastics movement inaugurated by "*Turnvater*" Friedrich Ludwig Jahn, who envisioned the physical culture of gymnastics as the seedbed of a vigorous anti-Napoleonic nationalism. Jahn established the Berlin *Turnplatz* in 1811 and Lieber was one of his early students; alongside many other young *Turner*, he served as a teenaged volunteer in the Prussian army and was wounded at Waterloo. Under Jahn's guidance, these student volunteers were also instrumental to the beginnings of the *Burschenschaften*, student societies that promoted a unified German state with a popular constitution. Lieber was involved in the Berlin Burschenschaft in its early days and was close to Karl (Charles) Follen, the more radical founder of the Giessen Burschenschaft. Jahn promoted a unified, reconstituted Germany that retained some aspects of Germany's patchwork of monarchies but was grounded in popular representation. He envisioned "a corporate body elected from a number of professional categories, a balanced assembly reflecting the complexity of society, and not the medieval three-estate type of representation"; his *Burschenschaftler* followers expanded and radicalized his ideas; some, most notably the Follens, endorsed an explicitly republican government.[49]

[48] François Zourabichvili, *Deleuze: A Philosophy of the Event*; together with *The Vocabulary of Deleuze*, Greg Lambert and Daniel W. Smith, eds., trans. Kieran Aarons (Edinburgh: University of Edinburgh Press, 2012), 141–42.

[49] Rolland Ray Lutz, "'Turnvater' Jahn and His Teacher-Revolutionaries from the German Student Movement," *Journal of Modern History* 48, no. 2 (On-Demand Supplement) (1976): 7–8.

Prussian (and other German) authorities were wary of the *Burschenschaften*, whose republican politics and highly elaborated structures made them de facto shadow states; the societies were formally banned (and went underground) after the 1819 assassination of the playwright and diplomat August von Kotzebue by the *Burschenschaftler* Karl Sand. In the wake of the murder, Lieber and Follen were both imprisoned and questioned; Jahn was arrested as well.[50] In response, the Prussian state imposed the Carlsbad decrees, which "outlawed all liberal or national activities that aimed at establishing constitutional government and national unity."[51] The *Burschenschaften* were forced underground and Follen went into exile in Switzerland, where he drafted a revolutionary constitution for Germany and planned "a German revolution that would violently overthrow the existing structures of rule, abolish all hereditary rights and all forms of unchecked exercise of political power."[52] After a stint in Paris, he emigrated to the United States, where he would be a crucial ally for Lieber upon his subsequent arrival.

Follen had already invested considerable effort in constitutional thinking. As Maike Oergel writes, he viewed the *Burschenschaften* "as prototype free states, governed publicly by the general will of their members/citizens" and authored the *Ehrenspiegel* (1816), a constitution for student associations that included an internal justice system. Moreover, he and his brother August drafted a German constitution, grounded in the principle of popular sovereignty, during 1817–18.[53] Both within the context of the *Burschenschaften* and in a wider political sphere, Follen's writing was deeply concerned with modeling political associations. Like Jahn's vision of a national assembly as a complex corporate body, Follen's draft constitution attends to multiple levels of coherent political activity, meticulously detailing "democratic consensus at all levels…from village to Reichstag." Follen, as Oergel demonstrates, envisioned democracy as both multileveled and pluralistic: "all levels have fora of discussion and decision-making, including decisions on all functionaries and officials (parishes can pass a vote of no confidence on their vicars, §11), even 'die Gemeine ist ein Freistaat' (§22, 'the parish is a free state'), one of the many free states Follen envisaged existing and interlinking in the new Germany."[54]

Due to his involvement in the *Turner* and *Burschenschaft* movements, Lieber was denied admission to Prussian universities (he studied at Jena and was subsequently called back to the Prussian University of Halle, where he was closely watched), and was imprisoned alongside other politically active students. After an abortive attempt to volunteer in the Greek War of Independence, a stint in Rome,

[50] Freidel, *Francis Lieber*, 25–26, 42; Ernest Nys, "Francis Lieber: His Life and his Works, Part 1," *The American Journal of International Law* 5, no. 1 (1911): 97.

[51] Maike Oergel, "Constitutionalism and Cultural Identity as Revolutionary Concepts in German Political Radicalism 1806–1819: the Case of Karl Follen," *Comparative Critical Studies* 15, no. 2: 185.

[52] Oergel, "Constitutionalism and Cultural Identity," 196.

[53] Oergel, "Constitutionalism and Cultural Identity," 190–91.

[54] Oergel, "Constitutionalism and Cultural Identity," 192.

where he became the protégé of the statesman and historian Barthold Georg Niebuhr, and continued persecution upon his return to Prussia, he emigrated, first to England (in 1826) and then to the United States. Aided by his fellow *Burschenschaftler* exiles Charles Follen and Charles Beck, and bearing letters of recommendations from Niebuhr and Jahn, Lieber accepted a position as the instructor of a gymnastics and swimming school in Boston and quickly made inroads with Boston elites.[55] Lieber's biographer Frank Freidel argues that even before Lieber's arrival in the United States, mentor Niebuhr had "transform[ed] the revolutionary-minded man into a cautious, moderate social scientist." In any case, Lieber's political principles, like Follen's, certainly looked different in German and American contexts: "the same middle-class liberalism that had plunged Lieber into Prussian prisons made him a 'safe' companion of the Kents, Biddles, and Storys."[56] I would argue, however, that Lieber's American writing, editing, and networking reveals continuity with his youthful involvement in the *Turner* and *Burschenschaft* movements. Indeed, Lieber's early review of Jahn's *Gymnastics* (in Beck's translation) mentions Beck and Follen and details much of the still-fresh political history, even as it stresses the utility of Jahn's physical education program in an American context.[57]

Lieber's experience in the *Turner* and *Burschenschaft* movements—movements grounded in the power of voluntary association and committed to political change (on a liberal nationalist model), sometimes by revolutionary means—shows in his conceptualization of associations and their relation to the state.[58] (Indeed, the conservative student associations against which the Burschenschaften would position themselves were known as *Korps*, short for *Korporationen*, a name that "implied that an informal organization had been superseded by one characterized by formal bylaws and procedures."[59]) This milieu thus gave him both a theoretical understanding of and practical experience with the social and political potential of voluntary associations. The *Burschenschaft* movement was at once a carefully guarded elite network of elite volunteers and an experimental microcosm of a transformed Germany. It is not hard to recognize the lineaments of Jahn and Follen's political theorizing—and the highly self-conscious culture of association among *Turner* and *Burschenschaftler*—in Lieber's description of the nation as the "great corporation," constituted by and as an organized concatenation of relatively autonomous corporate bodies. What had been radical, even

[55] Nys, "Francis Lieber"; Freidel, *Francis Lieber*. Lieber recounts some of the history of the *Turner* movement in his review of Beck's translation of Jahn's *Treatise on Gymnastics* in Francis Lieber, "*A Treatise on Gymnastics, Taken Chiefly from the German of F. L. Jahn*," *American Quarterly Review* 3 (1828): 126–50.

[56] Freidel, *Francis Lieber*, 37, 62.

[57] Lieber, "*A Treatise on Gymnastics.*"

[58] Rolland Ray Lutz, "The German Revolutionary Student Movement, 1819–1833," *Central European History* 4 (1971): 215–41; Lisa Fetheringill Zwicker, "The Burschenschaft and German Political Culture, 1890–1914," *Central European History* 42 (2009): 389–428.

[59] Lutz, "German Revolutionary Student Movement," 216.

revolutionary theorizing in a German context could pass as respectable general knowledge in the *Americana.*

From Corporation to State

> "The state is, in principle, no association, but a society."
>
> Lieber, *Political Ethics*[60]

Although Lieber's career as a theorist of the corporation was brief, his *Americana* article heralded a persistent attention to other kinds of association, from Girard College, whose constitution and curriculum he framed, to the state.[61] Turning to his texts from the 1830s allows us to discern both a taxonomy of associations and an account of the processes of assembly—whether formal, by deliberate action and statute, or spontaneous, as a manifestation of human nature. While many of Lieber's insights into the legal and social contours of corporations and related associations resonate with his contemporaries, his understanding of association as irreducibly political makes his work both distinctive and prescient.[62] While the *Americana* article offers a glimpse of the theory of the corporation as political entity, his theory of political associations does not reach its full development until the *Manual of Political Ethics* (1838–39). At the center of *Political Ethics* is a double observation: association springs up spontaneously wherever there is human plurality, and such association constitutes the basis of the political.

On August 15, 1837, Story wrote to Lieber, who had sent him the first part of *Political Ethics*. The judge singled out for particular praise Lieber's chapter on "the state" as "by far the fullest & most correct development of the true theory of what constitutes a state, that I have ever seen" and "one of the best Theoretical Treatises on the true nature & object of Government, which has been produced in modern times."[63] As both Story and Lieber recognized, this theory of the state was the heart of Lieber's *Political Ethics*. Lieber was famously frustrated that his treatise was neither enthusiastically consumed like the *Americana* nor recognized as his magnum opus. Part of the problem was marketing: although the subtitle of *Political Ethics* presented it as a textbook for law students, it was at its core a work of political theory.[64]

60 Lieber, *Political Ethics*, Vol. 1, 191.

61 Francis Lieber, *A Constitution and Plan of Education for Girard College for Orphans, with an Introductory Report, Laid before the Board of Trustees by Francis Lieber* (Philadelphia: Carey, Lea and Blanchard, 1834).

62 Tocqueville, in contrast, distinguishes political from civil associations. Tocqueville, *Democracy in America*, 595–96.

63 Joseph Story to Francis Lieber, MSS LI 3271, Francis Lieber Papers, Huntington Library.

64 Lieber complained to Hilliard about the notices it received in leading periodicals, which found it either incomprehensible or trivial. Joseph Story to George Hilliard, MSS LI 2072, Francis Lieber Papers, Huntington Library.

The theory of the state that Lieber develops in *Political Ethics* builds on his framing of the nation as "the great corporation."[65] For Lieber, states, like other sorts of associations, emerge from spontaneous association and human plurality rather than explicit contract. For Lieber, the similarity of states and corporations occasions neither indistinction nor despair. Rather than simply conflate the two, Lieber uses state and corporation to theorize one another—and to theorize association more broadly. In doing so he emphasizes some features of political assemblages—the shape of relations among their constituents—and minimizes others—the legalistic performativity of the constitutions and charters that call them into being.

His theory of the state is centered on neither originary contract nor absolute power, but rather on the forms of relationality that underlie groups: "The state is a society. What is a society? A society is a number of individuals, between all of whom exists the same relation—the same, as to its principle, however modified it may be in other respects, or it is a number of individuals who have the same interest, and strive unitedly for it."[66] Lieber's perceptive account of plurality and relationality anchors the distinction he draws between societies and associations, a distinction that can be too easily masked by the conventional use, in his time and ours, of the term "society": "Societies may be temporary unions with stated objects, or they may rest on relations not entirely, or not at all controllable by the members—on *given* relations, with general objects chiefly to be learned from the fundamental relations themselves between the members. By way of greater distinction, I would call the former associations (companies), the latter, by way of excellence, societies. Insurance companies, charitable societies, academies of science, are associations; nations, states, communities, are societies."[67]

Associations (or companies) are temporary, voluntary, and constituted to pursue deliberate ends; societies are durable and characterized by ends that emerge from relations rather than preceding them. Nonetheless, both derive their nature from their plurality, which allows them to constitute law in their own right. Whereas associations—business, charitable, and cultural institutions—are governed by explicit, voluntary charters, societies, in Lieber's narrow sense, are premised on relations that precede and exceed members' explicit will. For Lieber,

[65] Angell and Ames echo Lieber's notion of the nation as great corporation: "Nations, or states, are denominated by publicists bodies politic; and are said to have their affairs and interests, and to deliberate and resolve in common. They thus become as moral persons, having an understanding and will peculiar to themselves, and are susceptible of obligations and laws. In this extensive sense, the United States may be termed a corporation; and so may each State singly; so the king of England is a corporation; and so is Parliament." Angell and Ames, *Treatise on the Law of Private Corporations Aggregate*, 10–11.

[66] Lieber, *Political Ethics*, Vol. 1, 163.

[67] Lieber, *Political Ethics*, Vol. 1, 164.

these two features—priority and excess with regard to particular ends—make a view of the state as a contract among individuals untenable.[68]

Various kinds of societies, he contends, arise on the basis of various kinds of relations, such as economic or religious. He proceeds to argue, however, that every relation between people, regardless of the sphere in which it originates, "becomes…a relation of right, either claiming to be enforced or to be protected against infringement."[69] If all human relations are essentially relations of right—what Lieber goes on to term *jural* relations—the only institution is fundamentally attuned to them is the state. He defends his terminology as necessary to make explicit an implicit concept of politics: "Should I say that the state is a political society? This is nothing but arguing in a circle."[70] If "political" is redundant, "legal," which points to statutory law (*lex, Gesetz, loi*) rather than a more fundamental conception of right (*jus, Recht, droit*), is insufficient. Although jural relations precede the formal institution of the state, they depend on the state to give them force:

> All relations existing in the state, or, all strictly political relations are relations of right—jural relations. The individual *demands* of the state that his right—his jural relation to others be maintained inviolate, and the state *demands* that the individual do not interfere with the right of others, or, in other words, do not disturb their jural relations. Finally, the individual, being unable to obtain those ends for which he was placed on earth or made a man, in a state of insulation, but who shall and must, of necessity founded in his very nature, live in society, it is matter of right that he obtain through and conjointly with society, what he cannot obtain singly, and what, nevertheless, is essential to his well-being as a man. The state, therefore, has the right and the duty to obtain all these ends by the combined energy of society for each individual.[71]

As this excerpt makes clear, for Lieber the state is not simply one institution among many. Rather, as the institution that confronts both human plurality and the demand for justice, it is the instrument that secures, as Hannah Arendt would put it more than a century later, the "right to have rights."[72] The state thus plays a unique role as "the society of societies."[73] That is, the state is a society whose laws necessarily permeate all other spheres of life because they are grounded in the

[68] Lieber's account of constitutive plurality is akin to Arendt's conception of action as unpredictable human activity arising from plurality, and thus "the political activity par excellence." For Arendt as for Lieber, the open-endedness of genuinely political action distinguishes it from cyclical labor and teleological work. Hannah Arendt, *The Human Condition* (Chicago: University of Chicago Press, 1958), 9.

[69] Lieber, *Political Ethics*, Vol. 1, 169.

[70] Lieber, *Political Ethics*, Vol. 1, 174.

[71] Lieber, *Political Ethics*, Vol. 1, 176–77.

[72] Hannah Arendt, *The Origins of Totalitarianism* (New York: Harcourt, Brace & World, 1968), 296.

[73] Lieber, *Political Ethics*, Vol. 1, 169, 180.

demand and capacity for justice that Lieber sees as pervading all human relations.[74] Although the state resembles other associated bodies, "society of societies" indicates the way it both comprises and surpasses them.

While Lieber's "society of societies" departs from familiar contractarian models of the state, it hews quite close to the theories of association with which he was immersed in the *Turner* and *Burschenschaft* movements. His view of the state flows naturally from Jahn and Follen's project of assembling a nation-state from other associated bodies—and of using voluntary associations like *Burschenschaften* as "prototype free states." Follen's careful attention to democratic and judicial processes in the *Burschenschaften* was specifically suited to Germany's political landscape, in which the promise of national unity lay in the interarticulation of numerous small states into a unified constitutional whole. Transplanted to the United States, Follen's revolutionary theorizing could pass for a more conventional account of the federal constitution of the nation. Yet seen in its German context, Lieber's theory of both the corporation and the state highlights the surprising fluidity that could allow voluntary associations, provided with jural means, to assume the mantle of the state. Like Follen, Lieber recognized the state-likeness of gymnastic and student associations as well as parishes, and could see an incipient if flawed model of their concatenation in the plural composition of the German Confederation.

Lieber's "society of societies" thus offers a vivid contrast to Hobbes's monolithic image of the corporate state as "Artificial Man." Lieber refuses to reduce the essential plurality of the state to an individual, even a virtual one—a fact that may help explain why he gives such short shrift in "Corporation" to the notion of corporate personhood. Invoking and rejecting Louis XIV's notorious "L'état c'est moi," Lieber underlines the fundamental sociality of the state. Later in *Political Ethics* he reiterates this contrast in terms of autarchy and (his neologism) hamarchy: "I call autarchy that state in which public power, whole and entire, unmitigated and unmodified, rests somewhere, be this in the hands of a monarch, or the people, or an aristocracy.... Hamarchy, on the other hand, is that polity, which has an organism, an organic life, if I may say so, in which a thousand distinct parts have their independent action, yet are by the general organism united into one whole, into one living system."[75]

This figure of an organism composed of "a thousand distinct parts" echoes and amplifies the modular structure implied by Lieber's "society of societies" or "concatenation of corporations," which may comprise a "living system" without

[74] "[T]he individual, being unable to obtain those ends for which he was placed on earth or made a man, in a state of insulation, but who shall and must, of necessity founded in his very nature, live in society, it is matter of right that he obtain through and conjointly with society, what he cannot obtain singly, and what, nevertheless, is essential to his well-being as a man." *Political Ethics*, Vol. 1, 176–77.

[75] Lieber, *Political Ethics*, Vol. 1, 411.

centralization.[76] As a "society of societies," the hamarchic state is, paradoxically, both like and quite unlike a business corporation. Whereas the Lieber of *Americana* looks at the corporation from the perspective of politics, the Lieber of *Political Ethics*, several years later, looks at the state from the perspective of associations. A common thread, then, links the "concatenation" that for Lieber characterizes both particular corporations and "the great corporation" and his critique, in *Political Ethics*, of social contract theory's presumption of presocial individuals free to enter into a compact. It is Lieber's very attention to the corporateness of the state that allows him resist a vision of the "great corporation" as a business company or voluntary association. Theorizing the corporation ultimately allows Lieber more flexibly to theorize plurality—and the plurality of pluralities.

Lieber categorizes associated bodies by the type of relations among members on which they are based. Consanguinity grounds the family; exchange—"catallactic relation," in Lieber's parlance—grounds economic relations (due to their importance, he writes, "the society founded upon [them] has…been mistaken for the state")[77]; the relation of "comity" grounds "social intercourse"; and "intellectual relations" ground "the strong ties of a common language and literature, of the fine arts, sciences, and national custom."[78] The jural relation grounds the state.

Lieber thus argues that social contact theory errs fundamentally in grounding the state in the catallactic relation of contract. He dramatizes the distinction between jural and catallactic relations with reference to a corporate entity familiar to his readers: the insurance company.[79] "The state," he writes, "has been compared to an insurance company, in which property forms the share each citizen holds. Sad indeed would be that state where this principle should be attempted to be acted out." First, the state's sovereignty extends beyond the protection of property rights—"For how is it, that the state legislates also over those who have no property, and that they have a right to ask not only protection, but all the benefits guaranteed by human society." Even more fundamentally, to treat the state as an insurance company radically misstates the role of the individual member: "How is it that no one has a right to withdraw from this insurance company, and say, 'I am my own insurer;' in other words, 'I renounce your protection, I can take better care of myself; give up, therefore, all claims you make on me; do not

[76] On Lieber's interest in "decentralized institutions," see also Steven Alan Samson, "Francis Lieber: Transatlantic Cultural Missionary," ed. Charles R. Mack and Henry R. Lesesne, *Francis Lieber and the Culture of the Mind* (Columbia: University of South Carolina Press, 2005), 129–42, esp. 129–32. On the thread connecting "institutional liberty" to Lieber's broader interest in associations, see James Farr, "From Moral Philosophy to Political Science: Lieber and the Innovations of Antebellum Political Thought," in *Francis Lieber and the Culture of the Mind*, ed. Charles R. Mack and Henry H. Lesesne, (Columbia, SC: University of South Carolina Press, 2005), 113–26, esp. 119–21.

[77] Lieber, *Political Ethics*, Vol. 1, 165.

[78] Lieber, *Political Ethics*, Vol. 1, 166.

[79] See Butterfield, *The Making of Tocqueville's America*, particularly 130–48 on the evolving conceptions of insurance companies and membership.

consider me any longer amenable to your laws.'" The state, he concludes, consists not of property but of human beings. If the state were essentially an insurer, "men possessed of such enormous property as the marquis of Westminster, the duke of Buccleugh, the Portlands and Bedfords, ought to have each a hundred votes at least in parliament."[80] Yet we can recognize Lieber's rejected metaphor both in Locke's insistence that "the great and chief end...of men's uniting into commonwealths...is the preservation of their property" and in Emerson's sublimely liberal disavowal of society as a "joint stock company, in which the members agree, for the better securing of his bread to each shareholder, to surrender the liberty and culture of the eater."[81] (In fact, the reviewer for the *Boston Quarterly Review* chides Lieber for failing to recognize that "Society is, in short, a great joint-stock concern" centered on the disposition of property.[82]) As Lieber's account reveals, Emersonian self-reliance relies on a model of spiritual rights that reduces the basis of social belonging to property insurance.

For Lieber, in contrast, societies (in his narrow, elevated sense) are not the result of contracts but rather their condition of possibility. The state, he contends, emerges not from an explicit agreement but from the ethical relations intrinsic to human collectivity. It "is founded on the relations of right; it is a *jural* society, as a church is a religious society, or an insurance company a financial association. The idea of the just, and the action founded upon this idea, called *justice*, is the broad foundation and great object of the state."[83] Here, finally, is the heart of Lieber's political theory: the state is a) a corporate body that b) exceeds contractual belonging (that is, is a society rather than an association), and c) is fundamentally grounded in relations between members on the basis of justice. In contrast to Lockean contract theory, Lieber's state does not presume possessive individuals as its precondition; in contrast to Hobbesian contract theory, it does not give rise to a unitary authority that subsumes originary plurality. This vision of the state—grounded neither in sovereignty nor in contract but in the reciprocated demand for justice—is akin to the real entity theory of the corporation, which finds the corporation's basis in the relations intrinsic to the corporate body rather than the granting of its charter or the rights of corporators. Although Judge Story praised Lieber's theory of the state, Story's own ascendant theory of corporations was poorly equipped to recognize the plurality and the relations among members shared by corporate and political bodies.

Lieber's account of the state departs sharply from contractarian narratives of the commonwealth's emergence from a state of nature or a state of war. Because the state's fundamental concern is justice, and because jural relations are co-originary

[80] Lieber, *Political Ethics*, Vol. 1, 190.
[81] John Locke, *Second Treatise* §124. Ralph Waldo Emerson, "Self-Reliance," *Essays and Lectures*, ed. Joel Porte (New York: Library of America, 1983), 261.
[82] "Lieber's Political Ethics," *Boston Quarterly Review* 2 (1839): 120.
[83] Lieber, *Political Ethics*, Vol. 1, 171.

with mankind itself, the state is at once primordial and preeminent: "The state is aboriginal with man; it is no voluntary association, no contrivance of art, or invention of suffering, no company of shareholders; no machine, no work of contract by individuals who lived previously out of it; no necessary evil, no ill of humanity which will be cured in time and by civilisation; no accidental thing, no institution above and separate from society, no instrument for one or a few—the state is a form and faculty of mankind to lead the species toward perfection—it is the glory of man."[84]

While Lieber acknowledges the similarity of state and corporation on one register, their difference is evident here. Consider the contrast between the *Americana* article on corporations, which emphasizes the statelikeness of corporate/chartered/constitutional form, and the article on joint-stock companies, which emphasizes the financial incentives for organizing such an association.[85] Lieber's account of the nation in *Political Ethics* brings both halves of the story together: business corporations are *associations*, and thus a kind of society (in Lieber's broad sense), but the state is a *society* (in the narrow sense) whose fundamental principle is right and whose co-origination with humanity marks it as "society of societies."[86] While state and corporation are essentially indistinguishable on the level of formal organization, they are radically distinguished by the state's role as the "form and faculty of mankind" that responds to the ethical demands of plurality and justice.

For Lieber, the state is not an insurance company because the a priori collectivity of the state cannot, as the metaphor of contract suggests, be opted out of—not because sovereignty precedes the liberal individual, but because the jural relations between persons—the fundamental concern of state—are co-originary with individuals. Lieber's anthropological and quasi-theological idioms—"aboriginal with man," "a form and faculty of mankind," "the glory of man"—separate the state from the artifices, machines, and contracts; they also undercut claims to the superiority of "civilized" to "aboriginal" peoples on the basis of political organization. Yet Lieber acknowledges that the state is quite like the types of organizations he's catalogued, even though its necessity and inevitability make it qualitatively different. The state, he suggests, realizes the potential latent in any kind of association—from the most venal company to the most casual gathering. If "society of societies" begins as a technical definition—the state at once *comprises* other social relationships and *governs* them—the phrase soon takes on the transcendent, even theological resonance latent in its redoubled grammatical structure.

[84] Lieber, *Political Ethics*, Vol. 1, 183. [85] *Encyclopaedia Americana*, Vol. 7, 242–43.

[86] Before even entering his analysis of "society," he asserts, "All civilized nations are now agreed, that the state is a society; no man will be so bold as to pretend that an individual, a monarch, can be the state, as Louis XIV, when a boy, asserted of himself" (Lieber, *Political Ethics*, 163). In addition to disputing Louis XIV's "L'état c'est moi," Lieber implicitly distances himself from Hobbes's theory of the state as an "artificial man"—an individual.

Although Lieber concedes that the state is a means, not an end, he describes it in terms that anticipate something like political theology:

> On the other hand, the state stands incalculably above the individual, is worthy of every sacrifice, of life, and goods, of wife and children, for it is the society of societies, the sacred union by which the creator leads man to civilisation, the bond, the pacifier, the humanizer, of men, the protector of all undertakings in which and through which the individual has received its character, and which is the staff and shield of society. Not that I am guilty of the egregious folly of believing that everything in the state is good...but the state, as the chiefest of human unions, is a sacred institution, and deserves each man's faithful devotion, to serve where it is right, to improve where wrong.[87]

As this elaboration shows, "society of societies" transposes the political theology of "king of kings" into a republican key: instead of gods or monarchs, "unions" and "institutions" demand faithful devotion. (It is telling that Lieber invokes "the creator" in the context of the state's sacredness and transcendence.) For Lieber, the primacy of the state is intrinsic to its dual role as both the "sacred institution" or "great corporation" that comprehends and connects all other associations and the entity that authorizes and protects them. (In this sense, he anticipates the Fourierist proposals for perfectly harmonized institutions that I treat in chapter 5.)

While Lieber's chapter on the state emphasizes its ontological priority and ethical supremacy, elsewhere in *Political Ethics* he characterizes association less as a kind of entity (*an* association) than as a *force* that emerges from plurality: "Division of labor and combination of labor, energy or means, or the tendency of association are...two of the main elements of all civilization." From this definition of association as dynamic combination Lieber deduces that "Despotism naturally dislikes association; yet each association, if not carefully regulated, bears within it the germ of more or less despotism, either towards others or its own individual members, for the simple reason, even if there were no other, that it increases intensity of action, and separates, in some degree at least, the associated members from the rest of the community, and subjects them to separate rules of action."[88]

Lieber's warning about associated despots recalls the radical politics of the *Burschenschaft* movement and resonates with Tocqueville's contemporaneous statements on the tyranny of the majority. It also adumbrates our own era of corporate power. Lieber sees associations as potentially despotic in two directions—toward members and toward outsiders—as they subject these groups to "separate

[87] Lieber, *Political Ethics*, Vol. 1, 180–81.

[88] Lieber, *Political Ethics*, Vol. 2, 338.

rules of action." (Along these lines, he devotes much of the chapter to arguing against trade unions, which he views as impediments to a fair labor market.) He then offers a catalogue of associations that resembles contemporaneous lists by Angell and Ames and Tocqueville. Lieber's catalog, however, is noteworthy in pointing to a middle ground between private associations for the public interest and government per se:

> We have associations for the promotion of mutual interest, such as insurance companies, of public convenience, or objects of public spirit, or, as is frequently the case, of both ends united; associations for the promotion of knowledge in the higher spheres, such as academies of sciences, or for the diffusion of general knowledge, common schools, &c.; associations for the promotion of charity or other moral ends, such as the prison societies, temperance societies, societies to assist shipwrecked people, or the promotion of vaccination; religious associations, such as the monastic orders, and bible societies; and political associations. These may be, either for mutual protection, for instance, in times of great danger, or feebleness of government, which may be unable to perform certain acts, which are nevertheless necessary for men,—for instance, administering justice, or common protection in general;—or for the obtaining of certain rights or privileges; or, finally, for the opposing and ultimate change of a government. These are generally and necessarily for a time secret societies.[89]

Unlike the contemporaneous catalogues of American associations I've compiled above, Lieber's associations do not sit neatly alongside the state; their purposes range from insurance to revolution. In contrast to those earlier lists, with their neat separation of civil and business associations from political entities, Lieber frames association itself as a form of immanent, and potentially disruptive, power. And again, his immediate model would appear to be the *Burschenschaften* in Follen's most radical articulation: revolutionary underground societies that have carefully demonstrated their ability to carry out relations of political representation and justice.

It is the lineaments of these associations—representative, jural, and thus ready to serve as governments in a pinch—that Lieber identifies (and no doubt romanticizes) in the proto-states he observes on the frontiers of the United States. In contrast to Tocqueville, he sees the same spirit animating organized institutions and the seemingly anarchic formations beyond the government's reach. In *Letters to a Gentleman in Germany* (1834), his memoir of travels and observations in the United States, Lieber sees institutions operating even "beyond the boundaries of organized society":

[89] Lieber, *Political Ethics*, Vol. 2, 338–39.

> The great interest of this country lies in its institutions. There the observer of society and student of mankind finds enough with which to occupy himself. You may observe at once, in this country, some of the boldest applications of principles, the most recently developed, and the first manifestations, the first pulsations, so to speak, of those [p]rinciples of life which lie at the bottom of every political society. You may see in the farthest west, beyond the boundaries of organized society, the incipient stages of political relations, of law and justice laid bare, as if prepared for the student of history, and of the gradual development of man as a member of political society. Perhaps all this would become clearer to you, should I write you about the *regulators* and the manner in which communities, beyond the limits of established law, meet the imperious necessity of dealing out justice; of this kind was one of the most interesting cases that ever came to my knowledge, when, lately, the assembled men of a district, arrested, tried, and executed a murderer. By what right?—By the right to punish crime, natural, indispensable and inalienable to every society, and growing out of the necessity, both physical and moral, of punishment.[90]

In contrast to Crèvecoeur's famously unflattering portrait of "back settlers" as "unsociable" and "lawless," in contrast to whom "[t]he manners of the Indian natives are respectable," Lieber presents regulators—the vigilante enforcers of the "farthest west"—as exemplifying both the "institutions" of the United States and the "principles . . . at the bottom of every political society."[91] Despite his enduring respect for the legitimacy and supremacy of the state, he endorses "the right to punish crime" extrajudicially as an expression of the "indispensable and alienable" rights not of individuals but of "every society."

Lieber describes an even more primitive version of this institutional impulse in Pony Clubs, organizations of white thieves on the borders of Indigenous lands devoted to stealing Native people's horses. A note in *Political Ethics* draws the reader's attention to "an article of great interest with regard to this subject"—political associations emerging in the absence of state institutions—"on Pony Clubs among the Indians."[92] In a commonplace book, Lieber affixes this article under the heading "Indians Pony Club Lawlessness. Cut from N. Gazette of Oct. 21, 1833." Titled "Intruders upon Indian Lands," the article describes borders of Indian territories as ruled by force alone, and describes how some white intruders form groups devoted to stealing and reselling Indians' horses: "To but offer one example in support of these assertions, it is only necessary to name the Pony Club, that has existed for years notoriously, on the borders of the Cherokee

[90] Lieber, *Letters to a Gentleman in Germany*, 17–18.

[91] J. Hector St. John de Crèvecoeur, *Letters from An American Farmer and Sketches of Eighteenth-Century America*, ed. Albert E. Stone (New York: Penguin, 1981), 76–77.

[92] Lieber, *Political Ethics*, Vol. 1, 189.

nation." Below the article, Lieber references his other entries on "'*Regulators*' in the West," and describes their relevance:

> In the most western counties or parts of the U.S. recently settled, where political organization has not yet extended to, the most influential or substantial men often unite for taking the law into their own hands; they are called *regulators.* They try a person, whip him if guilty and send him away, under high penalty, should he return. This [illegible] as Germans might call it, springs from the same source—the necessity of some justice between man & man—from which the *Fehmengerichte* [vigilante tribunals] in the middle ages sprung. Unite a band of pirates, and a kind of administration of justice immediately springs up among them; revolted people, troops &c immediately have a kind of authority—a kind of admiralty justice among them[.] [93]

The extreme example of Pony Clubs—of proto-institutional power, however brutal and cynical—leads Lieber to his understanding of the political: "[T]o return to the first: we see in those regulators (who spring up wherever men are together; in marriage it is the husband.—you find regulators even in prisons) the beginning of *states*; it is the idea of justice, and I have said in another place which is the beginning of all government, because even where the administration of justice is handled by one, more, by assumed authority, the idea of justice is *always* founded upon equality."[94]

In other words, despite the "lawlessness" and predation of Pony Clubs and regulators, Lieber sees in them the origins of jural relations—the emergence of justice from the foundation of equality—and thus the political essence of mankind.

Political theorist Jason Frank has convincingly delineated a "revolutionary tradition of popular constitutionalism, whereby the authorizing voice of the people was claimed by self-created associations—committees, conventions, popular juries, and crowds—alongside and sometimes against the duly constituted—that is, republican, government."[95] Frank emphasizes the relations between formal articulations of constituent power ("We the people") in revolutionary and post-revolutionary America and "the proliferation of groups claiming to speak in the people's name" in the postrevolutionary US, associations that "emerged alongside, and sometimes against, the constituted authorities of the postcolonial republican states."[96] Like Lieber, Frank emphasizes the political claims of vigilante and resistance groups as evidence of their claims to democratic legitimacy. If anything, Lieber's context—which looks to the world of German voluntary

[93] MSS LI 31 (the "Green Book"), Francis Lieber Papers, Huntington Library, 65.

[94] MSS LI 31, 66.

[95] Jason Frank, *Constituent Moments: Enacting the People in Postrevolutionary America* (Durham: Duke University Press, 2010), 24.

[96] Frank, *Constituent Moments*, 25.

associations as well as US revolutionary history and republican theory—suggests a more pluralistic genealogy for nineteenth-century manifestations of radical democracy. Lieber's examination of Pony Clubs and regulators might likewise reorient the Deleuzean political idiom. Whereas Deleuze and Guattari memorably describe "war machines," characterized by "another dynamism, a nomadic ambition over against the State," Lieber convincingly frames nomadic war machines as not anti-states but proto-states.[97]

The other of the state, according to Lieber, emerges in a more prosaic and ostensibly more civilized context: the arbitrary association of passengers aboard a steamboat:

> The foundation of the state lies too deeply in the human soul, in man's whole nature, to be explained simply by selfishness. It is no accidental mass of atoms, it is an organism. Observe a steamboat full of passengers, all collected for one purpose, to reach a certain point as soon as possible, all in the same condition, having paid their fare, and equally interested in the safety of the vessel. Besides these points, every passenger forms an isolated individual. Is this the picture of a state? What a society do they form! with what utter selfishness every one acts and struggles for himself. Is this a society: an organised thing, with life and energy, with moral elasticity, with power, which can rest on close union alone? with an elevating, a humanizing, character? Are there no other considerations than those of protection of property and life, which unite us into a state? Then how unwise to sacrifice either for liberty![98]

Lieber's steamboat, full of passengers pursuing a shared but limited interest, is a demoralizing vision of the state reduced to "utter selfishness," a set of "isolated individual[s]" rather than "an organised thing, with life and energy." In other words, the Lockean, contractarian view of the state as a vehicle for protecting individual interests—the insurance company theory of the state—is precisely what Lieber laments as hollow, powerless, and formless—even in comparison to a band of white supremacist horse thieves. As I discuss in chapter 6, Melville, knowingly or not, takes up Lieber's formulation of society as a steamboat in *The Confidence-Man*.[99] While the novel foregrounds the selfishness of the assembled passengers, it nonetheless draws quite different conclusions about this mobile body's mode of collectivity.

Lieber's description of the steamboat as not-yet-political (because merely catallactic) returns us to familiar descriptions of corporate modernity characterized by

[97] Gilles Deleuze and Felix Guattari, *A Thousand Plateaus*, 366.
[98] Lieber, *Political Ethics*, Vol. 1, 191.
[99] Herman Melville, *The Confidence-Man: His Masquerade* (1857) (Evanston: Northwestern UP, 1984).

narrow conceptions of interest like shareholder primacy. Yet there is a key difference. Lieber's emphasis on the political aspects of association distances him from Tocqueville, whose emphasis on voluntary association dovetails more easily with a (neo)liberal worldview and a politics grounded in contract theory. Lieber's emphasis on the fundamental jural relations between persons and the involuntary nature of political belonging makes the title of liberal so often bestowed on him an odd fit.[100] By emphasizing the corporateness of the state, on the one hand, and the differences between different kinds of societies and associations, on the other, he presents association not as a particularly American trait but rather as a portable toolbox for political collectivity. (Indeed, as I discuss in chapter 5, Fourier and his successors would follow similar intuitions about association, collectivity, and human nature to conceive of a socialist order radically at odds with existing civilization.)

As these diverse examples show, Lieber's interest ranges from networks that assemble themselves more or less spontaneously (regulators, pony clubs) to those, like the steamboat, that stop short of such assembly. These particular examples push back somewhat against Lieber's scheme of organic societies and deliberate, but limited associations. For organic networks also appear in places where we might have expected only economic and intellectual exchange. A brief episode in *Letters to a Gentleman in Germany* finds just such a self-assembling network in the book trade, which appears here as less a deliberate economic contrivance than as a quasi-organic, globe-spanning network of commercial and intellectual exchange: "I also found, at the bookseller's a number of the Chinese Register, published in Canton. In this number was a review of an article on Canton, in the Encyclopedia Americana, which is founded on the German Conversations-Lexicon. What an intercourse, at present, exists between the different parts of the world!"[101] We're back to the *Americana* as a study in contrasts and an allegory of politics. Lieber's editorial imprimatur fails spectacularly in imposing autarchy over its sprawling contents; its hamarchic nature is clear in the arbitrary but poignant associations to which it gives rise (Locke and the lobster, Shakers and Shakespeare). Like these accidental associations, Lieber's examples outrun his theory. If his political theory favors the spontaneous (society) over the deliberate (association), his eye for assemblage reveals the ways spontaneous order emerges between the cracks of authority, whether editorial or political.

Lieber's conception of corporations and associations thus yields a fruitful language for both theorizing the state and recognizing the political potential of spontaneous societies—themes to which I return in chapters 5 and 6. Chapter 3 examines how the novelist and physician Robert Montgomery Bird, through very

[100] Freidel, *Francis Lieber*; W. David Clinton, *Tocqueville, Lieber, Bagehot: Liberalism Confronts the World* (New York: Palgrave, 2003).

[101] Lieber, *Letters to a Gentleman in Germany*, 146.

different means, presents a model of plurality that we might put in conversation with Lieber's. Bird's novel *Sheppard Lee*, in exploring the mechanisms of corporeality and corporate succession, generates an idiom flexible enough to address contemporaneous debates over the status of banking corporations and the contested citizenship of African Americans and link these debates to perennial questions of individuality and plurality.

The Corporate Forms of Antebellum US Literature. Peter Jaros, Oxford University Press. © Peter Jaros 2026.
DOI: 10.1093/9780198996491.003.0003

3

The Faculties of Law

Constituting Persons in Robert Montgomery Bird's *Sheppard Lee*

The dénouement of Robert Montgomery Bird's *Sheppard Lee, Written by Himself* (1836) is as disappointing as the novel's premise is titillating. The hero of Bird's metaphysical picaresque discovers that he has the power to transfer his soul into any recently deceased body, and he subsequently occupies a series of roles—a gouty millionaire, a penniless dandy, a miser, a Quaker philanthropist, a contented slave who turns revolutionary, and a mentally unstable member of the Southern gentry—before being miraculously restored to his own body. Or rather, before being informed by his physician that he never left it in the first place: Lee's metempsychic tour of Jacksonian America, punctuated by leaps from body to body, is finally revealed to be a delusion. Still, it is difficult to dismiss Lee's journey as superstition, false consciousness, or medical disorder. In its play with reanimation, mortality and immortality, and embodiment and disembodiment, the novel addresses not only metaphysics and medicine but also the legal mechanics underpinning what Colin Dayan has called the making and unmaking of persons and what Yann Thomas has identified as the "legal artifice" of the person.[1]

This chapter situates *Sheppard Lee*'s play with medical and philosophical questions of life, death, and personal identity amid contemporaneous debates about the legal and political faculties of personhood. As recent readers have observed, *Sheppard Lee* is a text obsessively concerned with the constitution of persons.[2]

[1] Colin Dayan, *The Law Is a White Dog: How Legal Rituals Make and Unmake Persons* (Princeton, NJ: Princeton University Press, 2011), xii. Yann Thomas, "The Subject of Right, the Person, Nature: Remarks on the Current Criticism of the Legal Subject," in *Legal Artifices: Ten Essays on Roman Law in the Present Tense*, ed. Thanos Zartaloudis and Cooper Francis (Edinburgh: Edinburgh University Press, 2021), 119. On the importance of recognizing "the incommensurability of 'person' and 'human'" in the context of slavery and abolition, see Jeanine Marie DeLombard, "The Claims of the Humanitarian, Legally Considered," in Jeffrey Insko et al., "Abolition's Afterlives," *American Literary History* 35 (2023): 1776–85.

[2] Christopher Looby shows how Bird plays on Enlightenment theories of personal identity, particularly Hume's reduction of identity to a bundle of associations. Christopher Looby, "Introduction" to Robert Montgomery Bird, *Sheppard Lee, Written by Himself*, ed. Christopher Looby (New York: New York Review Books, 2008), xviii–xx. Page references to Bird's novel will appear parenthetically in the text. Looby suggests that Bird's novel constitutes "a meditation on the bodily basis of political life" (xx). Justine S. Murison reveals the ways in which medicine and fiction alike asserted racialized forms of interiority and undermined racial theory by revealing surprising symmetries between slave owner and slave. *The Politics of Anxiety in Nineteenth-Century American Literature* (Cambridge: Cambridge

These critics' attention to contemporaneous philosophical, medical, political, and racial discourse shows how *Sheppard Lee* registers transformations of personhood particular to the institutions of Jacksonian America. Yet their accounts engage only glancingly with the law, the institution most centrally concerned with articulating the structure of personhood. *Sheppard Lee*'s play with the philosophical and physiological foundations of personhood, I will argue, can best be understood with reference to contemporaneous processes and provisions that granted and withdrew aspects of legal personhood. Bird grounds his narrative and metaphysical play with personhood in two concrete forms of institutional power: banking corporations and racialized political belonging. Like Francis Lieber's contemporaneous texts on associations, corporations, and states, then, Bird's novel is concerned with the ways authority emerges from various forms of associated plurality.

The common law had long drawn a distinction between natural persons (human beings) and artificial persons (corporations); the politics of Jacksonian America put both categories under pressure. Revised state constitutions expanded the franchise, giving large groups of (predominantly white) men political agency for the first time. Expansion of the franchise, along with gradual abolition in the North, precipitated the question of African Americans' political inclusion or exclusion, often replacing class distinctions with racial ones.[3] At the same time, debates over the rights of corporations—particularly banks—brought attention to the ways in which the law accorded or rescinded its recognition of artificial persons. For Bird's readers, I argue, the novel's persistent focus on bodies—natural or artificial, legally aggregated or medically dismantled—called up these

University Press, 2011), 17–46. Samuel Otter, in *Philadelphia Stories: America's Literature of Race and Freedom* (Oxford: Oxford University Press, 2010), shows how the racialized violence of Jacksonian Philadelphia—legally enforced racism and extralegal rioting—shape the narrative though they are elided in it. Chad Luck, "The Sum of All Tears: *Sheppard Lee*, Utilitarian Reading, and the Problem of Aggregation" (paper presented at the American Literature Association, Hyatt Regency, San Francisco, May 26, 2012), reads the novel as a reductio ad absurdum of the logic of utilitarianism and its leveling theory of happiness. Jordan Alexander Stein carefully tracks the novel's attention to the political effects of reading and textual circulation and concludes that the novel "implicitly disputed the fervor of Jacksonian individualism by strongly criticizing the kinds of contradictions…that can inhere in persons" and thus "seemed to align itself with more impersonal institutions, to the extent that these would not be subject to historical foibles." Jordan Alexander Stein, "The Whig Interpretation of Media: *Sheppard Lee* and Jacksonian Paperwork," *History of the Present* 3, no. 1 (2013): 29–56, 37. Stein's antinomy of the personal and the impersonal, in particular, echoes Bird's contemporary Alexis de Tocqueville, for whom nothing could be more American than individualism, on the one hand, and voluntary—and frequently incorporated—associations, on the other. Alexis de Tocqueville, *Democracy in America: And Two Essays on America*, ed. Isaac Kramnick, trans. Gerald Bevan (New York: Penguin, 2003), 587, 596. Most recently, James D. Lilley has read *Sheppard Lee*'s "Gothic economies of exchange and conversion" as revealing the mutual dependence of agrarian ideology, commodity capitalism, and the racial logic of slavery in "the systematic transformations of personhood and property" in Jacksonian America. James D. Lilley, *Common Things: Romance and the Aesthetics of Belonging in Atlantic Modernity* (New York: Fordham University Press, 2014), 106, 110.

[3] On race and franchise in Jacksonian America, see Christopher Malone, *Between Freedom and Bondage: Race, Party, and Voting Rights in the Antebellum North* (New York: Routledge, 2008). On the Jacksonian ideology of the "white republic," see particularly pages 63–64.

legal phenomena and revealed their shared logic at a moment when the state's constitution of so-called natural and artificial persons was in flux.[4] In the context of the legal animation of artificial persons and the civil death of racially marked persons, Sheppard Lee's "faculty of reanimating dead bodies" looks less like a supernatural fantasy than a legal thought experiment.[5] Despite the traditional legal separation of persons and property, the law of slavery and the law of corporations both provided for beings that were treated as persons in some contexts and property in others. The uncanny likeness of these two forms of personhood is central to *Sheppard Lee*'s engagement with legal categories. Reading Bird's Philadelphia-centered novel alongside the controversies that came to a head in the 1837–38 Pennsylvania Constitutional Convention reveals its remarkable superimposition of two complementary crises of personhood: one corporate and one racial. Attending to *Sheppard Lee*'s legal imaginary affords a glimpse of a remarkable reimagining of personhood commensurate to Jacksonian America's momentous institutional changes that goes beyond the era's familiar partisan politics and withering satire.

In this chapter, I first summarize the 1830s debates on corporate and racialized personhood that animated the Pennsylvania convention. I then trace Bird's discussion of "faculties" in *Sheppard Lee* and in other, rarely examined works to show how Bird, by linking the seemingly disparate registers of medicine, law, and the supernatural, reframes debates over personhood. I show how *Sheppard Lee*, through its protagonist's remarkable faculty of metempsychosis, both echoes and expands contemporaneous legal reasoning. With particular reference to the Zachariah Longstraw episode (book 5), I show how the novel brings contemporaneous transformations of corporate and racialized personhood—transformations that had remained separate in legal and political discourse—into figurative proximity. Finally, I consider the novel's work in light of Bird's ambiguous and disturbing comments on race, jurisdiction, and civil death.

As the preceding chapters have shown, the economic power of banks and other business corporations, combined with their dual legal identity as inviolable contracts and immortal persons, invited both political controversy and literary speculation. The corporate form thus lent fresh relevance to the Enlightenment theories of personal identity that critics have recognized as touchstones for Bird's

[4] Bird's interest in the law is evident both within and beyond *Sheppard Lee*. Frustrated by his lack of remuneration from foreign editions of his work, for instance, he became something of an expert on international copyright. See Curtis Dahl, *Robert Montgomery Bird* (New York: Twayne, 1963), 22–23, 25. On Bird's reading in law and political theory, see Nancy Jane Buffington, "From Freedom to Slavery: Robert Montgomery Bird and the Natural Law Tradition" (PhD diss., University of Arizona, 1998), 33–34, 74. The Robert Montgomery Bird Papers (RMBP) (Rare Book and Manuscript Library, University of Pennsylvania, MS Coll. 108) contain extensive writings on copyright as well as miscellaneous legal papers.

[5] Bird, *Sheppard Lee*, 423.

novel. “Person,” as John Locke reminds readers, “is a forensic term.”[6] The law of persons, he explains, assumes certain capacities, such as memory and moral choice, required for assigning moral agency and responsibility. David Hume, in *A Treatise of Human Nature*, argues in contrast that personal identity is a heterogeneous bundle of thoughts and experiences lacking an identifiable center.[7] Corporations, at once persons in law and messy collectives, recapitulated this debate about the coherence of identity with heightened political and economic stakes.

As business corporations accrued power and prominence, the legal theory of the corporation attracted increased attention and controversy. Drawing momentum from the Bank War, critics questioned the status of banking corporations, particularly the Bank of the United States (BUS), and the legal premises on which they rested. Jacksonian Democrats condemned banks as the instruments of an “artificial aristocracy of wealth” and demanded limits on them.[8] Critics like the Boston businessman and politician David Henshaw and the Philadelphia lawyer and legislator Charles Jared Ingersoll argued that the sanctity of corporate charters granted by *Dartmouth College* gave banks too much power and too little accountability. Around the same time, *Dartmouth College* began to look vulnerable as one of the first major decisions of the Taney Court, *Charles River Bridge v. Warren Bridge* (1837), limited corporations’ claim to vested rights.[9] Both law and public opinion seemed ripe for major changes, particularly in Pennsylvania. After President Jackson vetoed Congress’s rechartering of the BUS in 1832, the state’s legislators worked to grant the bank a charter, which was issued shortly before the federal charter expired in 1836.[10] The controversy around the BUS was central to the calling of a state constitutional convention, endorsed by Pennsylvania voters in 1835 and held in 1837–38.[11]

[6] John Locke, *An Essay Concerning Human Understanding* (1689), ed. Roger Woolhouse (London: Penguin, 1997), 2.27.26.

[7] David Hume, *A Treatise of Human Nature* (1739), ed. Ernest C. Mossner (London: Penguin, 1969), 299–311; Looby, *Sheppard Lee*, xvii–xx.

[8] James Clarke, quoted in Roy H. Akagi, “The Pennsylvania Constitution of 1838,” *Pennsylvania Magazine of History and Biography* 48, no. 4 (1924): 301–33, 324.

[9] On the novelty of this ruling, see Stanley I. Kutler, *Privilege and Creative Destruction: The Charles River Bridge Case* (Baltimore, MD: Johns Hopkins University Press, 1989).

[10] *An Act to Incorporate the Stockholders of the Bank of the United States, by the State of Pennsylvania* (Philadelphia: Printed by Joseph and William Kite, 1836). As convention member James Madison Porter pointed out in a speech subsequently printed as a pamphlet, the Bank’s charter likely would not have passed the legislature had it not been wrapped into a massive bill that repealed unpopular taxes and funded railroads and canals. James Madison Porter, *Speech of James Madison Porter, of Northampton, in the Convention of Pennsylvania, on the Subject of the Right to Annul Charters of Incorporation. Delivered November 20, 1837* (Philadelphia: Peter Hay & Co., 1837).

[11] The Reform Convention of 1833 had promoted constitutional revisions aimed at breaking free from the vestiges of aristocratic government: limiting appointed offices and abolishing offices for life, extending the franchise, and increasing direct election of legislators (Akagi, “The Pennsylvania Convention,” 308). The ensuing Constitutional Convention, approved by the legislature in April 1835 and by voters in October 1835, was part of a nationwide trend of refashioning state institutions in the image of Jacksonian democracy. Charles Sellers, *The Market Revolution: Jacksonian America,*

The convention debated two apparently separate questions. First, should the state legislature be able to repeal the charters of corporations, particularly banking corporations, which had enjoyed legal protection as both artificial persons and inviolable contracts? Second, were African Americans to be considered "freemen" with voting rights in Pennsylvania? These two controversies coexisted uncomfortably. Critiques of banking corporations depicted them as unnaturally constituted entities preying on common people—the very people whose sovereignty was rhetorically and practically central to the new state constitutions of the Jacksonian era. Debates over racialized political rights, on the other hand, revealed that recognizing "natural persons" as a sovereign people was itself an ineluctably political process.

Although the convention is now best remembered for limiting the franchise by adding "white" to the description of eligible voters, it was the status of "*corporate bodies*, particularly the *banks*" that generated the most debate, both in anticipation of the convention and on its floor. While delegates finally steered away from allowing the legislature to revoke charters, they passed limitations on new corporate charters.[12] Meanwhile, racial politics, and the question of the racialized franchise, engendered increasing legal and practical contention. As Samuel Otter has shown, Philadelphia became a particular flashpoint for racial politics due to its large free Black population and its political and business ties to the slaveholding South. Mob violence against African Americans erupted on the city's peripheries in 1829 and 1834 and would recur throughout the 1830s and 1840s.[13] While violence threatened African Americans' social belonging from one side, sporadic access to the franchise challenged it from another. Tocqueville, who observed the mismatch between Black Pennsylvanians' statutory voting rights and their practical disenfranchisement, presented extralegal suppression of the Black vote as a prime example of majority tyranny.[14] Before 1835, a patchwork of de facto policies governed Black suffrage: African Americans had typically voted in some areas, like Bucks County, but stayed away from the polls, usually under implicit threats, in others, particularly Philadelphia.[15] At the Convention of 1837–38, delegates initially discussed the franchise in terms of democratic expansion—reducing residency and tax qualifications—but debate eventually centered on the question of race. While many delegates supported universal suffrage without regard to taxation or race, Benjamin Martin of Philadelphia took advantage of controversies around the Black vote contemporary with the convention—particularly the lawsuit

1815–1846 (New York: Oxford University Press, 1991), 107–8, 126–27, 200; Sean Wilentz, *The Rise of American Democracy: Jefferson to Lincoln* (New York: Norton, 2005), 354, 468. Delegates were elected in 1836 and the convention began in May 1837 (Akagi, "The Pennsylvania Convention," 310–11).

[12] Akagi, "The Pennsylvania Convention," 323, 325.

[13] Otter, *Philadelphia Stories*, 131, 134–35. [14] Tocqueville, *Democracy*, 295.

[15] "Evidence suggests that blacks had been voting in the state since the Revolutionary years in at least seven counties in the state. But blacks were increasingly intimidated from the polls in other regions." Malone, *Between Freedom and Bondage*, 90.

brought by William Fogg, denied the vote in Luzerne County—to insert the notorious qualification of "white" in defining the class of voters; delegates approved by a 77–45 margin.[16]

These debates over corporate charters and racialized citizenship mirrored each other uncannily. Both concerned the state's power to grant and revoke attributes of legal personhood: in one case to artificial persons with outsized influence and in the other to human individuals with precarious access to political power. But political expediency kept critical accounts of corporate and racialized personhood divided along partisan lines. Jacksonian Democrats criticized banks as monstrous and detrimental to the interests of common people but relied on a rhetoric of white male equality predicated on the exclusion of Black Americans. Their opponents, many of whom represented the banking interest and minimized its dangers, included advocates for the Black franchise such as Thaddeus Stevens. As Sean Wilentz writes, "Although Whigs and Democrats shared in the Negrophobia dominant among all whites in the 1830s, northern Democrats did take the lead in disenfranchising blacks…, even as they celebrated the growing political participation of lower-class white men." Because a significant minority of Whigs opposed slavery and Black disenfranchisement, "the propensity of Democratic leaders to see antislavery agitation in partisan terms led them to equate, falsely, political ambition and opportunism with genuine humanitarianism."[17] Thus, despite their shared concern with the law of persons, partisanship ensured that the debates over corporate charters and the racialized franchise did not cross on the convention floor.[18]

The connections between Black and corporate personhood would reemerge in the 1840s and 1850s in a number of Supreme Court cases concerning diversity jurisdiction, the principle that gave jurisdiction over disputes between citizens of different states to federal courts. The Taney Court ruled in *Letson* (1844) that corporations could sue in diversity because a corporation was "capable of being treated as a citizen of that state, as much as a natural person."[19] As historian Austin Allen has shown, the quasi-citizenship granted to corporations appeared to extend to others: "If corporations had access to the federal courts, then free blacks probably did as well. And if the court protected their rights as it did corporate rights, then the South's system of racial rule faced a grave threat." The Taney Court's subsequent jurisprudence, up to and including Taney's notorious opinion

[16] *Proceedings and Debates of the Convention of the Commonwealth of Pennsylvania to Propose Amendments to the Constitution, Commenced and Held at Harrisburg on the Second Day of May, 1837, Reported by John Agg, Stenographer to the Convention, Assisted by Messrs. Wheeler, Kingman, Drake, and M'Kinley* (Harrisburg: Packer, Barrett, and Parke, 1837–38), Vol. 10, 106, 132–34. Akagi, "The Pennsylvania Convention," 318–19.

[17] Wilentz, *The Rise of American Democracy*, 512.

[18] The franchise was debated June 19–28, 1837, and January 16–17, 1838; corporate charters primarily from November 19 to December 29, 1837. Akagi, "The Pennsylvania Convention," 317, 323.

[19] *Louisville, Cincinnati & Charleston R. Co. v. Letson*, 43 US 497 (1844), 558.

in *Dred Scott v. Sandford* (1857), was thus tailored both to preserve corporate access to federal courts and to maintain the status quo of slavery by denying Black citizenship and legal standing. As Allen writes, the racist excess of Taney's *Dred Scott* opinion "underscored that blacks' historical and legal experience placed them in a category different from that of other quasi-citizens."[20]

Two decades before *Dred Scott*, however, the discourses of corporate and racialized personhood converged in less rigid, productively disorienting terms in *Sheppard Lee*. Bird himself was neither lawyer, banker, nor politician—though he would later serve as a bank director and make an abortive bid for Congress as a Delaware Whig—but as an elite Philadelphia resident he could hardly have avoided the debates over corporate charters and racialized citizenship.[21] Written during the run-up to the 1837–38 convention, *Sheppard Lee* traces various characters interested in the questions of personhood it would address, including a stock-jobber, a quasi-abolitionist Quaker philanthropist, and an enslaved African American. Through Lee's changing status—living and dead, singular and plural, person and property—*Sheppard Lee* both dramatizes the legal doctrines on which Jacksonian America's crises of personhood centered and resituates them by revealing the surprising symmetries in the ways they structured persons.

Faculties of a Most Marvelous Nature

Even as it traverses the registers of law, medicine, and the supernatural, *Sheppard Lee* anticipates John Dewey's account of the person as a "right-and-duty-bearing unit."[22] For Dewey, Maitland's insight that corporate personality is a set of powers and liabilities heads off fruitless metaphysical questions about essence of the persons, whether "natural" or "artificial." While Lee initially frames his personhood as a metaphysical or (pseudo-)scientific quandary, Bird's novel ultimately endorses a theory of personhood as a set of affordances or capacities.

In this respect, the novel can be illuminated by an unlikely source: a lecture Bird likely wrote and delivered while teaching at the Pennsylvania College of Medicine. In "Apparitions," Bird brings medical reasoning to bear on apparently supernatural phenomena under the subtle rubric of "faculties."[23] Bird argues for natural explanations of apparently supernatural phenomena in order "to demolish a creed, that formerly sent its *few* victims to the grave, and its many to the

[20] Austin Allen, *Origins of the Dred Scott Case: Jacksonian Jurisprudence and the Supreme Court, 1837–1857* (Athens, GA: University of Georgia Press, 2006), 73, 161.

[21] Dahl, *Robert Montgomery Bird*, 29–30.

[22] John Dewey, "The Historic Background of Corporate Legal Personality," *Yale Law Journal* 35 (1926): 656.

[23] On Bird's medical lectures, see Mary Mayer Bird, "Life of Robert Montgomery Bird," *University of Pennsylvania Library Chronicle* 12 (1944): 71–92, 97–120; 13 (1945): 3–30; 33–56; 61–95, 13: 79. A note in Bird's hand on the title page mentions reading it in November 1842.

madhouse."[24] Yet he treats the phenomenology of apparition with great respect: "there have been many apparitions *of the most genuine character*, which were proved, to the satisfaction of those most interested—the *seers of them*—to have arisen *from causes within themselves*,—the progeny of their own *false sensations*."[25] Bird's juxtaposition of genuine apparitions and false sensations is ontologically subtle: the immateriality or virtuality of a phenomenon does not compromise its authenticity. He reasons, moreover, that such false sensations are not simply a liability of the weak-minded but rather the results of "a very peculiar, and wonderful, power in the Organs of Sense (and especially in the nobler organs of sight and hearing,) to perform their several functions (in a greater or less degree of perfection) *independent of all material causes of sensation*; the power to see without sight, to hear without hearing."[26] He thus places the error of the ghost-seer on a continuum with the visionary power of the romantic genius: "It is among *imaginative* classes of men, (and, above all, *painters* and *poets*) that the *power* of Independant [*sic*] Sensation rises to the dignity of a *faculty*, (which, in the case of the visual organ, may be called the *Poetic*, or *Inner, Sight*)."[27] False sensation, which first appears as a disability, is elevated to the level of a faculty, "a power *subjected to the will*."[28]

Following this twist in Bird's lecture, we might read *Sheppard Lee* as depicting not only a nervous disorder but also a corresponding faculty analogous to "poetic sight." Lee himself uses the language of faculties to insist on the plausibility of his story: "why should it not be granted that an individual should possess the power of transferring his spirit from body to body at will[?]" (*SL*, 423). After all, he points out "there are several different faculties of a most marvellous nature"—he mentions ventriloquism and animal magnetism—"with which a few individuals in the world are mysteriously endowed, while the great mass of men are entirely without them; and to the number of these supernatural endowments there is scarce a year passes by without adding a new one" (*SL*, 422).[29] Lee proceeds by analogy: "In the same way, it is not improbable that other persons besides myself may possess the faculty of reanimating dead bodies, without suspecting it; for I can scarce believe the faculty should be confined entirely to myself" (*SL*, 423). As in "Apparitions," Bird invites the reader to make a double move: first, to doubt Lee's insistence that his (or magnetizers' or ventriloquists') endowments are supernatural and thus to seek their natural origins; second, to analyze the phenomena in their own terms rather than reducing them to their material causes.

[24] RMBP, box 22, folder 278,"Apparitions": Lecture and Notes, undated, 3.
[25] Bird, "Apparitions," 20. [26] Bird, "Apparitions," 22. [27] Bird, "Apparitions," 23–24.
[28] Bird, "Apparitions," 22.
[29] Alongside these extraordinary cases, it should be noted, appear others too good to be true, like quack homeopaths "who, by shaking a bottle in a peculiar way, give to its contents a medical virtue which did not exist before, and which another man,—the patient, for example,—might shake till doomsday without imparting" (422).

But while "Apparitions" asserts that a "barrier of clouds and darkness and funeral adamant" separates the living and the dead and assures auditors that "the midnight graveyard" will "lose [its] terrors" in the face of enlightened understanding,[30] *Sheppard Lee*, a novel that begins its play with life, death, and personal identity in a graveyard at midnight, suggests that some terrors are not so easily dispelled.

Justine Murison, astutely in tune with Bird's interest in materialist explanation, has described the epistemological and political stakes of *Sheppard Lee* as a narrative of hypochondria, a nineteenth-century diagnosis that both medicalized aesthetic subjectivity and paralleled the power dynamics of race, mastery, and slavery.[31] Her account, however, hardly exhausts the "faculties" on which Lee's voyage, whether imaginary or supernatural, can shed light. As both Murison and Christopher Looby have pointed out, the novel depicts moral character as inseparable from bodily fact. Yet it also playfully dematerializes bodily fact into legal fiction. Given Bird's medical training, it might seem perverse to seek legal sources for phenomena that ought to have natural explanations. The novel is full of physicians, yet their appearances frequently open conduits between medical and legal registers, suggesting a rich field of analogies between natural and artificial persons, the corporeal and the incorporated. In fact, the doctors in *Sheppard Lee*—Higginson's Dr Boneset, Megrim's Dr Tibbikens, and the mysterious Dr Feuerteufel—provide some of the most compelling illustrations of Lee's extraordinary experience as a case of aggregate personhood. Early in his tenure in Higginson's body, Lee seeks treatment for his gout. As Dr Boneset explains, "The gout…has as great an affection for the human body as a cat has for a house in which she has been well treated…once it finds itself at home, in a good wholesome corporation of a man, there you may expect to find it a tenant for life" (*SL*, 79). Describing Higginson's body as a "corporation," Dr Boneset effaces the distinction between natural and artificial bodies, and between medical and legal terminology: Lee-as-Higginson is at once corpulent, corporeal, and corporate.

Lawyers and the law, moreover, crop up around every corner in *Sheppard Lee*. Early in book 1, we learn that one of Lee's college friends has "become a great lawyer in an adjacent state" (*SL*, 24). Lee-as-Higginson, imprisoned for murdering Lee, is advised to retain counsel: "My friend Sharphead, I think, will be your best man" (*SL*, 65). Mr. Cutclose, another lawyer, is one of Lee-as-Higginson's wealthy neighbors. As the penniless dandy I. Dulmer Dawkins, Lee describes law as "a respectable profession" among gentlemen "because it keeps down the mob, or people, by keeping them constantly by the ears, and because it makes money" (*SL*, 161). Still another lawyer gets involved when Samuel Wilkins, Lee-as-Dawkins's uncle, devises a scheme to marry off his progeny so as best to preserve his estate (*SL*, 214). And during Lee's tenure as the Quaker philanthropist Zachariah

[30] Bird, "Apparitions," 37. [31] Murison, *Politics of Anxiety*, 19–27.

Longstraw, his protégé Abel Snipe works his way through the courts into prison before a petition from his benefactor frees him (*SL*, 260–61).

The extraordinary "faculties" of ventriloquism and animal magnetism to which Lee refers are also suggestive in their legal resonance. Ventriloquism, as Lee describes it, consists of "throwing the voice into places and things afar from the operator," whether animate or inanimate (*SL*, 422). The law has long recognized such voice-throwing: a lawyer (as agent) speaks for another (the principal), personating him or her as a "mouthpiece," what Hobbes calls a "*Feigned* or *Artificiall person*"—with the implication that capacities (here, the capacity of speech) do not inhere in individuals but rather can float between them.[32] More broadly, of course, this situation is the basis of the theory of agency, central to the law of corporations and the subject of a major treatise by Joseph Story.[33] Animal magnetism, similarly, presents a model of agency that redistributes the capacities of an individual: "the magnetizer, who, by flourishing his digits about your body, now cures your rheumatism, and now sets you sound asleep" or "the magnetized slumberer" gains mysterious abilities—reading unseen letters or "render[ing] oraculous responses to any question" (*SL*, 423).[34] These faculties offer two analogs for Lee's experience: he can be conceived of as a voice that moves from body to body while retaining its identity (an interpretation that accords with Locke's theory of personal identity) or as a force that transcends individual bodies, which become its medium. However marvelous (or dubious) these faculties may be, their creation and distribution of agency is matched by the law, which through processes including incorporation, enfranchisement, and disenfranchisement creates, extinguishes, distributes, and reconstitutes identity and rights. The law of persons thus offers a particular key to Lee's remarkable ability.

No Longer of the Singular Number

As discussed in chapter 1, Blackstone describes the corporation is an apparatus for circumventing the legal inconvenience of mortality: "As all personal rights die with the person; and, as the necessary forms of investing a series of individuals, one after another, with the same identical rights, would be very inconvenient,

[32] James J. Paxson, *The Poetics of Personification* (Cambridge: Cambridge University Press, 1994), 18; Thomas Hobbes, *Leviathan*, ed. Richard E. Flathman and David Johnston (New York: Norton, 1997), 88.

[33] Joseph Story, *Commentaries on the Law of Agency, as a Branch of Commercial and Maritime Jurisprudence, with Occasional Illustrations from the Civil and Foreign Law* (Boston: Little and Brown, 1839). The law of principal and agent was a frequent heading in the *American Jurist*'s regular digest of recent cases. See also William Paley, *Treatise on the Law of Principal and Agent* (Exeter, NH: 1822).

[34] On the phenomenon of animal magnetism, see Russ Castronovo, *Necro Citizenship: Death, Eroticism, and the Public Sphere in the Nineteenth Century United States* (Durham, NC: Duke University Press, 2001), 101–50; John Lardas Modern, *Secularism in Antebellum America* (Chicago: University of Chicago Press, 2011), 119–81.

if not impracticable; it has been found necessary...to constitute artificial persons, who may maintain a perpetual succession, and enjoy a kind of legal immortality."[35] The inconvenience of mortality, in Blackstone's story, gives rise to a remarkable innovation: "artificial persons" characterized by succession and immortality. Chief Justice John Marshall's opinion in *Dartmouth College* likewise describes corporations as "artificial being[s], invisible, intangible," and characterized by "immortality" and "individuality," "properties, by which a perpetual succession of many persons are considered as the same, and may act as a single individual...like one immortal being."[36] Drawing on Blackstone and Marshall, among others, Joseph K. Angell and Samuel Ames, in the first major American text on corporate law, present the legal artifice of the corporation as the creation of persistent unity from messy mortality and multiplicity: "a body, related by law, composed of individuals united under a common name, the members of which succeed each other, so that the body continues the same, notwithstanding the change of the individuals who compose it, and is, for certain purposes, considered as a natural person."[37] The corporate form ensures that "any number of persons...consolidated and united into a corporation...are then considered as *one person*, which has but one will," even as this unity stretches the conceptual boundaries of persons and bodies.[38]

The hallmarks by which these jurists identify the corporation—unity in multiplicity and immortality through succession—aptly describe the eponymous narrator of *Sheppard Lee*, published just four years after Angell and Ames's *A Treatise on the Law of Private Corporations Aggregate*. While Bird's narrator takes on a new name and distinct characteristics in each incarnation, he retains a certain formal unity.[39] Like a corporation, Lee retains a single name in the formal accounting: the chapter titles, like that of the novel, refer only to Lee, not to any of his avatars: "Sheppard Lee's introduction to his wife, and his suspicion that all is not gold that glistens"; "In which Sheppard Lee finds every thing black about him" (*SL*, 79, 331). Yet even as his name unifies the narrative, it coexists with a multiplicity that precedes even Lee's discovery of his power of metempsychosis. After mortally wounding himself while digging for treasure, Lee finds himself a disembodied spirit looking down on his own body:

> *There* I lay on the ground, stiff and lifeless; and *here* I stood on my feet, alive, and surveying my own corpse, stretched before me. But I forgot my extraordinary

[35] William Blackstone, *Commentaries on the Laws of England*: Book I: Of the Rights of Persons *(1765–69)*, 455.

[36] *Trustees of Dartmouth College v. Woodward*, 17 US (4 Wheat.) 518 (1819), 636.

[37] Joseph K. Angell and Samuel Ames, *A Treatise on the Law of Private Corporations Aggregate* (Boston: Hilliard, 1832), 1.

[38] Angell and Ames, *Treatise*, 7.

[39] Looby identifies Lee's dramatic changes with each new body as a challenge to the republican "ideology of disembodiment." Looby, "Introduction," xxxvi.

> duality in my concern for myself—that is to say, for that part of me, that *eidolon*, or representative, or duplicate of me, that was stretched on the grass...My condition, or *conditions* (for I was no longer of the singular number) at this time, can be understood only by comparing my confusion of senses and sensations to that which occurs in a dream, when one beholds himself dead, surveys his body, and philosophizes or laments, and is, all the time, to all intents and purposes, without being surprised at it, *two persons*, one of which lives and observes, while the other is wholly defunct. (*SL*, 48)

This Cartesian meditation on the "extraordinary duality" of body and soul transposes the plurality of the corporation to the corporeal register even as it borrows metaphors from Platonic metaphysics (*eidolon*), politics (representative), and secretarial work (duplicate). Lee's "condition, or *conditions*" align him with the corporation sole, an office like king or bishop that conveys rights or privileges distinct from those incumbent on its occupant as a natural person.[40] (Angell and Ames note that "Sole Corporations, it is believed, are not common in the United States"; Bird's novel offers a provocative counterexample.)[41]

Lee's apparently playful claim to be "no longer of the singular number" suggests that human individuals are always potentially divisible—or potentially corporate. Transposing the dialectic of individuation and aggregation from the metaphysics of law to metaphysics *tout court*, Bird raises provocative questions about identity and number. Here, the law of property punctuates the metaphysics of persons. As Lee's spirit looks enviously at the recently deceased body of John H. Higginson, he proposes "tak[ing] possession of a tenement which there remained no spirit to claim, and thus, uniting interests together, as two feeble factions unite together in the political world, become a body possessing life, strength, and usefulness" (*SL*, 52). "Body" does double duty here, naming both Higginson's inert corpse (metaphorically presented as real estate—a quirk to which I will return) and the vital combination of two "feeble" units. Comparing the combination of spirit and body to a political alliance, Lee figures both spirit and flesh as "factions." The resulting "body possessing life, strength, and usefulness"—what would appear to be an individual—is thus presented as a coalition composed of collectives. If Lee's mechanics of succession echo the corporation sole, then, his self-description as an association echoes the form of a corporation aggregate. Thus, while readers like Looby have convincingly read *Sheppard Lee* as a thoroughgoing exploration of embodiment, the novel refuses any naturalistic

[40] Kantorowicz famously describes this notion as the king's two bodies. Maitland famously dismisses the corporation sole as "either natural man or juristic abortion," which he distinguishes from "a true corporation, a corporation aggregate." Frederic W. Maitland, *State, Trust, and Corporation*, ed. David Runciman and Magnus Ryan (Cambridge: Cambridge University Press, 2003), 30, 28.

[41] Angell and Ames, *Treatise*, 19.

sense of what a body is. It asks us, rather, to consider "the body" in a sense capacious enough to include beings "no longer of the singular number."

If Lee's plural "conditions" make him metaphorically corporate, his incarnations are also metonymically linked to 1830s corporations, including banks, joint-stock companies, and philanthropic organizations.[42] His interactions with corporations highlight their characteristic combination of unity and multiplicity: legally, they are grounded in the aggregation of persons; economically, they are subject to a complementary disaggregation into multiple, fungible shares. As the wealthy brewer Higginson, his possessions include a "pocketbook...full of banknotes" as well as "bank-stock and coal-mines" (*SL,* 71, 83). As Abram Skinner, a note-shaver, stock-jobber, and miser drawn in broad and likely anti-Semitic caricature, Lee fancies himself "the very devil among the fancy stocks" (*SL,* 208). Defined by a nineteenth-century "reformed stock gambler" as stocks "of no particular or known value" that "represent worthless or embarrassed corporations, which have failed in the undertakings for which capital was contributed," fancy stocks provide "the *materiel* which forms the basis of the antagonistical operations of bulls and bears."[43] (With their basis in "fancy" or imagination, they also recall Bird's theory of the faculty of independent sensation.) Rising from the ashes of troubled businesses, they are reincarnated by the likes of Skinner as an abstracted, easily manipulated form of value: "I have known a pet stock to be tossed up and down like a ball, while every ascent and downfall served the purpose of filling the pockets of the fraternity [of stock-jobbers] and emptying those of the victims" (*SL,* 208–9). And as the Quaker Longstraw, Lee is at once a proud sponsor of incorporated charities, a befuddled victim of stock schemes, and a commodity himself.

The double dynamic of aggregation and disaggregation, then, undergirds both Lee's metempsychosis and the financial misconduct and misfortune he meets in various encounters with economic modernity. It emerges with particular clarity in book 5, in which Lee inhabits the wealthy but hapless Longstraw and is defrauded by his nephew Jonathan and protégé Abel Snipe. The ex-convict Snipe is practiced in such malfeasance: "he had borrowed from the hoards of his

[42] While stock companies were newly prominent and anxiety-provoking in Jacksonian America, they were hardly new in a larger historical sense. Miles Ogborn and Mary Poovey, among others, have examined the discourses of joint-stock companies and practices like stock-jobbing in late seventeenth-century and early eighteenth-century England. Miles Ogborn, *Indian Ink: Script and Print in the Making of the English East India Company* (Chicago: University of Chicago Press, 2007), 157–97; Mary Poovey, *Genres of the Credit Economy: Mediating Value in Eighteenth- and Nineteenth-Century Britain* (Chicago: University of Chicago Press, 2008).

[43] William Armstrong, *Stocks and Stock-Jobbing in Wall-Street, with Sketches of the Brokers, and Fancy Stocks* (New York: New York Publishing Company, 1848), 13. Skinner boasts of his skill in "the management of small stocks, and especially those that were good for nothing, and more especially still in southern mining-companies," as well as "*cornering*" and "*selling on time*" (208–9)—two of "those peculiar, mysterious, keen, spicy, and rascally transactions" of which Armstrong warns novice investors (*Stocks,* 12).

employers (the president and directors of a certain stock-company, in whose office he had a petty appointment), and thus, perforce, made charitable an institution that was chartered to be uncharitable" (*SL*, 260). His fraud, which blurs the boundary between charities and businesses, recalls recent legal history. Although the *Dartmouth College* ruling centered on the status of a charitable corporation and Marshall and Story's opinions principally discussed such associations, the case became, perforce, a cornerstone for the business corporations included in Story's broad construction of private corporations—the very corporations whose profusion called for Angell and Ames' treatise. By the 1830s, critics of banks would argue that the decision had made the corporate form too powerful and that its application to businesses was a mistake.

In the *Commentaries*, Blackstone had divided lay corporations aggregate into "two sorts, civil and eleemosynary. The civil are such as are erected for a variety of temporal purposes," among which he counts both institutions of governance (the crown itself, municipal governance) and bodies "for the advancement and regulation of manufactures and commerce" or "for the better carrying on of divers special purposes"—the category comprises what we would today recognize as both public agencies and private companies. Eleemosynary corporations have a much narrower scope: they "are constituted for the perpetual distribution of the free alms, or bounty, of the founder of them to such persons as he has directed," and include hospitals and colleges.[44] Blackstone's scheme predates the more familiar private/public distinction articulated in *Dartmouth College*. (The Marshall Court would classify Dartmouth College, not uncontroversially, as a private eleemosynary corporation.)[45] While civil corporations straddle our public/private divide, Blackstone's explanation makes clear their purpose of providing a public benefit—a standard to which American corporations were held until the era of general incorporation.[46]

The rapid rise of business corporations in early nineteenth-century America challenged both corporations' traditional role as an instruments of public good and the fiction of their "existing only in intendment and consideration of law."[47] Democratic writers and politicians argued that different kinds of corporations deserved separate legal and moral consideration. Business corporations, they

[44] Blackstone, *Commentaries*, 458–9.

[45] Blackstone identifies the Universities of Oxford and Cambridge as *civil* corporations, because professors' and administrators' salaries "are rewards *pro opera et labore*, not charitable donations only," but identifies the colleges comprised by the universities as eleemosynary corporations, because they were established for the support of poor students, "imparting assistance to the members of those bodies, in order to enable them to prosecute their devotion and studies with greater ease and assiduity." Blackstone, *Commentaries*, 459. The Marshall Court's identification of Dartmouth College as an eleemosynary corporation follows the letter of its name rather than the spirit of its charter.

[46] Eric Hilt, "Early American Corporations and the State," ed. Naomi R. Lamoreaux and William J. Novak, *Corporations and American Democracy* (Cambridge, MA: Harvard University Press, 2017), 40.

[47] Blackstone, *Commentaries* 458–59, 464.

contended, could hardly be understood or regulated in the eighteenth-century terms that had grounded the *Dartmouth College* decision. Ingersoll looked back a generation to contrast Hamilton's view of corporations "as absurd creations of imagination" with the "great independent substantive things, political engines of peculiar magnitude and moment" they had become by the 1830s.[48] For Ingersoll, Blackstone's taxonomy of corporations—sole and aggregate, ecclesiastical and lay, civil and eleemosynary—is inadequate in an age of banking power. In an 1836 pamphlet addressing Pennsylvania's chartering of the BUS, he asserts that "bank charters, and above all, the charter of that bank, may be repealed by an act of Assembly, without a Convention; and such act will not be contrary to the Constitution of the United States." There is an essential difference, he writes, between charters in general and those "incorporat[ing] bodies for the sole purpose of gain."[49] His statement reflects the pre-*Dartmouth College* conventional wisdom that "it seems very difficult to conceive of a corporation established for merely private purposes" without "the establishment of some public good or purpose."[50] He thus rejects the *Dartmouth College* doctrine "that bank charters are contracts, within the meaning of the constitution" and asserts that "it is a common error to confound all charters of incorporation."[51] An anonymously published 1837 pamphlet by David Henshaw similarly urges a new taxonomy: "Corporations, in America, may be divided into three classes: Municipal, eleemosynary, and business corporations. The first embraces our towns, cities, and the like; the second, hospitals, colleges, &c.; and the third, manufacturing, banking, rail-roads, wharves, hotels, stage companies, and the like." By identifying business corporations as a distinct category, he departs from legal authorities both traditional and contemporary and concludes that "the legislative power creates the charter, and that power can modify or repeal it."[52]

As noted in chapter 1, Henshaw's and Ingersoll's discussions of banks both recall and recast the distinction between natural and artificial persons. Whereas

[48] Charles Jared Ingersoll, "Speech of Charles J. Ingersoll, Esq., in the Convention of Pennsylvania, on Legislative and Judicial Control over Charters of Incorporation," *Democratic Review* 5 (1839): 97–144, 111. Ingersoll alludes to Hamilton's opinion on Congress's power to charter a national bank, in which Hamilton rejects the notion of the corporation as "some great, independent, substantive thing" in favor of a more abstract view: "a quality, capacity, or means to an end." Alexander Hamilton, "Opinion on the Constitutionality of an Act to Establish a Bank" (February 23, 1791), *The Papers of Alexander Hamilton Digital Edition*, ed. Harold C. Syrett (Charlottesville, VA: University of Virginia Press, Rotunda, 2011, accessed December 16, 2013, https://rotunda.upress.virginia.edu/founders/default.xqy?keys=ARHN-chron-1790-1791-02-23-6.

[49] Charles Jared Ingersoll, *Opinion of Charles J. Ingersoll, Esq. "with Reference to the United States Bank and the Question of Vested Rights"* (Philadelphia: 1836), 1–2.

[50] *Trustees of the University of North Carolina v. Foy*, 1 Murphy 58 (NC 1805), 88–9; R. Kent Newmyer, *Supreme Court Justice Joseph Story*, 132.

[51] Ingersoll, "Speech," 100.

[52] David Henshaw, *Remarks Upon the Rights and Powers of Corporations, and the Rights, Powers, and Duties of the Legislature toward Them. Embracing a Review of the Opinion of the Supreme Court of the United States, in the Case of Dartmouth College, in New Hampshire, Given in 1819* (Boston: Beals and Greene, 1837), 5.

the law classifies persons as natural (human beings) or artificial (corporations), Henshaw contrasts well-regulated "business corporations," the "natural offspring" of republicanism, to "banks and all large corporations for trading in money," which, "if they are to be placed beyond legislative control, and are thus to become monopolies and perpetuities, . . . assume an aspect the reverse of this, and become alarming excrescences upon the body politic."[53] Ingersoll, likewise, decries an emergent corporate aristocracy as a "fungus grown upon government, upon property, upon liberty and equality."[54] Both politicians elevate the natural/artificial distinction from a technicality of the law of persons to a normative judgment.[55]

Such critiques can help us understand Lee-as-Longstraw's confusion and misfortune in the world of corporate supremacy. While a Whig like Bird might be expected to resist Jacksonian antibank rhetoric, he characteristically aims his satire in all directions, at once echoing antibank writers' characterization of business corporations and suggesting how blurry the distinction between different kinds of corporations could be in practice. The Longstraw episode, in this light, occupies the cusp between older and newer instantiations of the corporate form. On the one hand, Lee-as-Longstraw enthusiastically collects charters for philanthropic charities: "I instituted some half a dozen charitable societies, to supply fuel, clothing, food, and employment to the suffering poor; as well as others to exhort them to economy, industry, prudence, fortitude, and so forth. I formed societies even among themselves, classing divers isolated creatures into bands, who wrought in common, and disposed of their wares, either in a shop kept for the purpose, or at fairs. I established schools to keep the children of the poor out of mischief, and one in particular I supported solely from my own, that is to say, Zachariah Longstraw's pocket" (*SL*, 275–76).

Longstraw's charitable activity shades into business, as Snipe's job description makes clear: "accountant, or secretary, collector of rents, dispenser of secret charities, and, in general, factotum and fiduciary at large" (*SL*, 261). It's clear that Snipe's résumé—"ma[king] charitable an institution that was chartered to be uncharitable" suits the job perfectly. At the same time, as the former employee of "a certain stock-company," Snipe is at home in the milieu of business corporations and finance capital, a world in which Longstraw is lost. It thus comes as little surprise when Snipe and Jonathan lure Longstraw into a stock market swindle on the pretext of reforming profit-seeking into charity. When Longstraw protests

[53] Henshaw, *Remarks*, 9. [54] Ingersoll, "Speech," 111.

[55] Defenders of banking corporations such as Nicholas Biddle (president of the Second Bank) and John Pendleton Kennedy, by contrast, stressed corporate metaphors of mechanical order and associated their opponents with mob violence and anarchy. John Pendleton Kennedy, *Strictures on the Letter of Charles J. Ingersoll, Esq. Touching the Right of a Legislature to Repeal a Charter. With an Appendix, Containing the Letters of Mr. Ingersoll, of Mrs. Dallas, of Mr. Forward, and of Mr. Biddle, in Illustration of the Subject Discussed. By a Citizen of Maryland* (Baltimore, MD: Joseph Neal, 1836). The *American Jurist*, the most important American legal periodical of the 1830s, noticed Henshaw's pamphlet and James Madison Porter's rebuttal to Ingersoll.

that trading stocks is "neither honest nor humane" because "it is practiced at the expense of the ignorant, and often the needy," Snipe retorts,

> "It shall be at the expense of the rich and niggardly—the man that is a miser and uncharitable—the broker and the gambler—the bull and the bear. Our dealings shall not be with the poor and ignorant man that dabbleth in stocks; but him we will charitably pluck from the grasp of the covetous, and thus protect, while drawing from the covetous man those alms of benevolence which he would never himself apply to the use of the afflicted."
>
> "Verily," said I, pleased with the idea, "if we can make the covetous man charitable, it will be a good thing; and if we can protect the foolish ignorant person from his grasp, it will be still better." (*SL*, 291)

Longstraw then worries that stock speculation is a form of gambling, but Snipe convinces him that "money, bagged up in stocks and other investments [is] as merchandise" (*SL*, 291). Jonathan strikes the decisive rhetorical blow when he casts the plan as a de facto tax that remediates "the crying evil arising from money that is chartered in stocks" by "do[ing] what the commonwealth should be doing; we will impose a tax upon the gains of chartered money, and distribute the proceeds among the needy" (*SL*, 291–92). Creative accounting, Jonathan suggests, might force corporations to serve the common good by reducing "bodies for the sole purpose of gain" to charitable institutions.

In Bird's arch satire, this debate about corporate profits is itself part of the swindle. Abel's and Jonathan's ensuing scheme closely resembles the "manœuvres" that the "reformed stock gambler" Armstrong would detail a decade later in *Stocks and Stock-Jobbing in Wall-Street*. Abel fakes a "sudden bankruptcy" and blames it on "Speculation, speculation—bad speculation!" (*SL*, 293), until Jonathan turns state's witness against him and makes off with Longstraw's inheritance, bestowed in a moment of ill-considered gratitude. Snipe's and Jonathan's conspiracy thus both recapitulates and cynically borrows contemporary antibank critique.[56] Bird's portrayal of the appropriation of antibank rhetoric, like his send-up of "Hurrah boys" elsewhere in *Sheppard Lee*, certainly operates as anti-Jacksonian satire. But by emphasizing the parallels between their criminal scheme and banks' more genteel malfeasances, Bird takes aim at the banks as well. Clothing the pursuit of profit in the guise of charity, Snipe and Jonathan make the same move that American corporations made en masse in the wake of *Dartmouth College*, which extended the privileges of charitable corporations to

[56] It thus echoes the position of anti-BUS businessmen who stood to gain immensely by the failure of the BUS by "promoting cheap money, obtaining a share of the federal deposits held by the BUS, or taking over the national bank's functions themselves," of whom Henshaw was "the most energetic." Wilentz, *Rise of American Democracy*, 364.

corporations of all sorts. By the end of the episode, the logic of chartered money has prevailed, anticipating the twentieth-century doctrine of shareholder primacy, according to which "maximizing profit and shareholder value was treated as the proper goal of corporate enterprise."[57] While Lee-as-Longstraw may be convinced by smooth-talking apologists for the new financial order, Bird invites readers to remain skeptical.

Converted by Scientific Processes

The Longstraw episode ends with another, quite different juxtaposition of personhood and property. After a series of reversals instigated by Snipe's faux-bankruptcy, Lee-as-Longstraw is kidnapped to be sold—and eventually lynched—in Louisiana as "a great abolitionist" (*SL*, 317–18). Thematically and geographically, his capture marks the crossing between the logic of corporate capitalism and the logic of slavery, from the hazards of mysterious investments to the fate of a human investment. As both a virtual slave and sophisticated but dubious product of finance capitalism, Longstraw is a human fancy stock, evidence of the symmetry between "money, bagged up...as merchandise" and his own bagging up—a symmetry from which Bird's contemporaries averted their eyes. Critics' accounts of *Sheppard Lee*'s engagement with slavery have generally focused on Lee's stints as the enslaved Tom and the slaveholding Arthur Megrim.[58] Less frequently examined, however, are episodes that unfold the mysterious operations that turn persons into property (and vice versa).[59] Anchored by the imperfect yet suggestive symmetry between slavery and stock corporations as institutions centered on the interconvertibility of person and property, these moments are mediated by rich collection of metaphors that Lee uses to describe body, soul, and their relationship.[60]

At the nadir of despair as the money-lender Abram Skinner, financially and emotionally ruined by a faithless son, Lee is ready to transfer his soul into any other body. Finding a drunk apparently dead on the ground, he thrusts money and silver spoons in the pockets of this "body to be taken possession of" (*SL*, 234). Yet the apparent corpse turns out to be merely unconscious; he awakens and

[57] Naomi R. Lamoreaux and William J. Novak, "Corporations and American Democracy: An Introduction," *Corporations and American Democracy*, 24.

[58] Looby, "Introduction," xxix–xxxv; Otter, *Philadelphia Stories*, 102–5; Murison, *Politics*, 17–46.

[59] In his insightful analysis of "thingified spirits and spiritualized matter" in *Sheppard Lee*, James D. Lilley discusses a number of these moments, particularly Dr. Feuerteufel's experiments, as critiques of Enlightenment knowledge, commodity capitalism, agrarian democracy, and racial ideology as "fictions rooted in a violent economy of alienation and enslavement, an economy that metempsychotically circulates the fragmented stuff of personhood" (105, 111). His compelling account of the economy of personhood, however, is incomplete without attention to the law of persons.

[60] As Looby has pointed out, Lee's metaphors of embodiment are copious and baroque: "'tenement,' 'natural dwelling,' 'fleshly casing,' 'corporation,' 'fleshly matrix,' or 'mould,'" Looby, "Introduction," xvii.

shambles off with his pockets full of Skinner's silver. Lee-as-Skinner responds: '"You villain!" said I, running after him, 'give me back my property. I'm a free man,' said the sot; 'I'm no man's property. And so, Charlie, don't go for to disturb me, for I knows my way home as well as anybody'" (*SL*, 235).

Confusing Lee-as-Skinner's claim to movable property as a claim to his own person, the drunkard tellingly reframes a dispute about possession as a question of mastery and slavery. His words aptly, if ironically, echo Lee-as-Skinner's plan, just a moment before, to "take possession" of his body as a new "tenement" (*SL*, 232). This frequently repeated word, one of Lee's favored figures for bodies-as-possessions, suggests that spirits are the owners or occupants of the bodies they occupy—if only, sometimes, by squatter's rights. It reappears ironically—again in the context of race and slavery—when Longstraw, slumlord and philanthropist, lends "a little tenement that belongeth to me"—an actual habitation in this case—to John Smith, the caricatured free Black man who eventually kills him (*SL*, 241). The tenement metaphor suggests that bodies, while not as easily alienated as a pocketful of silver, can be understood as real property.[61] (In contrast, both chattel slaves and stocks, legally speaking, were personal property.)

Lee's other favorite figure for bodies—"casing"—comes from his father's successful sausage-making business (*SL*, 9, 52, 200, 227, 239). Casing portrays the body as a different kind of property: movable and consumable, perishable rather than durable, a housing that imposes unity on mixed, minced, and fungible stuff instead of sheltering a titled proprietor. These two metaphors deform personal identity in complementary ways: as a tenement, the body is a piece of transferable, habitable property while the soul retains its identity as owner and inhabitant. As a casing, the body is a generic vessel that gives shape to an otherwise formless and heterogeneous interior mass. Figuring bodies as various kinds of property, these tropes subject persons metaphorically both to possession and to disaggregation and thus provide telling analogs for the legal mechanics regulating enslaved persons and corporations as person-property hybrids. The legal title transforming a slave's body into property consolidates the mastery of the proprietor; the "casing" of a corporate charter grants legal "individuality" to an aggregate.

With the narrative juxtaposition and figurative similarity of property in stocks and slaves, Bird situates the corporation as a revealing counterpoint to slavery's reconfigurations of personhood. The law of slavery relied on the distinction between person—a legal subject—and human. As Jeannine DeLombard has argued, the humanity of enslaved people was not in doubt, even as their status as legal persons was fleeting: "As civilly incapacitated human property, the slave had no standing under civil law to own property, enter into contracts, initiate lawsuits, marry, claim custody of children, and so on. Yet for purposes of social

[61] "Tenement" also embraces holdings that are not owned outright, such as land granted by a feudal lord. Blackstone, *Commentaries*, Vol. 2, 16, 59.

control, the slave was a person with rights and duties under criminal law." Thus, "when...we realize the incommensurability of "person" and "human," we begin to see why...appeals to shared humanity have been largely irrelevant."[62] Unlike contemporaneous political discourse, whether pro- or antislavery, *Sheppard Lee* frames the legal mechanisms of slavery and the corporation as perverse reflections in the mirror of the law: the slave was a human individual deprived of key aspects of legal personhood, the corporation an inhuman legal person. Both were subject, in quite different ways, to fragmentation or disintegration: enslaved persons to physical violence, natal alienation, and family separation, corporations to division into and exchange as fungible shares. Lee's experiences, from Skinner's nearly claiming a person as property to Longstraw's slide from financial dupe to quasi-slave, repeatedly suggest a link between these two legal artifices. During his captivity, Lee-as-Longstraw hears that Sheppard Lee's body has been commodified, fragmented, and reassembled as a medical exhibit assembled by the dubious Dr Feuerteufel: "Alas! what an ending for poor Sheppard Lee! His body subjected to the knife of an anatomist, his bones scraped, boiled, bleached, hung together on wires, and set up in a museum, while his spirit was wandering about from body to body, enduring more afflictions in each than it had ever mourned even in that unlucky original dwelling it was so glad to leave" (*SL*, 317).

This imagined dismemberment recapitulates not only the commodification of enslaved bodies but also conjures grotesque violence against enslaved persons and the arbitrary divisibility of company stock. Reflecting on these rumors inspires a "touch of indignation and grief; which...I should have expressed, had there not arisen...an occasion to exercise those feelings on my own immediate behalf" as kidnapping victim (*SL*, 317). Yet rather than imagine the cruel operations of anatomist's knives or hangman's nooses, Lee-as-Longstraw decries the opaque and unscrupulous pricing of commodities: "the manner in which my merchants designed giving value to their merchandise not inherent and intrinsic to it (for, of a truth, my abolition principles...had never been carried to the point of notoriety, or even notice)" (*SL*, 318). His weak and oblique critique of chattel slavery arises from his vantage point as a fraudulent asset.[63]

These episodes map the overlap between persons and property as the site of dismantling bodies—whether into fraudulent goods, lynched corpses, or preserved organs. Lee's redescription of slavery in terms of stock market sleight-of-hand aligns the two practices as instances of the broader interconvertibility of persons

[62] DeLombard, "Claims of the Humanitarian," 1777–78.

[63] It should not be forgotten, of course, that many of the financial innovations of modernity arose in the service of the slave trade. See, for instance, Ian Baucom, *Specters of the Atlantic: Finance Capital, Slavery, and the Philosophy of History* (Durham, NC: Duke University Press, 2005); Ian Baucom, "Financing Enlightenment, Part Two: Extraordinary Expenditure," in *This Is Enlightenment*, ed. Clifford Siskin and William Warner (Chicago: University of Chicago Press, 2009), 336–56; Jennifer Rae Greeson, "The Prehistory of Possessive Individualism," *PMLA* 127 (2012): 918–24.

and property that the novel so richly if ambivalently presents. By the logic of *Sheppard Lee*, then, legal, financial, and scientific technologies are best understood as equivalent processes of aggregation, disaggregation, and interconvertibility. This play reaches its climax in Dr Feuerteufel's scientific exhibition, which transforms human beings into something both inanimate and immortal: "It consisted of an infinite variety of fragments from the bodies of animals and human beings, imitations, as I supposed at first, in wax, or some other suitable substance, and done to the life; but Tibbikens assured me they were real specimens, taken from animal bodies, and converted by scientific processes, known only to the exhibiter, into the substances we now saw" (*SL*, 399).

Feuerteufel's specimens are both scientific curiosities and economic novelties, aimed at transforming the funeral industry by transforming the abject stuff of mortality—"de exhalation and de miasm, de effluvium from de decay animal and vegetable "—into everlasting objects (*SL*, 404). His masterpiece is Lee's own body, "converted into a mummy by a new process, for the especial benefit of science and the world" (*SL*, 406). Feuerteufel's process, like the doctrine of incorporation, confers immortality on persons by remaking them as things—and even promises to confer a public benefit in the bargain.

The Name and Most of the Privileges of Freemen

If "scientific processes" can turn persons into things, might they also turn things into persons? The climax of Feuerteufel's demonstration in the unanticipated revivification of Lee's mummified body brings Lee's journey full circle, anticipating the famous chiasmus Frederick Douglass announces in his *Narrative* nine years later: "You have seen how a man was made a slave; you shall see how a slave was made a man."[64] Reading Bird's text alongside Douglass's highlights the motion of bodies into and out of slavery in *Sheppard Lee*: Longstraw shelters a freedom seeker in Philadelphia, only to assist unwittingly in his recapture; and of course Lee-as-Longstraw is captured as a mock slave and then nearly lynched before Lee flees his body for that of Tom, an enslaved African American who leads a revolt, in which incarnation he is all too predictably lynched. Later, Lee's reanimated corpse charts the course of a freedom seeker, fleeing Virginia for his New Jersey home with prodigious speed to avoid recapture as Feuerteufel's possession. Lee's legal and metaphysical metamorphoses, like Douglass's, often accompany geographic crossings.

[64] Frederick Douglass, *Narrative of the Life of Frederick Douglass, an American Slave*, ed. Houston Baker (New York: Penguin, 1982), 107. Consider also Stowe's original subtitle for *Uncle Tom's Cabin: "The Man That Was a Thing."* Murison has pointed out, with a different emphasis, how *Sheppard Lee* resonates with Douglass's chiasmus. Murison, *Politics of Anxiety*, 35.

A more ironic crossing occurred on the level of authorial biography: only months before Douglass fled Maryland for New York, Bird began to plan a move from Philadelphia to the Eastern Shore of Maryland.[65] On January 20, 1838, Bird wrote to his friend Samuel Groome, a resident of Cecil County, Maryland. In his letter, Bird reminisces about their last conversation, some years past, and its bearing on his present hopes: "I had then some thoughts of turning clodhopper and setting up my stakes on the Eastern Shore; and I have now a stronger tendency that way than ever; for our blackguards in the Convention are actually debating the propriety of admitting the negroes to the right of suffrage,—a measure that will drive me out of Pennsylvania, were the alternative the other side of the Rocky Mountains, and the very thought of which—though I believe there is not much fear of its actual occurrence—sharpens my desire to be off."[66]

Of course, the Pennsylvania Convention, during which Bird wrote this letter, did not give African Americans the vote but took it away; the letter stands as evidence of Bird's susceptibility to the racist fear and confusion drummed up by politicians like John Sterigere and Benjamin Martin in the wake of a controversial lawsuit and a contested election.[67] Yet Bird's letter's juxtaposition of racialized citizenship and border-crossing also echoes the jurisdictional issues he had explored two years earlier in *Sheppard Lee*.

Lee's transformations—from free man to chattel, from mummified corpse to living man—parallel his movement through various states and often reflect the legal status of those states' Black residents. Indeed, some of the names Bird considered for his protagonist suggest a pointedly racialized identity: "Niggaby Low…Niggaby Long…Niggaby Leake. (Nigby Low.)"[68] Moreover, *Sheppard Lee*'s opening and closing in New Jersey and movement through Pennsylvania and Virginia trace a map of variations in the law of race and slavery. Early nineteenth-century transformations in state law, including gradual abolition and disenfranchisement statutes, had created an uneven landscape of political and legal status for African Americans. Lee's home state of New Jersey enacted gradual abolition in 1804 and became the first state to disenfranchise African Americans in 1807; by 1830 it was

[65] Bird purchased a farm in Cecil County 1839 and finally occupied it in 1840. Clement E. Foust, *The Life and Dramatic Works of Robert Montgomery Bird* (New York: Knickerbocker Press, 1919), 114–15.

[66] RMBP, box 1 folder 62. A letter from Samuel Groome to Bird of January 26, 1838 (RMBP, box 1 folder 63) responding to and quoting this letter suggests that the recipient (John C. Groome) and year (1837) normally assigned to Bird's letter are in error. Bird's biographer Curtis Dahl has pointed out this letter's racial irony: "The author of the antislavery play *The Gladiator*, it should be remembered, was also the man who wished to move out of Pennsylvania if Negroes were given the franchise there!" (Dahl, *Robert Montgomery Bird*, 109). Bird's biographers attribute the move to physical and mental exhaustion. See M. M. Bird, *Life*, Vol. 13, 61; Foust, *The Life*, 114–15.

[67] Malone, *Between Freedom and Bondage*, 63, 91–98.

[68] RMBP, box 11, folder 259. (*Sheppard Lee*, Fragments and Notes, undated).

home to two-thirds of the enslaved Blacks in the North.[69] Given *Sheppard Lee*'s primary setting in Philadelphia, Otter notes that "The logical body for Lee to enter would not have been a Virginia slave but a member of Philadelphia's African American aspiring classes."[70] Yet while *Sheppard Lee* features slaves, slaveholders, and their analogs, it only glancingly touches on the plight of free Black Pennsylvanians.

Until 1838, Black Pennsylvanians were in legal and political limbo. Their de facto disenfranchisement in Philadelphia and other areas, along with the absence of explicit racial qualifications in Pennsylvania's 1790 Pennsylvania Constitution, created a patchwork of local practices but suspended the larger question of political rights. But in the 1830s, contests over Black voting rights forced delegates decisively to extend the vote or to strip it—and in doing so to take a clear position on the definition of "freeman." In 1835, William Fogg, a Black resident of Luzerne County, was turned away from the polls; he subsequently sued for the franchise. While the case was initially decided in his favor, it was appealed to the state Supreme Court, which put off ruling on this sensitive case until the convention had voted on suffrage. Close to the same time, the narrow victory of a Whig candidate in Bucks County, attributed to the Black vote there, mounted a challenge to decades of one-party politics in Pennsylvania. At the convention, an initial vote in June 1837 failed to add the word "white" to suffrage requirements, but a second vote in January 1838—with *Fogg v. Hobbs* (1837) and the Bucks County controversy fresh in the minds of delegates and the public—succeeded in adding the racial qualification. Convention delegates cited Judge Fox of the Pennsylvania Supreme Court, who asserted that African Americans had never been included among the "freemen" or citizens of Pennsylvania. Yet only after the convention's vote did Judge Gibson of the Pennsylvania Supreme Court hand down the final verdict.[71] This cynical game of legal hot potato allowed both court and convention to treat the disenfranchisement of African Americans as an established—indeed, a natural—fact rather than a condition they had enacted. *American Jurist* reported the decision in *Fogg v. Hobbs* but did not note the racial restriction of the franchise in its summary of the convention. Publications by leading members of Pennsylvania's African American communities protesting a racially restricted franchise, in contrast, addressed the convention rather than the courts.[72]

[69] Pennsylvania, in contrast, enacted gradual abolition in 1780. Edgar J. McManus, *Black Bondage in the North* (Syracuse, NY: Syracuse University Press, 1973), 184, 161. Douglas Harper, "Slavery in New Jersey," *Slavery in the North*, accessed June 20, 2013, http://www.slavenorth.com/newjersey.htm.

[70] Otter, *Philadelphia Stories*, 103.

[71] Malone, *Between Freedom and Bondage*, 90–91, 97–98.

[72] "Digest of American Cases," *American Jurist* 19 (1838): 462; "Constitution of Pennsylvania," *American Jurist* 18 (1837–38): 263–64; *Memorial of the Free Citizens of Color in Pittsburg and its Vicinity Relative to the Right of Suffrage: Read in Convention July 8, 1837* (Harrisburg, PA: Thompson and Clark, 1837); Robert Purvis, *Appeal of Forty Thousand Citizens, Threatened with Disenfranchisement, to the People of Pennsylvania* (Philadelphia: Printed by Merrihew and Gunn, 1838).

As the course of disenfranchisement in Pennsylvania indicates, Black Americans' shifting status often hinged on the contested meaning of "freeman." A word that had ambiguously signified emancipation, land ownership, and citizenship thus became a demand for political rights in an era of franchise-expanding constitutions.[73] In *Sheppard Lee*, as in Jacksonian America more broadly, the term sometimes contrasts with "slave" and thus implicitly embraces free Blacks (including freedpeople); at others, it marks a qualification for political participation, sometimes tied to property ownership, which became increasingly prominent as democratic pressure eroded voting requirements.[74] Both sides of the term are visible in *Sheppard Lee*'s Longstraw episode. Lee-as-Longstraw, unaware that he has been carried across the Mason-Dixon line, sees a group of shackled African Americans and, philanthropically forgetting his own captivity, cries out, "Are these people slaves or freemen? and why dost thou conduct them thus in chains through the free state of Pennsylvania?" (*SL*, 312). Later, rallying a crowd in preparation for Longstraw's lynching as an abolitionist, a local politician hails his audience as "Gentlemen—fellow-freemen of Virginia!" (*SL*, 323). The term's utility in conjuring antithetical political positions depends, of course, on its variable racialization. Alternately signifying the mere absence of enslavement (for Blacks) and a claim to democratic but racially restrictive citizenship (for whites), it bears witness to the ways Quaker toleration, local opinion, and mass violence in 1830s Pennsylvania brought the question of Black political participation and marginalization to a head.

As the historian Christopher Malone has shown, whites in antebellum Pennsylvania displayed complex racial attitudes, overwhelmingly aiding freedom seekers even as they restricted the rights of free Blacks.[75] And as DeLombard points out, even among Garrisonian abolitionists, it was "easier...to affirm Black humanity than to achieve consensus regarding the equal status of African Americans in US law and culture."[76] This ambivalence is visible in *Sheppard Lee* and in Bird's remarks on race beyond the novel. Bird satirizes white abolitionists' hypocrisy by presenting Longstraw as "the African's friend" in theory but averse to African Americans in practice, with all the marks of conventional racist

[73] In an address given before numerous audiences, the working-class radical Seth Luther proclaimed, "We are not only determined to have the name of freemen, but that we will LIVE FREEMEN and DIE FREEMEN." *An Address to the Working Men of New England, on the State of Education, and on the Condition of the Producing Classes in Europe and America. With Particular Reference to the Effect of Manufacturing (as Now Conducted) on the Health and Happiness of the Poor, and on the Safety of Our Republic*, 2nd ed. (New York: Published at the Office of the Working Man's Advocate, by George H. Evans, 1833), 32.

[74] As Hoang Gia Phan has pointed out, the erasure of indentured servants meant that freedom and servitude were increasingly mapped onto—and naturalized as—race. Hoang Gia Phan, *Bonds of Citizenship: Law and the Labors of Emancipation* (New York: New York University Press, 2013), 20. Bird uses "freeman" in several political pieces, including the anonymously published "To Governor M'Duffie," *New-England Magazine* 8 (1835): 138–41. See Buffington, "From Freedom to Slavery," 244; Samuel Jones, *A Treatise on the Right of Suffrage, with an Appendix* (Boston: Otis, Broaders, 1842).

[75] Malone, *Between Freedom and Bondage*, 81–82.

[76] DeLombard, "Claims of the Humanitarian," 1779.

antipathy. He counts among the objects of his charitable activities "that other class of poor creatures, called negroes, whom, although allowed the name, and most of the privileges of freemen, their white brethren refuse to take to their bosoms, merely because they have black faces, woolly heads, and an ill savour of body" (*SL*, 276).[77] Bird's early notes for the novel offer a still harsher vision of philanthropic hypocrisy, in which Lee as "the Abolitionist" attends "a rendezvous for the Missionaries of Freedom," whom Bird portrays as cynical northern merchants, likely modeled on prominent American Anti-Slavery Society leaders Arthur and Lewis Tappan.[78] "Here they discuss the *reasons* for abolishing—1st. Slavery is against the laws of God; 2d. against the interests of man.—It is highly desirable to get rid of our black population altogether—1st because the [*sic*] eat so much corn as to make breadstuff high; 2dly. because they constitute a large portion of our population who are of no benefit to the New York shopkeepers,—whereas 2 mils. white men would buy at least 10 mils. of dry goods and groceries."[79]

This position is amplified in an enigmatic, undated text, reminiscent of Jefferson's *Notes on the State of Virginia*, written on a paper bearing the address of Bird's brother Henry: "Slavery is the moral cancer which is eating its way into the vitals of this otherwise healthful country; and, like the phisical [sic] disease, will, if not, in time, extirpated, root & branch, put a period, & a dreadful one, to its existence. Slavery should not be merely abolished,—there should be no negroes in the country. Few of their greatest friends would be willing to allow them *all* the privileges of the white man: but in time they may demand these."[80] "The text's language—"the privileges of the white man," "their greatest friends"—echoes Lee-as-Longstraw's: "the privileges of freemen," "the African's friend." Even more than in *Sheppard Lee*, geography is asked to supplement law. Bird sketches a "*Plan* to get rid of our negro popltn":

> March them west of the Stoney Mountains and form of a colony & nation at the mouth of the Columbia. Build them towns—furnish them with agricultl. implts. &c &c. Give them a white governor, to preside in a council of their own representatives—(Establish schools, &c.) And in a few generations when they will be able (as they soon will,) to take care of themselves, recognize them as an independent nation, and ratify with them a treaty of eternal amity. They will make good friends—they are bad foes....

[77] As noted above, he also harbors a freedom seeker but then assists in his recapture after he steals Longstraw's silver; Longstraw subsequently reports that his house was burned down in retribution by "the free Africans in town," a perverse reversal of the racial violence that periodically rocked 1830s Philadelphia. See Otter, *Philadelphia Stories*, 131–209.

[78] The Tappans were prominent New York silk and dry-goods merchants. Not only did AASS leadership include businessmen; "the 1830s AASS resembled a modern business enterprise." Teresa A. Goddu, *Selling Antislavery: Abolition and Mass Media in Antebellum America* (Philadelphia, PA: University of Pennsylvania Press, 2020), 10.

[79] RMBP, box 11, folder 259.

[80] RMBP, box 22, folder 296 (Politics: Writings, undated).

> The expense of this colony would be comparatively nothing; its difficulties few; its advantages incalculable....
>
> This plan is good—There is only one that would be easier or more effectual—& that is to murder 'em all.[81]

Is this fragment a burlesque of Jefferson's equivocation over slavery, or perhaps of the American Colonization Society, meant for inclusion in *Sheppard Lee* or another satirical text? Is its final gesture a sardonic jab at self-interested abolitionists, or perhaps at their political enemies, the white working-class perpetrators of mob violence? Or is the genocidal impulse Bird's own? Echoing both his arch depiction of abolitionist hypocrisy and his professed desire to flee the possibility of "admitting the negroes to the right of suffrage," it resists easy categorization as earnest or ironic, opinion or fiction.

In any case, in the stark alternatives it outlines for African Americans—expulsion via colonization or violent death—the fragment offers a chilling perspective on both Bird's flight south and *Sheppard Lee*'s play with life and death. Bird's move to Maryland, we might say, was precipitated by the imagined political reanimation of the disenfranchised, an operation that resembles nothing so much as Lee's final resuscitation, accomplished through galvanism and metempsychosis and consolidated by crossing state lines. The novel's exploration of Lee's simultaneous occupation of the "conditions" of death and life and his successive inhabitation of varied bodies is thus all the more remarkable in light of Bird's demands elsewhere for clear lines of demarcation: the "barrier of clouds and darkness and funeral adamant" that separates the living from the dead or the Rocky Mountains that might separate Blacks from whites.

"Ruined Accordg. to Law"

What happens, then, when the barrier between life and death is itself reduced to a legal fiction? Bird raises this question in an episode that he outlined in his notes for *Sheppard Lee* but excluded from the finished novel. He proposes that Lee inhabit the body of an ill-fated reformer: "A legislator from Maine—the maker of the law of 1835, for substituting life imprisonment, & *civil death*, for capital punishment. He is convicted of an offence of which he is not guilty, & the sentence takes effect. He is soon discovd. to be innocent, & pardoned; but his *wife has taken another husband, his children his property*, &c. & they laugh at his claims. Every body pities him, but he is ruined accordg. to law."[82]

[81] RMBP, box 22, folder 296 (Politics: Writings, undated).

[82] RMBP, box 11, folder 259.

How humane, this episode asks, is the substitution of a life sentence for the death penalty? Rather than consider the misfortunes of incarceration itself, the proposed episode centers on the consequences of legal status.[83] Civil death, traditionally reserved for outlaws and members of religious orders, renders a person dead in law while still alive in body. Bird's note emphasizes its key features: forfeiture of property and corruption of blood (inability to bequeath property or title). As Dayan has argued, civil death provided the framework for the inclusion of slavery in the Common Law, particularly insofar as attainder (the formal judgment of outlawry) was associated with the "taint" of racialized blood.[84] Stripped of legal connections to his wife, children, and property, the Maine legislator is a monk or a slave translated into the idiom of reformist, Protestant New England. Deprived of a bundle of fundamental legal capacities—marriage, property, heritability—he presents a negative image of Dewey's conception of personhood as a set of rights and duties—or to use Bird's term, faculties.

More clearly than any character in the finished novel, the Maine legislator figures the legal structure homologous to Sheppard Lee's metaphysical predicament. Life after civil death nightmarishly mirrors Lee's wondrous "faculty" of surviving his own demise. Perhaps Bird excluded the episode not because its politics were too local but rather because it offered too vertiginous a mis-en-abîme of *Sheppard Lee*'s central conceit. (It's worth noting that civil death, not mentioned in the Maine law, was Bird's own flourish.)[85] Lee, after all, maintains consciousness, memory, and narrative persona—the Lockean requirements for personhood—despite physical death and finds resurrection in a series of physical bodies up to and including his own; the Maine legislator retains bare life after his civil death but unlike Lee cannot resume his civil identity or reestablish the relationships and property bound to it. While Lee's immortality-by-succession resembles the "faculties of a most marvellous nature" produced by the corporation's extension of identity beyond the death of individual corporators, the Maine legislator episode reveals the corresponding possibility raised by the legal structures of civil death and slavery: bare survival in the face of the loss of central affordances of legal personhood—ruin according to law.

[83] The notes for *Sheppard Lee* also include planned episodes in which characters meet in prison. RMBP, box 11, folder 259.

[84] Dayan, *Law* 45–48.

[85] Looby suggests that Bird discarded the episode as "too local and time bound" (Looby, "Introduction," xxviii). Contemporaneous sources suggest that Maine's death penalty reform was widely reported and emulated in part by Massachusetts. Maine: Legislature, Committee on Capital Punishment, *Fifteenth Legislature. No. 25. House. Report of the Committee to Whom Was Referred the Several Memorials and Petitions for the Abolition of Capital Punishment* (Augusta, ME: William J. Condon, 1835); T. Purrington, *Report on Capital Punishment, Made to the Maine Legislature in 1836, by Hon. T. Purrington*, 3rd ed. (Washington: Gideon & Co., 1852), esp. 30. 46. See also John F. Galiher, Larry W. Koch, David Patrick Keys, and Teresa J. Guess, *America without the Death Penalty: States Leading the Way* (Lebanon, NH: Northeastern University Press/University Press of New England, 2002), 53–78.

This sketched episode, with particular poignancy, highlights the symmetry between the two legal structures that framed debates over personhood in 1830s Pennsylvania and the antebellum United States more broadly. By revealing the shared logic that governed newly ascendant corporations and politically excluded African Americans, Lee's metaphysical journey draws connections that the delegates of the 1837–38 convention could not—or dared not—articulate. Like Bird's "Apparitions," in which the mechanism of poetic sight underlies both the liability of false sensation and the faculty of imaginative genius, *Sheppard Lee* comes into clearest focus when it anatomizes the ways that the marvelous faculties of corporate power; the liabilities of disenfranchisement, slavery, and civil death; and even the naturalness of the so-called natural person are wrought by the law. If Lee's capacities and incapacities are the stuff of ghost stories or science fiction, they nonetheless crystallize the legal artifice—and the corresponding mutability—of the person that came to the fore in the 1830s.

In attending to the disorienting effects of what Mussawir and Parsley call the "discrete and self-conscious techniques of shaping the legal person" in the context of Jacksonian America, *Sheppard Lee* dramatizes the way both the law of racialized citizenship and the law of corporations, in strangely entangled ways, at once revealed and reshaped the legal affordances of personhood.[86] The next chapter, which turns its focus from the corporate person to the corporate form more broadly, is likewise centrally concerned with the corporation's faculties. In Irving's *Astoria*, a work of bombastic corporate propaganda that could hardly differ more from Bird's playful satire, the affordances of corporate form at the imperial scale—and the possibilities of a literary form that attempts to mirror and capture them—emerge with particular clarity.

The Corporate Forms of Antebellum US Literature. Peter Jaros, Oxford University Press. © Peter Jaros 2026.
DOI: 10.1093/9780198996491.003.0004

[86] Edward Mussawir and Connal Parsley, "The Law of Persons Today: At the Margins of Jurisprudence," *Law and Humanities* 11 (2017): 45.

4

Irving's *Astoria* and the Forms of Enterprise

Washington Irving's *Astoria, or Anecdotes of an Enterprise beyond the Rocky Mountains* (1836) is usually read, when it is read at all, as a lament for an unrealized empire and a call for US territorial expansion. The wide-ranging text narrates John Jacob Astor's designs for a Pacific fur empire, the foundation of the American Fur Company (AFC), the two voyages—by sea and by land—that he commissioned to found a trading fort at the mouth of the Columbia River, and the eventual sale of Fort Astoria during the War of 1812 to the Montreal-based North West Company. Near the end of *Astoria*, Irving sounds an elegiac note: "In a word, Astoria might have realized the anticipations of Mr. Astor, so well understood and appreciated by Mr. Jefferson, in gradually becoming a commercial empire beyond the Mountains, peopled by 'free and independent Americans, and linked with us by ties of blood and interest.'"[1] The tension between national identity and commercial empire that marks Jefferson's words also pervades Irving's text.

Critics have located *Astoria* among what Peter Antelyes describes as "tales of adventurous enterprise": narratives that conceived of the US as "a literary form, and American literature, the vehicle by which its boundaries were discovered, explored, expanded."[2] At the same time, *Astoria* appeared years before the Oregon Treaty and John O'Sullivan's famous coinage of "manifest destiny"; the events it recounts took place decades earlier yet. This chronology suggests that its national frame is retrospectively imposed on the political and historical situation Laura Doyle calls "inter-imperiality," the "conditions created by the violent histories of plural interacting empires and by interacting persons moving between and against empires."[3] In the years around 1810, the Columbia basin, occupied principally by Indigenous people, rich in furs, and distant from imperial metropoles, was less a proto-national space than a "strategic inter-imperial [zone]" in which British,

[1] Washington Irving, *Astoria: Or Anecdotes of an Enterprize beyond the Rocky Mountains*, in *Three Western Narratives*, ed. James P. Ronda (New York: Library of America, 2004), 596. Subsequent references in parentheses.

[2] Peter Antelyes, *Tales of Adventurous Enterprise: Washington Irving and the Poetics of Western Expansion* (New York: Columbia University Press, 1990), 17–18.

[3] Laura Doyle, "Inter-Imperiality: Dialectics in a Postcolonial World History," *Interventions* 16, no. 2 (2014): 160.

American, and Russian companies competed for the opportunity to profit as middlemen between Indigenous trappers and traders and global markets.[4]

While Irving's text sometimes imagines an expanding nation, it more frequently narrates a networked economic and political enterprise that is only incidentally national, with nodes including Astor's New York and Fort Astoria as well as Montreal, London, Hawaii, St. Petersburg, and Canton. Astute readers of *Astoria*, from the early reviewer Edward Everett to recent critics like Stephanie LeMenager and David Watson, have pointed out how the text both invokes the rhetoric of national expansion and veers outside the nation. For LeMenager, *Astoria* reveals "the unexpected results of...commercial imperialism: racial and ethnic mixing, dislocation, even de-nationalization" and thus presents "an alternate version of US manifest destiny...as imperialist, commercial, and anachronistically postnational."[5] Watson argues further that *Astoria* dramatizes two imperial logics, "territorial expansion" and "transnationally located" commerce, sometimes clashing but sometimes symbiotic: "the corporation deterritorializes the nation-state...while the nation-state grounds the corporation."[6] Such accounts echo a broader current in Americanist literary and cultural studies that has replaced national stories with imperial stories, reframed the romance of manifest destiny as the messy and brutal work of empire, and situated US continental hegemony in the contexts of hemispheric and overseas imperial projects.[7]

[4] Doyle, "Inter-Imperiality: Dialectics," 163. See also Frederick Merk, *The Oregon Question: Essays in Anglo-American Diplomacy and Politics* (Cambridge, MA: Harvard University Press, 1967); James P. Ronda, *Astoria and Empire* (Lincoln, NE: University of Nebraska Press, 1990). As Mary Louise Pratt has argued, "Every sphere of life in [the Americas] has been shaped by the layering and entanglement of empires and...by their long, lingering afterlives." "Language and the Afterlives of Empire," *PMLA* 130, no. 2 (2015): 349.

[5] Stephanie LeMenager, "Trading Stories: Washington Irving and the Global West," *American Literary History* 15, no. 4 (2003): 687, 684.

[6] David Watson, "Lawless Intervals: Washington Irving's Astoria and the Procession of Empire." *American Studies in Scandinavia* 42, no.1 (2010): 10, 21.

[7] Brian Harding suggests that *Astoria* exhibits the contradiction between "the belief that commerce was morally and culturally elevating" and its "story of greed, jealousy, and unscrupulous exploitation of the Indians by whites." "Washington Irving's Great Enterprise: Exploring American Values in the Western Writings," *Making America/Making American Literature: Franklin to Cooper*, ed. A. Robert Lee and W. M. Verhoeven (Amsterdam: Rodopi, 1996), 215. Eric Sundquist calls the literature of exploration and expansion constitutes "the new republic's first national literature"; he notes that Irving "minimize[s] the economic failure of the enterprise not only in order to glorify Astor himself as an exponent of Jacksonian capitalist energy but also to signal the coming American dominion over the continent." Eric Sundquist, "The Literature of Expansion and Race," *The Cambridge History of American Literature*, ed. Sacvan Bercovitch, Vol. 2 (Cambridge: Cambridge University Press, 1995), 129, 139. Patricia Roylance emphasizes the ways writers of antebellum imperial histories invoked not only the teleology of manifest destiny but also narratives of imperial eclipse and supersession. Patricia Roylance, *Eclipse of Empires: World History in Nineteenth-Century U.S. Literature and Culture* (Tuscaloosa, AL: University of Alabama Press, 2013), 3. See also Amy Kaplan, *The Anarchy of Empire in the Making of U.S. Culture* (Cambridge, MA: Harvard University Press, 2002); Amy Kaplan and Donald E. Pease, ed., *Cultures of United States Imperialism* (Durham, NC: Duke University Press, 1993).

As scholars of Indigenous America remind us, the seemingly natural connections between land, sovereignty, and nationhood are contingent products of colonial-Indigenous entanglement. Scholars in Native and Indigenous studies have long "recognize[d] land as more than property or territory," even as they have highlighted the ways that conceptions of territorial sovereignty have been used to strip Indigenous people of land since the Supreme Court cases known as the Marshall Trilogy, which recognized Native people as "domestic dependent nations," sovereign but subject to Federal jurisdiction, and lacking defensible territorial claims.[8] Those decisions, and their conception of Federal-Indigenous relations grounded in territorial control, fell between the events of *Astoria* and the book's 1836 publication. Its nationalist framing notwithstanding, Irving's text makes clear that control over land was marginal to both Indigenous and colonial conceptions of the Columbia basin. The great colonial fur trading companies—the Hudson's Bay and North West Company along with Astor's American Fur Company—occupied the space that historians of Indigenous America have called the "Native Inland Sea," a "middle ground" characterized by of hybrid networks of trade and overlapping and negotiation of Indigenous and colonial political and economic protocols.[9] At the same time, they represented a form non- (or not yet) territorial imperial power along the lines of the British East India Company (EIC), whose descendants include not only colonial states (the United States and Canada, British India) but also non-territorial multinationals, particularly oil and other resource extraction companies, that have operated in and shaped colonial landscapes.[10]

Although *Astoria*, which links its era's most celebrated writer and most celebrated capitalist in an imperial narrative of epic sweep, might appear a paradigmatic text for considerations of the literary history of US empire, Irving's text has remained relatively peripheral to such accounts. It regularly elicits frustration and distaste in the manner of Hugh Egan's succinct assessment: "*Astoria* does not possess the unity Irving thinks it does."[11] Assembled by Irving and his nephew Pierre Munro Irving from "the various papers, letters, and journals in the possession of Mr. Astor, written by various persons who have been in his

[8] Mishuana Goeman, "Land as Life: Unsettling the Logics of Containment," in *Native Studies Keywords*, ed. Stephanie Nohelani Teves, Andrea Smith, and Michelle H. Raheja (Tucson, AZ: University of Arizona Press, 2015), 72. The Marshall Trilogy comprises *Johnson v. McIntosh*, 21 U.S. 543 (1823); *Cherokee Nation v. Georgia*, 30 U.S. 1 (1831); *Worcester v. Georgia*, 31 U.S. 515 (1832). Marshall refers to tribes as "domestic dependent nations" in *Cherokee Nation v. Georgia*, 17.

[9] Ned Blackhawk, *The Rediscovery of America: Native Peoples and the Unmaking of U.S. History* (New Haven, CT: Yale University Press, 2023), 106–38; Richard White, *The Middle Ground: Indians, Empires, and Republics in the Great Lakes Region, 1650–1815*, Twentieth Anniversary ed. (New York: Cambridge University Press, 2011).

[10] See, for instance, Stephanie LeMenager, *Living Oil: Petroleum Culture in the American Century* (Oxford: Oxford University Press, 2014); Philip J. Stern, *Empire Incorporated: The Corporations That Built British Colonialism* (Cambridge, MA: Harvard University Press, 2023).

[11] Hugh Egan, "The Second-Hand Wilderness: History and Art in Irving's *Astoria*," *ATQ* 2 (1988): 266.

employ," including published and unpublished firsthand accounts, *Astoria* might fairly be described as a patchwork.[12] Indeed, the scale and shape of the AFC challenged both Astor's managerial control and Irving's narrative consolidation. Irving, Egan writes, presents Astor as an "armchair genius" whose supposedly "great scheme of commerce and colonization" is unequal to the messiness of Western commercial empire.[13] Irving's difficulty reining in his work thus parallels Astor's compromised management of his company. I would suggest that *Astoria*'s marginality—its unreadability or its unreadness—is inseparable from its grappling with the dynamics of corporate empire. It thus comes into clearer focus when we consider a third term alongside nation and empire: the corporation.

A reading of *Astoria* centered on the corporate form can reveal the ways Irving's text confronts both the facts of empire and the challenges inherent to narrating an entity that is neither an individual nor a state. Recent scholarship on *Astoria* frequently cites Irving's lament that despite efforts at permanent settlement in the West, "a great part of it will form a lawless interval between the abodes of civilized man" and give rise to "new and mongrel races, like new formations in geology, the amalgamation of the 'debris' and 'abrasions' of former races, civilized and savage" (*A*, 359). Invoking conflict, hybridity, and anarchy, not to mention racial anxiety, this moment works against Irving's appeals elsewhere to national identity and imperial teleology.[14] Such disorder, LeMenager argues, also marks the text's form: "what Irving called the 'disjointedness' of *Astoria* has to do with the fact that this nationalist, imperial history does not involve the occupation of land."[15] While such scholarship rightly emphasizes the corrosion of national and literary form in the face of empire, it only glancingly addresses the corporate form underlying both Astor's commercial empire and *Astoria*'s generic and narratological quirks. Attending to the corporation, located at the intersection of law, politics, and narrative, can reorient the dialectic of form and formlessness that critics have identified in *Astoria*. As a nominally unified but practically multifarious organizational structure, the corporate form afforded Astor both direct command and diffuseness; as a mode of governance only loosely attached to particular territory and reducible neither to the individual or the nation, it offered a flexible mode of imperial governance but struggled to achieve unity. Both company and book, then, are premised on the theoretical coherence of the

[12] Pierre Munro Irving, *The Life and Letters of Washington Irving* (New York: Putnam, 1862), Vol. 3, 63. Subsequent references in parentheses.

[13] Egan, "The Second-Hand Wilderness," 257, 264.

[14] Egan points out that *Astoria* is anchored by two topoi: conflict—among trading companies, native inhabitants, and rival empires—and hybridity. Egan, "The Second-Hand Wilderness," 257. LeMenager argues that *Astoria* discloses "a gap in…agrarian ideology," revealing how "multinational efforts toward profit" outweigh "the incorporation of lands…into the US." "Trading Stories," 684. Watson highlights the way Irving depicts "contamination by 'savagery'" as "at once the risk of colonial enterprises like Astor's and the pragmatic consequence of such commercial ventures." "Lawless Intervals," 8.

[15] LeMenager, "Trading Stories," 701.

corporation but marked by its practical multiplicity: the AFC consolidated varied commercial and imperial activities under the legal unity of its corporate name; *Astoria*, as corporate biography, imposes a retrospective unity on the company's fragmented history. We might thus, in a certain sense, consider Astor's corporation and Irving's text as mutually authorizing fictions. While legal doctrine had described the corporation as an artificial person and novelists and satirists had personified corporations as caricatures, mythical antagonists, or bit players in the lives of human protagonists, such portrayals rarely afforded the corporation its own life story. In this light, *Astoria* is unusual both in granting the corporation a narrative form and in attending to its ability to transcend the nation.[16]

Reading *Astoria* by way of the corporate form brings into focus what might otherwise seem disparate threads in recent studies of empire, and can illuminate the "anarchy" that Amy Kaplan identifies as integral to both empire itself and "the representation of U.S. imperialism."[17] Even the most laudatory narratives of empire, she notes, must contend with imperial violence and the conceptual and narrative instability to which it gives rise. As she suggests, early US imperialism foreshadows Michael Hardt and Antonio Negri's characterization of contemporary empire as "a *decentered* and *deterritorializing* apparatus of rule" mediated by multinational corporations.[18] On a related note, scholars including Lauren Benton, Philip Stern, and Joshua Barkan have shown the centrality of imperial trading companies to early modern formations of sovereignty and empire. Their work bolsters Paul Giles's claim that our "current transnational phase"—characterized more by multinational corporations than national empires—"actually has more in common with the so-called early national period... when national boundaries and habits were much less formed and settled."[19] This perspective casts Astor's business as an heir to early modern merchant companies as well as a precursor of today's multinational corporations.

Corporate in both subject and structure, *Astoria* tells a corporation's story at the same time as it models a capacious literary form in which assemblage, collectivity, and dispersed management take the place of coherence, singularity, and individual authority. In what follows, I examine *Astoria*'s central figure of *enterprise* and

[16] On late-nineteenth- and twentieth-century novels centered on corporate protagonists, see Siraganian, *Modernism and the Meaning of Corporate Persons* and Mueller, *The Corporation in the Nineteenth-Century American Imagination.*

[17] Kaplan, *Anarchy of Empire*, 13.

[18] Michael Hardt and Antonio Negri, *Empire* (Cambridge, MA: Harvard University Press, 2000), xii (italics original).

[19] Paul Giles, "The Deterritorialization of American Literature," *Shades of the Planet: American Literature as World Literature*, ed. Wai Chee Dimock and Lawrence Buell (Princeton, NJ: Princeton University Press, 2007), 54–55. Giles contests a transhistorical understanding of US imperialism that "seems often to extrapolate a view of American influence abroad from the realist epistemologies associated with the nationalist era at home, thereby simply extending the familiar domain of U.S. nationalism around the globe"; he argues that David Harvey's account of an antagonistic "dialectic between a territorial and a capitalist logic of power," mediated by deterritorialization, is fundamental to understanding contemporary empire (57).

its relations with three other key terms: *sovereignty*, *excursivity*, and *savagery*. *Enterprise* is what William Empson called a complex word, with linked and layered meanings and contexts that amount to a "compacted doctrine," and it anchors a network of keywords, in Raymond Williams's sense of a resonant, if contested, vocabulary.[20] Reading Irving's text through these keywords highlights the aspects of Astor's corporation that emerge from the company's form and constitute it as a compelling if baffling narrative protagonist. Irving presents the company as at once an animating spirit and an organizational structure (enterprise), as imperial actor (sovereignty), as form that outruns its own boundaries (excursivity), and as an entity that embraces imagined wildness rather than imposing metropolitan order on it (savagery). Approaching the text through this vocabulary highlights the composite, networked shapes shared by Irving's and Astor's "enterprises" and, more broadly, can orient us toward the intersection of literary and corporate forms. The characteristics of the corporation enabled Irving and Astor to recast commercial colonialism in terms that heroically and paradoxically synthesized metropolitan management and Indigenous ungovernability. *Astoria* thus showcases the affordances of the corporation both as a rhetorical strategy and as a form of governance.

Romancing Enterprise

Irving cared enough about the subtitle of *Astoria, or Anecdotes of an Enterprise beyond the Rocky Mountains* to carp about the "unwarranted liberties" his British publisher Richard Bentley took in truncating it to *Astoria; or, Enterprise beyond the Rocky Mountains*.[21] For contemporaneous readers, this change, along with the title page's identification of Irving as "author of 'The Sketch Book,' 'The Alhambra,' &c.," distanced *Astoria* from Irving's histories of the late 1820s and early 1830s and framed it as a romance.[22] The *London Spectator*'s notice registered surprise: "Instead of a novel, which the title, on its first announcement seemed to propose, *Astoria* is the history of as grand and comprehensive a commercial enterprise as ever was planned with any well-grounded prospect of success" (*LL*, 93). The *London and Westminster Review*'s reviewer recounts being "spell-bound by its many and varied beauties" while reminding readers that *Astoria* is "not a romance, but a plain, though exquisitely skilful description of a mercantile speculation."[23]

[20] William Empson, *The Structure of Complex Words* (London: Chatto & Windus, 1951), 41; Raymond Williams, *Keywords: A Vocabulary of Culture and Society* (1976) (new ed., New York: Oxford University Press, 2015), xxvii.

[21] Quoted by Ronda in Irving, *Three Western Narratives*, 985.

[22] *A History of the Life and Voyages of Christopher Columbus* (1828), *Voyages and Discoveries of the Companions of Columbus* (1831).

[23] Review of *Astoria; or an* [sic] *Enterprise beyond the Rocky Mountains* by Washington Irving (London: Bentley, 1837), *London and Westminster Review* 26 (1837): 320.

This confusion—feigned or otherwise—over *Astoria*'s genre indicates the different inflections "enterprise" could take in the 1830s. The term could refer, as Bentley had shrewdly recognized, to a narrative or a business. It could also indicate a character trait, a meaning on which Irving often relies. Indeed, "enterprise" holds *Astoria* together even as the word's multivalence threatens to fragment it. Irving writes to his nephew of his plan to write "a history of [Astor's] great colonial and commercial enterprise" (*LL*, 62). He lauds both "the enterprize and perseverance of a single merchant" (*A*, 195) and the spirit of the men Astor headhunted from the North West Company: "men seasoned to hardships, who cared for neither wind nor weather. They could live hard, lie hard, sleep hard, eat dogs!" and "were ready to do and suffer any thing for the good of the enterprize" (*A*, 214).[24] On the one hand, then, "enterprise" identifies Astor's AFC and, with it, the problem of telling a corporation's story. On the other, the term's semantic slipperiness suggests the difficulty of identifying it with a particular organizational or literary entity, even as it highlights the shared features of corporation and text. Associated with individual character and imperial undertaking as well as Astor's business, "enterprise" serves as the text's central figure yet draws attention away from the business entity at *Astoria*'s heart.

"Enterprise" already held a privileged place in literary accounts of the West when *Astoria* was published. In 1834, Robert Baird characterized Westerners' "*spirit of adventurous enterprise*: a willingness to go through any hardship or danger to accomplish an object," particularly "trade."[25] Irving's Western texts—*A Tour on the Prairies* (the first volume of *The Crayon Miscellany*, 1835), *Astoria*, and *The Adventures of Captain Bonneville* (1837)—were instrumental, according to Antelyes, in enshrining "tales of adventurous enterprise" as a literary genre that aligned individual bravery with commercial and territorial expansion. Featuring protagonists who were at once "adventurers…encountering 'hardship or danger'" and "enterprising opportunists" pursuing "profitable trade," such tales enabled "enterprise" to indicate "both the national mission…and a quality of individual character."[26] Irving's still more capacious use of "enterprise" allowed him to depict the AFC in antithetical ways: boldness and bureaucracy, private company and imperial mission, animating force and wide-ranging form.

This strategic ambiguity foreshadows the ambivalence that has long marked critics' accounts of *Astoria*'s merit and its genre. Early reviewers eventually recognized *Astoria* as history, yet later ones remained skeptical. With judgments ranging

[24] As the *OED* notes, "enterprise" has long comprehended any "bold, arduous, or momentous undertaking," particularly when it takes the form of "a firm, company, or business," while also signifying the "disposition or readiness to engage in undertakings of difficulty, risk, or danger."

[25] Robert Baird, *View of the Valley of the Mississippi, or the Emigrant's and Traveler's Guide to the West* (Philadelphia: H.S. Tanner, 1834), 102. I am indebted to Antelyes for identifying Baird's early use of "adventurous enterprise."

[26] Antelyes, *Tales of Adventurous Enterprise*, 2, 22.

from "hack work" to "romantic history in the mode of nineteenth-century scholarship," most twentieth-century scholars regarded *Astoria* more as a historiographical failure than an aesthetic success.[27] K. A. Spaulding concludes that Irving "imposed on the facts his own melodramatic fiction" to produce "a tale of adventure."[28] Wayne R. Kime, for one, defends *Astoria* as "both a scholarly and an artistic success," but acknowledges that the text quickly developed a "reputation as a 'non-history.'"[29] Subsequent historians have likewise challenged Irving's flattering presentation of Astor and his business.[30]

To characterize *Astoria*'s historiographical shortcomings as fiction, however, asserts an epistemological difference between fiction and history in place of a subtler aesthetic or generic distinction. Early nineteenth-century historians insisted that "the re-creation of the Past requires imaginative and literary skill" and regularly lionized Sir Walter Scott.[31] Moreover, because fiction and historiography alike aspired to literary authenticity—and had to contest claims of fraudulence—a flawed history hardly amounted to a fiction.[32] In histories from *A History of New York* onward, Irving reflects playfully and pointedly on the generic and aesthetic basis of history and even "consolidate[s] the various agents and events into repetitive patterns… [that] turn through the narrative like orbiting constellations."[33]

[27] Egan, "The Second-Hand Wilderness," 254.

[28] K. A. Spaulding, "A Note on *Astoria*: Irving's Use of the Robert Stuart Manuscript." *American Literature* 22.2 (1950): 152–53.

[29] Wayne R. Kime, "Washington Irving's Revision of the *Tonquin* Episode in *Astoria*," *Western American Literature* 4.1 (1969): 58, 51. Hiram Chittenden also defends *Astoria*'s historicity against Bancroft's charges of sycophancy, plagiarism, and dilettantism. *The American Fur Trade of the Far West*, 2 vols. (Stanford, CA: Academic Reprints, 1954), 1: 239–246. Kime acknowledges the many purposes Irving's historiographical writing served—from advocating for aggressive US policy on the Oregon question to consolidating his status as a professional writer and funding the construction of his Tarrytown estate. "The Author as Professional" 238, 247).

[30] See Merk, *The Oregon Question*; Ronda, *Astoria and Empire*, esp. 342. On the question of *Astoria*'s fictionality or historicity, see Kime, "Washington Irving's Revision," 51, n. 1; Egan, "The Second-Hand Wilderness," 254.

[31] David Levin, *History as Romantic Art: Bancroft, Prescott, Motley, and Parkman* (Stanford, CA: Stanford University Press, 1959), 9, 11. While early works of romantic history, like Weems's *Life of Washington* and Irving's own *History of New-York*, challenged readers' generic expectations, this mode was familiar "by the 1830's." George H. Callcott, *History in the United States, 1800–1860* (Baltimore, MD: Johns Hopkins University Press, 1970), 22. Eileen Ka-May Cheng contends that "early national historians at once defined truth in opposition to the novel and were influenced by the novel in their understanding of truth." *The Plain and Noble Garb of Truth: Nationalism and Impartiality in American Historical Writings, 1784–1860* (Athens, GA: University of Georgia Press, 2008), 52. This conception was challenged by the emerging professional historians of the late nineteenth century, who rejected their predecessors' "model of literary presentation." Peter Novick, *That Noble Dream: The "Objectivity Question" and the American Historical Profession* (Cambridge: Cambridge University Press, 1988), 45.

[32] As Lara Langer Cohen has argued, the antebellum ascendancy of imaginative literature occurs in tandem with a "literary discourse… obsess[ed] with fraudulence." Lara Langer Cohen, *The Fabrication of American Literature: Fraudulence and Antebellum Print Culture* (Philadelphia: University of Pennsylvania Press, 2012), 5.

[33] Jerome McGann "Washington Irving, *A History of New York*, and American History," *Early American Literature* 47.2 (2012): 359. As McGann points out, Irving's 1848 revisions to *A History* invoke Lewis and Clark and "the seeds of empire": an "ominous American story" that "Irving himself

It is thus unsurprising that *Astoria*'s early reviewers frame Irving's historiography in terms of literary aesthetics: the *London Spectator* praises *Astoria*'s "arrangement" as possessing "all the art of a fiction, yet without any apparent sacrifice of truth or exactness" (*LL*, 93). Fictionality, in this context, is a matter of aesthetic form or ingenuity, not truth-value; it suggests a homology between a well-wrought narrative and an auspiciously chartered corporation.

This understanding of fictionality as artful arrangement chimes with Simon Stern's contention that legal and literary notions of fictionality are neither identical nor entirely distinct. The term "legal fiction" is traditionally understood to indicate the law's incorporation of a "consciously false assumption" obtain a desired legal result while restricting the consequences that would follow from recognizing the assertion as true in fact.[34] As Stern points out, however, legal fictions rarely operate so clearly and restrictively: "the significance of the legal fiction lies not only in its starting point but also in what flows from it," such that "the fiction holds the seed of a plot," a "latent narrative potential."[35] Fictionality, in this sense, illuminates what Astor's corporation and Irving's book have in common: both are strategically crafted entities constructed from and productive of plots.

Reviewers' praise for Irving's craftsmanship echoes Irving's own admiration for the ingenious legal and rhetorical groundwork of the AFC, which artfully linked Astor—and the men, ships, and stores of furs that materially constituted his business—to the governments of New York and the United States. From its inception, the AFC was designed to impress partners, rivals, and governments as both well-grounded and fleet-footed. In 1808, New York State granted Astor license "to form a trading company" for the purpose of "carrying on an extensive trade with the native Indian inhabitants of America," which put it directly into competition with the Hudson's Bay and North West Companies. The charter's preamble insists that "an undertaking of such magnitude would require a greater capital than any individual or unincorporated association could well furnish."[36] Yet as Astor's biographer Kenneth Wiggins Porter notes, "the fact that Astor furnished all the capital [one million dollars] for the purposes of this Company" makes clear "the disingenuousness of the reason for its incorporation."[37] Even Irving acknowledges that Astor, "in fact, constituted the Company": "...for though he had a board of directors, they were merely nominal; the whole business was conducted

retells...often, most notably in *The Life and Voyages of Christopher Columbus, The Voyages and Discoveries of the Companions of Columbus*, and finally in *Astoria*" (372).

[34] Simon Stern, "Legal and Literary Fictions," *New Directions in Law and Literature*, ed. Elizabeth Anker and Bernadette Meyler. (Oxford: Oxford University Press, 2017), 316. Stern cites Lon fuller's notion of legal fiction as "consciously false assumption." "Legal Fictions." *Illinois Law Review* 25 (1930): 363–99.

[35] Stern, "Legal and Literary Fictions," 317.

[36] Kenneth Wiggins Porter, *John Jacob Astor: Business Man* (Cambridge, MA: Harvard University Press, 1931), Vol. 1, 413–14.

[37] Porter, *John Jacob Astor*, Vol. 1, 413.

on his plans, and with his resources, but he preferred to do so under the imposing and formidable aspect of a corporation, rather than in his individual name; and his policy was sagacious and effective" (*A*,197–98).

The charter goes on to propose that Astor's company will "conciliate the good will and affections of the Indian tribes toward the government and people of the United States, and may conduce to the peace and safety of our citizens inhabiting the territories bordering on the native Indian tribes"—a romantic account of US-Indigenous relations that contrasts with the shrewd bargaining and shifting alliances familiar to Astor from his early days in the "middle ground" of the fur trade.[38] It is the very tenuousness of Astor's rhetorical alignment of individual and national interest that prompts Irving's judgment of sagacity. Moreover, while the charter emphasizes national and continental contexts, Astor's aspirations were global. In 1810, with three Canadian and four American partners, he established the Pacific Fur Company (PFC) as a subsidiary of the AFC, with the purpose of founding a Pacific establishment for buying and processing pelts for the lucrative Russian and Chinese markets and warding off the North West and Hudson's Bay companies, which controlled most of the North American trade.[39] For Irving's purposes, the AFC's carefully narrated rationale and the "imposing and formidable aspect of a corporation" carry narrative weight beyond the legal consequences of incorporation. In its two aspects—as person and quasi-state—the corporation affords Astor an interface between individual and imperial forms of power.

This origin story can clarify *Astoria*'s depiction of the AFC as alternately authoritarian and anarchic, an extension of the nation-state and an alternative to it. Sometimes the Company appears as an imperial venture on the model of the East India Company or a national project aimed at continental dominance. At others, it is the inflated silhouette of Astor, a shrewd capitalist hero who would be at home in today's neoliberal discourse: "What government failed to effect...was at length brought about by the enterprize and perseverance of a single merchant, one of its adopted citizens; and this brings us to speak of the individual whose enterprize is the especial subject of the following pages" (*A*,195). Repeated here within a single sentence, "enterprize" links Astor's vigor and his company—and opposes both to sluggish bureaucracy. A few pages later, however, Astor's business appears as the leading edge of an imperial project both corporate and national: "A scheme of this kind...was too vast and hazardous for individual enterprize; it could only be undertaken by a company, under the sanction and protection of a

[38] Porter, *John Jacob Astor*, Vol. 1, 414. Incorporating also won Astor an expression of federal "approbation" that implied military support. Ronda, *Astoria and Empire*, 40. As I discuss below, such protection failed when it was most needed, when the United States abruptly withdrew the frigate *Adams*, which was to have accompanied Astor's ship *Enterprize* to Astoria. Blackhawk frames Astor as both a product of the networked, hybrid world of the fur trade as well as a harbinger of US territorial sovereignty. *The Rediscovery of America*, 216–18.

[39] Ronda, *Astoria and Empire*, 58, 62.

government" (*A*,203).[40] In this light, Astor's "sagacious and effective" charter strategy and Irving's "arrangement" of *Astoria* with "all the art of a fiction" indicate analogous, tactically (perhaps deviously) structured contrivances. Perhaps Bentley's subtitle—"Enterprise beyond the Rocky Mountains"—troubled Irving because it foregrounded this shared penchant for expedient romance.

In contrast, Irving's subtitle—"Anecdotes of an Enterprise beyond the Rocky Mountains"—emphasizes *Astoria*'s narrative challenge: to render a coherent "enterprise" from a multiplicity of meandering "anecdotes" that include business transactions, exploratory and quasi-diplomatic missions, and tales of wilderness hardship and fortitude. The book's stunning range, which spans from minute accounting for the *Tonquin*'s voyage via the Falkland Islands and Hawaii to ethnographic investigations of North American tribes and abstract speculation on imperial extraction economies, follows the vectors of the AFC's organizational and geographic dispersal. "Enterprise" indicates a heterogeneous network of company employees, indigenous allies and adversaries, and legal and political frameworks; it can name a complex whole (the AFC) even as it isolates particular, representative nodes (Astor, Fort Astoria, the maritime expedition leader Jonathan Thorn, and the overland expedition leader Wilson Price Hunt).

The tension between portraying "various hardy and eventful expeditions" of the Astorians and making the whole work cohere is evident throughout the text (*A*, 209). Chapters leap between different expeditionary groups; transitions are framed as excursions and returns. Frequent instances of prolepsis and analepsis promise but rarely deliver narrative coherence at a grand scale. At the end of the first volume, for instance, Irving foreshadows the adventures of the second: "Little did they dream of the hardships and perils by land and water, which were yet to be encountered in the frightful wilderness that intervened between them and the shores of the Pacific!" (*A*, 400). References to earlier events evidently tax the writer's memory as well as the reader's; at least seven times he uses conventional phrases such as "It will be recollected" or "the reader will perhaps recollect" (*A*, 338, 492). Irving describes his labor as "linking together the parts of this excursive narrative" (*A*, 538). Like Astor—"the master spirit of the enterprize, who regulated the springs of Astoria, at his residence in New York" (*A*, 475)—he is less a solitary genius than the operator of a complex mechanism. If Irving overstates Astor's mastery, he emphasizes the challenges of such orchestration in portraying his own authorship.

Irving regularly relies on the word "enterprise" as he moves between disparate episodes and scales: "[W]e will return for a moment to the master spirit of the enterprize" (*A*, 475); "[W]e...shall leave them to their fortunes, promising to take

[40] If anything, Irving understates the case: as historian James Ronda writes, "Astor had very nearly made the Pacific Fur Company another branch of government, placing himself at the cabinet table." *Astoria and Empire*, 52.

them up again at some future page, and to close the story of their persevering and illfated enterprize" (*A*, 496). At such moments, the tenuous connective tissue of *Astoria* is reduced to a single word. Yet to call *Astoria* a failure on these grounds would be to recapitulate its early reviewers' aesthetic criteria while reversing their judgment. Rather, through the text's oscillation between small-group ventures, the collective enterprise of the AFC/PFC, and the enterprising "master spirit," Irving highlights the homology between the narrative form adequate to corporate biography and the legal and organizational form of the corporation itself. While "enterprise" sometimes invokes virile agency (whether in New York or the Rocky Mountains, the fur trade or the book trade), the word's appearance at the narrative joints of *Astoria* indicates a network in which agency is distributed, mediated, and diluted, in which Irving's narrative management of the far-flung company parallels Astor's remote executive management.

The slippage in Irving's use of "enterprise" suggests not so much a lack of form as a form with manifestations at various scales—individual, company, state—yet irreducible to any one of them. This structure, I contend, emerges from the genealogy of the corporation and its imbrication in commercial empire. Like the corporate form itself, Irving's narration is artificial as means of representation yet effective as a form of power.

Commercial Empire and Corporate Sovereignty

Since the early modern era, the corporate form has been central both to the management of empire and to the constitution of sovereignty. As the English legal theorist Frederic Maitland reminds us, corporations served as agents of empire and nascent states: "an English joint-stock company which happed into a rulership of the Indies, . . . another English company which while its charter was still very new had become the puritan commonwealth of Massachusett's [sic] Bay."[41] Because corporations have acted as "a form of state and sovereign," Philip Stern points out, we need to recognize "a range of corporate communities"—his central example is the EIC—alongside the familiar categories of nation-state and empire in "the history of state formation and political thought."[42] Considered in this way, the corporation is at once a tool of the state and an alternative to it, occupying, in Barkan's words, "the ambiguous position of being closely intertwined with law while simultaneously formally separate from (and even opposed to) state power." This paradox, Barkan argues, arises from the early modern doctrine of police

[41] Frederic Maitland, "Translator's Introduction," Otto von Gierke, *Political Theories of the Middle Age* (1900) (Boston: Beacon, 1958), x.

[42] Philip J. Stern, *The Company-State: Corporate Sovereignty and the Early Modern Foundations of the British Empire in India* (New York: Oxford University Press, 2011), 14.

power: the delegation of the managerial work of governance via corporate charters that provide for "the extension of law as well as . . . suspensions, privileges, and immunities from law."[43] Because charters construed corporations as sovereign yet also subjected them to existing sovereigns, the corporation deserves particular attention in analyses of sovereignty, empire, norm, and exception.[44]

The AFC's charter allowed it to operate transnationally, nominally for the benefit of the United States, but practically as a sovereign entity in its own right. *Astoria* grapples with this doubleness by offering two contrasting models for the relationship between state and corporation. On the one hand, Irving shows how the North West Company (NWC) and AFC served as proxies for Britain and the United States and how, in consequence, Fort Astoria became a token of their rivalry in the War of 1812. On the other, by attending to the way Astor's enterprise and its competitors were by turns private, national, and transnational, he reveals that companies were not simply agents of states. As LeMenager rightly notes, "the power [Irving] discerned in Astor's trading venture was more amorphous and more dangerous than that of an imperial state."[45] In an 1840 review in the *Knickerbocker Magazine*, Irving recruits Astor into a narrative of "the progressive steps of discovery and occupation by which we [the United States] acquired an indefeasible right to the Oregon territory." He complains that "Astoria, our original seat of empire, has been turned into a British fortified post and trading-house" occupied by "a mere trading company." In a moment to which LeMenager draws attention, Irving impugns Congress for failing to assert American claims against "wily Commerce," which he fears "will have woven its web over the whole country."[46] Yet his argument for US territorial sovereignty in the Northwest conveniently omits what *Astoria* makes plain: Astor, too, ran a trading company that wove a web of its own.

Despite Irving's explicit invocation of national and territorial frameworks, *Astoria* presents a layered and networked landscape in which individual, tribal, corporate, and national authority overlap. If Irving laments "the fact that the US had missed the glory days of mercantilism, when companies had the powers of nations and merchants were kings," *Astoria* nonetheless reveals the surprising persistence in the nineteenth century of the remnants of "an early modern world defined . . . [by] intersecting empires, pluralistic legal cultures, and a variety of shapes and forms of hybrid and competing jurisdictions."[47]

Early in *Astoria*, Irving turns his focus to the AFC's primary competitor, the NWC. Based in Montreal but exercising control over strategic trading routes and forts across North America, the Company exemplified the layered and networked

[43] Joshua Barkan, *Corporate Sovereignty* (Minneapolis, MN: University of Minnesota Press, 2013), 8.
[44] Barkan, *Corporate* Sovereignty, 37. [45] LeMenager, "Trading Stories," 702.
[46] Irving, "The 'Empire of the West'" (1840), *Miscellaneous Writings, 1803–1859*, Vol. 2: *Prose Writings, 1829–1855*, ed. Wayne R. Kime (Twayne, 1981), 135–36; LeMenager, *Trading Stories*, 689.
[47] LeMenager, *Trading Stories*, 702; Stern, *The Company-State*, 9.

sovereignty that historian Lauren Benton has described. Irving situates the NWC in a genealogy of sovereign corporations, comparing its "lordly sway over the wintry lakes and boundless forests of the Canadas" to "that of the East India Company over the voluptuous climes and magnificent realms of the Orient" (*A*, 188–89). (He leaves unanswered the question of how "boundless forests" might be governed.) Edward Everett's notice in the *North American Review* extends this comparison:

> Talk of Alexander and Cæsar, of Napoleon and Wellington; the British East India Company, the incorporate hero, the chartered despot of modern days, outshines them all.... truly astounding as the work of British power, achieved under the sanction of British laws;—as if it had been the object of her statesmen, out of her free institutions of constitutional liberty at home and her stupendous tyranny at the Antipodes, to build up the grandest political dualism the world has ever seen.... We are not quite so far from Astoria, in these discursive suggestions, as might at first be thought.[48]

Emerson's brief history identifies the "chartered despot" as the apotheosis of imperial sovereignty and tyranny. Like the EIC, the "incorporate hero" of *Astoria* was chartered as a trading company but quickly outgrew its nominal purpose. While the EIC's charter was eventually revised to grant it jurisdiction in its areas of operation, however, the fur companies' imperial ambitions centered, despite Irving's insistence, not on territory but on controlling strategic points and routes in the global trade.

A consideration of the AFC and its competitors reveals that networked commercial empire is not reducible to anarchy, de-civilization, or exception.[49] Imperial "discourse about lawlessness," Benton points out, relied on "ideas about wildness and barbarism, categories contrasted to civility as a property of Christendom or of particular European political communities," and did not simply reflect an existing legal order (or disorder). Such discourse often reveals more about ideology than it does about law or its absence: "the supposedly empty box of lawlessness," she contends, "was in fact full of law."[50] As Benton and others have argued, the binary of norm and exception thus offers a poor fit for the landscape of corporate empire. In place of this binary, recent historiography of empire stresses the "variety of individuals and corporate groups" involved in establishing and governing empires

[48] Everett Emerson, Review of *Astoria, or Anecdotes of an Enterprise beyond the Rocky Mountains*, by Washington Irving (Philadelphia: Carey, 1836), *The North American Review* 44 (1837): 203.

[49] See, for instance, Watson's suggestion that Irving's "lawless interval" is not simply a feature of the ungovernable West but also a figure for the way the AFC "operates within a state of exception produced by the nation-state" as "an extralegal, extra-national entity" even as it "continue[s] by other means the state's imperial mission." Watson, "Lawless Intervals," 19.

[50] Lauren Benton, *A Search for Sovereignty: Law and Geography in European Empires, 1400–1900* (Cambridge: Cambridge University Press, 2010), 31, 32–33.

through "an array of often-powerful legal prerogatives."[51] The imperial geography over which corporations exercised power comprised enclaves, corridors, and "areas of partial or shared sovereignty," conditions that engendered what Benton calls "layered sovereignties" and "[p]ockets of legal anomaly" rather than uniform, clearly demarcated spaces.[52] Neither Irving's frame of territorial empire nor recent critics' binaries of norm and exception, law-giving metropole and lawless colony fully capture the shape of Astor's enterprise. *Astoria*'s diverse and interconnected episodes reflect the deterritorialized networks and inter-imperial competition that these frameworks can obscure. Indeed, Irving's text offers a term that captures the convoluted relations of inside and outside, law and lawlessness that characterize both the AFC's vectors of power and the narrative vectors of the text itself: not exception but excursivity.

Excursivity

Irving opens the final chapter of *Astoria* with a promise "to gather up a few loose ends of this widely excursive narrative and conclude" (*A*, 589). "Excursive narrative" describes, in narratological terms, both *Astoria*'s digressive, unbounded narrative discourse and its narrated story, including the "trading excursions," "sporting excursions," and "hunting excursions" undertaken by Astor's agents and the Indigenous people with whom they came, often violently, into contact. At one point, Irving suggests that the introduction of Spanish horses transformed Indigenous nations into fearsome nomads just before apologizing for "wandering…into excursive speculations." Shortly thereafter he describes the "daring and excursive habits, and great dexterity in horse stealing" of the Crow or Apsáalooke nation, "savages, through whose mountain haunts the party would have to pass" (*A*, 361). The dynamic of excursivity is capacious enough to embrace Indigenous peoples and commercial imperialists, Astor's undertaking and Irving's text. It gathers what might otherwise seem radically different things—heroic narrative, historical speculation, nomadic corporate commerce, and violence between Indigenous peoples and company traders—under a shared figure of movement: running out into a realm of danger.

This keyword can illuminate the apparent paradox whereby Astor's commercial empire appears as both a projection of US power and the remnant of the law's withdrawal from an extraterritorial corporation. While the world *Astoria* pictures

[51] Benton, *A Search for Sovereignty*, 31. Philip Stern describes "a medley of companies and corporations, *conquistadores*, explorers, privateers, proprietors, and itinerant merchant, family, and religious networks." Stern, *The Company-State*, 10; Doyle highlights the "mutually serving if contested infrastructures" created by states and merchants even when as they "opposed or sabotaged each other." "Inter-Imperiality and Literary Studies in the Longer *Durée*," *PMLA* 130, no. 2 (2015): 340.

[52] Benton, *A Search for Sovereignty*, 2, 31, 287.

looks formless and lawless from the perspective of territorial, national sovereignty, it is structured by the excursive patterns of exploration, trade, and narrative to which nomadic corporate capitalism gives rise. The deterritorialized nature of the AFC—the aspect in which it looks least like a state—highlights its resemblance to Indigenous political formations that historians have come to acknowledge as empires—and which figured in racist, nationalist rhetoric as the savage foils to the spread of civilization.[53] Irving's descriptions of both corporate and Indigenous actors as excursive implicitly acknowledge this similarity.

Irving links the Astorians' disparate trajectories by figuratively traveling alongside them. At one point, he "propose[s] to accompany" a "little handful of adventurous men…in its long and perilous peregrinations" (*A*, 479–80); after two chapters, he "leave[s] them to their fortunes, promising to take them up again at some future page, and to close the story of their persevering and illfated enterprize" (*A*, 496). He tropes these departures and arrivals as returns—"we will return," "To return from this digression"—to an expedition party, a neglected storyline, or New York and Astor (*A*, 247, 364). Beside these excursions in his narration, Irving tracks the irregular circulation of narratives themselves. An emblem of this movement is the "tin case of despatches" that company clerk John Reed attempts to convey to Astor. The metal box attracts the attention of the indigenous inhabitants of Wish-ram and never reaches its destination (*A*, 468). Elsewhere, indigenous people enable narrative excursions, as when Wilson Price Hunt, en route to the mouth of the Columbia, learns of the establishment of Astoria from Indigenous interlocutors: "From these people Mr. Hunt for the first time received vague, but deeply interesting intelligence of that part of the enterprize which had proceeded by sea to the mouth of the Columbia. The Indians spoke of a number of white men who had built a large house at the mouth of the Great River, and surrounded it with palisades. None of them had been down to Astoria themselves; but rumours spread widely and rapidly from mouth to mouth, among the Indian tribes, and are carried to the heart of the interior by hunting parties and migratory hordes" (*A*, 446). A crucial part of the AFC's communications network, that is, comprises Indigenous people whom Irving denigrates as "savages" even as he stresses their observant narration: "It is surprising to notice how well this remote tribe of savages had learnt through intermediate gossips, the private feelings of the colonists at Astoria; it shews that Indians are not the incurious and indifferent observers that they have been represented" (*A*, 446–47). Astor's enterprise both engenders excursively circulating stories and conducts its business through them.

Although Irving playfully foregrounds *Astoria*'s disunity, its wanderings are modest compared to those of its sources. Three firsthand accounts by Astorians

[53] Pekka Hämäläinen, *The Comanche Empire* (New Haven, CT: Yale University Press, 2008).

appeared in the nineteenth century: Gabriel Franchère's *Narrative of a Voyage to the Northwest Coast of America in the Years 1811, 1812, 1813, and 1814* (1820 in French, 1854 in English), Ross Cox's *Adventures on the Columbia River* (1831), and Alexander Ross's *Adventures of the First Settlers on the Oregon or Columbia River* (1849). Disregarding *Astoria*'s nominal goal of formal unity and its national teleology, these texts veer more eccentrically across imperial, corporate, national, and tribal locations and identifications. Their publication history reveals how tenuously Astor's business was inserted retrospectively in a national teleology. All of these narratives first appeared outside of the United States: Franchère's *Relation* in Montreal and Cox's and Ross's texts in London (a US edition of Cox's work appeared in 1832). The works also feature occasional materials—Franchère's Chinook vocabulary, Cox's dedication to Lord Gower, and Ross's Chinook vocabulary and "Table of Weather at the Mouth of the Columbia"—that later editions omit. These paratexts project a landscape of transnational economic and cultural exchange rather than national teleology.[54] They indicate the networked texture of commercial enterprise that belies Irving's assertion of a "lawless interval" between stable narrative or governmental structures.

Franchère's *Narrative* offers a particularly illustrative foil to *Astoria*. First published in Montreal in 1820, it relates the author's journey aboard the *Tonquin* and his overland return to Montreal, his encounters with figures like King Kamehameha and John Young in the Pacific and fellow French Canadians in backcountry posts—a complex weave of the cross-currents of maritime commercial empire rather than a narrative of national development. The *Narrative* presents the Astoria enterprise as a tissue of excursions beyond the nation-state, emblematized by The *Tonquin*'s cosmopolitan crew of Hawaiians, Spaniards, Americans, Scotsmen, Portuguese, French, and "an Indian from Bombay," who had been "for the most part strangers to one another; but arrived at the river Columbia we were all friends, and regarded each other almost as brothers."[55]

[54] The writers' biographies likewise illustrate the inadequacy of the nation and the company as totalizing frames. Franchère returned to Montreal in 1814, where he was the AFC's chief local agent from 1828–34. He subsequently served the AFC and Pierre Chouteau's fur company in Sault Ste. Marie and New York, and eventually founded his own business in Brooklyn, though he maintained ties to Montreal and French Canada throughout his life. Cox, who worked for the NWC after the sale of Fort Astoria, eventually returned to his native Ireland, where he died in 1853. Ross also worked for the NWC, on behalf of which he was posted at Fort Okanagan, at the confluence of the Okanogan and Columbia Rivers. He married an Okanagan woman, Sally as a "country wife" (and eventually with formal recognition). After the North West/Hudson's Bay Company merger, he served the HBC and eventually managed the Red River colony (in present-day Manitoba), where he mediated between the HBC, Native Americans, and American trappers in pragmatic but unorthodox fashion—frequently struggling with authorities and contravening the HBC's official trade monopoly. He wrote two subsequent volumes covering his NWC and HBC careers: Alexander Ross, *The Fur Hunters of the Far West* (London, 1855); Alexander Ross, *The Red River Settlement* (London, 1856).

[55] Gabriel Franchère, *Narrative of a Voyage to the Northwest Coast of America in the Years 1811, 1812, 1813, and 1814, or the First American Settlement on the Pacific*, trans. J. V. Huntington (New York: Redfield, 1854), 68, 95.

When Franchère frames his journey historically, he does so in terms of comparative empires, juxtaposing his own travels with Napoleon's impending defeat at Waterloo: "On the 18th of June (a day which its next anniversary was to render for ever celebrated in the annals of the world), we re-embarked at an early hour: and the wind rising, spread sail, a thing we had not done before, since we quitted the river Columbia."[56] By placing his own 1814 descent of the Saskatchewan River and the Astorians' navigation of the Columbia beside Napoleon's fall, Franchère implicitly contrasts the expansive prospects of North American trading companies to the decline of European territorial empire. While Astor's company has lost the battle, Franchère suggests that commercial empire is winning the war.

By the time of the *Narrative*'s 1854 translation and publication in New York, Franchère had become, like Astor, an "adopted citizen" of the United States and a friend of the expansionist US senator Thomas Hart Benton. The preface to the second edition, published in New York in the wake of the 1846 Oregon Treaty, retrospectively situates Franchère's text in "the historical literature of the great country, which by adoption has become mine" and emphasizes the extension of US sovereignty over "a vast territory, which at no distant day may add two more bright stars to our national banner."[57] The translation occasionally inserts retrospective footnotes that shoehorn the national language of the 1850s into the messier landscape of the 1810s. Franchère annotates his description of the Nor'wester David Thompson's failed attempt to block the foundation of Astoria: "The consequence of this step would have been his taking possession of the country, and displaying the British flag, as an emblem of that possession and a guarantee of protection hereafter. He found himself too late, however, and the stars and stripes floating over *Astoria*. This note is not intended by the author as an after-thought: as the opinion it conveys was that which we all entertained at the time of that gentleman's visit."[58]

As Irving had done in 1840, Franchère rewrites the history of the Columbia valley as a story of US territorial sovereignty rather than inter-imperial competition in Indigenous territory. The disjunction between Franchère's rambling 1820 narrative of the fur trade and his subsequent attempt to reframe it for a midcentury US audience reveals, more starkly than *Astoria*, the distance between Astor's commercial project and its subsequent recuperation as a national narrative.

Savage Corporations

Recovering the excursive shape of the Astoria enterprise from these subsequently imposed national narratives reveals an underlying doubleness. In his accounts of

[56] Franchère, *Narrative of a Voyage*, 325.

[57] Franchère, *Narrative of a Voyage*, 4, 5–6.

[58] Franchère, *Narrative of a Voyage*, 122–23.

conflict among imperial corporations and Indigenous peoples, Irving repeatedly juxtaposes commerce and warfare. Although he sometimes opposes these two terms, they might better be understood as dialectically intertwined. War and commerce appear in two characteristic syntheses, one admirable and the other contemptible. The former nostalgically looks back to Astor's imperial corporation. In this scheme, violence and wilderness are not simply features of the landscape in which the AFC exercises commercial power but also the very forces that animate the corporation. By framing the Astorians' land and sea expeditions in martial language, Irving presents them as more heroic than mere trade. Astor appears as a capacious manager, anchored in the commercial metropole but enlivened by the frontier. In its combination of commercial daring, martial grit, and imperial ambition, his enterprise figures as the heir to the very "savage life" it threatens. In contrast, Irving presents the imperial brinksmanship and bargaining between the United States and Britain, from the handover of Fort Astoria to the strategic deferral of the Oregon question, as cynical mercantile calculation in military drag. His decided preference for the nostalgic and the heroic—for the savage corporation over the shrewd nation—underscores *Astoria*'s function as a retrospective view of a residual form of corporate empire rather an optimistic narrative of the incipient continental expansion of the United States.

In one sense, Irving's nostalgic tone recalls his earlier contributions to the myth of the Vanishing Indian. In *A History of New York* and the *Sketch-Book*'s "Traits of Indian Character" and "Philip of Pokanoket," Irving had critiqued triumphalist accounts of settler colonialism, deploying the figure of the noble savage doomed to disappearance even as he presented the extirpation of Northeast Native people as contingent colonial violence rather than historical necessity.[59] Despite this sympathetic portrayal, Irving's Indian romances ultimately endorsed what Jean O'Brien calls "the master narrative of…replacing 'uncivilized' peoples…illogically rooted in nature, tradition, and superstition" with "the 'civilized' order of culture, science, and reason," a narrative linked to the termination of New England tribes' political status in the nineteenth century.[60] *Astoria*, with its endorsement of commercial colonialism and colder portrayal of Indigenous people, diverges from his earlier texts.[61] While Irving contrasts savage virtues to the corruption of commercial life, he decouples these character traits from ethnicity. He represents savagery, embodied by white and Indigenous actors alike, as a form of romantic heroism threatened by modernity. NWC partners are

[59] Washington Irving, *A History of New York* (1809), ed. Michael L. Black and Nancy B. Black (Boston: Twayne, 1984); Washington Irving, *The Sketch Book of Geoffrey Crayon, Gent.* (1819-20), ed. Haskell Springer (Boston: Twayne, 1978).

[60] Jean M. O'Brien, *Firsting and Lasting: Writing Indians Out of Existence in New England* (Minneapolis, MN: University of Minnesota Press, 2010), xxi.

[61] Andrew Burstein argues that *Astoria* and *Captain Bonneville* mark a major shift in Irving's treatment of Native Americans. *The Original Knickerbocker: The Life of Washington Irving* (New York: Basic Books, 2007), 287, 343.

cast as noble savages, "ascend[ing] the rivers in great state, like sovereigns making a progress: or rather like highland chieftains navigating their subject lakes"; the accompanying "Canadian voyageurs, as obedient as highland clansmen," are curious hybrids, with "dress...half civilized half savage" and "language...of the same pyebald character, being a French patois, embroidered with Indian and English words and phrases" (*A*, 191, 212).[62] Framing savagery not as the unspoiled other of corporate empire but as the hybridity to which it gives rise, Irving describes company agents as heroically and tragically wild: "But we are talking of things that are fast fading away! The march of mechanical invention is driving every thing poetical before it. The steamboats which are fast dispelling the wildness and romance of our lakes and rivers and aiding to subdue the world into the commonplace, are proving as fatal to the race of the Canadian voyageurs as they have been to that of the boatmen of the Mississippi" (*A*, 213). Commercial empire emerges as the refuge of primitive valor in a changing world—and eventually as an object of nostalgia in itself.

Likewise, Irving identifies savage hybridity as the chief qualification for participants in Wilson Price Hunt's overland expedition: "the proper kind of men were American hunters, experienced in savage life and savage warfare and possessed of the true game spirit of the West" (*A*, 292). He contrasts them to Indigenous people corrupted by commerce, who are "worthless dogs" inhabiting "noted fishing places...which, like our great cities, may with propriety be called the head quarters of vitiated principles" (*A*, 261–62).[63] Rather than an unspoiled wilderness, the West, for Irving, is a zone of overlapping imperial, racial, and even species claims. Indigenous trappers, he writes, make "deadly war upon that sagacious, but ill fated animal"—the beaver—"who in general lived in peaceful insignificance among his Indian neighbors, before the intrusion of the white trader" (*A*, 444). He approvingly quotes a prediction of the decline of the fur trade: "In North America, the animals are slowly decreasing.... They recede with the aborigines, before the tide of civilization; but a diminished supply will remain in the mountains and uncultivated tracts of this and other countries, if the avidity of the hunter can be restrained within proper limitations" (*A*, 609).[64] Here the atavistic "avidity" of hunters, whether white or Indigenous, functions ironically as the leading edge of the "tide of civilization." The global demand for furs appears in

[62] Franchère notes similarly that "our Canadian boatmen, having their hats decorated with particolored ribands and feathers, [were] taken by the Americans for so many wild Indians." Franchère, *Narrative of a Voyage*, 25. Richard White devotes extended attention to the role of the fur trade and *voyageurs* and *coureurs de bois*. White, *The Middle Ground*, 94–141.

[63] Irving's unnamed source recalls Jefferson: "Corruption of morals...is the mark set on those, who...depend for [their subsistence] on the casualties and caprice of customers." Thomas Jefferson, *Notes on the State of Virginia* (1781), ed. William Peden (Chapel Hill, NC: University of North Carolina Press, 1996), 165.

[64] This article appears as part of Gideon Algernon Mantell's *The Wonders of Geology* (London: Relfe and Fletcher, 1838) and in "The World We Live in, no. IV.," *Blackwood's Edinburgh Magazine* 41 (1837): 163–72.

the guise of hunters' savagery, penetrating the abode of metonymically linked "animals" and "aborigines."

Elsewhere, however, Irving offers a more conventional account of the Vanishing Indian, paraphrased from AFC partner Hunt. Hunt laments the "continual war" of "the most harassing kind" between tribes on the Missouri River and spins it into a Hobbesian vision that exonerates genocidal "civilization" by blaming the nature of Native people themselves:

> The lonely hunter, the wandering wayfarer, the poor squaw, cutting wood or gathering corn, was liable to be surprized and slaughtered.... That the race of red men should diminish from year to year, and so few should survive of the numerous nations which evidently once peopled the vast regions of the west, is nothing surprising; it is rather matter of surprize that so many should survive, for the existance of a savage in these parts seems little better than a prolonged and all besetting death. It is, in fact, a caricature of the boasted romance of feudal times; chivalry in its native and uncultured state, and knight errantry run wild. (*A*, 310–11)

If Hunt's theory of "knight errantry run wild" helps Irving to explain the wildness of the West, it also contrasts with Irving's predominant account of the feral, hybrid capitalism embodied by white hunters and fur companies.[65] While Irving laments the decline of Indigenous peoples, he envisions the reincarnation of the "spirit of the West" in a corporate body.

A striking microcosm of atavistic enterprise arises during Hunt's overland expedition when PFC member Joseph Miller gives up his stake in the company for "the rude life of a hunter." His fellows are astonished: the urbane Miller appears "little fitted" for his new vocation, with its "precarious and slender profits... beneath the prospects of one who held a share in the general enterprize" (*A*, 405). Yet Miller, as Irving portrays him, does not abjure business for the wilderness but rather enters a different—if less profitable—line of work. The hunting party's expedition—"their undertaking" or "their enterprize" (*A*, 405)—appears as a microcosm of Astor's Company. The seemingly wild West is traversed by a corporate network: "small knots of trappers and hunters... distributed about the wilderness by the fur companies"; at the same time, these commercial agents are wild, "like cranes and bitterns, haunt[ing] its solitary streams" (*A*, 405). Irving's trope of the savage corporation offers a vision of enterprise as heroically excursive at the disparate scales of individual character and imperial company. As he presents things, the agents of colonial capitalism prove themselves the rightful heirs to declining noble savages, not as avatars of civilization but as a dialectical synthesis of archaic savagery and capitalist modernity.

[65] Compare Tocqueville's account of native Americans' "uncivilized independence." Alexis de Tocqueville, *Democracy in America*, trans. Gerald Bevan (New York: Penguin, 2003), 373.

This pattern continues in the episode of the *Tonquin*'s destruction, which further complicates the commonplace opposition of white commerce and Native valor. Irving follows the ship to Neweetee (now Victoria, British Columbia), a port whose inhabitants are experienced in trade with British and American coasting vessels. Irving describes the *Tonquin*'s captain Jonathan Thorn, "a plain, straightforward sailor, who never had two minds nor two prices in his dealings," as "totally wanting in the chicanery of traffic" (*A*, 266). When the savvy Salishan elder Nookamis refuses to bargain with him, the captain humiliates chief by pushing him overboard. In retaliation, Nookamis's men attack the ship under the pretense of a trading visit. Ultimately the ship's clerk Lewis carries out a plan "to decoy as many of the savages on board as possible, then to set fire to the powder magazine, and terminate his life by a signal act of vengeance," killing "upwards of a hundred savages" (*A*, 270). His companions on land are killed in retribution "with all the lingering tortures of savage cruelty" (*A*, 271). Although Irving reserves the term "savage" for Indigenous actors, he portrays both whites and Indigenous people as adhering to an ethic of honor and revenge that overrides considerations of commercial or national interest. In the wake all this destruction, he draws a pragmatic moral: "It is a catastrophe that shows the importance in all enterprizes of moment, to keep in mind the general instructions of the sagacious heads which devise them" (*A*, 271). His talk of "enterprizes of moment" and "sagacious heads" resituates the *Tonquin* disaster in the sphere of commerce and prioritizes capitalist rationality over violence. Yet Irving's repeated insistence on Astor's commercial daring suggests a synthesis of savagery and sagacity, a dynamic that emerges particularly in Irving's account of the handover of Fort Astoria to the North West Company.

In January 1813, NWC partner John George McTavish arrived at Astoria with startling news: the United States and Britain were at war, and the armed ship *Isaac Todd* was on its way to Astoria to consolidate British claims over the Northwest Coast. The fort lacked supplies and defense, and its occupants were losing hope in the anticipated return of supply ship *Beaver*, carrying Hunt and needed trade goods. Managing partners Duncan McDougall and Donald McKenzie determined "to abandon the establishment in the course of the following spring" (*A*, 551). Citing "the 16th article of the Company's agreement," Irving stresses the technical legitimacy of the decision but casts doubt on McDougall's motives (*A*, 560). In October, McDougall handed over the fort and sold its inventory of fur to McTavish and the NWC for "about a third of its real value" (*A*, 583). McDougall soon became a partner of the NWC leading AFC partners and Astor himself to entertain "strong doubts as to his loyal devotion to the cause" (*A*, 558). Franchère writes more bluntly that McDougall would be marked by "the charge of treason to Mr. Astor's interests."[66] In Irving's account, the last word belongs to

[66] Franchère, *Narrative of a Voyage*, 204.

Astor: "Had our place and our property...been fairly captured, I should have preferred it. I should not feel as if I were disgraced" (*A*, 584). Presenting the perspectives of diverse parties, including the crew of the British warship *Racoon*, NWC employees, and the Chinook leader Concomly—the Astorians' most important indigenous interlocutor—Irving ultimately stresses their consensus: McDougall's compromised sale of Astoria reveals the superiority of martial to commercial ethics.

The crew of the *Racoon* likewise registers "disappointment...when they learnt that their warlike attack upon Astoria had been forestalled by a snug commercial arrangement; that their anticipated booty had become British property in the regular course of traffic" (*A*, 586). The commercial tail wags the imperial dog as "shrewd men of traffic" reduce military men to mere tools. This perspective casts the "sagacious" Astor in an ambiguous light. As Irving notes, Astor had successfully petitioned the US government for a naval escort for his supply ship *Enterprize*, which was withdrawn when the frigate *Adams* was diverted to combat British ships on Lake Ontario. While Irving usually endorses Astor's insistence on the synthesis of commercial and national interest, the poignant synecdoche of "the Enterprize...unloaded and dismantled" (*A*, 563) reveals the point at which they diverge.

Particularly illuminating is Concomly's perspective, which Irving uses in order to contrast romanticized Indian chivalry and commercial cowardice. Concomly had consolidated his bonds with the AFC with the marriage of his daughter to McDougall. The "Indian warriors" he supplies "to repel the strangers" look scornfully on the sale of Astoria: "It was explained to them as being a friendly arrangement and transfer, but they shook their heads grimly and considered it an act of subjugation of their ancient allies....As to Concomly he no longer prided himself upon his White son in law, but, whenever he was asked about him shook his head and replied that his daughter had made a mistake, and, instead of getting a great warrior for a husband, had married herself to a squaw" (*A*, 588).

If Irving savors Concomly's picturesquely patriarchal rhetoric, he also endorses the Natives' excoriation of McDougall and highlights Concomly's similarity to Astor. While Concomly, like Astor himself, is a man of trade, both use the rhetoric of chivalric (and misogynistic) honor to defuse charges of self-interest. Irving even offers Astor's wealth as proof of his noble intentions: "Indeed it is due to him to say that he was not actuated by mere motives of individual profit. He was already wealthy beyond the ordinary desires of man, but he now aspired to that honorable fame which is awarded to men of similar scope of mind, who by their great commercial enterprizes have enriched nations, peopled wildernesses, and extended the bounds of empire" (*A*, 205). His reluctance to abandon Fort Astoria, expressed in a letter to Hunt, bolsters this appeal: "If my object was merely gain of money I should say think whether it is best to save what we can and abandon the place, but the very idea is like a dagger to my heart" (*A*, 541). By distancing Astor from the vulgarity of gain, Irving frames him as Concomly's moral equal; at the same time, by highlighting Astor's synthesis of commerce and warfare he justifies his ascendancy at a moment in which Concomly's warrior ethic seems destined to fade. Irving thus implies that Concomly's martial spirit can only survive in the form of the deterritorialized imperial corporation. By this logic, Astor's company inherits Indigenous heroism even at the expense of Indigenous lives.

As this carefully presented equivalence of one chivalric patriarch in tragic decline and another destined for power and fame suggests, Irving's portrayal of fur traders as at once an atavistic remnant and the advance guard of empire is no mere romantic quirk. Rather, the romance of "savage life" closes the gap between the spirit of the West and the spirit of enterprise, the tragic trope of the Vanishing Indian and the ascendant trope of the adventure capitalist. The violence that might mar Astor's enterprise ultimately elevates it above mere commerce; the martial ethic that Irving attributes to Indigenous people is tragically doomed, except when it is taken up by or sublated as the deterritorialized imperial corporation. The form of the imperial corporation, in other words, affords Irving the imaginative means to reconcile romantic nostalgia and uncompromising economic and territorial expansion. Ironically, it is the disgraced McDougall, a commercial man in imperial clothing, who bears an uncanny resemblance to Astor. Presenting him instead as a foil enables Irving to deemphasize the commercial and transnational aspects of the enterprise—and to write Astor into a history of territorial, national empire. Yet just as *Astoria* inherits the rambling, excursive shape of commercial empire, Irving's vision of martial-commercial heroism reveals its origins in the era of corporate sovereignty.

Astoria, like the corporation at its center, thus juxtaposes a number of contrasting, if contemporaneous, visions of US/Indigenous relations. On the one hand, it relies on the topos of the Vanishing Indian and its implied story of civilizational succession. On the other, it frankly acknowledges the commercial and violent entanglements of Indigenous and colonial actors in Western North America, beyond the reach of US territorial sovereignty. Further, by presenting the savage corporation as the dialectical synthesis of Indigenous "savagery" and Western "civilization," it cynically justifies the dispossession of Native people even as it departs from the linear master narrative of civilizational progress. In doing so, it cruelly mirrors (and implicitly legitimates) the fate of the so-called Five Civilized Tribes, whose legal status as sovereign but dependent nations failed to stand in the way of Indian Removal. But we need not endorse Irving's conclusions to recognize the insight in his presentation of Native nations and corporations as uncanny doubles, contrasting incarnations of the paradox of sovereignty and dependence.

Conclusion: Corporate Authorship

In narrating a merchant's embodiment of the savage spirit of the West in an imperial corporation, *Astoria* tells something like its own origin story: the incorporation of an anarchic archive by an enterprising manager who balances imposed order and excursive sprawl. On September 15, 1834, Irving wrote to his nephew Pierre that Astor, anxious to "secure…the reputation of having originated the enterprise and founded the colony that are likely to have such important results in the history of commerce and colonization," had "applied to me repeatedly" to write an account of the AFC (*LL*, 60). Busy with other projects, Irving demurred until he found a solution suited to Astor's managerial logic: he asked Pierre "to take this subject in hand; to collate the various documents, collect verbal information, and reduce the whole to such perfection that I might be able to dress it up advantageously, and with little labor, for the press" (*LL*, 60–61). Pierre offered his services to Astor for $2000; Astor raised the figure to $3000 (*LL*, 62). Ensconced at Astor's Hell Gate estate on the then-bucolic Upper East Side of Manhattan, Pierre collated Astor's vast collection of materials—including company and private archives as well as Franchère's and Cox's published narratives—into a "crudely prepared" text for his uncle (*LL*, 61, 63). While Pierre would also receive a "special compensation from Mr. Irving for my literary jobwork," he was granted no authorial recognition; as his uncle wrote, "it is a sine qua non with Mr. Astor that my name should be to the work" (*LL*, 63). Irving, in turn, received payment only from his publishers (Carey, Lea & Blanchard in Philadelphia; Bentley in London) and thus avoided the charge of paid hackwork.[67] This division of labor and compensation, which allowed the Irvings to undertake the labor of research and publication on a rapid schedule without endangering the interest or reputation of any of the parties involved, recalls Astor's own managerial ingenuity and self-promotion. Pierre's research and Washingtons's reputation coalesced in a composite persona, unified under Irving's name yet irreducible to Irving himself. *Astoria*'s author was corporate in all but charter.

Although they could not have known the details of this arrangement, the Astorians who wrote back to Irving's text were suspicious of its well-connected author and highly mediated authorship. Alexander Ross sharply contrasts his own account to Irving's: "It is not an arm-chair narrative, derived from hearsay tales, but the result of practical experience on the spot. From beginning to end, I had personally to act my part in the scenes described; they passed under my own eyes; and the account altogether may derive more value from being authentic

[67] Pierre defends Irving from "the imputation [promulgated by Henry Schoolcraft]…that Mr. Astor gave the author five thousand dollars to take up his manuscripts" (*Life and Letters*, Vol. 3, 87). Yet as Antelyes notes, this assessment would persist: Hubert Howe Bancroft called *Astoria* a "well paid panegyric." Bancroft, *Tales of Adventurous Enterprise*, 152.

than from any adventitious embellishment bestowed on it."[68] Of course, the very faults Ross identifies—the mediation of "hearsay tales" and the "adventitious embellishment" of literary polish—constitute the value added by Irving's corporate authorship. Franchère similarly complains of "a long list of inaccuracies, more or less grave or trivial, in the beautifully written work of Mr. Irving," though he grants that "it would be tedious to go through the whole of them."[69]

I propose that we view these complaints less as signs of *Astoria*'s epistemological, ethical, or aesthetic failure than as evidence of its absorption of corporate management. In this light, the text's apparent formal lapses become indices—or affordances—of the distributed, incorporated form that structured author, text, and company alike. If *Astoria* is more coherently networked than it first appears, Irving's text also reveals that the corporate form can be messier and less monolithic than we might imagine. In our own era of multinational corporations that exercise virtual sovereignty in the wake of territorial empires, we would do well to attend to the literature of commercial empire—both for its perspectives on corporate power and for its vivid record of the narrative and rhetorical affordances and consequences of the corporate form.

Reading *Astoria*, then, tends to upset the neat periodization of the history of the corporation: the residual form of imperial merchant companies extends longer than has been recognized, and the emergent form of corporations as deterritorialized sovereigns predates modern multinationals. At the same time, the arc that leads from the EIC and AFC to twenty-first century corporations is not an inexorable progression but one path among many. As the following chapter demonstrates, such contingency is nowhere clearer than in the antebellum period's most ambitious projections of an incorporated future, as proposed by the Fourierist socialists of the Associationist movement.

The Corporate Forms of Antebellum US Literature. Peter Jaros, Oxford University Press. © Peter Jaros 2026.
DOI: 10.1093/9780198996491.003.0005

[68] Alexander Ross, *Adventures of the First Setters on the Oregon or Columbia River: Being a Narrative of the Expedition Fitted out by John Jacob Astor, to Establish the "Pacific Fur Company;" with an Account of Some Indian Tribes on the Coast of the Pacific* (London: Smith, Elder and Co., 1849), iv. Some subsequent critics concur: as I. S. MacLaren points out, Irving's efforts to make Astor the protagonist of the work run up against the stubborn fact of his distance from nearly all of its action: "More a Penelope than an Odysseus figure, he could only be seen in a romance of Astoria as a stay-at-home; with respect to action, the mainstay of romance, Astor can appear as little more than a paralysed, remote, sedentary, frustrated dreamer, desperately willing his men on." "Irving's Problems with History and Romance in *Astoria*," *Canadian Review of American Studies* 21, no. 1 (1990).

[69] Franchère, *Narrative of a Voyage*, 374.

5

A Company of Socialists

The Corporate Imaginary in Associationist Print

In 1843, the American socialist Albert Brisbane launched *The Phalanx* to energize, publicize, and connect country's nascent socialist movement. The periodical's title page presents an ambitious four-point program that includes "explain[ing] the system of universal Association…discovered by CHARLES FOURIER," offering "a frank and impartial criticism of the present false system of Society," treating "social, political, and religious questions on the broadest grounds of universality and impartiality," and "keep[ing] a general record of the progress of the doctrine of Association, and of social movements in different parts of the world" as well as serving as "the principal medium of communication between the Associations themselves and between them and the Public."[1] This mission cast Associationists, as American devotees of Fourier styled themselves, as both a pragmatic communications network and as a revolutionary vanguard. As Brisbane's sneering reference to the "present false system of Society" suggests, the periodical critiques capitalist modernity, yet it does so in a strikingly ambivalent fashion. In its third issue, a brief piece titled "Tyranny of Capital" and an article expounding the "Tendency of the Age to a Commercial Feudalism" are followed by a plea "To Capitalists," inviting investment in the recently founded American Phalanx, an intentional community on the banks of the Ohio River. While the former article denounces the "complete and revolting…tyranny exercised by Capital over the Laboring Classes under the present system of Hired Labor," the latter insists that "Association offers to the capitalist a mode of investment both safer and more profitable than can often be found in our existing state of society."[2] From its early days, the Associationist movement both framed capitalists as enemies and addressed them as investors.

Beyond mere opportunism or unexamined inconsistency, this contrast registers an acute double vision. This chapter argues that Associationists' apparently contradictory view of capitalism can be explained by their orientation toward the corporation, which from our perspective might seem naïve or incomprehensible. Like their contemporaries, Brisbane and his collaborators understood how powerful a vehicle for capitalist accumulation the corporate form could be. At the same time, they had not lost sight of its other uses—the manifold aims of association

[1] *The Phalanx* 1, no. 1 (October 5, 1843), 1.
[2] *The Phalanx* 1, no. 3 (December 5, 1843): 34, 43.

that contemporaries like Francis Lieber, Joseph Angell and Samuel Ames, and Alexis de Tocqueville had enumerated. Such a perspective has become vanishingly difficult to imagine in our age of corporate capitalism, in which the economic promise of capitalist investment and the catastrophic consequences of capitalist social organization are equally manifest. Associationists, however, held that a world violently transformed by capitalist organizations could be saved only by more efficient reorganization that retained the benefits of "Civilization" (the Associationist term of disparagement for nineteenth-century capitalist modernity and its accompanying social fragmentation) while rejecting its cruelties and inefficiencies.

The most canonical literary account of Associationism famously distances itself from social pronouncements. Nathaniel Hawthorne's preface to *The Blithedale Romance* frankly acknowledges the novel's debt to his time at Brook Farm but insists that *Blithedale*'s object is neither the particular persons he knew there nor the theories on which it was founded. Hawthorne acknowledges that "many readers will probably suspect a faint and not very faithful shadowing of Brook Farm, in Roxbury, which (now a little more than ten years ago) was occupied and cultivated by a company of socialists," and he "does not wish to deny, that he had this Community in his mind, and that (having had the good fortune, for a time, to be personally connected with it) he has occasionally availed himself of his actual reminiscences, in the hope of giving a more lifelike tint to the fancy-sketch in the following pages."[3] I will return, later in the chapter, to Hawthorne's play with memory and fancy, representation and aesthetic liberty; and to the overlaps and distinctions between Hawthorne's romantic aesthetics and Associationist theories of imagination. First, however, I'd suggest that the questions Hawthorne explicitly invites (How true a representation of Brook Farm is *Blithedale*? To what degree should we accept his disavowal of representing actual individuals or evaluating socialist theory?) can distract us from the more fundamental tension in his description of Brook Farm: is it "a company" or a "community"?

If "a company of socialists" intimates the casual association a company of revelers, it also calls up the grim pragmatism of a manufacturing company. "Community," on the other hand, suggests something holistic, rooted, and organic, if also more idealistic or utopian. Hawthorne's terms recall Lieber's distinction between "associations" (voluntary, temporary) and "societies" (which arise organically "from the fundamental relations themselves between the members"), even as the nature of an intentional community, at once holistic and deliberate, complicates Lieber's paradigm.[4] It's not surprising that "community" has become

[3] Nathaniel Hawthorne, *The Blithedale Romance* (1852), ed. Annette Kolodny (New York: Penguin, 1983), 1. Subsequent references in parentheses. On *Blithedale* and Brook Farm in the context of utopian movements, see Ashley Rattner, "No Such Faery Land, So Like the Real World," *Nathaniel Hawthorne Review* 47 (2021): 231–49.

[4] Francis Lieber, *Manual of Political Ethics: Designed Chiefly for the Use of Colleges and Students at Law* (Boston: Little, Brown, 1838), Vol. 1, 164.

the traditional term for discussing Brook Farm and related projects, which promised a collective life that was socially, affectively, and economically fulfilling. In this sense, "community" encapsulates Hawthorne's—and his narrator Miles Coverdale's—aesthetics of romantic longing, of rich if compromised nostalgia. Yet participants in both Fourierist phalanxes and non-Fourierist communities like the Hopedale and Northampton Associations carefully distanced themselves from the term "community." To mid-nineteenth-century ears, its associations with Shakers and Owenites suggested their scandalous notions of communal property and unorthodox sexual relations.[5] Brook Farm's official designation underwent a series of shifts: first an "Institute," then an "Association," and finally a "Phalanx." Its four successive founding documents established it as a joint-stock company, an organizational form it preserved when it was reorganized as a Fourierist Phalanx and chartered as a corporation by the Massachusetts Legislature.[6]

By describing *Blithedale* as a "fancy-sketch," Hawthorne foregrounds imagination as the central term of his literary aesthetics and a mechanism that grants him distance from both Brook Farm and socialist theory. Yet the imagination was also theoretically central to Associationists. *Pace* Hawthorne, we need not turn away from the less familiar "company" aspect of Associationism, with its cold overtones of business and military regimes, its emphasis on the organizational over the organic, its framing of membership as contractual rather than natural. While Brook Farm and related projects have been amply documented in the history of intentional communities, this chapter situates them amid nineteenth-century theories and practices of the corporation, particularly the print culture pioneered by religious and reform societies. And while Brook Farm plays an important role—both as a prominent Association and as one of the major centers of Associationist print culture and intellectual life—my object here is less a particular company of socialists than the Associationists' habit of both building and theorizing companies and organizational forms, with whose aesthetic, affective, and imaginative facets they, like Hawthorne, were fascinated.

It can be difficult to read early nineteenth-century socialist thought without interposing the lens of Marx, who derided Fourier and his contemporaries as utopian socialists. Associationists, including *Phalanx* editor and Fourier protégé Albert Brisbane, *New York Tribune* editor Horace Greeley, and Brook Farmers George and Sophia Ripley, Charles A. Dana, and John S. Dwight, have repeatedly

[5] A piece printed in the *Harbinger* is representative: "The principles which we Associationists profess have no connexion whatever with the Rappites, the Shakers, the Zoarites, or the Community system, either in their internal government, or professions of Faith." "Association—National Reform—Freedom of the Soil," *Harbinger* 4: 257.

[6] Sterling Delano notes the initial "Articles of Agreement," the "Articles of Association" of September 29, 1841, and the "Constitution" of January 18, 1844, which reorganized Brook Farm along explicitly Fourierist lines, and the revised constitution of March 20, 1845; incorporation took formal effect on May 1 of that year. Sterling Delano, *Brook Farm: The Dark Side of Utopia* (Cambridge, MA: Belknap Press, 2004), 351, n. 5, 142, 207.

been characterized as utopians, and their practical experiments—like the American Phalanx and longer-lived communities like Brook Farm and the North American Phalanx—as attempted utopias. Although some, like Ripley, self-consciously set out to found a "city of God," the epithet "utopian" is misleading. As Holly Jackson writes, "Ripley and his colleagues regarded their movement not as a utopian experiment but as a practical agenda for the fight against capitalism."[7] Associationist communities were not so much retreats from the world as laboratories for reengineering it. As Brisbane recognized early, both business corporations and municipal corporations offered frameworks for a transformed social order. Associationist communities organized themselves as joint-stock companies and frequently incorporated, appreciating both the security of state recognition and the order provided by corporate bylaws. As I will argue, Associationists made considerable investments, both theoretical and practical, in the corporate form. In their calls for capitalist investment in a post-capitalist future, Associationists can seem either perversely naïve or cravenly cynical. Yet their simultaneous embrace and critique of capital can help us see the daylight between the corporation, as legal and organizational form, and capitalism, as an entrenched formation of ownership, power, and economic production. Perhaps no social movement was either more dramatically opposed to *or* more closely aligned with mid-century corporate capitalism.

Recognizing the Associationist movement as a form of corporate life reveals the movement's worldliness, its attunement not only to abstract theory but also to contemporaneous practices of organization. Associationists recognized business corporations as powerful forms of social administration and extolled their organizational innovations even as they denounced the zero-sum economic and social order that those corporations anchored. Rather than escape from a fallen world, they boldly planned to reincorporate it by means of twin strategies: the deliberately ordered phalanx, a community of 1,600 harmoniously organized people, and a multi-tiered propaganda machine for the mass distribution of printed materials, aimed at bringing about a secular millennium.

Associationists' persistent attention to the intersections of the corporate form, aesthetic form, and social form can help us understand what both companies and socialism have to do with the circuits of print culture, the rhetorical and organizational strategies of propaganda, and the aesthetics of imagination. As this chapter argues, the most company-like facets of Associationism are in fact tied to the very aspects of socialist communities that Hawthorne described as conducive to romance: "essentially a daydream, and yet a fact—and thus offering an available foothold between fiction and reality." Although they were often derided as impractical visionaries, Associationists deliberately harnessed theories of affect

[7] Holly Jackson, *American Radicals: How Nineteenth-Century Protest Shaped the Nation* (New York: Crown, 2019), 116.

and imagination in order to formulate their practical appeal to a collective imaginary via mass media. In the Fourierist Association's multifaceted and intensely theorized relationship to both the corporation and the imagination we can see sustained attention to the performative constitution of social forms and the vivid fleshing out of a corporate imaginary. Historians of the Associationist movement including Charles Beecher, Carl Guarneri, and Sterling F. Delano have devoted considerable attention to Associationist theories of community. More recently, Kenneth Lipartito has pointed out how intentional communities both borrowed the corporate and joint-stock forms and left an organizational legacy for subsequent business corporations.[8] But the threads connecting Associationist theory, romantic aesthetics, and the corporate form have remained largely unexplored. Attending to them suggests a conception of romantic aesthetics grounded less in individual subjectivity than in the world-transforming practices of collective imagination.

This chapter examines the ways Associationists both theorized social forms—the joint-stock company, the township, the phalanx, the associated world—and embraced strategies of community organization, mass publication, and affective and aesthetic power. Attending to the ways that Associationists conceived of communities as companies—and vice versa—can reveal their underacknowledged contributions to the corporate imaginary as well as their consideration of social forms as both incubators for and manifestations of the imagination itself.

False and True Association

Associationists recognized a difference between corporatism and capitalism that has since become difficult to discern.[9] As Carl Guarneri notes, "In the 1840s, joint-stock organization was not yet identified exclusively with capitalist corporations but could be seen as a 'mutualist' mechanism, much like workers' benefit societies, which pooled individual risks and resources to enable a common good."[10] Corporations could be charities, voluntary associations, or powerful business

[8] See Carl Guarneri, *The Utopian Alternative*; Delano, *Brook Farm*; Jonathan Beecher, *Charles Fourier: The Visionary and His World* (Berkeley, CA: University of California Press, 1986); Kenneth Lipartito, "The Utopian Corporation," in *Constructing Corporate America: History, Politics, Culture*, ed. Kenneth Lipartito and David B. Sicilia (Oxford: Oxford University Press, 2004), 94–119. For an updated treatment of Associationism, centered on Brook Farm, see Jackson, *American Radicals*, 107–22.

[9] Associationists' ambivalence about the corporate form and aversion to conflict contrasts starkly to Marxist socialism. See, for instance, Brynnar Swenson, "The Prostitute to the King: The Corporate Form, Subsumption, and Periodization," *Cultural Critique* 89 (2015): 61–82, which follows Marx in treating the corporate form as a function of capitalism even as it attends to the corporate form as a systematic principle and not simply the shape of a single organization.

[10] Guarneri, *The Utopian Alternative*, 126. On mutual benefit societies, see also Kevin Butterfield, *The Making of Tocqueville's America: Law and Association in the Early United States* (Chicago: University of Chicago Press, 2015), 160–71.

and banking companies; they united members (sometimes substantively involved in their operation, sometimes only nominal) and investors (whose managerial participation was less significant than their financial stake); they governed their operations and guarded their status with constitutions and charters. Thus, while Fourierist Associations were not business corporations, the two species belonged to a shared genus, and their uncanny likeness emerged even where their differences became pronounced. Joint-stock companies claimed Associationists' attention because they "attested to the power of collective organization"; "large corporations and trade unions" indicated that "capitalists and workers were preparing for Harmonic society without even knowing it."[11]

Such preparation, however, hardly followed a linear course. Associationists emphasized both the similarities and the differences between capitalist forms of organization such as the Lowell Mills and industrial associations on Fourier's model. In a striking 1846 *Harbinger* article titled "False Association, Established by the Capitalists, Contrasted with True Association," Brisbane anatomizes the differences between capitalist and Associationist joint-stock entities even as he presents the two forms as variations on a theme. Although "our joint-stock manufacturing system, as it is now being established by the capitalists of our land" drew Brisbane's censure, it nonetheless demonstrated the viability of Associationist organizational principles.[12] Business on a mass scale created the conditions that demanded the establishment of a harmonious society even as it offered an imperfect model of that harmony: "It is to be borne in mind that these large manufactories are *Associations;* for they are established by joint-stock companies, and worked by large numbers of people, so that they combine two characteristics of associations, union of laborers and union of capitalists; they are, in addition, *industrial* associations, for they are engaged in one great branch of industry—manufactures. We state this particularly, because we wish to contrast them with the industrial associations which we aim at establishing."[13] While Brisbane emphasizes this contrast, from a twenty-first-century perspective the neglected similarities between Fourierist communities and business corporations may be more revealing. Because we have come to regard the corporate form as exclusively directed toward profit-making, Brisbane's characterization of capitalist manufacturing can seem at once caricatured and naïve: "Attention should be called to these false and oppressive industrial Associations, in which the sweat and blood of the producing classes are slowly transmuted into gold, a sacrifice to satiate the lust of mammon, the main spring of action of this age; and a remedy should be proposed before the system becomes universal and all powerful."[14] His critique is moral rather than structural. Singling out the effects of greed in "false and oppressive industrial Associations" sharpens his consternation that it constitutes "the main

[11] Guarneri, *The Utopian Alternative*, 144–45.
[12] *Harbinger* 3: 365–66.
[13] "False Association," *Harbinger* 3: 366.
[14] "False Association," *Harbinger* 3: 366.

spring of action of this age," on its way to becoming "universal and all powerful." Yet this moral language drives toward a strangely formal question, informed by Fourier's theory of the passions: how to divert destructive passions and reorganize the dynamic "system" powered by this "spring."

For Brisbane, capitalist manufacturing corporations shape a broader social system that he sometimes describes as unprecedented, but at others aligns with its precapitalist precursors: sovereigns and subjects, lords and serfs. Manufacturing corporations, he warns, may bring about "an *Industrial Feudalism*, or a gigantic system of industrial monopoly, in which Capital, with a rapacity and selfishness which have no term of comparison, will reign supreme, with a monied aristocracy for sovereign, and the laboring classes as its miserable serfs and hirelings."[15] Fourier had famously insisted that human desires could be made the engines of a just and egalitarian society. With his depiction of the artificial desires of artificial persons, Brisbane adopts Fourier's conception of passional attraction while also gesturing toward its limits. The unparalleled "rapacity and selfishness" of Capital are attributes of a carelessly constructed artificial being, rather than the passions of a natural one.

Although Brisbane's rhetoric is heated, its consistency suggests that his political idiom of feudal rule is neither fanciful nor metaphorical. Capitalists aren't *like* sovereigns; they *are* sovereigns. So, by his logic, are Associationists: "And now we ask opponents, which is the best system of Association, that which we propose, or that which your capitalists are establishing? Or, if this alternative of a true or false system of Industrial Association be denied, then, restricting the question to its narrowest limits:—Which is the most just and human organization, a joint-stock manufactory with its boarding-house arrangements such as our 'wise and humane rich' are establishing, or an Association such as our 'visionaries' and 'infidels' propose?"[16] Like Lieber in the *Encyclopaedia Americana*, Brisbane's corporate imaginary conceives of the corporate form as always already a political form. Joint-stock manufactories, like Fourierist Associations, are commonwealths in miniature. Sovereignty is neither simply imposed from above nor generated by social contract; rather, it inheres in organizational form itself. Thus, rather than reminding us of the business company's uncanny and parasitic statelikeness (as does Hobbes), Brisbane proposes that associations—whether "False Associations" or "True Associations"—are de facto political bodies. The boldness of his position can be difficult to recognize because of his repeated insistence that "our ills are social, not political"—his ascription, that is, of the label "political" only to the partisan politics with which he was disillusioned. But his expansive use of "social," which describes formal systems, associations, and assemblages at all scales, embraces the capacities of organizing and governing life.

[15] "False Association," *Harbinger* 3: 365.

[16] "False Association," *Harbinger* 3: 366.

Brisbane situates capitalist feudalism as a stage in a symmetrical historical order that recalls an explanatory diagram in *Social Destiny of Man* (Fig. 5.1): "Civilization commenced with a feudalism, and if there are not devotion and intelligence enough in the people to prevent such a catastrophe, it will, according to the law of contact of extremes, terminate in a feudalism." This transformation is inevitable, he warns, "if a true system of Association is not established"—which is to say, only the explicit structures of Association can protect against the superhuman passions and forces of capitalist avarice.[17] His view is noteworthy beyond its dramatization of Fourier's theory of history. While some nineteenth-century writers saw a residual feudalism in slavery, Brisbane posits a reemergent feudalism in capitalist wage-labor itself. He thus contrasts the bad joint-stock form of Lowell and Manchester manufacturing—in which capitalists exert unchecked sway—to the good joint-stock form of Association—in which members participate in and enjoy the joint-stock arrangement rather than simply being subject to it.

In Brisbane's scheme, the corporate form structures not only individual businesses but also larger systems. By centering his analysis on "our joint-stock manufacturing system, as it is now being established by the capitalists of our land," he frames corporate politics as at once an entrenched order and a work in progress.[18] The boundaries of such a system can be hard to establish: *a* corporation, *a* manufactory, *an* association take singular indefinite articles, but (capital-A) Association and the "manufacturing system" exist at higher and more abstract levels. While Brisbane contrasts two systems here, his focus on systematicity brings out a shared principle: the networked, modular structure that industrial capitalism and Association share.

As I have noted, despite denouncing capitalists as feudal overlords, Brisbane and his associates recognized the necessity of courting wealthy capitalist investors. E. P. Grant's prospectus for the American Phalanx, in its address "TO CAPITALISTS," captures some of Associationists' ambivalence toward this class: it acknowledges that "Of these, it is doubtless to be regretted that but few can be enlisted in any plan of radical reform." Yet the organizers warn investors lest their political objections get in the way of their business sense: "The sums which have been lost in civilization, after being invested in its choicest and most favored modes, almost defy computation or estimate. Witness its banks, insurance companies, and other similar institutions, the capital of many of which has been annihilated, while that of very few remains unimpaired. The capitalist who has trusted the plighted faith of sovereign States, has been scarcely less unfortunate."[19]

For its promoters, the American Phalanx not only shares organizational structures with the banks, insurance companies, and sovereign states that make up Civilization; it is also their direct competitor for investment. By promising a

[17] "False Association," *Harbinger* 3: 367.
[18] "False Association," *Harbinger* 3: 365–66.
[19] *Harbinger* 1: 44.

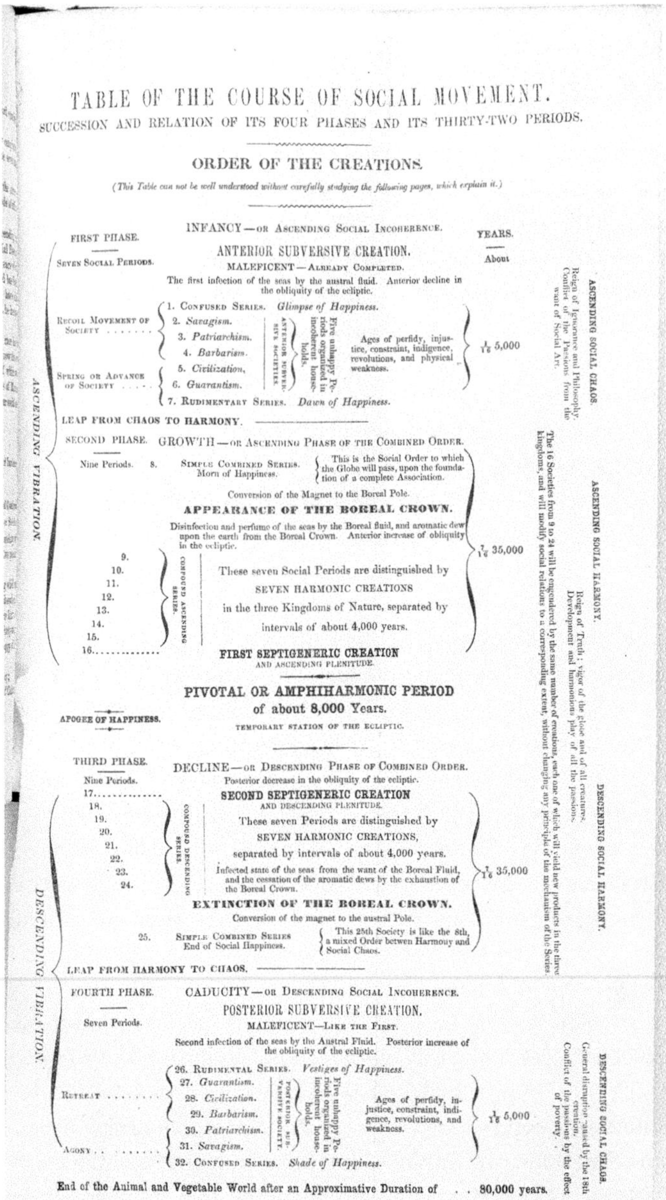

TABLE OF THE COURSE OF SOCIAL MOVEMENT.

SUCCESSION AND RELATION OF ITS FOUR PHASES AND ITS THIRTY-TWO PERIODS.

ORDER OF THE CREATIONS.

(This Table can not be well understood without carefully studying the following pages, which explain it.)

FIRST PHASE. — Seven Social Periods.

INFANCY—or Ascending Social Incoherence.

ANTERIOR SUBVERSIVE CREATION.

MALEFICENT—Already Completed.

The first infection of the seas by the austral fluid. Anterior decline in the obliquity of the ecliptic.

YEARS. About

Recoil Movement of Society . . . .

1. Confused Series. *Glimpse of Happiness.*
2. *Savagism.*
3. *Patriarchism.*
4. *Barbarism.*

Spring or Advance of Society . . . . .

5. *Civilization,*
6. *Guarantism.*
7. Rudimentary Series. *Dawn of Happiness.*

Anterior subversive societies. Five unhappy Periods organized in incoherent households. Ages of perfidy, injustice, constraint, indigence, revolutions, and physical weakness. — $\frac{1}{16}$ 5,000

ASCENDING SOCIAL CHAOS. Reign of Ignorance and Philosophy. Conflict of the Passions from the want of Social Art.

LEAP FROM CHAOS TO HARMONY.

SECOND PHASE. — Nine Periods.

GROWTH—or Ascending Phase of the Combined Order.

8. Simple Combined Series. Morn of Happiness. — This is the Social Order to which the Globe will pass, upon the foundation of a complete Association.

Conversion of the Magnet to the Boreal Pole.

APPEARANCE OF THE BOREAL CROWN.

Disinfection and perfume of the seas by the Boreal fluid, and aromatic dew upon the earth from the Boreal Crown. Anterior increase of obliquity in the ecliptic.

9. 10. 11. 12. 13. 14. 15. 16. . . . .

Compound ascending series. These seven Social Periods are distinguished by SEVEN HARMONIC CREATIONS in the three Kingdoms of Nature, separated by intervals of about 4,000 years. — $\frac{7}{16}$ 35,000

FIRST SEPTIGENERIC CREATION AND ASCENDING PLENITUDE.

ASCENDING VIBRATION.

APOGEE OF HAPPINESS.

PIVOTAL OR AMPHIHARMONIC PERIOD of about 8,000 Years.

TEMPORARY STATION OF THE ECLIPTIC.

ASCENDING SOCIAL HARMONY. DESCENDING SOCIAL HARMONY. Reign of Truth; vigor of the globe and of all creatures. Development and harmonious play of all the passions.

The 16 Societies from 9 to 24 will be engendered by the same number of creations, each one of which will yield new products in the three kingdoms, and will modify social relations to a corresponding extent, without changing any principle of the mechanism of the Series.

THIRD PHASE. — Nine Periods.

DECLINE—or Descending Phase of Combined Order.

Posterior decrease in the obliquity of the ecliptic.

17. . . . . SECOND SEPTIGENERIC CREATION AND DESCENDING PLENITUDE.

18. 19. 20. 21. 22. 23. 24.

Compound descending series. These seven Periods are distinguished by SEVEN HARMONIC CREATIONS, separated by intervals of about 4,000 years.

Infected state of the seas from the want of the Boreal Fluid, and the cessation of the aromatic dews by the exhaustion of the Boreal Crown. — $\frac{7}{16}$ 35,000

EXTINCTION OF THE BOREAL CROWN.

Conversion of the magnet to the austral Pole.

25. Simple Combined Series. End of Social Happiness. — This 25th Society is like the 8th, a mixed Order betwen Harmony and Social Chaos.

LEAP FROM HARMONY TO CHAOS.

FOURTH PHASE. — Seven Periods.

CADUCITY—or Descending Social Incoherence.

POSTERIOR SUBVERSIVE CREATION.

MALEFICENT—Like the First.

Second infection of the seas by the Austral Fluid. Posterior increase of the obliquity of the ecliptic.

26. Rudimental Series. *Vestiges of Happiness.*

Retreat . . . .

27. *Guarantism.*
28. *Civilization.*
29. *Barbarism.*
30. *Patriarchism.*

Agony . . . .

31. *Savagism.*
32. Confused Series. *Shade of Happiness.*

Posterior subversive society. Five unhappy Periods organized in incoherent households. Ages of perfidy, injustice, constraint, indigence, revolutions, and weakness. — $\frac{1}{16}$ 5,000

DESCENDING VIBRATION.

DESCENDING SOCIAL CHAOS. General disruption caused by the 18th creation. Conflict of the passions by the effect of poverty.

End of the Animal and Vegetable World after an Approximative Duration of . . 80,000 years.

Spiritual death of the Globe. End of nutation and rotation of the axis. Shifting of the Pole to the Equator. Natural death; fall and dissolution in the Milky Way.

Fig. 5.1 "Table of the Course of Social Movement." Charles Fourier and Albert Brisbane, *The Social Destiny of Man, or Theory of the Four Movements; with A Treatise on the Functions of the Human Passions and an outline of Fourier's System of Social Science* (New York: DeWitt and Blanchard, 1857). Courtesy, American Antiquarian Society.

guaranteed dividend to investors ("*the subsistence of the members alone* being preferred to their claim of seven per cent."), Grant's pitch both acknowledges the pragmatic necessity of outside capitalization and suggests that the avaricious passions of Civilization might be rechanneled into a socially productive and morally beneficent force. In this respect, it echoes Fourier's understanding of the power of the passions and their changing valences in different social orders: "If God had not intended all of you to live in a state of well-being, why would he have endowed all civilized peoples with an insatiable desire for wealth. The cupidity that you take for a vice is, on the contrary, a God-given drive which stimulates you to seek social states other than civilization, in which you recognize happiness without being able to enjoy it. It is now available to you, since the theory of Attraction opens before you the way to harmony."[20]

Some Associationists, like Hugh Doherty, the premier British exponent of Fourier, envisioned an even smoother transition from capitalist to Associationist political economy. More sanguine than Brisbane about corporate capitalism, Doherty emphasized the "associative power" of big business. In a letter to the *Harbinger* presenting a prospectus for the Associative Institute, devoted to the study and promotion of Fourier's social science, Doherty argued that the joint-stock form's advantages were palpable in the proliferation of businesses and voluntary associations alike. Despite the "imperfections" of existing organizations, he writes, "The advantages of combination are obvious. Joint-stock companies are rapidly supplanting individual enterprise, and the question of associative power is forcing itself *practically* on public attention." He thus insists that Associationists turn their attention to the proliferating associations around them: "In this, as in most other cases of true progress, theory comes after practice, to develop germs which have grown up spontaneously. Clubs and partnerships, societies and joint-stock companies, spring into life; and then the study of the new phenomena becomes imperative. Thus it is at present with associative science."[21] The editors of the *Harbinger* would come to agree. In a "Statement of Principles" printed under the masthead of issue 7, Volume 4, they lay out a broad Associationist program, a crucial section of which outlines the centrality of the joint-stock form to social reform. First, they emphasize pragmatic benefits of powerful collective coordination, what they call "The advantages and economies of combination in partnerships and companies." Further, the joint-stock form harnesses collective power without sacrificing individual autonomy over property, as did the schemes of collectivists like Shakers and Owenites, against whom the Associationists insistently defined themselves: "the individual reserves the

[20] Charles Fourier, *The Utopian Vision of Charles Fourier: Selected Texts on Work, Love, and Passionate Attraction*, trans. and ed. Jonathan Beecher and Richard Bienvenu (Boston: Beacon Press, 1971), 213.

[21] *Harbinger* 3: 319.

right to invest in that department in which he is specially interested; and to withdraw at any time after giving due notice." This individualist interpretation of joint-stock belonging highlights the similarities between businesses and communities and thus claims the joint-stock form as the harbinger for social transformation: "[T]he joint stock partnerships of capital, labor and skill" comprise "the matrix in which the serial organization is to crystalize."[22] By this reckoning, the joint-stock form was both advantageous in itself and integral to an Associationist conception of historical progress. In contrast to Marx's dialectics or Brisbane's earlier rhetoric of feudalism, according to which the existing order exacerbates a social crisis to its breaking point, they came to see an increasingly incorporated present as the "matrix" of a coming Associated age.

The problems endemic to Civilization, *The Harbinger*'s editors argued, emerged from its incomplete realization of an associative impulse and the wasteful animosity that ensued. Association would change all that: "the distinctive feature of Phalansterian partnership, is, that instead of associating capital against labor, as in the manufacturing companies; or labor against capital, as in the trades' unions; it associates them together" and can "thus [convert] to the welfare of all, the reciprocal faculties possessed by each."[23] From this perspective, the joint-stock or corporate form demonstrated the power of collective organization even as it revealed its limits amid the social misery and moral degradation of capitalist "Civilization." The very forms of association pioneered by antagonistic bodies—manufacturing companies, trade unions—constituted the groundwork for mass social transformation. In this sense, the "Statement of Principles" echoes Lieber's earlier insight that the same dynamics of association animate conventional organizations and revolutionary societies. This multivalent intellectual and aesthetic investment in the corporation—as paradigm, as contrast case, as practical strategy, and as matrix for future crystallization—can explain why Associationist writers treated it as both the most problematic aspect of Civilization and a bridge to an Associated future.

Media and Millennialism

Associationists also borrowed enthusiastically from another, very different group of companies: the great religious charitable organizations of the early nineteenth century. These groups, including the American Bible Society, the American Tract Society, and the American Sunday School Union, instigated an "organizational revolution" as important as the contemporaneous market revolution.[24] As historians

[22] *Harbinger* 4: 111. [23] *Harbinger* 4: 111.

[24] Peter Dobkin Hall, "Religion and the Organizational Revolution in the United States," in *Sacred Companies: Organizational Aspects of Religion and Religious Aspects of Organizations*, ed. N. J. Demerath III et al. (New York: Oxford University Press, 1998).

of religion and book historians have recognized, many of the most important businesses in the antebellum United States, particularly in the realm of print publication and distribution, were not commercial enterprises but rather charities. As David Paul Nord aptly writes, Bible and tract societies "launched their products into the currents of commerce, but against the flow," refusing the law of supply and demand in favor of totalizing, well-organized distribution; in doing so they pioneered not only the nonprofit sector but fundamental facets of both mass media and the business corporation. Their media strategy—the centralized production of imprints supported by dispersed mechanisms of funding and distribution—was so effective that other reform organizations, including temperance and antislavery societies, soon followed in their organizational footsteps.[25] Like these societies, the Associationist movement invited elite investment, embraced organizational models that coordinated centralized bodies with far-flung auxiliaries, and mobilized print culture at the mass scale to reach a broad audience.

The great religious and reform charities not only pioneered mass media techniques but also recognized mass media themselves as spiritually transformative. Scholars including Peter Dobkin Hall, David Paul Nord, Paul C. Gutjahr, and John Modern have demonstrated how their systematic organization, innovative use of print technology, and scientific apprehension of audiences marked evangelical publication societies as pioneers of an inspired corporate modernity. The nineteenth-century Presbyterian historian Robert Baird captured their vision in bold terms: "These arts of printing that multiply the Word of God literally with every minute; these accumulations of capital still active, still accumulating; these means of communication over sea and land, through the broad earth—who does not hear the voice of God in all of these?"[26] As evangelical mass media practices became "the privileged vehicle for applying scientific principles to the population in order to secure the humanity of those within it," they embraced and shaped the technological and governmental networks of nineteenth-century modernity.[27]

Associationist publications borrowed both the infrastructure of religious mass media and the structures of feeling that Modern has described as "evangelical secularism."[28] They evinced the power of print culture both to articulate a

[25] David Paul Nord, *Faith in Reading: Religious Publishing and the Birth of Mass Media in America* (New York: Oxford University Press, 2004), 7. See also Paul C. Gutjahr, *A History of the Good Book in the United States, 1777–1880* (Stanford, CA: Stanford University Press, 1999); David Paul Nord, "Benevolent Books: Printing, Religion, and Reform," in *The History of the Book in America*, Vol. 2, ed. Robert A. Gross and Mary Kelly (Chapel Hill, NC: University of North Carolina Press, 2010); Teresa A. Goddu, *Selling Antislavery: Abolition and Mass Media in Antebellum America* (Philadelphia, PA: University of Pennsylvania, 2020).

[26] Quoted in John Lardas Modern, *Secularism in Antebellum America* (Chicago: University of Chicago Press, 2011), 63.

[27] Modern, *Secularism*, 68.

[28] "Rather than being the antithesis to religiosity, evangelical secularism was constituted by those feelings, expectations, and practices that animated definitional categories about religion and was manifest in the deployment of those definitions at the level of the population." Modern, *Secularism*, 54.

population via systematic distribution and transform it at the level of the individual reader. In July 1846, the *Harbinger* offered a breathless description of the American Union of Associationists's (AUA's) lecture campaign: "The great work of Apostleship could not have had a more auspicious beginning. The Sowers are in the field; the Heavens bless their labors; the Truth will have its increase, and rejoicing multitudes will bear home the harvest."[29] The idiom of evangelical publications offered them a way to frame radical social theory for a readership versed in religious tracts—and to counter Fourier's reputation for godlessness in the bargain. Thus, despite their conventional image as at once utopian and irreligious, Associationists adapted the systematic organization and distribution of evangelical mass media to promulgate a visionary secularism. Rather than register surprise at the apparently theological residues in Associationist theory and media, we might follow Talal Asad's recognition that "The secular... is neither continuous with the religious that supposedly preceded it... nor a simple break from it."[30] Nowhere is this pattern clearer than in Associationists' adoption of the millennial idiom of epochal transformation.

Proclamations of the coming era of Harmony present a boldly secular conception of social evangelism: an imminent moment of conversion precipitated by the diffusion of inspired print material through a scientifically apprehended population. The AUA framed their 1846 constitution in terms of evangelical means put to social ends: "1. To indoctrinate the whole People of the United States, with the Principles of Associative Unity; 2. To prepare for the time, when the Nation like one man, shall reorganize its townships upon the basis of perfect justice."[31] Laying the groundwork for a messianic age of "perfect justice," the AUA transposes the proven innovations of the religious societies from a theological to a social key. Media-savvy millennialism offered the armature for the radical hope and faith necessary to imagine an Associated future against all apparent odds. As this document makes clear, the AUA's vision was singularly ambitious: not just the transformation of readers' spiritual lives or the construction of an organization outside the demands of the marketplace, but a thorough reordering of social and economic relations from Civilization to Harmony, to be achieved by a reorganization of the nation and the world, township by township, into an orderly series of phalanxes.

Identifying the township as the unit of transformation was both strategic and resonant. This familiar unit of municipal governance (and, as Jonathan Beecher Field has pointed out, of settler colonialism) was familiar to American audiences

[29] *Harbinger* 3: 80.

[30] Talal Asad, *Formations of the Secular: Christianity, Islam, Modernity* (Stanford, CA: Stanford University Press, 2003), 25. At the same time, Associationist millennialism bears out Asad's insistence that "secular redemptive politics" diverges from a theological model of "a redeemer saving sinners through *his* submission to suffering" (61–62).

[31] *Harbinger* 3: 14.

and theorists of American politics.[32] Brisbane envisioned Association on a modular pattern derived from municipal government: "It is evident, then, that the whole question of a *universal* Social Reform and the establishment of a true Social Order upon the earth, resolves itself into *the right organization of one single township.* If this organization is known (and we declare that Fourier has discovered it), it is clear that there will be no difficulty reforming the present system of Society and establishing a true one in its place."[33] Brisbane's "Means of Spreading Association and Rendering it Universal" is rooted in the township as a unit of spatial and political organization and self-government that can be iterated ad infinitum. Although he retains Fourier's terminology of phalanxes, phalansteries, and passional attraction, he softens it via translation into this idiom. Echoing Lieber's description in the *Americana* of the nation as a "concatenation" of various corporations, he envisions a concrete plan to rebuild society by artful concatenation, one township at a time.

Tocqueville had characterized the township both as both a spontaneous assemblage—"the grouping so close to man's nature that wherever men gather together township automatically comes into being"—and, particularly in its New England form, as a distinctive political institution animated by "a community spirit" and possessed of "independence and authority."[34] In this sense, the township occupies the borderline between organic bodies (Lieber's "society," Hawthorne's "community") and deliberate ones (Lieber's "association," Hawthorne's "company"). The Associationist project of reconstituting townships as phalanxes can thus be understood as a scheme for dialectically resolving the natural and artificial facets of social forms.

Even at its most extravagant, Associationists' evangelical rhetoric demonstrates a consistent logic, earnestly cashing out prophecy in worldly plans. The Associationist and Unitarian minister William Henry Channing introduces his periodical *The Spirit of the Age* as dedicated to "the Peaceful Transformation of human societies from isolated to associated interests, from competitive to co-operative industry, from disunity to unity. Amidst Revolution and Reaction it advocates Reorganization." By reconciling conflict through "an orderly arrangement of all relations, in the Family, the Township, the Nation, the World," Channing writes, his paper "would…aid to introduce the Era of Confederated Communities, which in spirit, truth and deed shall be the Kingdom of God and his Righteousness, a Heaven upon Earth."[35] Even when he wraps up the periodical

[32] Jonathan Beecher Field, *Town Hall Meetings and the Death of Deliberation* (Minneapolis, MN: University of Minnesota Press, 2019), 17.

[33] Albert Brisbane, *Association; A Concise Exposition of the Practical Part of Fourier's Social Science* (New York: Greeley & McElrath, 1843), 74.

[34] Alexis de Tocqueville, *Democracy in America* and *Two Essays on America*, ed. Isaac Kramnick, trans. Gerald Bevan (New York: Penguin, 2003), 72, 80.

[35] William Henry Channing, "Prospectus of *The Spirit of the Age*," *The Spirit of the Age* 1: 32.

a few years later, disappointed and "brain-sick," Channing insists that the nineteenth century's technical and social innovations are signs of spiritual transformation.[36] He prophesies a world transformed by political revolution and technological interconnection, manifestations of a new law of love:

> Ere the next quarter of a century has rolled away—however terrible the intervening struggle—fetters will be struck forever from the limbs of bondsmen, and Slaves in America, and serfs in Europe will stand erect in freedom; the Working-Classes of all civilized lands will be confederated, through a system of coöperative labor, equitable exchange, and just distribution, into a Commonwealth of Industry; hereditary dignities, the pride and power of money, the subtle sway of diplomacy, the tricks of professional politics, the sword's infernal tyranny, will be humbled before the Law of Brotherhood, declared through a Congress of Nations allied in the Republic of Christendom; and on an earth interlinked by railroads, steamboats, telegraphs, into one body, will be manifested that life of Universal Unity, which is the indwelling of God with Man.[37]

Framing technological, economic, and social change in messianic terms, Channing envisions social, political, and infrastructural networks as reconstituting the earth as "one body" animated by the "life of Universal Unity"—reincorporating it as a fit site for a regenerate mankind. At the climax of this techno-utopian iteration of the trope of the Church as the body of Christ, Channing emphasizes the secular, material networks—"railroads, steamboats, telegraphs"—that will constitute the bond of perfection. This materialist theology of love thus recasts both Christian doctrine and Fourierist Harmony as the perfect synergy of philanthropic passions and concrete infrastructural arrangements.

The most palpable of these material infrastructures was Associationist print itself, a multifaceted but deliberately orchestrated network, in which far-flung printers like U. P. James in Cincinnati and the Brook Farm Press in West Roxbury worked alongside Greeley's well-funded and widely distributed *New York Tribune*, which printed Brisbane's Associationist columns.[38] This approach is aptly illustrated by the publisher J. S. Redfield's advertisement on the back cover of the tract *What is Association*—itself distributed wholesale at the price of $1 per hundred (see Fig. 5.2). Following up on a mention, in the tract's text, of Brisbane's *Concise Exposition* of Fourier's principles, the advertisement offers the eighty-page pamphlet for sale (18¾ cents single copies, 12½ cents wholesale); it also presents Brisbane's forthcoming treatise, *Social Destiny of Man* (500 pages, $1)

[36] William Henry Channing, "To Meet Again!," *The Spirit of the Age* 2: 264.

[37] Channing, "To Meet Again!," 2: 265.

[38] Brisbane purchased a front-page column in Greeley's *Tribune* for $500. Greeley had also produced Brisbane's first Associationist periodical, *The Future*, in 1841. Guarneri, *The Utopian Alternative*, 32–33.

PAMPHLET ON ASSOCIATION.

A CONCISE EXPOSITION

OF THE

DOCTRINE OF ASSOCIATION.

(*Based on Fourier's theory of universal Association.*)

BY A. BRISBANE.

This pamphlet of 80 large pages, double columns, contains a clear and concise description of the system of Association discovered by CHARLES FOURIER.

Price 18 3-4 cents single copies; 12 1-2 cents wholesale. Published by J. S. Redfield, corner of Nassau and Beekman streets, New York.

THE SOCIAL DESTINY OF MAN, 1 vol. 500 pages, by A. Brisbane. Price $1. This is a larger and more comprehensive work upon Association. (In press.)

THE PHALANX,

OR

JOURNAL OF SOCIAL SCIENCE

DEVOTED TO THE

Cause of Association and a Social Reform

AND THE SOCIAL ELEVATION OF THE HUMAN RACE.

THE PHALANX will explain the System of Association and the Principles of a true Social Order discovered by CHARLES FOURIER, in regard both to practical details and universal Theory.

Political, Philosophical and Religious questions will be discussed on the broadest grounds of universality and impartiality, and with reference to their bearing upon the Social interests and welfare of mankind.

THE PHALANX will enter into a frank and impartial criticism of the present Order of Society, called "Civilization," and will analyze its evils and expose the defects of such of its institutions as are false and require reform. Searching and thorough expositions will be made of our Repugnant Ill-requited and Degrading System of Industry and our menial system of Hired Labor or Labor for Wages—of Free Competition, or false rivalry and envious strife and anarchy in the field of Commerce and Industry—of our complicated and wasteful system of Commerce; in short, every question concerning the interests and welfare of society will be dwelt upon for the purpose, not of exciting discontent and inflaming the passions of men, but of awakening public attention to the causes of the evils which exist, and pointing out a practical, safe and effectual REMEDY.

The Phalanx will contain regularly translations from the Works of Fourier, the whole of which it is designed to translate in time. The Phalanx will also contain extracts from the Paris and London Journals, devoted to the cause of Association, and will keep a general record of the progress of the doctrine, of practical experiments, and of all movements connected with Association.

The Phalanx will be published at $2 per annum—$1 for six months. Subscriptions can be sent *free* of postage through Postmasters.

Address Editors of the Phalanx, or

J. S. REDFIELD,

Publisher and Bookseller, corner of Beekman and Nassau streets, New York. General Depot for the sale of works on Association by Fourier and his disciples.

Fig. 5.2 Albert Brisbane, *What Is Association?* (New York: [J. S. Redfield], 1843–44), back cover. Courtesy, American Antiquarian Society.

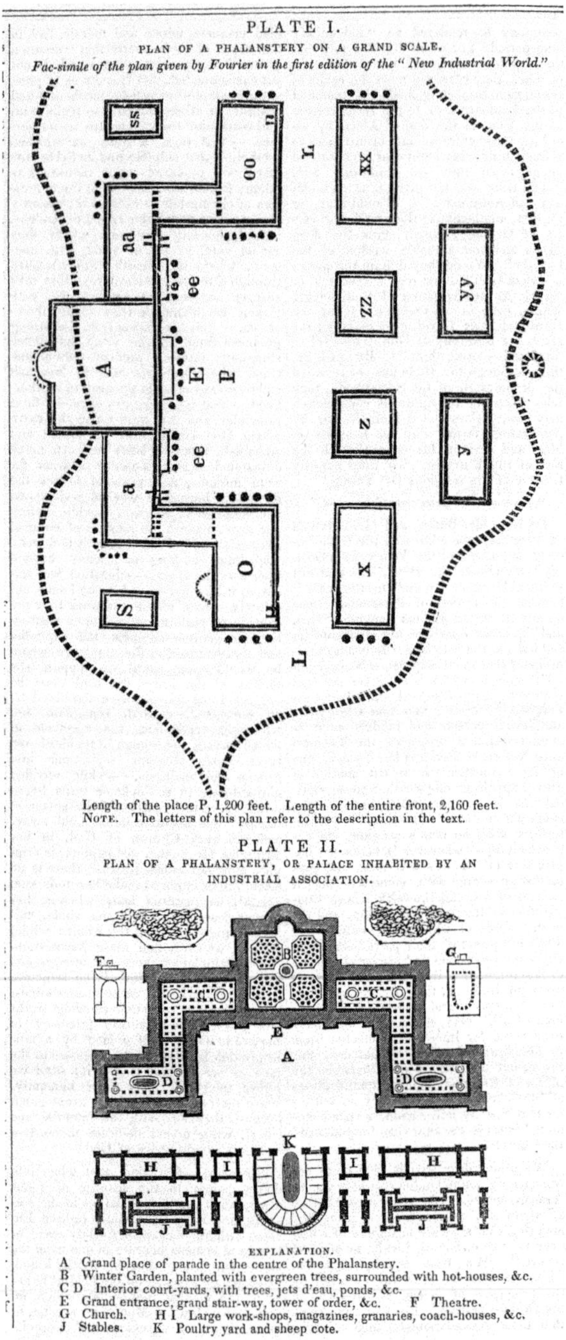

Fig. 5.3 Illustrations to Charles Fourier, "On the Unitary Distribution of Edifices," an installment of "The New Industrial World." *The Harbinger* 2:406 (June 6, 1846). Courtesy, American Antiquarian Society.

and his periodical, *The Phalanx* (announced as the *North American Phalanx* in the first edition of the *Concise Exposition*), at a rate of $2 per year.[39] In its graduated pricing and thorough consideration of a segmented readership, this brief catalogue illustrates a propaganda strategy as meticulously designed as the phalanstery plans so often featured in Associationist publications (see Fig. 5.3).

One scholar has argued that Fourier's theory offered "no practical mechanism for bringing the utopian future into being."[40] Yet American Associationists, informed by Fourier's theory of the passions and cutting-edge media strategies, found in print culture itself their practical mechanism for diffusing knowledge and affect. In frequently published articles detailing the production and distribution of Associationist print and oratory, Brisbane and his peers framed a bold plan for disseminating Fourierist theory with organizational clarity and affective punch. In this regard they echoed evangelical tract writers: "There is a way of representing divine truth which renders it striking, and makes it penetrate the mind, and arrest the attention. With this view, strong, pithy expressions, lively representations of truth and pathetic addresses, are here quite in point."[41] Because Fourier's theory of the passions elaborated the very affective mechanisms on which evangelical and reformist media relied, Associationist propaganda both promulgated his doctrine and counted on it as a tool for social transformation. This feedback loop—harnessing affect via print aesthetics and thereby promulgating a doctrine of social transformation through mass media—has often gone unnoticed. Associationist leaders attended carefully to the means of aesthetic and affective appeal and their expected return: the conversion of readers and crystallization of the public into a new social organization. Although their strategies failed to achieve change on the scale they imagined, they underscore the movement's investment in aesthetics and affect in strategic, rather than merely theoretical, terms.

Reorientation, Reorganization, and Romance

In their attention both to the effects of mass media on a passionately susceptible public and to the aesthetic dynamics of social forms themselves, Fourierist socialists were deeply attentive to aesthetic phenomena. Associationist print culture thus shares more than has been recognized with the questions that Hawthorne

[39] A later item in the *Harbinger* lists Brisbane's pamphlet as available for 18 cents and Godwin's for 25 cents in Cincinnati. *Harbinger* 4: 257.

[40] Craig White, "A Utopia of 'Spheres and Sympathies': Science and Society in *The Blithedale Romance* and at Brook Farm," *Utopian Studies* Vol. 9, no. 2 (1998): 88.

[41] Beilby Porteus, *An Address to Christians Recommending the Distribution of Cheap Religious Tracts. With an Extract from a Sermon, by Bishop Porteus* (Charlestown, MA: Samuel Etheridge, 1802), 12–13.

raises in his writing on aesthetics. Hawthorne famously privileges romance as a mode that can accommodate both reality and imagination. As many critics have noted, his account of romance—"a neutral territory, somewhere between the real world and fairy-land, where the Actual and the Imaginary may meet"—derives its effect from the very familiarity it evokes.[42] Despite his renunciations of representing reality conventionally, the romantic artist seduces the reader, as Michael Davitt Bell has argued, "into accepting his 'strange dreams' by making them *look* like the sort of truth to which the reader is accustomed."[43]

Hawthorne's playful furtiveness about depicting reality through the "atmospherical medium" and "legendary mist" of romance pervades *Blithedale*'s preface. Here, Hawthorne pushes his aesthetic theory further by identifying it not only with the visual effects of moonlight, mist, and mirror-photographs but with autobiographical memory: "the Author has ventured to make free with his old, and affectionately remembered home, at BROOK FARM, as being, certainly, the most romantic episode of his own life–essentially a daydream, and yet a fact–and thus offering an available foothold between fiction and reality" (*BR*, 2). Viewing the familiar world through an unfamiliar medium—whether a daguerreotype, the distance of memory, or the daydream phenomenology of Brook Farm—offers a tantalizing form of redoubled experience. While the transformation Hawthorne describes is individual and subjective, Associationists rely on collective social imagination to provide a "foothold between fiction and reality." By presenting capitalist modernity—"Civilization"—through the defamiliarizing medium of Fourierist theory, Associationists evoke an aesthetic "atmosphere of strange enchantment" that might render "Faery Land" and "the real world" indiscernible and thus animate a new era by reorienting the facts of "Civilization" in accordance with the daydreams of Association.[44] Their language suggests that a renovated social order might emerge not from the destruction of what preceded it but by a subtle reorientation in which existing forms take on new capabilities.

"Our evils are social not political," Brisbane asserted in his 1840 treatise, *The Social Destiny of Man*.[45] The phrase would reappear as an epigraph to Associationist periodicals and tracts for years thereafter. Despite its irenic tone, Brisbane's maxim has radical implications: it takes aim at society's structural arrangements rather than mere partisan conflict. *Social Destiny* unpacks this view with an

[42] Nathaniel Hawthorne, "The Custom-House: Introductory to the Scarlet Letter" (1850), in *The Scarlet Letter and Other Writings*, 2. ed., ed. Leland S. Person (New York: W. W. Norton & Co., 2017), 28.

[43] Michael Davitt Bell, *Culture, Genre, and Literary Vocation: Selected Essays on American Literature* (Chicago: University of Chicago Press, 2001), 43.

[44] Nathaniel Hawthorne, *The House of the Seven Gables* (1851), ed. Milton R. Stern (New York: Penguin, 1981), 1–2; Nathaniel Hawthorne, *The Blithedale Romance* (1852), ed. Annette Kolodny (New York: Penguin, 1983), 2.

[45] Albert Brisbane, *Social Destiny of Man: or, Association and Reorganization of Industry* (Philadelphia: C. F. Stollmeyer, 1840), 27. Subsequent references in parentheses.

optimistic eye toward human capacity: "Industrial Association is . . . a faculty of man: to what extent then can it be carried in agriculture, manufacture and commerce, and above all in our domestic organization—which, with its system of incoherent, isolated households, causes such incalculable waste and expense?" (*SDM*, 13). To the economic, affective, and aesthetic evils of wasteful redundancy, isolation, and incoherence, Brisbane proposes the solutions of consolidation, combination, and cooperation. Recurrently frustrated by bad organization, he proclaims: "The root of the evil is in the social organisation itself; and, until we attack it there, no permanent or beneficial reforms can be expected. The great fundamental question, therefore, which should occupy the attention of men, is a re-organization of society" (*SDM*, 27). His vision of reorganization ties the sense of radical contingency afforded by a "foothold between fiction and reality" to the possibilities of the corporation as a means of social and political organization.

Brisbane repeatedly insists that reform is essentially rearrangement, including the rearrangement of "domestic organization." While he concedes the difficulty of consolidating households (and thereby shields himself from the familiar critique that Association would undermine marriages or families), he stresses the feasibility of consolidation by gesturing toward financial institutions: "Association, although impossible between two or three families in their domestic operations, is not impossible in other affairs: we see it exist in certain branches of commerce, such as Banking and Insurance Companies, and in other enterprizes, in which the number of Stockholders may amount to one or two thousand persons"(*SDM*, 13).

The analogy of corporate economies of scale allows Brisbane to make Fourier's vision of a top-to-bottom rebuilding of society both concrete and palatable. By framing the benefits of consolidation in the apparently neutral terms of scale and efficiency, he glosses over the different reasons for seeking them: profit or social benefit. Brisbane's account risks reducing structural critique to bureaucratic strategy. Yet it also allows him to frame a socialist transformation of society that unobjectionably highlights the "unity of interests resulting from the system of joint-stock property of Association."[46]

Fourier himself had recognized the likeness between the phalanx and the business corporation: "A person may be a member without being a stockholder, or a stockholder without being a member."[47] The empowerment of a nonresident stockholder class reveals the tension between the Association's dual roles as company and community, enterprise and polity, and evokes competing visions of corporate membership: the residual form of an association of participatory members (the member corporation) and the emergent form of a body of passive shareholders separated from managerial control (the property corporation).[48]

[46] Brisbane, *Association*, 33. [47] Qtd. Brisbane, *Association*, 32.

[48] David Ciepley, "Member Corporations, Property Corporations, and Constitutional Rights," *Law & Ethics of Human Rights* 11 (2017): 31–60.

(This contrast between residents and investors also recalls the declining power of municipal corporations that accompanied the ascendancy of business corporations.[49])

The mass-audience tract *What Is Association?* frames social reorganization as a movement from the many "institutions in society" that are "partial Associations" to total Association proper. The problem with extant state and corporate forms, the pamphlet insists, is their messiness and incompleteness. Brisbane recalls Lieber's characterization of the nation as the "great corporation" when he notes that "the State or Government itself is but an Association of the whole body of the people—a great Political Association." But, he complains, all these forms of association are "extremely imperfect and defective, as the principle of association is but partially and fragmentally applied."[50] Existing institutions are characterized by competing interests, and these flaws of "*imperfect* and *incomplete* association" can only be righted by "*embrac*[ing] *all interests under a perfect organization*...., that is, by means of a complete and integral system of Association, universal in its application and embracing all interests."[51] He credits joint-stock companies—his examples include railroad, canal, banking, and insurance companies—with "extensive development" of "the principle of Association," and praises these "partial or special associations, formed for the purpose of prosecuting undertakings of a financial, commercial or industrial character more effectually and profitably than can be done by individual efforts and means.... [A]ll the power and usefulness of these institutions arise from the union and concentration of capital."[52]

Brisbane goes beyond his precursors' observations of the power and ubiquity of the corporate form by imagining an incorporated arrangement that transcends competing interests. While he celebrates corporate organization, he laments the fragmentation created by private interests that has kept the joint-stock form from reaching its potential: "The *isolated* corporation or Association, like the *isolated* family, is selfish and grasping; and standing in an antagonistic and hostile relation to other interests in society, it frequently resorts to fraud, injustice and duplicity to increase its prosperity, wealth and power."[53] Characterizing corporate villains as products of isolation, fragmentation, and misdirected passions allows him unreservedly to endorse association itself as a formal and affective remedy. In contrast to domestic ideology's framing of the family as antidote to capitalist business, Brisbane aligns family and corporation as instances of excessive privacy. By his logic, the evils of corporate capitalism arise from insufficient, rather than excessive, corporateness. Capitalist antagonism will be overcome not through the destruction of the corporate form but through its perfection:

[49] Gerald Frug, *City Making: Building Communities without Building Walls* (Princeton, NJ: Princeton University Press, 1999).

[50] Albert Brisbane, *What Is Association?* (New York: J. S. Redfield, 1843–44), 2–3.

[51] Brisbane, *What Is Association?*, 3.

[52] Brisbane, *What Is Association?*, 3.

[53] Brisbane, *What Is Association?*, 4.

> These Companies or Corporations compete, often, with individuals for supremacy in business, and possessing greater resources and power—the effect of the principle of association—they cripple and crush them, and monopolize the branch of trade or industry in which they are engaged. *For this reason Banks and other corporate bodies, or privileged leagues of capital, are so unpopular; but the abuse of power committed by these institutions should not induce us to condemn the principle which gives them their power*; it should show us what could be done if that power were rightly applied, that is, if it were so applied as to conduce and be advantageous to all interests, which can only be done by a system of association which will embrace all branches of business and industry, so that they will not be separated and left in opposition and antagonistic conflict.[54]

By this line of reasoning, the economic benefits of the corporation are but a promissory note on the political, aesthetic, affective, and moral transformation to be realized by true Association, which will surpass private interest: "a universal application of the principle of Association, will open a new era to the world, an era of universal prosperity and happiness."[55] By recasting corporations' crushing, monopolistic power as the first incarnation of a "principle" that will transcend conflict, Brisbane and his allies make the case for a formal solution to the ills of nineteenth-century capitalism.

Associationist Aesthetics

As I have argued, Fourier's theory of the passions as the fundamental ontology of the social led Associationists to theorize aesthetics and affect as forces for social change. In contrast to Hawthorne's idiom of the "fancy-sketch," in which individual aesthetic subjectivity temporarily transforms reality into the stuff of romance, Associationists conceived of imaginative sketches as draft blueprints of phalansteries to be constructed by a growing association of passionate readers. From this perspective, aesthetic experience is not a retreat from the social but rather constitutes both the means and the end of social transformation; it links imaginative activity to practical processes, from distributing propaganda to building institutions. Taking social organization itself as their subject and infusing it with prophetic importance, Associationist propagandists crafted a language that could describe both the wonders of the coming age of Harmony and the technologies that could constitute a network to produce and distribute feeling. They presented Association, that is, as both a creative medium and a world-historical collective actor, and Associationist print and oratorical culture, in tandem with the network

[54] Brisbane, *What Is Association?*, 4, emphasis added.
[55] Brisbane, *What Is Association?*, 4.

of nascent phalanxes, as a carefully crafted mechanism that could transmute affect and aesthetics into social transformation.

Civilization was not only unjust and inefficient, Brisbane insisted; it was also downright ugly. He was confident that the aesthetic dimension of social consolidation would guide observers beyond the disarray of "heterogeneous mass of small and separate houses of all sizes, shapes, colors, styles, and materials…a scene of confusion, incoherence, waste, and disorder."[56] His judgment adheres to Fourier's theory of passionate attraction, according to which the sense of aesthetic order and desire for social affiliation are varied manifestations of the same affect. "[P]assionate attraction," Fourier writes, "tend[s] toward three goals":

1. Toward luxury or the gratification of the five senses.
2. Toward the formation of groups and series of groups, the establishment of affective ties.
3. Toward the coordination of the passions, character traits, instincts, and consequently toward universal unity.[57]

The twelve passions he identifies include the five senses, four affectively charged groupings ("friendship," "ambition, corporative tie," "love," and "paternity or family"), and three "distributive passions" (cabalist, butterfly, and composite) that "establish the harmony of the passions in their internal and their external action."[58] Underlying this seemingly arbitrary taxonomy is Fourier's conviction that the passions share a common nature. This shared essence explains his insistence that apparent vices—the love of intrigue (cabalist), enthusiasm (composite), or variety (butterfly)—while destructive under the conditions of Civilization, "within families and corporate bodies," will blossom beneficially in the groups and series of Association. (In this respect Fourier can seem a Deleuze avant la lèttre: a relentless monist for whom varied phenomena ultimately resolve into assemblages and the affective intensities that traverse them.)

The Phalanstery's arrangement and its economies of scale are also calculated to optimize a variety of aesthetic pleasures in which all inhabitants, not only a privileged few, can partake—and turn those pleasures toward increased efficiency: "This elegance of working conditions will be an *industrial incentive*."[59] Because "[l]uxury assumes different forms and plays different roles at different stages of social development," the pleasures of Harmony are both economically and ethically preferable to those of Civilization: "In Harmony luxury is corporative; everyone wants his favorite groups and series to shine. This penchant is foreshadowed in some of the groups and corporations that exist today."[60] The

[56] Brisbane, *Association*, 74.
[57] Fourier, *The Utopian Vision*, 216.
[58] Fourier, *The Utopian Vision*, 217.
[59] Fourier, *The Utopian Vision*, 295.
[60] Fourier, *The Utopian Vision*, 293.

"corporative" pleasures of "groups and corporations" adumbrate a key feature of Association: recentering affect on the realm of economic activity, which will "endow productive work with all the lustre and the luxurious appurtenances which are today attached only to the unproductive functions."[61]

Infusing economic production with the aesthetic spirit of passionate attraction is what Fourier and his disciples call attractive industry. It undergirds the promised order, efficiency, and beauty of Phalansterian life and differentiates it from the ugliness and waste of Civilization. In Fourier's description of spaces designed to accommodate the social and industrial divisions of groups and series, architecture renders social structure visible with "halls for social relations... called *Seristeries* or places for the meeting and interaction of the passional series." In contrast to "our public rooms where ungraduated social relations prevail," a Seristery mirrors the carefully calibrated order of the series, which "always has its three, four or five divisions which occupy three, four or five adjacent locations."[62] More broadly, Fourier highlights the way the architectural and economic organization of the phalanx can overcome quotidian inconvenience and enable heightened aesthetic experience: "To spend a winter's day in a Phalanstery, to visit all parts of it without exposure to the elements, to go to the theater and the opera in light clothes and colored shoes without worrying about the mud and the cold, would be a charm so novel that it alone would suffice to make our cities and castles seem detestable."[63]

The aestheticized life of the phalanstery is characterized by its total permeability by the passions, which animate working conditions, sartorial habits, and explicitly artistic practices. By the same token, Fourier outlines a system of compensation for artistic and scientific producers that puts the economic coordination of the phalanx at the service of cultural ends: qualified series will judge "scientific discoveries and works of art" and phalanxes around the globe will coordinate their contributions through the "Congress of Spherical Unity" to compensate creators like Jean Racine and Benjamin Franklin for their contributions to science and culture.[64]

On the one hand, then, Associationists understood the aesthetics of social arrangement to act as a practical spur to artistic and scientific innovation, both by directing the passions that inspire cultural work and by supporting that work economically. On the other, the beauty and genius of phalanxes, groups, and series are conceived as sympathetically mirroring the formal beauty and genius of technical and literary wonders. This order is both incarnated and felt by corporate bodies at various scales: the group or series, the phalanx, and finally the political world constituted by concatenated phalanxes. The resulting vision of confederated order, powered by the fuel of twelve fundamental passions skillfully

[61] Fourier, *The Utopian Vision*, 295.
[62] Fourier, *The Utopian Vision*, 241.
[63] Fourier, *The Utopian Vision*, 245.
[64] Fourier, *The Utopian Vision*, 262–63.

distilled into "corporate sentiment," radicalizes Lieber's vision of the nation as a concatenation of corporations, reconceiving it as a single, infinitely articulated, and finely innervated corporate body.

In this spirit, Associationist writers also looked to the arts, particularly poetry, for an account of aesthetics consistent with Fourier's doctrine of passionate attraction and a visionary idiom for social renovation. The transplantation of *The Phalanx* from New York to Brook Farm and its reincarnation there as the *Harbinger* opened the way to increased literary and critical writing, including poetry, fiction, literary criticism, and music criticism, particularly by Brook Farmers like George Ripley, Dana, and Dwight.[65] While such work might initially appear to be genteel window dressing, the editors insisted upon literary writing's inseparability from Fourier's aesthetic and social theory.

Recognizing this theoretical investment in aesthetics can help reconcile Associationists' immersion in novel mass media strategies with the traditional framing of Associationist writers as occupying the fringes of an elite literary milieu. Given the overlap of central figures like Ripley and W. H. Channing and the ambivalence of Emerson, Thoreau, and Fuller toward the Associationist movement, it should not be surprising that literary and cultural histories treating Associationism have often considered the movement as a backdrop for, footnote to, or immature version of transcendentalism.[66] This approach, however, gives too New England- (and Brook Farm-) centric a picture of a movement initially centered on New Yorkers like Brisbane, Greeley, Godwin, and Macdaniel.[67] More importantly, this approach fundamentally mischaracterizes Associationist aesthetics and poetics by aligning Transcendentalism with visionary imagination and Associationism, by implicit contrast, with dull uniformity. While many of the founders of Brook Farm had been members of the Transcendentalist Club, they came to favor the mass print pioneered by newspapers like Greeley's *Tribune* and the religious and reform societies over the narrow circulation of publications like the *Dial*. Still, Associationist periodicals engaged extensively with literary production and aesthetic theory, often explicitly grounded in Fourier's theory of the passions. Sometimes, as in the serialized publication of novels by Eugène Sue and George Sand, the *Harbinger*'s editors proffered literary work by writers explicitly aligned with radical social critique. But just as frequently, they printed

[65] Clarence Gohdes, *The Periodicals of American Transcendentalism* (Durham, NC: Duke University Press, 1931), 150.

[66] F. O. Matthiessen, *American Renaissance: Art and Expression in the Age of Emerson and Whitman* (New York: Oxford University Press, 1941); Richard Francis, *Transcendental Utopias: Individual and Community at Brook Farm, Fruitlands, and Walden* (Ithaca, NY: Cornell University Press, 1997); Delano, *Brook Farm*; Gohdes, *The Periodicals*; Arthur Bestor, *Backwoods Utopias: The Sectarian Origins and the Owenite Phase of Communitarian Socialism in America, 1663–1829* (Philadelphia, PA: University of Pennsylvania Press, 1970).

[67] Delano, for instance, frames New York Associationists as meddling outsiders at Brook Farm in *Brook Farm*.

and reviewed literary material whose explicit commitments were aesthetic rather than theoretical, savoring the echoes between poetic and social accounts of passion, harmony, and form.

Poetry and criticism in the *Harbinger* repeatedly gesture toward the power of the imagination as a force of both aesthetic and social creativity. "The Ideal," a poem by William Wetmore Story (the poet, sculptor, and son of Justice Joseph Story) first published in volume 4 of the *Harbinger*, is exemplary. It presents a "soul by night subdued to harmony." The speaker turns his "inward eyes" to "one great hope, that time will never banish," succeeded by "phantoms of dreams.../ That mock my earthly grasp, yet never vanish." This experience inverts the speaker's sense of the real and the ideal:

> The Actual fadeth like a mountain mist,
> The Unreal is the Real and enduring;
> Upon the dizzy height of dreams I list
> To music-tones my inmost soul alluring.

Synesthetically seduced by the visions and tones of "the Unreal," Story's speaker laments the impossibility of transforming such sublime sense into a tangible product: "in the mould of art / The finest traits the hand forever loses." He resigns himself to artistic futility, "The vainness of all effort to attain / That which the secret thought forever blesses." Yet this consolation—tempering idealism in the name of possibility—is a retreat from his earlier platonic insistence that "The Unreal is the Real and enduring."[68] Given the familiar caricature of Associationism as airily visionary, it might seem rhetorically risky to hitch hopes for social reform to poetry that emphasizes the ideality and elusiveness of imaginative vision. Yet Story's poem goes even further than Hawthorne's aesthetics of "atmospheric medium." Identifying the Ideal with inward vision that "never vanish[es]" allows Story to desubstantialize the Actual into fading "mist." By retaining the romantic aesthetics of atmospheric effects but undoing the usual association of ideality and ephemerality, Story uses romantic vision to highlight the contingency of the Actual—or, in the editors' terms, of "Civilization." (The succeeding page doubles down on aerial aesthetics with a reprint of no less a paean to imagination and inevitable change than Shelley's "Ode to the West Wind").

It is in this relationship between the actual and the potential that the connections between Associationism and romantic aesthetics—and their orientation toward social transformation—emerge most clearly. A review in the same volume treats three recent books of poetry—by Emerson, William Ellery Channing (the nephew and namesake of the Unitarian minister), and Story himself—and

[68] *Harbinger* 4: 25.

explicitly aligns poetic and social vision.[69] The review lavishes the most attention on Emerson's poems, and sometimes sounds positively Emersonian itself in its account of poetry as a secular medium of spirituality: poetry is "only the stream traced nearer to its source, which is God, or Universal Love; and as this flows forth in definite directions, by its own perfect laws distributing itself through given spheres, through distinct natures and innumerable particulars, in such wise that all differ and yet all harmonize and make one living whole." Yet this living whole is not, as for Emerson's Poet, an individual in communion with the divine or the universe, but rather a social being enmeshed in vectors of passional attraction that embraces religious experience—"the human soul in its integral and fullest action is one love, or passion, or attraction towards Unity and God"—but also material, social and aesthetic affect: "and this is also in the human soul a complex love, distributed...towards the harmonies of the material, of the social or affective, and of the intellectual or abstract sphere of laws and principles; then again, secondarily towards the harmonies of each special sphere of passion embraced within these three, as the five senses, the four social attractions, and so forth."[70] By situating the sublime, the passions, sensory experience, and social belonging on the same plane, Fourierist theory carves out aesthetics as a worldly practice of the passions rather than a form of spiritual isolation, a route leading from harmonized passions to the harmonies of language and finally to social Harmony, in which quotidian domestic and economic activity is spiritualized.

The reviewer thus idealizes poetry in familiar romantic terms as "the highest reach of Intellect, eagerly noticing, contriving, publishing all affinities, contrasts, series and alternations, and every 'difference discreet' which makes up harmony, and makes the soul at home amid facts and its fellows." At the same time, he instrumentalizes it as a force for transforming the world, "not resting in the pastime of a mere intellectual conception or phantasmagoria, but from the heart's desire for these things, seeking earnestly their realization."[71] Emerson draws the reviewer's criticism precisely because he rejects the social realization of poetic vision—a judgment that suggests that his essays rather than his poems are the real target: "But by communing with his own heart alone, by absolute subjective consciousness, by isolated self-reliance, no man ever came near realizing that unity of which the heart whispers. No man ever brought himself into harmony with the whole in this way. With this gospel of self-reliance must be coupled that other of general mutual affiance, each to each; of a unity of system and organic solidarity, wherein no one can rely upon himself, or be himself, without the aid of all, completing the related character of all the faculties and tendencies which properly *are* himself."[72] By the standards of Associationist poetics, Emersonian

[69] Review of R. W. Emerson, *Poems*; William Ellery Channing, *Poems* (Charles C. Little and James Brown, 1843); W. W. Story, *Poems*, *Harbinger* 4: 91–94, 106–109, n. 6 and 7.

[70] *Harbinger* 4: 92. [71] *Harbinger* 4: 92. [72] *Harbinger* 4: 107.

self-reliance indicates not transcendent vision but a fundamental misunderstanding of the relationship between aesthetics and the social.[73]

Emerson's antisocial vision serves as a foil for the poetics of William Wetmore Story. Although he acknowledges the absence of any "distinct theory, or constructive vision of man's social destiny" in Story's poems, the reviewer lauds his "most clear faith in unity and recognition of the deep prayer and demand of this our age"—and closes with a long extract from "The Future," which projects a vision of human unity.[74] The highest praise is reserved for Story's poetics as realization of Fourier's theory of passional attraction: "Open the volume any where and read two lines; like a leaf dropped on a river, you sail down the page by an unconscious attraction, caught and possessed by something that commands you like good music, whether there be thoughts which you carry away or not."[75] A later essay titled "Tide Marks" spells out the socially transformative power of such unconscious effects: "All great social changes are preceded by the simultaneous rise in many minds, even the most conservative, and separated by position, circumstances and pursuits of all sorts of aspirations and suggestions incidental, fragmentary, momentary, which all however wear some shade of the common hue of the Idea which is at the bottom of said change." Signs of the coming age of Harmony are particularly evident in print culture and the conversation it animates: "It is the idea of the age; and like a tide it rises in all minds, before they are aware, and finds unconscious expression in them, even while they ignore and oppose the same idea as formally presented. The literature, the newspapers, the chance talk of men and women, are full of observations of which only an Associationist detects the full significance."[76]

Like Story's poetics, the tidal hydraulics of the "idea of the age" grow from unconscious perception and manifest in unconscious expression, a trend that a French contemporary describes as an "unconscious tendency" toward Association.[77] The way to the phalanstery, these articles suggest, runs through the aesthetic unconscious of a world of readers, in whom poetry elicits passions according to its own formal arrangement.

Constitutional Poetics

Associationist publications also foregrounded another, less familiar genre of writing. Association constitutions served as tools for both governance and

[73] Of course, as critics including Branka Arsić and Sharon Cameron have suggested, reducing Emerson's aesthetic program to individualism is misleading. Branka Arsić, *On Leaving: A Reading in Emerson* (Cambridge, MA: Harvard University Press, 2010); Sharon Cameron, *Impersonality: Seven Essays* (Chicago: University of Chicago Press, 2007). Guarneri calls Brook Farm "both an expression of Transcendentalist individualism and a reaction against it" *The Utopian Alternative*, 45.

[74] *Harbinger* 4: 109. [75] *Harbinger* 4: 108.

[76] *Harbinger* 5: 219. [77] *Harbinger* 5: 221.

propaganda. *The Phalanx* printed the constitutions or articles of incorporation of the American Phalanx, Brook Farm, the Union of Associationists, and the Fall River Association; it reported the receipt of constitutions from communities including the Leraysville, Adelphia, and Southport associations.[78] Sometimes the editors played coy, as when they printed the Notice and Introductory Statement to the revised Brook Farm Constitution but explained that "We omit the Constitution, which is for sale at J. S. Redfield's, corner Nassau and Beekman sts. New-York."[79] (They relented and printed the constitution in the next number.) The *Harbinger*, likewise, printed the constitution of the AUA and auxiliary unions: the Virginia No. 1 Union of Associationists and the Boston Auxiliary Union.[80] The AUA promoted constitution-making and provided templates; the *Harbinger*'s report of the Virginia auxiliary notes that the bulk of its constitution borrows "the form published in the Circular of the American Union."[81] In 1849, after the *Harbinger*'s demise, the North American Phalanx would incorporate under a charter from the New Jersey legislature; members characterized incorporation (along with the creation of paper currency) as "br[inging] the community closer to creating 'a complete commonwealth, embracing all the interests of the state, differing only in magnitude.'"[82] While Fourierist associations were hardly the only bodies to venerate and circulate articles, constitutions, or bylaws, Associationists used these documents to highlight both the functional and aesthetic aspects of organization. As the sampling above suggests, associational constitutions proliferated and circulated for varied purposes—as prototypes, as souvenirs, as fundraisers, and as promisory social contracts. They solicited investment from well-heeled well-wishers and broadcast a vision of Harmony to far-flung fellow travelers.

Associationist constitutions reveal how intimately Associationism's projects of aesthetics, reform, and corporate pragmatics were intertwined. The Articles of Association of the American Phalanx reveal a tension at the heart of any phalanx constitution. The document concludes with an explicitly Fourierist program of "Attractive industry rendered Productive" and projects a future at once bold and radically contingent: "And whereas we believe Social Science to be yet in its infancy, and are also conscious of our ignorance even of that portion of it which is revealed, as well as of the impossibility of realizing at once that harmonic organization to which we aspire:—We therefore further declare—...That these articles shall be regarded as provisional only, and shall be subject to such modifications, amendments, and additions as may from time to time be found necessary or proper to secure more perfectly the objects of this Association."[83] The aesthetics

[78] *Phalanx* 1: 48, 1: 80–82, 1: 167, 1: 307, 1: 68. [79] *Phalanx* 1:305–06.
[80] *Harbinger* 3: 14, 3: 269, 4: 26. [81] *Harbinger* 3: 269.
[82] Jayme Sokolow, *The North American Phalanx (1843–1855): A Nineteenth-century Utopian Community* (Lewiston, NY: Edwin Mellen Press, 2009), 146.
[83] *Phalanx* 1: 50.

of the provisional—what Melville would famously call "a draught of a draught"—is accompanied by legal language acknowledging vested interests that limits the amendment of *The Phalanx*'s articles.[84] Immediately following the pronouncement of mutability comes a disclaimer stipulating that "the shares of the net product herein awarded to Industry and Capital respectively shall not be varied or changed without consent of three-fourths in number and the majority in interest of those whose rights would be prejudiced by such change."[85] As the members of the incipient phalanx knew well, the practical bounds of radical social vision were marked by the investments that underwrote social reform. However radical their ambitions, their language recalls *Dartmouth College*'s reading of corporate charters as contracts protecting vested interests.

Brook Farm's printed constitutions carefully situate both the community and the Associationist movement in a world-historical transformation even as they outline the aesthetic and legal form of the single community. They frame Brook Farm as a model of aesthetic and organizational perfection, at the center of the ambitious project of crystallizing social relations worldwide. The articles existed in four versions: the Articles of Agreement drafted before members moved to West Roxbury (1840–41), the Articles of Association (September 1841), the Constitution of 1844, when Brook Farm was formally reorganized as a Fourierist Association, and the revised Constitution of 1845, shortly after its official incorporation by the Massachusetts legislature as the Brook Farm Phalanx. The first two documents served as guides for internal governance rather than publications addressing a wider audience (they were first reprinted in late nineteenth-century histories and biographies of the community and its founders).[86] The 1844 and 1845 constitutions, in contrast, were explicitly public-facing documents, published in Boston and New York for a national readership. Each constitution is more forthright than the last as an argument for Association and a plea for investment. The preamble to the 1844 Constitution, by Ripley, Minot Pratt, and Dana, takes clear aim at two groups: a broad "public" hailed as potential members or nonresident investors, and the New York Associationist elite (particularly Brisbane, Greeley, Godwin, and Macdaniel) who represented both the most powerful means of print distribution (Greeley's *Tribune* and associated printing and distribution networks) and, in Brisbane, a direct disciple of Fourier and a conduit to Fourierist movements in Britain and France, and thus the de facto imprimatur of the movement.

[84] Herman Melville, *Moby-Dick*, ed. Hershel Parker and Harrison Hayford (New York: Norton, 2002), 125.

[85] *Phalanx* 1: 50.

[86] The Articles of Agreement are reprinted in John Thomas Codman, *Brook Farm: Historic and Personal Memoirs* (Boston: Arena, 1896), 11–15; the Articles of Association are reprinted in Octavius Brooks Frothingham, *George Ripley* (Boston: Houghton, 1888), 112–16.

At the 1845 Convention of the New England Fourier Society, New Yorker Oliver Macdaniel presented Brook Farm, already the de facto center of the movement, as a catalyst for "hastening the era of this glorious transformation." Macdaniel argues on behalf of the convention that the Brook Farm Association "presents a bright promise of success and affords a healthy germ of that Divine Social Order that is soon to replace the societies of discord and suffering now existing on earth." Endorsing the strategy of "the successful establishment of one Model Phalanx [as] the surest means of hastening the era of this glorious transformation," he urges "the Associationists of the United States…to concentrate and direct their efforts, and apply their means and energies to the building up of the Brook Farm Association."[87] The national movement's investment in Brook Farm bespeaks its transformation from (in its directors' words) a "private experiment" that "has avoided rather than sought, the notice of the public" to a pressing matter of public interest. Fourierist social science provides the rationale for this turn to publicity: the necessity of promulgating "the doctrine of Association, which now fills the minds of intelligent people every where" had given the broader public a metaphorical stake in the community. The time had come, the directors write, for "all who have either a theoretical or practical knowledge of the subject to give their share to the stock of public information."[88]

This playful conception of the public as a shareholding body—capitalized with knowledge rather than money—dovetails with the preamble's call for members "who propose to connect themselves personally with the institution" as well as nonresident investors.[89] Beyond the immediate purpose of raising capital, it presents the joint-stock model as central to the community's self-conception. The appeal to a broader base of shareholders was no mere metaphor: the Brook Farmers reallocated shares and priced them at $100 after the initial share value of $500 proved so cumbersome that few members paid it in full.[90] Ripley's introduction to the 1845 constitution appeals even more explicitly for "capital to furnish sufficient means to enable us to develop every department to advantage" by "that increasing number, whose most ardent desire is to see the experiment of Association fairly tried."[91] Even more strongly than the 1844 preamble, Ripley's introduction ties an optimistic macrocosm—a rising tide of Associationist sympathy—to the struggling microcosm of Brook Farm. His ever-broader poetic license seems keyed to the community's increasingly desperate straits, reminding the Associationist elite in the United States and abroad of the community's

[87] *Phalanx* 21 (February 8, 1845): 310.

[88] *Constitution of the Brook Farm Association for Industry and Education, West Roxbury, Mass., with an Introductory Statement* (Boston: I.R. Butts, 1844), 3–4.

[89] *Constitution of the Brook Farm Association* (1844), 5.

[90] Delano, *Brook Farm*, 69–70.

[91] *Constitution of the Brook Farm Phalanx* (s.n., 1845), 3–4. Delano suggests that the explicitly Fourierist reorganization was a tactical plea for investment by Brisbane and his New York cohort. Delano, *Brook Farm*, 185–86.

suitability to serve as the movement's model phalanx and the need of additional resources to do so. Emphasizing sunk costs and lessons learned, he argues against the creation of a model phalanx from the ground up. (Ironically, the newly organized North American Phalanx would soon supplant Brook Farm in just that fashion.)[92]

Yet in comparing the body of the 1844 Constitution to the earlier iterations of Brook Farm's Articles, remarkably little has changed. (Even the initial articles, as reproduced by Codman, echo the Fourierist idiom of attractive industry and thus reinforce the view that Ripley had imbibed Brisbane's *Social Destiny* before formulating the community.[93]) Most provisions, outside the explicit commitments to Fourierist theory in section VI.2 and the reduced share prices, come from either the 1840–41 Articles of Agreement or the 1841 Articles of Association. The more significant change is aesthetic: instead of a pragmatic hodgepodge of provisions, the 1844 Constitution presents a hierarchically organized set of headings and subheadings that mimics the Associationist scheme of groups and series. The well-organized articles offer rhetorical and graphic proof of "the degree of order our organization has already attained" and thus evidence that it can sustain "an ultimate expansion into a perfect Phalanx."[94]

At the national level, Associationist print culture presented a coordinated and multi-tiered strategy. But at the local level of Brook Farm, things were catch-as-catch-can. When Brisbane's *Phalanx* and John Allen's *Social Reformer* joined efforts in 1845 as the *Harbinger*, Brook Farm arguably became the center of Associationist print, even though it lacked sophisticated capabilities available to the New Yorkers (most importantly, access to Greeley's *Tribune* and to stereotype technology). Printing had emerged as one of Brook Farm's chief industrial endeavors, alongside shoemaking, pewterware, and the manufacture of sashes and blinds. Its beginning is a revealing story of pragmatism under duress: Allen bartered the press on which he had printed *The Social Reformer*, one of the *Harbinger*'s precursors, for a membership stake in Brook Farm stock.[95] Ironically enough, the press's 1845 arrival coincided nearly perfectly with the departure of Pratt, the community's most experienced printer. Brook Farm's printing group was principally occupied with the production of the *Harbinger*; it occasionally produced pamphlet reprints from the periodical such as *Peace the Principle and Policy of Associationists* (1846), and undertook job printing, including currency for the community's use, as well.[96]

[92] Albert Brisbane moved his support from Brook Farm to the North American Phalanx (in Red Bank, NJ) in late 1845. $10,000 would be transferred to the North American Phalanx. Delano, *Brook Farm*, 251, 383, n. 1.

[93] Codman, *Brook Farm*, 11–15.

[94] *Constitution of the Brook Farm Association* (1844), 5.

[95] Delano, *Brook Farm*, 210, 223.

[96] Delano, *Brook Farm*, 258.

The printing group emblematizes the melancholy juxtaposition of Associationists' ambitions and the homely and overtaxed community of Brook Farm. There's a further irony: shortly after Brook Farm's adoption of the *Harbinger* and tentative assumption of a central role in the national Associationist movement, the community faced a series of severe trials: the withdrawal of national Associationist support and investment, crises that included a smallpox outbreak and a disastrous fire, and the eventual dwindling of community. Even the *Harbinger* would move to New York, and Ripley and Dana would ultimately go to work for Greeley's *Tribune*.[97] In the wake of these blows, however, the community would appear in its most poetic guise as the object of wistful romantic imagination. If it failed economically, Brook Farm nonetheless succeeded aesthetically, though not in its assigned role as model phalanx. Ironically, romantic melancholy achieved a resonance that the well-ordered prototype could not. As Story's glimpsed but ungraspable "Ideal" and Hawthorne's charged but misty account suggest, the aesthetics of retrospection threatened to supplant those of futurity.

An Available Foothold

Associationists had argued that art could offer visionary glimpses of Harmony, that Association would give artists their economic rewards, and that the phalanx itself constituted a form of aesthetic organization. This background recasts Hawthorne's insistence in *Blithedale* on separating social theory from the aesthetics of romance as a contrarian gesture. Hawthorne takes rhetorical pains to differentiate his "fictitious handling" of both "the Institution itself" and the affective and aesthetic life of his characters from a statement about Associationist theory and practice. Although his characters exhibit powerful faculties of imagination, desire, empathy, and storytelling—faculties they invest, not always wisely, in the project at Blithedale and in one another—he separates their imaginative work, like his own, from "serious" debate: "In short, his present concern with the Socialist Community is merely to establish a theatre, a little removed from the highway of ordinary travel, where the creatures of his brain may play their phantasmagorical antics, without exposing them to too close a comparison with the actual events of real lives." Yet he characterizes his own stay at Brook Farm in terms of a remarkable dialectic of real life and romancer's imagination: "the most romantic episode of his own life—essentially a daydream, and yet a fact—and thus offering an available foothold between fiction and reality" (*BR*, 2). Reversing the Associationist insistence that aesthetic experience could pave the way to the phalanstery, Hawthorne uses the phalanstery as means to aesthetic experience while dismissing the imagination's social implications.

[97] Guarneri, *The Utopian Alternative*, 345–46.

Hawthorne's characterization in *Blithedale*, however, undercuts this diffidence: the aesthetic and affective sensibilities of Coverdale, Zenobia, and Priscilla, their own failings notwithstanding, stand in sharp contrast to the straitened institutional imagination of Hollingsworth, with his "scheme for the reformation of the wicked by methods moral, intellectual, and industrial" (*BR*, 131), and the snake-oil messianism of Westervelt, with his talk of "a new era that was dawning upon the world; an era that would link soul to soul, and the present life to what we call futurity, with a closeness that should finally convert both worlds into one great, mutually conscious brotherhood" (*BR*, 200). Although these caricatures of Associationist millennialism are keyed to provoke suspicion, the novel repeatedly suggests that *Blithedale*'s critics attack it in bad faith: Coverdale notes the "pungent squibs" and "penny-a-liners" in newspapers denigrating *Blithedale*, only to disavow his connection to the whole enterprise as "only an experiment, on which I had staked no valuable amount of hope or fear; it had enabled me to pass the summer in a novel and agreeable way, had afforded me some grotesque specimens of artificial simplicity, and could not, therefore, so far as I was concerned, be reckoned a failure" (*BR*, 195). Between these poles—Hollingsworth's monomaniacal institutionalism and Coverdale's self-serving refusal to imagine the social—it is reductive to conclude, as did Oneida Community founder John Humphrey Noyes, that Hawthorne's depiction of Brook Farm "gave the enemies of Association the benefit of his talent for sneering."[98] Rather, *Blithedale*'s characters offer cynical or blinkered versions of the very forms of aestheticized sociality that Hawthorne's Associationist contemporaries elaborated more hopefully.

Hawthorne, who left Brook Farm long before its 1844 reorganization along Fourierist lines, was not the only community member to posit a special relationship between the community and the imagination. His preface resonates with the more explicit but rarely read account of Brook Farmer and frequent *Harbinger* contributor John S. Dwight. Like Hawthorne's preface, Dwight's article is a reminiscence, written late in 1846, a year that had seen the destruction of the phalanstery by fire and the withdrawal of the American Union of Associationists' support for Brook Farm.[99] Yet whereas Hawthorne frames his imaginative work as occasioned by but distinct from the socialist community, Dwight portrays Brook Farm itself as the imagination made manifest. In a *Harbinger* article titled "How Stands the Cause?," Dwight takes stock of the Associationist movement with particular attention to Brook Farm, which seems to be receding already into memory. With some melancholy, Dwight acknowledges Brook Farm's reduced

[98] Carol Weisbrod, *The Boundaries of Utopia* (New York: Pantheon, 1980), 83. Later critics join Noyes in rejecting Hawthorne's claims of distancing himself from social pronouncements. See Russ Castronovo, *Necro Citizenship: Death, Eroticism, and the Public Sphere in the Nineteenth-Century United States* (Durham, NC: Duke University Press, 2002), 101–50; Jennifer Greiman, *Democracy's Spectacle* (New York: Fordham University Press, 2011), 157–91.

[99] Delano, *Brook Farm*, 251, 265.

state—not "a great industrial Phalanx"—"In this it failed"—yet nonetheless "the intellectual and moral center of the movement" and home to the *Harbinger*, "the only printed organ which we have."[100] Here he waxes poetic: "even in its lowest estate, amid its worst embarrassments as a pecuniary and business operation, there is a feeling, so long as it lasts, that the cause of Association is not without 'a local habitation and a name.' "[101]

Dwight's brief quotation alludes to Shakespeare's account of poetic imagination as world-making in *A Midsummer Night's Dream*:

> The poet's eye, in a fine frenzy rolling,
> Doth glance from heaven to earth, from earth to heaven,
> And as imagination bodies forth
> The forms of things unknown, the poet's pen
> Turns them to shapes, and gives to airy nothing
> A local habitation and a name.[102]

The poet makes good on her "fine frenzy" by anchoring the "airy nothing" of vision in "A local habitation and a name." By Dwight's analogy, if the poet's eye is visionary Fourierist theory, the poet's pen corresponds to the Brook Farmers' labor—not least the pen-work and presswork behind the *Harbinger*. The publication itself thus constitutes proof of the convertibility of romantic imaginative capacity into the future form of society—even at a moment when its visions are melting into air.

Years before Hawthorne would question the commingling of socialism and poetry, Dwight's allusion offers a way to both amplify the Associationist social imaginary and ground it. In contrast to Hawthorne's caricature of Brook Farmers as dreamers in theory and plodders in practice, Dwight identifies the community as the node where celestial imagination becomes earthly realization, and leaps from a Shakespearean register of poetics to a Christian register of messianic incarnation culminating in the "coming of the great day of Unity." Thanks to Brook Farm, Association "is not without its holy-land, where pilgrimages may be made, with hope of more than the imaginary influence of seeing the spot where the dead Lord was laid, but of being quickened by a living spirit, warmed to a new hope, and filled with a clearer light, about the destinies of society and the duty of each towards so great a movement."[103]

[100] *Harbinger* 3: 350–51. In this respect, Dwight echoes Ripley's hopes that Brook Farm could continue to serve as the center of Associationist intellectual culture and publishing. Delano, *Brook Farm*, 265–66.

[101] *Harbinger* 3: 351.

[102] "A Midsummer Night's Dream," in *The Norton Shakespeare*, ed. Stephen Greenblatt et al. (New York: Norton 1997), 5.1, 7–17.

[103] *Harbinger* 3: 351.

Reading Dwight alongside Hawthorne reveals how the latter's account of the imagination is less a rejection than a revision of Associationist aesthetics. Hawthorne's argument closely follows his preface to *The House of the Seven Gables*, in which he resists the readerly desire to "assign an actual locality to the imaginary events of this narrative." To do so, he argues, "exposes the romance to an inflexible and exceedingly dangerous species of criticism, by bringing his fancy-pictures almost into positive contact with the realities of the moment."[104] Marcy Dinius has described this moment's ambiguity: "what appears, at first glance, to be a warning seems like an invitation with another, given the sincere duplicity of the persona that Hawthorne develops and performs in his prefaces."[105] The same double gesture marks Hawthorne's refusal, in *Blithedale*'s preface, "to illustrate a theory or elicit a conclusion, favorable or otherwise, in respect to Socialism" (1).

Yet as Dwight's article and Hawthorne's diffident prefaces reveal in different ways, romance aesthetics and socialist theory are not so easily disentangled. The relationship between the existing world and the potential world, whether conceived of in the Fourierist language of passions, Civilization, and Association or Dwight's Shakespearean idiom of poetic "bod[ying] forth," is predicated on a reordering as subtle as the effects of moonlight or an atmospheric medium. Hawthorne's description of his Brook Farm experience as "an available foothold between fiction and reality" acknowledges essentially the same thing. Coverdale, who shares Hawthorne's romantic sense of temporality if not his follow-through, puts things even more clearly when he describes his "summer in the country" as, "part of another age, a different state of society, a segment of an existence peculiar in its aims and methods, a leaf of some mysterious volume, interpolated into the current history which Time was writing off." This interpolated "segment of existence" exposes the status quo as radically contingent, even immaterial: "I had never before experienced a mood that so robbed the actual world of its solidity" (146). The heterotopian, heterochronic quality of *Blithedale* destabilizes the distinction between "the clouds overhead" and "the actual soil" (3).

We can thus read Hawthorne and Dwight—as offering closely related theories of the corporate imaginary as a transformative social force. It is Hawthorne's vehement insistence on the ephemerality of romantic vision—or perhaps his fear of what a more lasting collective vision would entail—that marks his distance from his Associationist contemporaries. He complains in the preface that in contrast to the poetic license accorded European writers, "Among ourselves... there is as yet no such Faery Land, so like the real world, that, in a suitable remoteness, one cannot well tell the difference, but with an atmosphere of strange enchantment,

[104] Hawthorne, *House of the Seven Gables*, 3.

[105] Marcy J. Dinius, *The Camera and the Press: American Visual and Print Culture in the Age of the Daguerreotype* (Philadelphia, PA: University of Pennsylvania Press, 2012), 51–52.

beheld through which the inhabitants have a propriety of their own. This atmosphere is what the American romancer needs" (2). Yet the atmosphere whose absence Hawthorne bewails in America is the air of poetic possibility that Dwight senses in Brook Farm. In Dwight's romance, unlike Hawthorne's, a compelling story can mobilize the collective imagination to transform the ephemeral into an earthly "habitation." Although the phrase is Hawthorne's, it is Dwight who most clearly envisions a romantic "foothold between fiction and reality" as a springboard for collective social transformation. Departing from the individual subjectivity of Hawthorne's Coverdale (or Emerson's "Poet"), Dwight shows his investment in a corporate imaginary that recognizes the community as both aesthetic form and collective aesthetic agent.

* * *

In recognizing the statelikeness of companies, the corporateness of communities, and the practical uses of the joint-stock form, Associationists captured the world-making possibilities of the corporate form with particular clarity. In their unrealized blueprints for a world of phalanxes they also offered a corporate imaginary through which to elevate considerations of the law and the state to the plane of the romantic aesthetics of the imagination—and presented society's institutions as subject to the very aesthetic and affective forces to which Hawthorne attended. Ironically, the very hopes that would be disdained by their successors as visionary were those that refused to limit themselves to ephemeral imagination but instead grounded themselves in the constitutional and legal poetics of companies and commonwealths.

Perhaps no text is more at odds with Associationists' messianic optimism than Melville's final novel, *The Confidence-Man*, which coldly examines social faith as a medium of opportunistic power. Yet as I show in the final chapter, Melville's attention to the formal and affective properties of collective bodies both formal and improvised—the "assembled companies" on which the novel repeatedly lingers—recalls Associationists' attention to social form even as it dispenses with their teleological narrative. In bearing witness to the formation and dissolution of overlapping collectivities, Melville's novel has more to say than we might imagine about the political possibilities of the corporate.

The Corporate Forms of Antebellum US Literature. Peter Jaros, Oxford University Press. © Peter Jaros 2026.
DOI: 10.1093/9780198996491.003.0006

6

Assembled Companies

The Corporate Forms of *The Confidence-Man*

A Mississippi riverboat might seem an odd stage for dramatizing the corporate form. Yet this setting both invokes a commonplace of eighteenth- and nineteenth-century theories of the corporation and illuminates their connections to persistent questions of philosophy and political theory. How are we to understand a corporation aggregate as a single unit? William Blackstone, in Commentaries on the Laws of England, offers a striking image: "for all the individual members that have existed from the foundation to the present time, or that shall ever hereafter exist, are but one person in law, a person that never dies: in like manner as the river Thames is still the same river, though the parts which compose it are changing every instant."[1] A corporation's individuality and immortality are constituted by this perpetual succession, no more tied to particular members than a river's identity is to particular particles of water. Grounding the law of artificial persons in a natural image, Blackstone's rhetoric reveals a doubleness in his theory of the corporation. While he explicitly defines corporate personality as a *legal* fact granted by a sovereign charter (the concession or artificial entity theory), the unity-in-multiplicity of the river analogy suggests an *ontological* basis for the corporation prior to legal recognition (the real entity theory).[2] While nineteenth-century American jurisprudence on the corporation, following Marshall's often-cited *Dartmouth College* opinion, most frequently articulates the artificial entity theory, contemporaneous theorists of associations attended to the forms and potentialities of assembled bodies beyond this narrow legal basis.

In *The Confidence-Man: His Masquerade* (1857), Herman Melville doubles down on Blackstone's figure. Early in the novel, Melville compares the ever-changing passengers aboard the *Fidèle* to the "strange waters" of "Rio Janeiro fountain," "overflowing with strange waters, but never with the same particles in every part."[3] And of course, this riverlike company of strangers floats down the

[1] William Blackstone, The Oxford Edition of Blackstone's: Commentaries on the Laws of England: Book I: Of the Rights of Persons *(1765–69)*, ed. David Lemmings (Oxford: Oxford University Press, 2016), 456.

[2] See Harold J. Laski, "The Personality of Associations," *Harvard Law Review* 29 (1916) 404–26. Henry S. Turner, *The Corporate Commonwealth* (Chicago: University of Chicago Press, 2016); David Runciman, *Pluralism and the Personality of the State* (Cambridge: Cambridge University Press, 1997).

[3] Herman Melville, *The Confidence-Man: His Masquerade* (Evanston, IL: Northwestern University Press, 1984). 8. Subsequent references in parentheses.

Mississippi River itself, which "unit[es] the streams of the most distant and opposite zones...in one cosmopolitan and confident tide" (*CM*, 9). If you want to understand the doctrine of the corporation, both Melville and Blackstone suggest, look at a river. Yet if Melville's river metaphor echoes a commonplace of corporation theory—a tradition to which I will return below—the company aboard a riverboat presents a more ambiguous spectacle. As discussed in chapter 2, the nineteenth-century polymath Francis Lieber briefly raises—and then rejects—"a steamboat full of passengers" as an emblem of the state or society. Outside of certain shared interests—"to reach a certain point as soon as possible, all in the same condition, having paid their fare, and equally interested in the safety of the vessel"—he writes, "every passenger forms an isolated individual....Is this a society: an organised thing, with life and energy, with moral elasticity, with power, which can rest on close union alone?"[4] Yet while Melville's *Fidèle* certainly serves as a stage for the enterprising cunning of isolated individuals, it also reveals entanglements among its passengers that belie Lieber's vision of the steamboat as atomistic and antisocial. As Blackstone's, Lieber's, and Melville's images suggest, corporate rivers, boat-societies, and riverlike corporations raise difficult questions about how to delimit and characterize entities. This ontological muddiness prompts what might seem an unsophisticated question: what kind of being or beings does Melville's novel depict? By putting *The Confidence-Man* into conversation with a seldom-read nineteenth-century investigation into the nature of the corporation, I'll suggest that the novel opens onto a richer and stranger field than we might realize. In doing so, moreover, it reframes some fundamental questions of politics in unfamiliar and revealing ways.

The Confidence-Man has, for a long time, both attracted and repelled readers with its dizzying play with character and identity. Does its title refer to a single protagonist who dons a series of disguises or a looser assemblage gathered under the rubric of a type—the confidence man? Or does it indicate, as Mark Noble has suggested, that mankind itself is the result of intersubjective confidence? Recently, scholars including Noble and Jennifer Greiman have read *The Confidence-Man* less as a satirical catalog blasting contemporary society than as a landscape of possible forms of sociality.[5] Thus for Noble, the novel's dismantling or evacuation of individual character does not indicate a "crisis" for "the coherence of social relationship" but rather reveals "the ground for social relationship," thus "afford[ing] something like a social ontology" of modernity.[6] In this chapter, I show how the

[4] Francis Lieber, *Manual of Political Ethics: Designed Chiefly for the Use of Colleges and Students at Law* (Boston: Little and Brown, 1838–39), Vol. 1, 191.

[5] Jennifer Greiman, "Theatricality, Strangeness, and the Aesthetics of Plurality in *The Confidence-Man*, in *Melville and Aesthetics*, ed. Samuel Otter and Geoffrey Sanborn (New York: Palgrave, 2011); Mark Noble, "Reading Melville Reading Character," *J19:* The Journal of Nineteenth-Century Americanists 4, no. 2 (2016): 237–47.

[6] Noble, "Reading Melville Reading Character," 238, 240.

novel articulates an ontology of associations and thus dramatizes the affordances of various associated and incorporated forms. In contrast to the Associationists' totalizing project of consolidating and perfecting the corporate form, *The Confidence-Man* offers readers a playbook—at once strategic, theatrical, and ludic for the age of corporations.

In pursuing this corporate ontology, I avoid the novel's "deep" question, whose exhaustion and inexhaustibility Peggy Kamuf made clear two decades ago: "To the question 'Whose is the face behind the mask?' every answer can be made credible by a reading of selected element."[7] As Kamuf suggests, *The Confidence-Man* can seem a trap designed to provoke suspicious reading even as the novel dramatizes the dangers of suspicion and credulity alike. The deck is stacked from the moment "a mute" steps aboard "[a]t sunrise on the first day of April" daring readers to be his April fools, whether simply gullible or overconfident in their own skepticism (*CM*, 3). The novel's ambiguous final line—"Something further may follow from this masquerade"—invites the same play of suspicion and credulity, explaining everything (so *that's* what this was—a masquerade!) and nothing (*CM*, 251). At the same time, its nod to "something further" evokes something like José Esteban Muñoz's conception of queer futurity as a "mode of desiring that allows us to see and feel beyond the quagmire of the present."[8]

Of course, the topos of masquerade, as Dror Wahrman has argued, foregrounds the playfulness and conventionality of identity rather than a logic of stable inner selves.[9] In this sense, Melville's language offers an oblique view of the legal form of the corporation, a collective artificial persona (masquerade) constituted by succession (following). The vocabulary of the corporation—artificial persons, piercing the corporate veil, etc.—is congenial to the idiom of the mask, but a corporation's legal persona is not a disguise or a hermeneutic puzzle. From this perspective, the relevant question is not *Who is the confidence man?* but *How do these masks operate, and what are they good for?* Reading *The Confidence-Man* in the context of the corporation, this chapter thus sets aside questions about some ultimate identity obscured by "the" confidence man's masquerade in favor of considering the forms of association encompassed by masquerade—a term that refers, after all, not to a single disguise but to an assembled company—in one character's words, "a pic-nic *en costume*" (*CM*, 133).

In this spirit, Sianne Ngai has aptly emphasized the way *The Confidence-Man* foregrounds assemblages or assemblies rather than individuals: "a throng of functionally ambiguous characters who endlessly combine and recombine with each

[7] Peggy Kamuf, *The Division of Literature: or the University in Deconstruction* (Chicago: University of Chicago Press, 1997), 207.

[8] José Esteban Muñoz, *Cruising Utopia: The There and Then of Queer Futurity* (2009), 10th Anniversary ed. (New York: New York University Press, 2019), 1.

[9] Dror Wahrman, *The Making of the Modern Self: Identity and Culture in Eighteenth-Century England* (New Haven, CT: Yale University Press, 2004).

other."[10] This network, she writes, is organized around the recurring figure of the operator who "convinces those with whom he 'assembles' that the feeling he invokes [i.e. confidence] is both fungible and possessible," thus transmuting affect, "feeling uncontained by the subject," into emotion, "something his dupes experience as occasioned within them."[11] As Ngai convincingly argues, this arrangement lays bare a fundamental affective structure of capitalism. Yet to identify capitalism as the meaning or motor of the novel's recombinant throngs risks repeating the familiar move of unmasking, short-circuiting the novel's intricate play with assembled companies by assuming that every company is a for-profit enterprise.

Rather, like the catalogs of examples of the corporate form that proliferated in the 1830s, *The Confidence-Man* offers a broad and varied landscape of associated bodies, including but not limited to the incorporated businesses that build capital from confidence. The consistent attention the novel devotes to the constitution of the various associations, from banks to reform societies, reveals the broad horizons of the corporate form beyond the seeming "teleological inevitability" of the modern, for-profit corporation.[12] Centering depictions of corporate collectivity means exchanging the questions of knowledge, faith, and doubt that typically animate readings of the novel for its prospect on the capacities of associated form. While readers of *The Confidence-Man* have long strained to see the face behind the mask, they have less frequently attended to the novel's compelling accounts of how corporate personae are crafted and companies called together. Melville's novel echoes the texts examined in earlier chapters in offering a rich sampling of the nineteenth-century corporate imaginary, yet the modes of association it presents do not simply reflect the mid-century corporate landscape. Rather, they amplify existing forms, drawing out their hidden consequences, and trace out possibilities for association unexplored in Melville's moment and forgotten in ours. They suggest, in particular, how corporate forms of plurality might offer unfamiliar perspectives on political belonging.

As discussed in chapter 2, Americans in the early decades of the nineteenth century were experts at the practical and legal techniques of association. The world of voluntary associations embraced mutual aid societies and turnpike companies, temperance societies and banks; a heterogeneous group that sprawls beyond contemporary notions of either voluntarism or the corporation. As Kevin Butterfield emphasizes, that culture of associations was deeply "law-minded": the founders and members of various societies and associations were versed in the legal genealogies and procedures of the corporation and the US Constitution; they tended to settle disputes among and within associations—the inclusion and exclusion of members, the formal standing of such bodies, etc.—through legal

[10] Sianne Ngai, *Ugly Feelings* (Cambridge, MA: Harvard University Press, 2007), 51.

[11] Ngai, *Ugly Feelings*, 61.

[12] Turner, *The Corporate Commonwealth*, 28.

channels.[13] This culture of associations provides the implicit backdrop for many of the questions raised in *The Confidence-Man*: what do the familiar shapes of the business corporation and the charitable association reveal about assembled bodies more broadly? What other shapes might such bodies take? What capacity do such bodies have—and what capacities *must* they have—to act as unified or singular beings? How do unincorporated bodies appear to the eye of the law—or the human eye? How might different sorts of assembled bodies traverse each other, and what happens when they come into conflict? Finally, to what degree does any assembled body—and not just a chartered corporation—constitute, as Hobbes feared, a nascent state, an *imperium in imperio*—or some other sort of entity? Taken together, these questions can help us see how persistently *The Confidence Man* is explores the possibilities of organizational, corporate, and political assembly. Rather than provide a focused critique of contemporaneous institutions or propose an alternate form of organization, it delves into the dynamic possibilities of assembled bodies—the good and ill they make possible, the salutary and corrosive ways they dismantle individuality. If, in some ways, it adumbrates the real entity theory of the corporation, it also asks readers whether so-called natural persons are any more real than the collectives they form.

The Age of Joint-Stock Companies

> "In former and less humanitarian ages—the ages of amphitheatres and gladiators—geniality was mostly confined to the fireside and table. But in our age—the age of joint-stock companies and free-and-easies—it is with this precious quality as with precious gold in old Peru, which Pizarro found making up the scullion's sauce-pot as the Inca's crown. Yes, we golden boys, the moderns, have geniality everywhere—a bounty broadcast like noonlight."
>
> (*CM*, 175)

In the introduction, I contrasted Emerson's view of society as a restrictive "joint-stock company" that strips the "liberty and culture" of each member with Ishmael and Queequeg's monkey-rope, a "joint stock company of two" that "merge[s]" individuality into intimate, if risky, interdependence. The Cosmopolitan, the second-act star of *The Confidence-Man* and the speaker of the quotation above, heralds both the ubiquity of companies the new forms of relation and affect to which they give rise. Like Emerson, he identifies the joint-stock company as one of the representative institutions of his age; unlike his precursor, however, he embraces the expanding "geniality" of "the age of joint-stock companies and

[13] Kevin Butterfield, *The Making of Tocqueville's America: Law and Association in the Early United States* (Chicago: University of Chicago Press, 2015), 37.

free-and-easies." The etymological senses of "geniality"—domestic intimacy and genital contact—resonate in the Cosmopolitan's references to "fireside and table" and particularly to "free-and-easies": saloons known for musical performance, homosocial intimacy, and sex work. By his account, the joint-stock age is less an era of compromised individuality than an age of expanded intimacy, networked connectivity, and exposed community—a huckster's version, perhaps, of Jean-Luc Nancy's notion of being-in-common.[14] The Cosmopolitan's account of ever-expanding geniality, "broadcast like noonlight," reads as perhaps a shade too sunny, not least because the analogy he draws to "precious gold in old Peru" suggests that the proliferation of a valuable thing in the commons devalues it—makes it common. He says precious little, however, about the kinds of exposure and alliance that commonality or community can produce.

More broadly, the Cosmopolitan's words bring into focus Melville's attention throughout *The Confidence-Man* to the ubiquity and plurality of corporate forms and the ways they condition subjectivity, affect, and social organization. *The Confidence-Man* not only presents a handful of notable companies; it also foregrounds, as do *Sheppard Lee* and *Astoria*, a corporate *narrative* subject, whether the titular confidence-man or the *Fidèle*. It's hard not to read the novel's unity (or lack thereof) as reflecting the viability or vulnerability of assembled, if unincorporated, bodies.[15] This attention to varied forms of association and assembly and their consequences—including the affects of confidence and charity to their dialectical twins skepticism and antipathy—ought to dissuade us from reading the book merely as the story of a character or type that instrumentalizes human interaction in the pursuit of profit.[16] As one skeptical observer within the novel points out, "Was the man a trickster, it must be more for the love than the lucre" (*CM*, 130). In other words, if there is *a* confidence man, and he is constituted like a corporation, we ought to situate him in the messy and expansive landscape of nineteenth-century corporations rather than assume that he will relentlessly pursue shareholder value. By design or by accident, these corporations produced many things other than profit—perhaps even love.

The remainder of this chapter turns to four corporate forms and phenomena on which *The Confidence-Man* dwells: the state, which incorporates a plurality into a body politic; the share, which partitions corporate assets into fungible commodities; the charity, which erases the political even as it is curiously structured like a political body; and a form I call, borrowing Melville's language, the assembled company—an assemblage with a life of its own that exceeds its concatenated parts even

[14] Nancy describes being-in-common as a "mode of being…presuppose[s] that there is no common being, no substance, no essence, or common identity, but that there is being *in* common." Jean-Luc Nancy, "Of Being-in-Common," in *Community at Loose Ends*, ed. Miami Theory Collective, trans. James Creech (Minneapolis, MN: University of Minnesota Press, 1991), 1–12.

[15] See Frederic Maitland, "The Unincorporate Body," in *State, Trust, and Corporation*, ed. David Runciman and Magnus Ryan (Cambridge: Cambridge University Press, 2003), 52–61.

[16] On these affective-epistemological complexes in *The Confidence-Man*, see Ngai, *Ugly Feelings*, 38–88; Kamuf, *The Division of Literature*, 167–222.

when it lacks formal recognition. In contrast to Emerson's depiction of "society" as the bad company from which we ought to disassociate, Melville's extensive and overlapping companies anticipate a "sociology of associations" that eschews hypostasizing society as a whole in favor of tracing the particular mechanisms of association.[17] In each of the episodes to which I now turn, Melville highlights a particular corporate form and posits a particular relationship between individual and association. Each form of collectivity offers a different means of apprehending a corporate body or assembly. Taken together, they suggest that thinking through the corporation can offer an idiom of human plurality more supple than traditional political, natural, or religious conceptions.

While the *Fidèle*'s voyage may seem remote from state power, Melville gestures early to an imagined *state* with a universal reach: an "Anacharsis Cloots congress" that might represent all humanity as a self-present political subject incorporated in a single body—and later introduces the Cosmopolitan, who does one better by figuratively federating all nations in a single person.

The *share* abstracts a company as exchange value, as a sum of fungible parts, constitutes the individual as owner rather than member, and renders collectivity invisible amid a world of atomized shareholders—in short, it prefigures the modern property corporation and its grounding abstraction of shareholder value while minimizing the exposure and experience of sharing. If the practice of speculating in shares has lost its strangeness in the intervening years, Melville's presentation of the Black Rapids Coal Company dramatizes the way the share effaces the corporate body and minimizes corporate belonging—even as its abstract rise and fall echoes theological tropes.

The *charity* exemplifies one of the dominant incarnations of the early nineteenth century corporation—from Dartmouth College to the Bible, temperance, and abolition societies that proliferated during the 1830s and 1840s. From the man in cream-colors's initial invocation of Christian charity in the language of 1 Corinthians to the man in gray's World's Charity, *The Confidence-Man* juxtaposes the virtue of charity with the corporations that borrow its name. By operationalizing St Paul's conception of love (*caritas/agape*)—the "bond of perfectness"—as an organizational strategy, the charity refigures Christian love as a form of governance that separates the body of a charity's organizers from its subject population.[18] The World's Charity presents a logical, if hyperbolic, development of the ambitious charities of Melville's day: by imagining the world's population as objects of charity, it frames a world state that (following the example of missionary work) translates love as governance while erasing the political subjectivity of the governed. At the same time, it incarnates what the man in gray calls the

[17] Bruno Latour, *Reassembling the Social*: An Introduction to Actor-Network Theory (Oxford: Oxford University Press, 2005), 9.

[18] Col. 3 :14 (King James Version).

"Wall street spirit"—a sharp metaphysical contrast to the trope of the "soulless corporation" (*CM* 40, 203).

While the state, the share, and the charity depend on the formal and legal unity of the corporation, the *assembled company* lacks such coherence. Yet Melville's description of the company assembled on board the *Fidèle* suggests that it would be erroneous *not* to consider it a body with properties of its own. His description of this singular but unchartered entity prefigures a number of later theoretical traditions: real entity theory, which sees in unincorporated bodies entities worthy of recognition even when they lack the indices of chartered corporations, as well as actor-network theory's account of association and Jean-Luc Nancy and Maurice Blanchot's accounts of a community that is constitutively incomplete and non-self-identical.[19] While the assembled company, as Melville presents it, constitutes a kind of substantive, if elusive, unity, it also unmakes the individuals who constitute this constantly transforming collective—a Heraclitean corporation that once again takes up the venerable trope of the river. The assembled company offers, I argue, a politics of plurality that departs from the dominant associational models of Melville's day—the state, the business corporation, and the charity—and the forms of sovereignty toward which they gesture. Yet it also offers a way to recognize the collective being of groups that liberal theorists had only understood as atomized individuals.

Humanity, Incorporated

In chapter 2, Melville closes a catalog of the *Fidèle*'s passengers with a memorable description: "a piebald parliament, an Anacharsis Cloots congress of all kinds of that multiform pilgrim species, man" (9).[20] These words echo Ishmael's characterization in *Moby-Dick* of the *Pequod*'s "Anacharsis Clootz deputation from all the isles of the sea, and all the ends of the earth."[21] In both moments, Melville playfully gestures towards the Prussian nobleman-cum-French Revolutionary Cloots's attempt to collect a representative ensemble that might embody the human race, as conceived in the *Déclaration des droits de l'homme et du citoyen*, as a world-state, the republic of mankind. Cloots's project, however utopian, offers a concrete vision of the human being as such as political subject and its

[19] Jean-Luc Nancy, *The Inoperative Community*, ed. Peter Connor, trans. Peter Connor, Lisa Garbus, Michael Holland, and Simona Sawhney (Minneapolis, MN: University of Minnesota Press, 1991); Maurice Blanchot, *The Unavowable Community*, trans. Pierre Joris (Barrytown, NY: Station Hill Press, 1988).

[20] As Walter Johnson points out, "it was a nineteenth-century literary commonplace to describe a Mississippi steamboat as a 'world in miniature.'" Walter Johnson, *River of Dark Dreams: Slavery and Empire in the Cotton Kingdom* (Cambridge, MA: Belknap Press, 2013), 127.

[21] Herman Melville, Moby-Dick (1851), ed, Hershel Parker and Harrison Hayford (New York: Norton, 2002), 107.

corollary, a universal state.[22] While Ishmael describes the *Pequod's* crew as an ad hoc "deputation," the *Fidèle* hosts a proper representative assembly, a "congress" or "parliament." And whereas Ishmael anchors the oceangoing *Pequod's* crew to "all the isles of the sea, and all the ends of the earth," the *Fidèle*, despite its inland setting, deterritorializes the body politic of migratory humanity, "that multiform pilgrim species." If, in one sense, the *Fidèle* realizes Cloots's vision, in another it radicalizes and destabilizes it through the image of a hybrid humanity on board a moving vessel. (Under the rubric of the assembled company, I'll return to the question of whether and how this hybrid assembly might form a commonwealth without any sort of declaration.)

Halfway through *The Confidence-Man*, the Cosmopolitan appears as the emblem of such an Anacharsis Cloots congress: he "federates, in heart as in costume, something of the various gallantries of men under various suns" (*CM*, 132) and attempts to draw the skeptics and loners among the *Fidèle's* passengers into his collective.[23] His appeal, though, smacks less of democracy than of cannibalism: "Is the sight of humanity so very disagreeable to you then? Ah, I may be foolish, but for my part, in all its aspects, I love it. Served up à la Pole, or à la Moor, à la Ladrone, or à la Yankee, that good dish, man, still delights me; or rather is man a wine I never weary of comparing and sipping; wherefore am I a pledged cosmopolitan, a sort of London-Dock-Vault connoisseur, going about from Teheran to Natchitoches, a taster of races; in all his vintages, smacking my lips over this racy creature, man, continually" (*CM*, 133).

This connoisseur of humanity disdains the "teetotal souls which relish not even the very best brands of humanity" (*CM*, 133). Here it's worth remembering Ishmael's words: "Men may seem detestable as joint stock-companies and nations" yet they earn his admiration when, as "meanest mariners, renegades, and castaways," they constitute a collective without stable national or corporate identity.[24] That stable identity is a little too prominent for the voracious Clootsian Cosmopolitan: "To you, an Ishmael," he says to one disagreeable interlocutor, "I came ambassador from the human race" (*CM*, 138). Acting on the premise of a human race that is constituted, consolidated, and sending forth ambassadors, he comes to Ishmaels and isolatoes as a dominating, ingesting force.

Although these colonizing pleas for confidence in mankind seem forced (particularly in his tête-a-tête with the "Mississippi operator" Charlie Noble), the Cosmopolitan's case for human interdependence is difficult to dispute. As the

[22] Cloots "adapt[ed] features central to the revolutionary polity: popular sovereignty, the general will, the single legislative chamber, and above all, national unity." Alexander Bevilacqua, "Conceiving the Republic of Mankind: The Political Thought of Anacharsis Cloots," *History of European Ideas* 38, no. 4 (2012): 550–69, 553.

[23] Hans-Joachim Lang and Benjamin Lease identify the Cosmopolitan as a portrait of the writer, traveler, and diplomat Bayard Taylor. "Melville's Cosmopolitan: Bayard Taylor in *The Confidence-Man*," *Amerikastudien/American Studies* 22 (1977): 286–90.

[24] Melville, *Moby-Dick*, 103.

Emerson-manqué figure Mark Winsome joins him in the seat recently occupied by Noble, the Cosmopolitan ruminates on the intimacy of heat exchange: "the genial warmth of whose person in part passes into yours, and whose genial hospitality meanders through you—be it so" (*CM*, 190). Both Winsome and his disciple Egbert—true to Emerson's rejection of society as joint-stock company—resist the Cosmopolitan's call to geniality. Yet the latter tacitly concedes his own porousness as he borrows his interlocutor's idiom of interconnection to acknowledge his debt to his sage in: "the voice of Mark Winsome is congenial to my larynx" (*CM*, 207). Whatever the Cosmopolitan's motives, he gestures repeatedly toward the adhesive power of congeniality, the dependence of individuals on larger social bodies, the ubiquity of artificial personation and role-playing. The principles of association and personation anchor his claim to ambassadorship; the "human race" marks not a natural species but a body politic whose unity is realized in the act of representation itself.

Shareholders

While the Cosmopolitan's Clootsian appeal is overbearing in both its affect and its scope, *The Confidence-Man* presents a more modest and convenient sort of corporatism in the form of company stock. Stocks come to the fore in chapter 4 when John Ringman, the man with a weed, persuades a merchant named Henry Roberts to give him a substantial banknote through a "tale of singular interest" (*CM*, 21) that recalls the operations of the "original confidence man."[25] In response to Roberts's gift, Ringman offers a stock tip: the president of the Black Rapids Coal Company is on board and, "having been subpoenaed as a witness in a stock case on the docket in Kentucky, has his transfer book with him" (*CM*, 22). Ringman lays claim to inside information: the company's stock, he insinuates, has fallen due to a selloff by "artful alarmists," but has bought back by the company, soon to be sold "at par" to investors: "For, the panic subsiding more and more every day, it will daily be seen how it originated; confidence will be more than restored; there will be a reaction; from the stock's descent its rise will be higher than from no fall, the holders trusting themselves to fear no second fate" (*CM*, 22). Like his earlier tale of woe, his stock tip dramatizes the emergence of corporate value from affect—panic and confidence, swerve and reaction, the hushed excitement of insider information. This relocation of value from the company's assets and prospects to the affective environment surrounding it is less

[25] The source of *The Confidence-Man*'s title, the so-called "original confidence man," went by William Thompson and a handful of other names, and was arrested in Manhattan in July, 1849; Melville read of him in 1855. Shortly after his arrest, the New York *Herald* published "'The Confidence Man' on a large Scale," which looked not to the Tombs but "the paths that lead to Wall street." Melville, *The Confidence Man*, 283.

a matter of the nature of this company than of the relatively novel form in which it appears.

Stock ownership in the mid-nineteenth century United States was understood less as a uniform practice than as a combination of speculation and participation. Historian John Majewski highlights one common divide: "speculative booms in banking, civic-minded investment in transportation companies."[26] Moreover, "shareholding in early corporations was not confined to a tiny urban elite but involved a broad occupational swath" of the population, particularly investment in corporations whose "aim was not quick profit, but long-term community development," particularly around transportation and infrastructure.[27] Thus, even as shareholding was emerging as a speculative practice, the most widespread forms of corporate investment were those furthest removed from speculation. Joined to the new vision of the shareholder as profit-seeker—and of the corporation as an instrument for maximizing shareholder gain—the share quantified the company's value even as it enabled that value to be abstracted so far from the company's operations that it could effectively float free of them.[28] While shareholding was a familiar and widespread practice by the mid-nineteenth century, trading and speculating in stocks retained novelty and mystery, as William Armstrong's pamphlet *Stocks and Stock-Jobbing in Wall Street* (1848) makes clear. Writing as "a reformed stock gambler," Armstrong warns that "it does not at all add to the business credit or reputation of a mercantile man to be known as an operator in stocks".[29]

As noted in chapter 3, he particularly cautions readers against the plentiful so-called "Fancy Stocks," which "represent worthless or embarrassed corporations, which have failed in the undertakings for which capital was contributed.... Their real worth, or rather worthlessness, is so little known, that it seldom interferes with an expansion or contraction in prices, as according to the wealth or talent employed on either side may preponderate."[30] Armstrong explains that stock

[26] John Majewski, "Toward a Social History of the Corporation: Shareholding in Pennsylvania, 1800–1840," in *The Economy of Early America: Historical Perspectives and New Directions*," ed. Cathy Matson (University Park, PA: Pennsylvania State University Press, 2006), 297.

[27] Majewski, "Toward a Social History of the Corporation," 312; John Majewski, *A House Dividing: Economic Development in Pennsylvania and Virginia before the Civil War* (Cambridge: Cambridge University Press, 200), 8.

[28] As Eric Hilt points out, in the early decades of the nineteenth century shareholding slowly spread beyond the elite circles of corporate directors and the public officials whose favor they sought; by the 1820s: "Shareholders and directors remained atypical of the population, but became less so over time as larger numbers of corporations were created." Eric Hilt, "Early American Corporations and the State," in *Corporations and American Democracy*, ed. Naomi R. Lamoreaux and William J. Novak (Cambridge, MA: Harvard University Press, 2017), 51.

[29] William Armstrong, *Stocks and Stock-Jobbing in Wall-Street, with Sketches of the Brokers, and Fancy Stocks* (New York: New-York Publishing Company, 1848), 6–7. Contrast Angell and Ames's 1832 assertion that "There is scarcely an individual of respectable character in our community, who is not a member of, at least, one private company or society which is incorporated." Joseph K. Angell and Samuel Ames, *Treatise on the Law of Private Corporations Aggregate* (Boston: Hilliard, 1832), 51.

[30] Armstrong, *Stocks and Stock-Jobbing*, 13.

fluctuations generally result from struggles between bulls and bears—or rather from "the wire pullers of either party," with the result that "outsiders are apt to suffer" when tempted by ballooning prices.[31]

On the one hand, the Black Rapids Coal Company constitutes the minimal assemblage of the company reduced to an object of exchange: a man—the Company president and agent, with his traveling-cap—and his "ledger-like volume" (*CM*, 46). Coal corporations had generated both impressive profits and considerable suspicion in the decades preceding *The Confidence-Man*. Because coal mining required significant investment capital (and entailed significant risks), it "became one of the first industrial pursuits to use the corporate form of organization." Coal company charters were contested for a number of reasons: anti-corporate sentiment was inspired by banking corporations, entrenched interests sought to exclude their competitors, and mining corporations were perceived as vehicles for speculation.[32]

Contemporaneous readers of *The Confidence-Man* would thus be ready to eye the Black Rapids Coal Company and its stocks with suspicion. To compound matters further, not only are the company's president and records under subpoena, but its oversized transfer book looks suspiciously like a register of souls purchased by the Devil and its booster Ringman promotes it in the language of Milton's Satan. In Book II of *Paradise Lost*, Satan urges the assembly at Pandaemonium to retake their heavenly place: "From this descent / Celestial Virtues rising, will appear / More glorious and more dread than from no fall / And trust themselves to fear no second fate."[33] In contrast to the falls and uprisings of banished angels, Ringman's description of stock prices can only seem bathetic: "from the stock's descent its rise will be higher than from no fall, the holders trusting themselves to fear no second fate" (*CM*, 22).

Even without these metaphysical warnings, the company bears the suspicious marks of a volatile fancy stock. While one investor casts a quick eye on the "small, printed pamphlet" that details the state of the company, readers learn nothing about the pamphlet's contents or the company's assets (does the company take its name from its location near the "black rapids" of a river? From the resemblance of coal veins to such rapids? From a metaphorical, infernal blackness?).[34] We read, rather, of the rise and fall of company stock, of bulls and bears, over- and undervaluation, all part of a reluctantly delivered sales pitch that recalls the

[31] Armstrong, *Stocks and Stock-Jobbing*, 20.

[32] Sean Patrick Adams, *Old Dominion, Industrial Commonwealth: Coal, Politics, and Economy in Antebellum America* (Baltimore, MD: Johns Hopkins University Press, 2004), 154, 165–66. Adams notes that Coal companies were long excluded from general incorporation statutes in Pennsylvania and Virginia (173).

[33] John Milton, *Paradise Lost* II: 14–17. *Complete Poems and Major Prose*, ed. Merritt Y. Hughes (Upper Saddle River, NJ: Prentice Hall, 1957), 232.

[34] "Sad Acheron of sorrow, black and deep" is one of the four rivers Milton depicts as feeding the "burning Lake" of Hell (II:578, 576).

"'money articles' in the leading papers of the day, which are often very elaborate productions... in most cases written by interested persons or by individuals who are bribed to write in a specified manner."[35] If the company statement goes virtually unread, its transfer-book is a talismanic object. While the man with the traveling-cap repeatedly protests that "it would hardly be the thing to convert this boat into the Company's office" (*CM*, 47), "Business [is] transacted" with a number of eager investors (*CM*, 49). The transformation of the corporation from a community of members to a commodity exchanged by shareholders redefines the company's substance as its exchange value.

As he tips his hand to the eager collegian, the man with the traveling-cap offers a glimpse of the corporation's two bodies: "we have been so very prosperous lately in our affairs—by we, I mean the Black Rapids Coal Company—that, really, out of my abundance, associative and individual, it is but fair that a charitable investment or two should be made, don't you think so?" (*CM*, 47). With his "we" and "My abundance, associative and individual," he speaks both as an officer of the corporation—an integral part of a corporate body—and a private investor—a beneficiary of the emergent, abstracted corporation of exchange value. The seeming oxymoron "charitable investment" highlights a related doubleness: the business corporation-as-membership-organization (in contrast to the business corporation-as-shareholder-abstraction) closely resembles the incorporated charity. "Investment" ambiguously gestures both ways: on the one hand, suggesting a merely financial interest; on the other, recalling the etymological roots of "investment" in clothing. After all, Melville's succession of characters resists abstraction or disembodiment through this literal investment precisely in being metonymically identified by articles of clothing: a weed, a gray coat, a traveling-cap (articles that, taken together, offer one gloss for the titular "masquerade"). At this moment, then, we see both the extreme of economic abstraction and the remnants of corporate embodiment. Only through the disembodiment of the corporation and its distillation into exchange value can one become an investor without investiture, a holder of shares rather than a member of a shared corporate body. Such abstraction underlies what Armstrong calls "those peculiar, mysterious, keen, spicy, and rascally transactions" that "constitute the greater part of the mysteries of Wall-street."[36] But its possibilities do not end there.

Objects of Charity/Objects of Sovereignty

The Confidence-Man's charitable companies present another form of corporate power. The charitable counterpart of the Coal Company president appears in

[35] Armstrong, *Stocks and Stock-Jobbing*, 16.

[36] Armstrong, *Stocks and Stock-Jobbing*, 12.

chapter 6 as the man in a gray coat and white tie, soliciting contributions for "a Widow and Orphan Asylum recently founded among the Seminoles" (*CM*, 28). Both appear as agents of faraway concerns; both are skilled in converting affect into cash, anchored by confidence in these remote entities. The representative of the Widow and Orphan Asylum, moreover, indicates the entanglement between association and state: the US Army's involvement in the Third Seminole War (1855–58), contemporary with *The Confidence Man*'s composition and publication, marks the Asylum as a *reductio ad absurdum* of charity. This institution is not a bulwark against state violence but a palliative to make it socially acceptable, the white man's burden in genocidal real time. Needless to say, the man in gray collects generous contributions from the white Americans in whose name the Seminole War is being carried out. The interweaving of these cutting satires, along with locutions like "the charity business" (*CM*, 38) and "charitable investment" (*CM*, 47), suggest how the boundaries between business, charity, and the state have blurred. In doing so, they recall Lieber's characterization of "the whole political system" as "a concatenation of various corporations, political, civil, religious, social, and economical," with the "nation itself" as "the great corporation, comprehending all the others."[37] Beyond stressing the parallels between various instances of the corporate form, Lieber's words indicate a corporate imaginary in which the corporation was not only a comprehensive unit but a part of a larger, coherent corporate assemblage.

As historic cases like *Sutton's Hospital* and *Dartmouth College* remind us, central facets of the law of corporations were built around charitable associations. Blackstone defines eleemosynary (charitable) corporations as those "constituted for the perpetual distribution of the free alms, or bounty, of the founder of them to such persons as he has directed."[38] The act of a founding donation, Blackstone writes, gives the founder lasting authority: whereas the king, as "sole founder," holds the right of visitation (i.e. oversight) for civil corporations, the "patron or endower," as "perficient founder" holds it for eleemosynary corporations.[39] In *Dartmouth College*, Justices Marshall and Story followed Blackstone's emphasis on corporate origins to articulate a far-reaching theory of private corporations. As Story wrote, "If…the foundation be private, though under the charter of the government, the corporation is private, however extensive the uses may be to which it is devoted, either by the bounty of the founder, or the nature and objects of the institution."[40] As discussed in earlier chapters, Story's theory of the private anchors the modern corporation's claim to private authority in the rights of charitable founders.

[37] Francis Lieber, "Corporation," in *Encyclopaedia Americana* (Philadelphia, PA: Carey & Lea, 1830), Vol. 3, 547.

[38] Blackstone, *Commentaries*, 459.

[39] Blackstone, *Commentaries*, 468–69.

[40] *Trustees of Dartmouth College v. Woodward*, 17 U.S. (4 Wheat.) Wheaton 518 (1819), 669.

Moreover, as the great religious and reform associations of the early nineteenth century demonstrated, charitable corporations rapidly took up technological and organizational innovations to become formidable businesses in their own right.[41] Yet Melville draws a contrast between business corporations and charities, which comes into particular focus in the World's Charity, the man in gray's speculative project. While the Black Rapids Coal Company minimizes the corporate form, reducing a complex assemblage of labor, capital, and subterranean resources to the fluctuations of a stock's value, the World's Charity presents a hypertrophied corporate body in expansive terms that approach a world state—albeit one quite different from Cloots's republic of mankind. (Despite its founder's claim to be "no Fourier, the projector of an impossible scheme," it more closely resembles American Associationists' vision of Harmony (*CM*, 39).) In contrast to the Black Rapids Coal Company's foregrounding of *homo economicus*, the locus of profit and loss, the World's Charity frames humanity not as political or economic subject but as the object of charitable governance. The charitable association triangulates ruthless imperial power and the Pauline vision of Christian charity offered by the mute in cream colors in the novel's opening. The World's Charity appears both as a form of imperial sovereignty, exercising power over subjects in the name of love, and as an inspirited entity that defies the image of the soulless corporation.

The man in gray delivers his pitch for the World's Charity to the sympathetic if skeptical man with gold sleeve-buttons, who keeps his white kid gloves immaculately clean by leaving his dirtier work to "a certain negro body-servant" (*CM*, 36). Why buttonhole a genteel slaveholder for a project that echoes the reformist associations of the 1840s and 1850s, particularly those aligned with temperance and abolition? One answer might be that the World's Charity imagines a world state governed by paternalistic oversight rather than democratic sovereignty. Like the Seminole Widow and Orphan Asylum, it constitutes the objects of charity as governed or captured subjects, but does so on a still grander scale. As such, it echoes the infamous *Dred Scott* decision's framing of Black Americans as objects of paternalistic concern and economic exchange, rather than political subjects. The man with gold sleeve-buttons laments the atomization of charity: "that so many benevolent societies as there were, here and there isolated in the land, should not act in concert by coming together, in the way that already in each society the individuals composing it had done, which would result, he thought, in like advantages upon a larger scale. Indeed, such a confederation might, perhaps, be attended with as happy results as politically attended that of the states"

[41] David Paul Nord, "Benevolent Books: Printing, Religion, and Reform," in The History of the Book in America, Vol. 2: An Extensive Republic: Print, Culture, and Society in the New Nation, 1790–1840, ed. Robert A. Gross and Mary Kelley (Chapel Hill, NC: University of North Carolina Press, 2010).

(*CM*, 37–38). Now, we might sniff some irony in a complacent slaveholder's praise, circa 1857, of federalism—but we might also note his approving citation of Lieber's figure of the concatenated corporate nation. The man in gray, responding to his argument with sympathetic "animation," proposes an elaborated vision of such a confederation: "a society whose members shall comprise deputies from every charity and mission extant; the one object of the society to be the methodization of the world's benevolence" by means of "one grand benevolence tax upon all mankind" (*CM*, 39). With its universal reach, the World's Charity gestures toward both Roman *imperium* and Christian sacred history: "as in Augustus Caesar's time, the whole world to come up to be taxed" (*CM*, 39). Charity promises to replace the state, with paternalism as its governing principle.

In presenting the World's Charity as akin to a form of government, Melville satirically amplifies one facet of nineteenth-century charities. The World's Charity, like the Associationists discussed in chapter 5, borrows the organizational and management strategies of the mega-charities that, with centralized corporate production and far-flung distribution networks, carried out the work of evangelism and social reform via print. Interdenominational religious societies—particularly the American Bible Society, American Sunday School Union, and American Tract Society—promulgated the vision of "general supply": "placing religious publications into the hands of every man, woman, and child in America."[42] These charitable societies harnessed the most advanced technologies of industrial production—stereotype printing and steam presses—and sophisticated management and accounting—centralized organizations sold books to numerous local auxiliaries, responsible for fundraising and distribution. The "millennial vision" of general supply was soon "exported into the realm of social reform," where the American Temperance Society and American Anti-Slavery Society used similar techniques of production, distribution, and organization.[43]

In the 1840s, the early nineteenth-century "bond of union" that linked interdenominational religious and reform societies gave way to increasing fragmentation, particularly as protestant denominations fractured over their positions on slavery.[44] In this light, the man in gray's project and the genteel slaveowner's lament for the era of federated charity recall a recent history of centralized corporate charity, and expand it from a national to a global scale. Moreover, the particular projects to be represented by the World's Charity gesture toward missionary societies, particularly the American Board of Commissioners for Foreign Missions, whose imperialist tactics Melville's Pacific novels had famously lampooned: "In brief, the conversion of the heathen, so far, at least, as depending on human effort, would, by the World's Charity, be let out on contract. So much bid for converting India, so much for

[42] Nord, "Benevolent Books," 236. [43] Nord, "Benevolent Books," 236, 239.
[44] Paul C. Gutjahr, *An American Bible*: A History of the Good Book in the United States, 1777–1880 (Stanford, CA: Stanford University Press, 1999), 195, 197.

Borneo, so much for Africa. Competition allowed, stimulus would be given" (*CM*, 40). Like the auxiliary societies carrying out the day-to-day work of the American Bible Society, American Sunday School Union, and American Tract Society—and like the white-gloved slaveowner's "negro body-servant"—the contractors for the World's Charity insulate a sovereign corporation from the messier aspects of imperial and racial domination with which the charity business is entwined—and for which serves as alibi. The imperial charity keeps its hands clean as it administers the world with a new law of love, operationalized as almsgiving on the model of the charitable corporation: the paternalistic provision of funds gives rise to a right of visitation that expands into universal sovereignty. Humanity is reconstituted as a messianic kingdom fit for the age of centralized management, its regeneration registered as "quicken[ing] with the Wall street spirit."

Quickening Spirits

As the man in gray expounds his project, the man with gold sleeve-buttons shrugs:

> "Well, I won't quibble any more. But, after all, if I understand your project, there is little specially new in it, further than the magnifying of means now in operation."
>
> "Magnifying and energizing. For one thing, missions I would thoroughly reform. Missions I would quicken with the Wall street spirit."
>
> "The Wall street spirit?"
>
> "Yes; for if, confessedly, certain spiritual ends are to be gained but through the auxiliary agency of worldly means, then, to the surer gaining of such spiritual ends, the example of worldly policy in worldly projects should not by spiritual projectors be slighted" (*CM*, 40).

The debate between the projector of the World's Charity and his auditor boils down to a debate about bodies and spirits: while the auditor sees nothing new in the project beside "the magnifying of means now in operation," the man in gray insists that "Magnifying and energizing" amounts to messianic *quickening*: "Missions I would quicken with the Wall street spirit." Blasphemy, it would seem: the worldly and the spiritual have switched places, such that the former animates the latter rather than vice versa: "if...certain spiritual ends are to be gained but through the auxiliary agency of worldly means,...the example of worldly policy in worldly projects should not by spiritual projectors be slighted" (*CM*, 40). From his perspective, the "worldly means" that animate spiritual projects—the technological, legal, and managerial innovations that energized the religious and reform societies—have inherited the place of the spirit, yielding a technocratic Christian community that operationalizes "charity" as a bond of managerial perfectness.

Put differently, the World's Charity runs on what John Modern has called evangelical secularism, "constituted by those feelings, expectations, and practices that animated definitional categories about religion and was manifest in the deployment of those definitions at the level of the population."[45] For the man in gray, the "Wall street spirit" involves deploying religious affects and practices via "the auxiliary agency of worldly means." In doing so, it also highlights the ontology afforded by financial instruments and the corporate form: an artificial and immortal, if nonetheless worldly, body.

The man in gray's locution plays on St Paul's language of bodies and spirits; in particular, it draws on his distinction between quickening spirit (*pneuma*) and natural soul (*psyche*): "And so it is written, The first man Adam was made a living soul; the last Adam was made a quickening spirit. Howbeit that was not first which is spiritual, but that which is natural; and afterward that which is spiritual."[46] Although his idiom of charity and "Christian community" seem to mark the man in gray as an exponent of Pauline doctrine, his theory of spirit turns Paul on his head by attributing life-giving force to corporate finance and management (*CM*, 32). What counts here as worldly or spiritual, body or spirit—or, for that matter, natural or artificial? Although the man in gray does not linger on these questions, by nudging Paul's distinction—natural/spiritual—toward the legal distinction of natural and artificial persons, he "pun[s] with ideas as another man may with words" (*CM*, 124).[47]

In contrast to Pauline metaphysics, in which spirit (*pneuma*) is the master term that links human life to the divine, the ontology of *The Confidence-Man* embraces various assembled bodies, and the various spirits that coincide with or emerge from them. What theology, and what new apostle, might offer purchase on the "Wall street Spirit"? Is the immortalized, apotheosized spirit of business, as Paul's language of "spiritual bodies" suggests, indistinguishable from the immortal body of the corporation? While the man in gray never answers these questions, his project gives the lie to the recurrent trope of the soulless corporation—and to the metaphysical squeamishness with which theorists of the corporation from Sir Edward Coke to what Joseph K. Angell and Samuel Ames consider corporate immortality—by offering a robust account of the soulful, or rather spirited, corporation. The "Wall street spirit" is, in any case, only one of many spirits that

[45] John Lardas Modern, *Secularism in Antebellum America* (Chicago: University of Chicago Press, 2011), 54.

[46] 1 Cor 15: 45–46 (King James Version). Christ as "quickening spirit" is a trope to which Paul repeatedly returns, most famously in "the letter killeth but the spirit giveth life (2 Cor. 3: 6). See also Romans 8: 11: "But if the Spirit of him that raised up Jesus from the dead dwell in you, he that raised up Christ from the dead shall also quicken your mortal bodies by his Spirit that dwelleth in you."

[47] It remains far from clear whether these terminologies are false friends arising from bad translation between the languages of theology and law or whether they might anchor a corporate political theology. While the King James version translates Paul's terms as natural and spiritual, his Greek terms are *psychikon/pneumatikon* (soulful/spiritual), and derive from a tripartite understanding of the human being as body, soul, and spirit, of which only the third part is associated with divinity. Thus "living soul" and "natural" both refer to the *psyche*.

The Confidence-Man conjures from corporate assemblies: we hear also of "spiritual projectors," "the inmost spirit of our contract," and "the dashing and all-fusing spirit of the West." If the means of Wall Street can serve as the spirit that quickens Charity (diminished, perhaps, as translation of *agape* but magnified as imperial power), we have at once a pre-Weberian recognition of the spirit of capitalism and an account of corporate theology—and the corporate soul—that theorists of the corporation would skirt until Amasa Mason Eaton's striking early twentieth-century assertion that a corporation is "nothing but a soul."[48]

River(boat) Corporations

If Anacharsis Cloots and the man in gray offer two contrasting accounts of incorporating humanity as a totalizing political entity—as a self-actualizing political subject or a governable object—Melville hides a more optimistic picture of incorporated plurality in plain sight in *The Confidence-Man*'s early pages. The *Fidèle* itself presents a corporate political subject that anticipates the real entity theory of the corporation even as it departs from conventional conceptions of identity.

As noted above, eighteenth- and nineteenth-century legal writers recurrently compared corporate bodies to rivers. Attending to their uses of this trope can show how the problem of corporate identity or assemblage restates persistent political and ontological questions. Blackstone's figure of the corporation-as-Thames invites ontology (which is to say, entity theory) into the common-law doctrine of the corporation; it also recalls the parallels between rivers and associations that philosophers and political theorists had long recognized. Although Blackstone does not explicitly identify the source of his image, later jurists would trace its genealogy. In his 1793 treatise, Stewart Kyd cites Grotius's river analogies alongside Blackstone.[49] And in *Thomas v. Dakin* (1839), New York Supreme Court Justice Esek Cowen, a onetime partner of Melville's uncle Wessel Gansevoort,[50] offers an erudite opinion connecting the dots from Heraclitus to Blackstone. In an 1839 case hinging on the question of corporate ontology—and in particular,

[48] "The First Book in English on the Law of Incorporation," (New Haven, CT: Ryder's Printing House 1903) (reprinted from the *Yale Law Journal*, March–April 1903), 11. Eaton's formulation echoes Hobbes's formulation in *Leviathan* that sovereignty is "an artificial soul." See Paul Downes, *Hobbes, Sovereignty, and Early American Literature* (Cambridge: Cambridge University Press, 2015).

[49] Stewart Kyd, *A Treatise on the Law of Corporations* (London: Printed for J. Butterworth, 1793), Vol. 1, 17–18.

[50] Anderson, George Baker, *Our County and Its People: A Descriptive and Biographical Record of Saratoga County, New York. Prepared and Published under the Auspices of the Saratogian* (Boston: The Boston History Company, 1899), 418, 507. Robert L. Gale describes Wessell Gansevoort as "a clever, often charming, occasionally quarrelsome alcoholic" who "studied and sporadically practiced law." Robert L. Gale, *A Herman Melville Encyclopedia* (Westport, CT: Greenwood, 1995), 169.

the status of unincorporated bodies, Cowen's opinion lights the way that Melville, likely without knowing it, would follow.

What is a corporation?—the question Blackstone had answered in theory—became an urgent practical matter for New York Supreme Court in *Thomas v. Dakin*. The case arose nearly two decades before *The Confidence-Man*, prior to the New York constitution of 1846 that the lawyer of "Bartleby" famously laments. Although the specifics of the case were moot by the time Melville wrote the novel, at the heart of the conflict and the court's ruling was a question that parallels *The Confidence-Man*'s investigations of corporate forms. Passed in 1838, New York's Free Banking Act broke with the practice of requiring legislative charters for banking corporations, instead authorizing general conditions for the creation of unchartered banking associations.[51] Whereas New York's 1821 constitution had required a supermajority of two-thirds of the legislature for all acts chartering corporations, the act skirted the constitutional issue by distinguishing the banking associations it authorized from chartered corporations. *Thomas v. Dakin* turned on a few related questions: whether these new banks were in fact corporations, whether they had legal standing to sue and be sued (per the act, the suit was brought in the name of Anson Thomas, the president of the Central New-York Bank), and whether the act authorizing them was constitutional, given the state constitution's two-thirds stipulation. In other words, *Thomas v. Dakin* offered an early confrontation between contrasting conceptions of the corporation. Was the bank a corporation for purposes of the law? If not, what sort of thing was it? How should the law address a corporation-like but unchartered body?

Writing for the majority, Chief Justice Samuel Nelson considers "the properties essential to constitute a corporate body" and concludes, echoing Blackstone, that its "distinguishing feature…is the capacity conferred, by which *a perpetual succession of different persons shall be regarded in the law as one and the same body, and may, at all times act in fulfillment of the objects of the association as a single individual*."[52] Because the new banks created by the act fulfilled this ontological criterion, Nelson ruled that they were corporations, regardless of nomenclature. Stressing the features of the corporation (perpetual succession, unity in multiplicity), rather than the performative grant of a charter, favored a view of corporation as entity rather than concession. In consequence, the court sided with the plaintiff in holding the Banking Act valid and constitutional, but refused to recognize the act's distinction between formally chartered corporations and generally authorized associations.[53] In blurring this distinction, it signaled a shift in the doctrine of the corporation, anticipating the contrast later theorists would make explicit between the concession (or artificial entity) theory of the corporation

[51] New York was early in its promotion of free banking. On the Free Banking Act, see Hilt, "Early American Corporations," esp. 61–67.

[52] *Thomas v. Dakin*, 22 Wend. 9 (NY Sup. Ct. 1839), 70–71.

[53] *Thomas v. Dakin*, 8–9.

(corporations derive their existence from state recognition) and the real entity theory (corporations have a life of their own; formal recognition is secondary).[54]

Cowen's extensive concurring opinion addresses the question "*what is a corporation?*" in order to answer the apparently recondite question of whether an "association" and a corporation are the same thing. Cowen cites legal authorities including Blackstone and Kyd but also turns to legal and philosophical sources beyond the common law tradition. He thereby insists on a historical basis for corporate ontology that overshadows the jurisdiction of the New York legislature. By showing how the law of corporations on which the legislature draws frames corporations broadly, he argues that the Banking Act's definition of a corporation is unjustifiably narrow.

Cowen's argument for the legal standing of unchartered associations draws on the river metaphor, particularly as formulated by the Dutch statesman, philosopher, and jurist Hugo Grotius. It thus highlights the shared genealogy of corporation and commonwealth. Cowen quotes Grotius repeatedly:

> "For these *artificial bodies* are like the *natural.* The natural body continues to be still the same, though its particles are perpetually upon an insensible flux and change, whilst the same form remains, as *Alphenus* from the philosophers, argues." In the second subdivision of the same section, he [Grotius] adopts the like comparison with Blackstone, between a corporation and the Thames. *Grotius* there quotes *Heraclitus,* who said, "We can not go down twice into the same river; which *Seneca* very judiciously explains, viz., the *name* of the river continues, though the *water* is continually gliding along. So Aristotle, comparing a river to the people, said, the river retains the same *name,* though some *water* is always coming and some going."[55]

The river, as Cowen demonstrates, serves as a durable figure for the persistence of corporate identity despite the "insensible flux and change" of constituent "particles."[56] It does so, moreover, for authors and contexts far beyond the scope of Anglo-American corporate law: Heraclitus, Aristotle, and Seneca; discourses of ontology and political theory; and entities, such as states, peoples, or being more broadly, that exceed the common-law corporation.[57] Although the figure of

[54] The concession theory, articulated most clearly by Chief Justice Marshall in *Dartmouth College,* was predominant in nineteenth-century American jurisprudence. Ruth H. Bloch and Naomi R. Lamoreaux, "Corporations and the Fourteenth Amendment," in *Corporations and American Democracy,* ed. Naomi R. Lamoreaux and William J. Novak (Cambridge, MA: Harvard University Press, 2017), 293–94.

[55] *Thomas v. Dakin,* 105.

[56] Rivers have also been recognized as legal persons in their own right, most notably the Whanganui River in Aotearoa New Zealand. Te Awa Tupua (Whanganui River Claims Settlement) Act 2017.

[57] On the state as corporation and vice versa, see Frederic Maitland, *State, Trust, and Corporation* (Cambridge: Cambridge University Press, 2003), 1.

the river has long accompanied the law of corporations, it exceeds the legal formula of a charter granted by sovereign prerogative. (Recall Chief Baron Manwood's syllogism: only God creates souls; the king creates a corporation; therefore corporations have no souls.)[58] But if a corporation's status as an entity does not depend on sovereign creation, might it lay a different kind of claim to a soul—a suggestion toward which Melville's "all-fusing spirit" points?

Although grounded in philological investigation, Cowen's argument ultimately leads away from terminological specificity. He notes that Grotius's Latin term *consociatio* "is translated, indifferently, *consociation* or *association*." This fluidity in translation of a key term allows him to argue against the terminological uniqueness of "corporation": "the word *association* used in the general banking law, so far from being incompatible with the common law idea of a corporation, is perfectly consistent with it, and has been used by a standard writer as signifying the same thing."[59] By arguing against a nominalist conception of the corporation, this position prefigures what late nineteenth- and early twentieth-century jurists including the German legal historian Otto von Gierke and his successors Frederic William Maitland and Harold J. Laski describe as the real entity theory of the corporation: the law should treat corporations as existing, associated entities *recognized* by the state, not legal fictions *created* by it; the distinction between incorporated and unincorporated bodies is only nominal.

If the trope of the river-corporation can illustrate real entity theory, it also leaves itself open to more unorthodox interpretations. In contrast to Grotius's and Blackstone's rivers, Melville's river and riverboat exhibit a more tenuous kind of unity, characterized by perpetual succession without sovereignty or unity of purpose. When Grotius cites Heraclitus, he does so in order to argue, with Aristotle and Seneca, against the kind of flux Heraclitus sees in rivers. But what might a corporate entity produced by perpetual succession but *without* the guarantee of a shared, sovereign spirit, a persistent self-identity, look like? What kind of entity theory might we fish out of Heraclitus's river? That is the question *The Confidence-Man* answers.

Presenting the river corporation at its most Heraclitean, Melville's novel resists Cowen's neat reduction of perpetual flux to persistent identity. The metonymic association of river, steamboat, and passengers allows the figure to move promiscuously among various registers: human and nonhuman, hydrological, botanical, and social. The stream of passengers, like the stream of the Mississippi, is produced by continuous replenishment and intermixture: "Though her voyage of twelve hundred miles extends from apple to orange, from clime to clime, yet, like any small ferry-boat, to right and left, at every landing, the huge *Fidèle* still receives additional passengers in exchange for those that disembark; so that,

[58] *Tipling v. Plexall*, 2 Bulstrode 233. [59] *Thomas v. Dakin*, 38.

though always full of strangers, she continually, in some degree, adds to, or replaces them with strangers still more strange; like Rio Janeiro fountain, fed from the Corcovado mountains, which is ever overflowing with strange waters, but never with the same strange particles in every part" (*CM*, 15).

This figure of constant exchange renders the *Fidèle*'s passengers not as individuals but as overflowing "particles" of a changing aggregate that somehow maintains a collective, if not constant, character (the novel's chapter on "original characters" notwithstanding). Melville's descriptions of river, vessel, and passengers are playfully indifferent to the distinction between human and nonhuman, both of which participate in the same kind of aggregations. After a long list of types assembled aboard and around the *Fidèle*, intermingling "high bluffs and shot-towers" with "bluff-looking Missourians and towering Kentuckians," the narrator concludes, "Here reigned the dashing and all-fusing spirit of the West, whose type is the Mississippi itself, which, uniting the streams of the most distant and opposite zones, pours them along, helter-skelter, in one cosmopolitan and confident tide" (*CM*, 17).

This spirit of (cosmo)political fusion echoes Justice Cowen's reminder of the shared genealogy of state and corporation: Grotius is "speaking of the state" when he "substantially furnishes Blackstone's idea of a corporation" as a river and describes its "one spirit" or "breath of life" as sovereign power.[60] By this measure, the *Fidèle* makes an odd body politic: it is characterized by perpetual but provisional succession, not filiation but embarkation and debarkation; the "spirit" that reigns on board is hard to square with a conventional vision of sovereignty. When the *Fidèle* speaks as an aggregate it does so not with "one spirit" but "conflictingly," as does the "miscellaneous company…assembled" on board, producing an irreconcilable aggregate of "epitaphic comments, conflictingly spoken or thought" (*CM*, 14). If the *Fidèle* has a reigning spirit, it lacks a *Volkgeist*, a sovereign "artificial soul," or even a Wall Street spirit; its fusion sounds more like a confusion of tongues. Yet Melville insists on depicting the steamboat, populated as it is by grifters and their marks, as something different in kind than Lieber's despairing picture of an atomistic steamboat society composed of nothing but the "utter selfishness" of "isolated individual[s]." Melville's steamboat, pace Lieber, is what the latter calls "an organised thing, with life and energy."[61] The *Fidèle* boasts a self-assembling company marked by confidence, charity, and a shared if ambiguous spirit. That these (not entirely innocuous) properties emerge from spontaneous assembly rather than being imposed from above suggests the distance between Lieber's and Melville's steamboats—and their corporate imaginaries. *The Confidence-Man* thus offers a glimpse of a world in which corporations are not only destabilizing threats to human personhood or totalizing systems of

[60] *Thomas v. Dakin*, 105. [61] Lieber, *Political Ethics*, Vol. 1, 191.

governance but also the means of generating, by means of perpetual succession, ever novel forms of aggregate sociality.

Insofar as the shifting company of the *Fidèle* constitutes a real entity, it presents a basis for recognizing human community that depends neither on bloodlines, sovereignty, nor a performative declaration. Association offers a mode of plural being (interdependent, intersubjective) that is irreducible to the "natural" belonging of a nation or a species. At the same time, it resists the atomism of a state of nature or a homogeneous, empty landscape populated by liberal individuals. In the *Fidèle*, Melville thus offers a vision of human plurality among strangers under the sign of association without recourse to either nature or the sovereign state.

Humanity, Inc.

What might follow from conceiving of the human race as such a corporation? Cowen offers a roundabout answer when he invokes the early modern English poet John Davies, who, as Cowen writes, likens the creation of a corporation "to the creative power of the Deity."[62] He quotes the following lines from "Immortality of the Soul":

> Of this we find some foot-steps in our law,
> Which doth her root from God and nature take;
> Ten thousand men she doth together draw,
> And of them all *one corporation* make.

Cowen conveniently fails to mention, however, that Davies's stanza comes in the midst of a discussion of divine omniscience and original sin. God, in "seeing the whole, each single part doth see," and thus "He looks at Adam, as a root, or well, / And on his heirs, as branches, and as streams: / He sees all men, as one man, though they dwell / In sundry cities, and in sundry realms." By Davies's reasoning, humanity needs a corporate charter to make the doctrine of original sin coherent.

Like Davies's mixed metaphors—tree, river, and corporation—his vision of humanity is vexed. Whereas a tree is a single living organism, it is the rare stream that proceeds from a single well. And the corporation is more troublesome still as a figure of unity. Once the law draws ten thousand men together, Davies writes,

> Yet these, and their successors, are but one;
> And if they gain or lose their liberties,

[62] *Thomas v. Dakin*, 104.

> They harm or profit not themselves alone,
> But such as in succeeding times shall rise.[63]

With the analogy of the corporate form, Davies thus figures artificial *successorship* rather than natural *heredity* as the means by which a multitude is linked over time. In other words, by emphasizing humanity as incorporated by divine law, the poem suggests that we understand human community as grounded in the artifice of law rather than the biopolitical nature of a species.

Like Davies, Melville imagines human collectivity as a corporation—though not a divinely chartered one. While Melville does not refer directly to Davies's verse, his Philosophical Intelligence Office man, in a convoluted discussion of the development of boys into men, draws a strikingly similar contrast between heredity and succession: "The second teeth follow, but do not come from the first; *successors, not sons.* The first teeth are not like the germ blossom of the apple, at once the father of, and incorporated into, the growth it foreruns; but they are thrust from their place by the independent undergrowth of the succeeding set—an illustration, by the way, which shows more for me than I mean though not more than I wish" (*CM*, 123, emphasis added). Like Davies's trope of humanity, incorporated, the figure of "successors, not sons" sidesteps the logic of reproductive futurism. In its unlikely way, the corporate form affords a vision of collectivity that offers an alternative to what Lee Edelman, in *No Future*, evocatively calls "the Ponzi scheme of reproductive futurism," a social order that enforces its coercive persistence through the sacralized figure of the child.[64] Yet rather than refuse futurity *tout court*, the novel's recurrent foregrounding of succession without identity offers an orientation toward a different futurity, perhaps a queer futurity in Muñoz's sense.[65] Admittedly, Muñoz's avowed utopianism is at odds with *The Confidence-Man*'s relentless lampooning of utopian projects like the World's Charity. But his insistence on a "a renewed and newly animated sense of the social" aptly captures the novel's equally relentless attention to social formations.[66]

To return to the novel's opening, the *Fidèle* is a well-fed stream that does not proceed from a single well: "like Rio Janeiro fountain, fed from the Corcovado mountains, which is ever overflowing with strange waters, but never with the same strange particles in every part" (*CM*, 8). Melville's metaphors ground collectivity not in a divine or performative origin but in a shared, promiscuous trajectory. He presents a collection of successors and strangers, bound together

[63] John Davies, "The Immortality of the Soul," *Select Works of the British Poets: From Chaucer to Jonson, with Biographical Sketches*, ed. Robert Southey (London: Longman, 1831), 694.

[64] Lee Edelman, *No Future: Queer Theory and the Death Drive* (Durham, NC: Duke University Press, 2004), 4.

[65] In this sense the novel anticipates something like the confrontation between Edelman's and Muñoz's accounts of queerness, temporality, and futurity. See Drew Daniel, "Trading Futures: Queer Theory's Anti-antirelational Turn," *Criticism* 52 (2010): 325–30.

[66] Muñoz, *Cruising Utopia*, 18.

with the shared fate of shipmates, animated by a spirit both "dashing"—at once charming, racing, violently smashing—and "and all-fusing." This collective body is marked both by divisibility and by disindividuation.

If this fused but fractured body is in part generated by the logic of individual economic interest, the novel keeps reminding us that it exceeds such interest. During the multichapter episode of the "boon companions," the Cosmopolitan—who has introduced himself as Frank Goodman—and the Mississippi Operator Charlie Noble converse over a bottle of port. Charlie urges Frank to drink while himself carefully abstaining. When Frank offers Charlie a cigar but the latter begs off, he wonders aloud if Charlie is concerned that "tobacco, when in league with wine…with certain constitutions tends to impair self-possession" (*CM*, 169). "To think that," Charlie responds, "were treason to good fellowship" (*CM*, 169). Self-possession is, rhetorically speaking, long gone by this point—it takes an unusually attentive reader to see who is talking at any given moment—but the conversation reaches its climax with a reassertion of self-possession: when Frank finally confides, "I am in want, urgent want of money" (*CM*, 178), Charlie responds with shocked coldness; he is only restored by Frank's playful show of ten gold half-eagles in a "magic-ring" (*CM*, 180). It may be tempting to reduce this moment to the unmasking of the cynical self-interest beneath Charlie's unctuous façade, yet to do so neglects the way the two, with their indistinguishable affect of overcooked conviviality, share a kind of genial existence. Geniality, certainly, is less than sincerity, kindness, or care; as Charlie himself says, "We have genial senators, genial authors, genial lecturers, genial doctors, genial clergymen, genial surgeons, and the next thing we shall have genial hangmen" (*CM*, 175). Yet, however artificial and morally neutral such geniality may be, it remains no less a mode of "liv[ing] together in the finest sense" (*CM*, 175): an affect and practice of conviviality altogether foreign to Lieber's steamboat of isolated individuals.

As Henry Turner argues, "the corporation may seem to resemble a little state…even as the state reveals itself to be a species of corporation on a large scale." If we take this analogy seriously, the corporation also "reveals to us the pluralistic, fragile, and assembled nature of *all* political entities; the corporation constantly dissolves into its networks and relays of substances, disperses itself into its collective pronouns, and borrows the mouths and bodies of its natural representatives, without which its personhood would never exist."[67] The company aboard the *Fidèle* foregrounds this "pluralistic, fragile, and assembled" nature: its dissolution is, paradoxically, its most consistent unifying feature: "the crowd, as is usual, began in all parts to break up from a concourse into various clusters or squads, which in some cases disintegrated again into quartettes, trios, and couples, or even solitaires; involuntarily submitting to that natural law which

[67] Turner, *The Corporate Commonwealth*, 114.

ordains dissolution equally to the mass, as in time to the member" (*CM*, 9). This inbuilt tendency toward decomposition pushes against sovereignty and instead emphasizes the assembled company's permanently provisional status.

As this chapter has argued, each of Melville's key examples takes a different iteration of the corporate form and expands it into a political conception of human plurality. In this way, *The Confidence-Man* can serve as a microcosm for the multifarious conceptions of the corporate form entertained by the nineteenth-century writers. It repeats on the level of fictional play what imperial companies and Fourierist Associationists had attempted in deadly earnest: the project of reincorporating the world. At the same time, *The Confidence-Man* washes the ground from beneath these totalizing forms of secular governance—shareholding, citizenship, empire, and charity—by framing them as contingent patterns that arise from the assembled and ever-reassembling company aboard the *Fidèle*. And with its central trope of masquerade, *The Confidence-Man* reframes the question of corporate personality in a fruitfully disorienting way: this is how we might imagine personhood, plurality, and succession without the bedrock of identity. Such a collectivity, "a pic-nic *en costume*" premised on "successors, not sons" offers an apt image of the corporation as a figure of political possibility. It suggests, as I have argued, an ontology of the collective that need not be grounded in national identity or natural reproduction any more than in theological or political sovereignty.

As I noted in the introduction, the constrained corporate imaginary of our own moment tends to treat as inevitable the powerful multinational business corporations that act as quasi-sovereigns even as we disavow their political nature. The hegemonic status of the business corporation in the twenty-first century is clear from its monopolistic claim to the epithet "corporate." This phenomenon is particularly poignant from the perspective of higher education, in which, as critics including Timothy Kaufman-Osborn and Wendy Brown have detailed, the logic of the neoliberal property corporation has increasingly shouldered aside other forms of governance and collective life—the phenomenon often, if imprecisely, described as the corporatization of the university.[68] Of course, the university's status as one of the oldest exemplars of the corporate form reminds us that this conception of the corporate is a narrow one, and to naturalize it is to forget the broader and messier genealogy of forms of corporate collectivity that this study has addressed.[69]

The antebellum corporate imaginary thus offers us resources that are untimely in Nietzsche's precise sense: "that is to say, acting counter to our time and thereby

[68] Timothy V. Kaufman-Osborn, *The Autocratic Academy: Reenvisioning Rule within America's Universities* (Durham, NC: Duke University Press, 2023), 30–46; Wendy Brown, *Undoing the Demos: Neoliberalism's Stealth Revolution* (New York: Zone Books, 2015), 175–200.

[69] Kaufman-Osborn, *The Autocratic Academy*, 47–60; Turner, *The Corporate Commonwealth*, 234–35.

acting on our time and, let us hope, for the benefit of a time to come."[70] Like Muñoz's resonant description of "queerness as a temporal arrangement in which the past is a field of possibility in which subjects can act in the present in the service of a new futurity," Nietzschean untimeliness locates hope, however tentative, in temporal dislocation and superimposition.[71] Something like that uncertain hope has animated my attempt to map a field of untimely possibility in the strange terrain of the nineteenth century. I thus end this study with questions rather than prescriptions. What forms of collectivity can we distill from the extravagant archive of the antebellum corporate imaginary? How might returning to this archive enable us to imagine both the future of collective forms and the future of the person differently? Like Ishmael and Queequeg joined by their monkey-rope, we cannot extricate ourselves from the danger of being-in-common. But like Ishmael afloat on Queequeg's coffin, we may nonetheless be buoyed up in unexpected ways by our entanglement in collectivity. As Melville reminds us in both *Moby-Dick* and *The Confidence-Man*, the salutary artificiality of the corporation affords the possibility of imagining plurality otherwise: the possibility, in other words, that something further may follow from this masquerade.

The Corporate Forms of Antebellum US Literature. Peter Jaros, Oxford University Press. © Peter Jaros 2026.
DOI: 10.1093/9780198996491.003.0007

[70] Friedrich Nietzsche, "On the Uses and Disadvantages of History for Life" (1874), *Untimely Meditations*, ed. Daniel Breazeale, trans. R. J. Hollingdale (Cambridge: Cambridge University Press, 2012), 60.

[71] Muñoz, *Cruising Utopia*, 16. Admittedly, I am stretching Muñoz's conception of futurity by taking it beyond the horizon of queer experience and critique.

Bibliography

Archives

Francis Lieber Papers. The Huntington Library, San Marino, California.

Robert Montgomery Bird Papers. Kislak Center for Special Collections, Rare Books and Manuscripts, University of Pennsylvania.

Periodicals

The Harbinger (Brook Farm, MA; New York), 1845–49.

The Phalanx (New York), 1843–45.

Cases

Bank of the United States v. Deveaux, 9 US 61 (1809).

Burwell v. Hobby Lobby Stores, Inc., 573 US 682 (2014).

Cherokee Nation v. Georgia, 30 US 1 (1831).

Citizens United v. Federal Election Commission, 558 US 310 (2010).

Dred Scott v. Sandford, 60 US 393 (1857).

Johnson & Graham's Lessee v. McIntosh, 21 US 543 (1823).

Louisville, C. & CR Co. v. Letson, 43 US 497 (1844).

Proprietors of Charles River Bridge v. Proprietors of Warren Bridge, 36 US 420 (1837).

Railroad Tax Cases. County of San Mateo v. Southern Pacific R. Co. (9th Cir. 1882).

Slee v. Bloom, 19 Johnson 456 (NY Supreme Court 1822).

Thomas v. Dakin, 22 Wend. 9 (NY Sup. Ct. 1839).

Tipling v. Pexall, 2 Bulstrode 233, 80 English Reports 1085 (1614).

Trustees of Dartmouth College v. Woodward, 17 US (4 Wheat.) Wheaton 518 (1819).

Trustees of the University of North Carolina v. Foy (NC 1805).

Worcester v. Georgia, 31 US 515 (1832).

Other Sources

"A Digest of the Cases Contained in the 19th Vol. of Johnson's Reports." *United States Law Journal* 1, no. 4 (1822): 461–510.

Adams, Sean Patrick. *Old Dominion, Industrial Commonwealth: Coal, Politics, and Economy in Antebellum America*. Baltimore: Johns Hopkins University Press, 2004.

Allen, Austin. *Origins of the Dred Scott Case: Jacksonian Jurisprudence and the Supreme Court, 1837–1857*. Athens, GA: University of Georgia Press, 2006.

Alterton, Margaret. *Origins of Poe's Critical Theory* (1925). New York: Russell and Russell, 1965.

"American Banks." *Port-Folio* 4th ser., 7 (1819): 352.

An Act to Incorporate the Stockholders of the Bank of the United States, by the State of Pennsylvania. Philadelphia, PA: Joseph and William Kite, Printers, 1836.

Anderson, Elizabeth. *Private Government: How Employers Rule Our Lives (and Why We Don't Talk about It)*. Princeton, NJ: Princeton University Press, 2019.

Anderson, George Baker. *Our County and Its People: A Descriptive and Biographical Record of Saratoga County, New York. Prepared and Published under the Auspices of the Saratogian*. Boston: The Boston History Company, 1899.

"Angell and Ames on Corporations." *American Jurist* 8 (1832): 105–11.

Angell, Joseph K., and Samuel Ames. *A Treatise on the Law of Private Corporations Aggregate*. Boston: Hilliard, 1832.

Antelyes, Peter. *Tales of Adventurous Enterprise: Washington Irving and the Poetics of Western Expansion*. New York: Columbia University Press, 1990.

Anthony, David. *Paper Money Men: Commerce, Manhood, and the Sensational Public Sphere in Antebellum America*. Columbus, OH: Ohio State University Press, 2020.
Arendt, Hannah. *The Human Condition*. Chicago: University of Chicago Press, 1958.
Arendt, Hannah. *The Origins of Totalitarianism*. New York: Harcourt, Brace & World, 1968.
Armstrong, William. *Stocks and Stock-Jobbing in Wall-Street, with Sketches of the Brokers, and Fancy Stocks*. New York: New-York Publishing Company, 1848.
Arsić, Branka. *On Leaving: A Reading in Emerson*. Cambridge, MA: Harvard University Press, 2010.
Asad, Talal. *Formations of the Secular: Christianity, Islam, Modernity*. Stanford, CA: Stanford University Press, 2010.
Avi-Yonah, Reuven. "The Cyclical Transformations of the Corporate Form: A Historical Perspective on Corporate Social Responsibility." *Delaware Journal of Corporate Law* 30 (2005): 767–818.
Baird, Robert. *View of the Valley of the Mississippi, or the Emigrant's and Traveler's Guide to the West*. Philadelphia, PA: Tanner, 1834.
"Banks and Banking." *Niles' Weekly Register* 16 (1819): 421–22.
Barkan, Joshua. *Corporate Sovereignty: Law and Government Under Capitalism*. Minneapolis, MN: University of Minnesota Press, 2013.
Baucom, Ian. "Financing Enlightenment, Part Two: Extraordinary Expenditure." In *This Is Enlightenment*, edited by Clifford Siskin and William Warner, 336–56. Chicago: University of Chicago Press, 2009.
Baucom, Ian. *Specters of the Atlantic: Finance Capital, Slavery, and the Philosophy of History*. Durham, NC: Duke University Press, 2005.
Beecher, Jonathan. *Charles Fourier: The Visionary and His World*. Berkeley, CA: University of California Press, 1986.
Bell, Michael Davitt. *Culture, Genre, and Literary Vocation: Selected Essays on American Literature*. Chicago: University of Chicago Press, 2001.
Benton, Lauren. *A Search for Sovereignty: Law and Geography in European Empires, 1400–1900*. Cambridge: Cambridge University Press, 2010.
Best, Stephen M. *The Fugitive's Properties: Law and the Poetics of Possession*. Chicago: University of Chicago Press, 2004.
Bestor, Arthur. *Backwoods Utopias: The Sectarian Origins and the Owenite Phase of Communitarian Socialism in America, 1663–1829*. 2nd ed. Philadelphia, PA: University of Pennsylvania Press, 1970.
Beuka, Robert. "The Jacksonian Man of Parts: Dismemberment, Manhood, and Race in 'The Man That Was Used Up.'" *Edgar Allan Poe Review* 3, no. 1 (2002): 27–44.
Bevilacqua, Alexander. "Conceiving the Republic of Mankind: The Political Thought of Anacharsis Cloots." *History of European Ideas* 38, no. 4 (2012): 550.
Biddle, Nicholas. *An Ode to Bogle*. Philadelphia, PA, 1889.
Binder, Guyora, and Robert Weisberg. *Literary Criticisms of Law*. Princeton, N.J: Princeton University Press, 2000.
Bird, Mary Mayer. "Life of Robert Montgomery Bird," edited by C. Seymour Thompson. *University of Pennsylvania Library Chronicle* 12, nos. 3–4 (1944): 71–92, 97–120; 13, nos. 1–3 (1945): 3–30, 33–56, 61–95.
Bird, Robert Montgomery. *Sheppard Lee, Written by Himself* (1836), edited by Christopher Looby. New York: NYRB Classics, 2008.
Bird, Robert Montgomery. "To Governor M'Duffie." *The New-England Magazine* 8 (February 1835): 138–41.
Blackhawk, Ned. *The Rediscovery of America: Native Peoples and the Unmaking of U.S. History*. New Haven, CT: Yale University Press, 2023.
Blackson, Robert M. "Pennsylvania Banks and the Panic of 1819: A Reinterpretation." *Journal of the Early Republic* 9, no. 3 (1989): 335–58.
Blackstone, William. *Commentaries on the Laws of England: Book I: Of the Rights of Persons (1765–69)*, edited by David Lemmings. Oxford: Oxford University Press, 2016.

Blair, Margaret M., and Elizabeth Pollman. "The Supreme Court's View of Corporate Rights: Two Centuries of Evolution and Controversy." In *Corporations and American Democracy*, edited by Naomi R. Lamoreaux and William J. Novak, 245–85. Cambridge, MA: Harvard University Press, 2017.

Blanchot, Maurice. *The Unavowable Community*. Translated by Pierre Joris. Barrytown, NY: Station Hill Press, 1988.

Bloch, Ruth H., and Naomi R. Lamoreaux. "Corporations and the Fourteenth Amendment." In *Corporations and American Democracy*, edited by Naomi R. Lamoreaux and William J. Novak. Cambridge, MA: Harvard University Press, 2017.

Bradford, Adam. "Inspiring Death: Poe's Poetic Aesthetics, 'Annabel Lee,' and the Communities of Mourning in Nineteenth-Century America." *The Edgar Allan Poe Review* 12, no. 1 (2011): 72–100.

Brisbane, Albert. *Association; Or, A Concise Exposition of the Practical Part of Fourier's Social Science*. New York: Greeley & McElrath, 1843.

Brisbane, Albert. *Social Destiny of Man: Or, Association and Reorganization of Industry*. Philadelphia, PA: C. F. Stollmeyer, 1840.

Brisbane, Albert. *What Is Association?* New York: J. S. Redfield, 1843.

Brown, Wendy. *Undoing the Demos: Neoliberalism's Stealth Revolution*. New York: Zone Books, 2015.

Brożek, Bartosz. "The Troublesome 'Person.'" In *Legal Personhood: Animals, Artificial Intelligence, and the Unborn*, edited by Visa A. J. Kurki and Tomasz Pietrzykowski. New York: Springer, 2017.

Buffington, Nancy Jane. "From Freedom to Slavery: Robert Montgomery Bird and the Natural Law Tradition." PhD diss. University of Arizona, 1998.

Burstein, Andrew. *The Original Knickerbocker: The Life of Washington Irving*. New York: Basic Books, 2007.

Butterfield, Kevin. *The Making of Tocqueville's America: Law and Association in the Early United States*. Chicago, IL: University of Chicago Press, 2015.

Callcott, George H. *History in the United States, 1800–1860*. Baltimore, MD: Johns Hopkins University Press, 1970.

Cameron, Sharon. *Impersonality: Seven Essays*. Chicago: University of Chicago Press, 2009.

Canady, Nicholas. "Poe's William Wilson." *The Explicator* 40, no. 2 (1982): 28–29.

Castronovo, Russ. *Necro Citizenship: Death, Eroticism, and the Public Sphere in the Nineteenth-Century United States*. Durham, NC: Duke University Press, 2002.

Channing, William Henry. "Prospectus of The Spirit of the Age." *The Spirit of the Age* 1, no. 2 (1849): 32.

Channing, William Henry. "To Meet Again!" *The Spirit of the Age* 2, no. 17 (1850): 264–65.

Cheng, Eileen Ka-May. *The Plain and Noble Garb of Truth: Nationalism and Impartiality in American Historical Writings, 1784–1860*. Athens, GA: University of Georgia Press, 2008.

Chittenden, Hiram. *The American Fur Trade of the Far West*. Stanford, CA: Academic Reprints, 1954.

Ciepley, David. "Beyond Public and Private: Toward a Political Theory of the Corporation." *American Political Science Review* 107, no. 1 (February 2013): 139–58. https://doi.org/10.1017/S0003055412000536.

Ciepley, David. "Member Corporations, Property Corporations, and Constitutional Rights." *The Law & Ethics of Human Rights* 11, no. 1 (May 2017): 31–59. https://doi.org/10.1515/lehr-2017-0001.

Clarkson, C. M. V. "Kicking Corporate Bodies and Damning Their Souls." *The Modern Law Review* 59, no. 4 (1996): 557–72.

Clinton, W. David. *Tocqueville, Lieber, and Bagehot: Liberalism Confronts the World*. New York: Palgrave, 2003.

Codman, John Thomas. *Brook Farm: Historic and Personal Memoirs*. Boston: Arena, 1896.

Coffee, John C. "'No Soul to Damn: No Body to Kick': An Unscandalized Inquiry into the Problem of Corporate Punishment." *Michigan Law Review* 79, no. 3 (1981): 386–459. https://doi.org/10.2307/1288201.

Cohen, Lara Langer. *The Fabrication of American Literature: Fraudulence and Antebellum Print Culture*. Philadelphia, PA: University of Pennsylvania Press, 2012.
"Constitution of Pennsylvania." *American Jurist* 18, no. 38 (1837).
Constitution of the Brook Farm Association for Industry and Education, West Roxbury, Mass. with an Introductory Statement. Second Edition, with the By-Laws of the Association. Boston: I. R. Butts, Printer, 1844.
Constitution of the Brook Farm Phalanx, 1845.
"Constitutional Law." *North American Review* 10 (1820): 83–115.
Conversations-Lexicon. 7. Aufl. Leipzig: Brockhaus, 1827.
Cox, Ross. *Adventures on the Columbia River, Including the Narrative of a Residence of Six Years on the Western Side of the Rocky Mountains, among Various Tribes of Indians Hitherto Unknown: Together with a Journey across the American Continent*. London: Henry Colburn and Richard Bentley, 1831.
Crevecoeur, J. Hector St John de. *Letters from an American Farmer and Sketches of Eighteenth-Century America*, edited by Albert E. Stone. New York: Penguin, 1981.
Dahl, Curtis. *Robert Montgomery Bird*. New York: Twayne, 1963.
Daniel, Drew. "Trading Futures: Queer Theory's Anti-Anti-Relational Turn." *Criticism* 52, no. 2 (2010): 325–30.
Davies, John. "The Immortality of the Soul." In *Select Works of the British Poets: From Chaucer to Jonson, with Biographical Sketches*, edited by Robert Southey. London: Longman, 1831.
Davis, Joseph S. *Essays in the Earlier History of American Corporations*. Cambridge, MA: Harvard University Press, 1917.
Dayan, Colin. *The Law Is a White Dog: How Legal Rituals Make and Unmake Persons*. Princeton, NJ: Princeton University Press, 2011.
Dayan, Joan. *Fables of Mind: An Inquiry into Poe's Fiction*. Oxford: Oxford University Press, 1987.
Dayan, Joan. "Poe, Persons, and Property." In *Romancing the Shadow: Poe and Race*, edited by J. Gerald Kennedy and Lilliane Weissberg. Oxford: Oxford University Press, 2001.
De Kay, Drake. "Encyclopedia Americana, First Edition." *The Journal of Library History (1966–1972)* 3, no. 3 (1968): 201–20.
Delano, Sterling F. *Brook Farm: The Dark Side of Utopia*. Cambridge, MA: Harvard University Press, 2004.
Deleuze, Gilles, and Félix Guattari. *A Thousand Plateaus: Capitalism and Schizophrenia*. Translated by Brian Massumi. Minneapolis, MA: University of Minnesota Press, 1987.
DeLombard, Jeannine Marie. "Debunking Dehumanization." *American Literary History* 30, no. 4 (November 2018): 799–810. https://doi.org/10.1093/alh/ajy038.
DeLombard, Jeannine Marie. "The Claims of the Humanitarian, Legally Considered." Forum: "Abolition's Afterlives." *American Literary History* 35, no. 4 (2023): 1776–85.
de Man, Paul. *The Rhetoric of Romanticism*. New York: Columbia University Press, 1984.
Dewey, John. "The Historic Background of Corporate Legal Personality." *Yale Law Journal* 35 (1926, 1925): 655–73.
"Digest of American Cases." *American Jurist* 19 (1838).
Dinius, Marcy J. *The Camera and the Press: American Visual and Print Culture in the Age of the Daguerreotype*. Philadelphia, PA: University of Pennsylvania Press, 2012.
Dodd, Edwin Merrick. *American Business Corporations Until 1860 with Special Reference to Massachusetts*. Cambridge, MA: Harvard University Press, 1954.
Douglass, Frederick. *Narrative of the Life of Frederick Douglass, an American Slave*. In *Autobiographies*, edited by Henry Louis Gates Jr. New York: Library of America, 1994.
Downes, Paul. *Hobbes, Sovereignty, and Early American Literature*. New York: Cambridge University Press, 2015.
Doyle, Laura. "Inter-Imperiality and Literary Studies in the Longer 'Durée.'" *PMLA* 130, no. 2 (2015): 336–47.
Doyle, Laura. "Inter-Imperiality: Dialectics in a Postcolonial World History." *Interventions* 16, no. 2 (March 2014): 159–96. https://doi.org/10.1080/1369801X.2013.776244.

Easterbrook, Frank H., and Daniel R. Fischel. "The Corporate Contract." *Columbia Law Review* 89 (1989): 1416–48.

Eaton, Amasa Mason. *The First Book in English on the Law of Incorporation*. New Haven, CT: Ryder's Printing House, 1903.

Edelman, Lee. *No Future: Queer Theory and the Death Drive*. Durham, NC: Duke University Press, 2004.

Egan, Hugh. "The Second-Hand Wilderness: History and Art in Irving's *Astoria*." *ATQ* 2 (1988): 253–70.

Elmer, Jonathan. *Reading at the Social Limit: Affect, Mass Culture, & Edgar Allan Poe*. Stanford, CA: Stanford University Press, 1995.

Emerson, Ralph Waldo. *Essays and Lectures*, edited by Joel Porte. New York: Library of America, 1983.

Emerson, Ralph Waldo. "Self-Reliance." In *Essays and Lectures*, edited by Joel Porte. New York: Library of America, 1983.

Empson, William. *The Structure of Complex Words*. London: Chatto and Windus, 1951.

"Erratum in Angell and Ames on Corporations." *American Jurist and Law Magazine* 11 (1834): 263.

Everett, Edward. Review of *Astoria, or Anecdotes of an Enterprise beyond the Rocky Mountains*, by Washington Irving. *North American Review* 44 (1837).

Farr, James. "From Moral Philosophy to Political Science: Lieber and the Innovations of Antebellum Political Thought." In *Francis Lieber and the Culture of the Mind*, edited by Charles R. Mack and Henry H. Lesesne, 113–26. Columbia: University of South Carolina Press, 2005.

Farrar, Timothy. *Report of the Case of the Trustees of Dartmouth College against William H. Woodward. Argued and Determined in the Superior Court of Judicature of the State of New-Hampshire, November 1817. And on Error in the Supreme Court of the United States, February 1819*. Portsmouth, NH: John W. Foster, 1819.

Ferguson, Robert A. *Law and Letters in American Culture*. Cambridge, MA.: Harvard University Press, 1984.

Ferguson, Robert A. *The American Enlightenment, 1750–1820*. Cambridge, MA.: Harvard University Press, 1997.

Field, Jonathan Beecher. *Town Hall Meetings and the Death of Deliberation*. Minneapolis, MA: University of Minnesota Press, 2019.

Fourier, Charles. *The Utopian Vision of Charles Fourier: Selected Texts on Work, Love and Passionate Attraction*, edited by Jonathan Beecher and Richard Bienvnenu. Boston: Beacon, 1971.

Foust, Clement E. *The Life and Dramatic Works of Robert Montgomery Bird*. New York: Knickerbocker Press, 1919.

Franchere, Gabriel. *Narrative of a Voyage to the Northwest Coast of America in the Years 1811, 1812, 1813, and 1814, or the First American Settlement on the Pacific*. Translated by J. V. Huntington. New York: Redfield, 1854.

Francis, Richard. *Transcendental Utopias: Individual and Community at Brook Farm, Fruitlands, and Walden*. Ithaca, NY: Cornell University Press, 2007.

Frank, Jason. *Constituent Moments: Enacting the People in Postrevolutionary America*. Durham, NC: Duke University Press, 2010.

Freidel, Frank. *Francis Lieber, Nineteenth-Century Liberal*. Baton Rouge, LA: Louisiana State University Press, 1947.

Freidel, Frank. "Lieber's Contribution to the International Copyright Movement." *Huntington Library Quarterly* 8, no. 2 (1945): 200–6.

Frothingham, Octavius Brooks. *George Ripley*. Boston: Houghton, 1888.

Frug, Gerald E. *City Making: Building Communities without Building Walls*. Princeton, NJ: Princeton University Press, 1999.

Fuller, Lon. "Legal Fictions." *Illinois Law Review* 25 (1930): 363–99.

Gale, Robert L. *A Herman Melville Encyclopedia.* Westport, CT: Greenwood, 1995.
Galliher, John F., Larry W. Koch, David Patrick Keys, and Teresa J. Guess. *America Without the Death Penalty: States Leading the Way.* Hanover, NH: Northeastern University Press/ University Press of New England, 2002.
Gibson, James J. *The Ecological Approach to Visual Perception.* Boston: Houghton, 1979.
Gierke, Otto. *Political Theories of the Middle Age.* Translated by Frederic Maitland. Boston: Beacon, 1958.
Giles, Paul. "The Deterritorialization of American Literature." In *Shades of the Planet: American Literature as World Literature,* edited by Wai Chee Dimock and Lawrence Buell. Princeton, NJ: Princeton University Press, 2007.
Goddu, Teresa A. *Gothic America: Narrative, History, and Nation.* New York: Columbia University Press, 1997.
Goddu, Teresa A. *Selling Antislavery: Abolition and Mass Media in Antebellum America.* Philadelphia, PA: University of Pennsylvania Press, 2020.
Goeman, Mishuana. "Land as Life: Unsettling the Logics of Containment." In *Native Studies Keywords,* edited by Stephanie Nohelani Teves, Andrea Smith, and Michelle H. Raheja. Tucson, AZ: University of Arizona Press, 2015.
Gohdes, Clarence L. *The Periodicals of American Transcendentalism.* Durham, NC: Duke University Press, 1931.
Gordon, Sarah Barringer. "The African Supplement: Religion, Race, and Corporate Law in Early National America." *The William and Mary Quarterly* 72, no. 3 (2015): 385–422.
Graham, Howard Jay. *Everyman's Constitution: Historical Essays on the Fourteenth Amendment, the "Conspiracy Theory," and American Constitutionalism.* Madison, WI: Wisconsin Historical Society, 2013.
Green, James N. "The Rise of Book Publishing." In *The History of the Book in America. Volume 2: An Extensive Republic: Print, Culture, and Society in the New Nation, 1790–1840,* edited by Robert A. Gross and Mary Kelley. Chapel Hill, NC: University of North Carolina Press, 2010.
Greene, Jody, and Sharif Youssef. *Human Rights after Corporate Personhood: An Uneasy Merger.* Toronto: University of Toronto Press, 2020.
Greiman, Jennifer. *Democracy's Spectacle: Sovereignty and Public Life in Antebellum American Writing.* New York: Fordham University Press, 2011.
Greiman, Jennifer. "Theatricality, Strangeness, and the Aesthetics of Plurality in The Confidence-Man." In *Melville and Aesthetics,* edited by Samuel Otter and Geoffrey Sanborn. New York: Palgrave, 2011.
Guarneri, Carl J. *The Utopian Alternative: Fourierism in Nineteenth-Century America.* Ithaca, NY: Cornell University Press, 1991.
Gutjahr, Paul C. *An American Bible: A History of the Good Book in the United States, 1777–1880.* Stanford, CA: Stanford University Press, 1999.
Halbertal, Moshe, and Avishai Margalit. *Idolatry.* Translated by Naomi Goldblum. Cambridge, MA: Harvard University Press, 1992.
Hall, Peter Dobkin. "Religion and the Organizational Revolution in the United States." In *Sacred Companies: Organizational Aspects of Religion and Religious Aspects of Organizations,* edited by N. J. Demerath III, Peter Dobkin Hall, Terry Schmitt, and Rhys H. Williams. New York: Oxford University Press, 1998.
Hämäläinen, Pekka. *The Comanche Empire.* New Haven, CT: Yale University Press, 2008.
Hamilton, Alexander. "Opinion on the Constitutionality of an Act to Establish a Bank (1791)." In *The Papers of Alexander Hamilton Digital Edition.* Charlottesville, VA: University of Virginia Press, 2011. http://rotunda.upress.virginia.edu/founders/ARHN-01-08-02-0060-0003.
Hammond, Bray. *Banks and Politics in America from the Revolution to the Civil War.* Princeton, NJ: Princeton University Press, 1991.
Handlin, Oscar, and Mary F. Handlin. "Origins of the American Business Corporation." *The Journal of Economic History* 5, no. 1 (1945): 1–23.
Harding, Brian. "Washington Irving's Great Enterprise: Exploring American Values in the Western Writings." In *Making America/Making American Literature: Franklin to Cooper,* edited by A. Robert Lee and W. M. Verhoeven. Amsterdam: Rodopi, 1996.

Hardt, Michael, and Antonio Negri. *Empire*. Cambridge, MA: Harvard University Press, 2000.

Harper, Douglas. "Slavery in New Jersey." 2003. Slavery in the North. http://www.slavenorth.com/newjersey.htm.

Hawthorne, Nathaniel. *The Blithedale Romance*. Edited by Annette Kolodny. East Rutherford, NJ: Penguin, 1983.

Hawthorne, Nathaniel. *The House of the Seven Gables*. Edited by Milton R. Stern. New York: Penguin, 1981.

Hawthorne, Nathaniel. *The Scarlet Letter and Other Writings*. Edited by Leland S. Person. New York: Norton, 2017.

Henshaw, David. *Remarks upon the Rights and Powers of Corporations, and the Rights, Powers, and Duties of the Legislature toward Them. Embracing a Review of the Opinion of the Supreme Court of the United States, in the Case of Dartmouth College, in New Hampshire, Given in 1819*. Boston: Beals and Greene, 1837.

Hilt, Eric. "Early American Corporations and the State." In *Corporations and American Democracy*, edited by Naomi R. Lamoreaux and William J. Novak. Cambridge, MA: Harvard University Press, 2017.

Hobbes, Thomas. *Leviathan* (1651). Edited by Richard Flathman and David Johnston. New York: Norton, 1996.

Horwitz, Morton J. *The Transformation of American Law, 1780–1860*. Cambridge, MA: Harvard University Press, 1977.

Horwitz, Morton J. *The Transformation of American Law, 1870–1960: The Crisis of Legal Orthodoxy*. New York: Oxford University Press, 1994.

Hume, David. *A Treatise of Human Nature* (1739). Edited by Ernest C. Mossner. London: Penguin, 1969.

Hurst, James Willard. *The Legitimacy of the Business Corporation in the Law of the United States, 1780–1970*. Charlottesville, VA: University Press of Virginia, 1970.

Ingersoll, Charles J. "Speech of Charles J. Ingersoll, Esq., in the Convention of Pennsylvania, on Legislative and Judicial Control over Charters of Incorporation." *Democratic Review* 5, no. 13 (1839): 97–144.

Irving, Pierre Munro. *The Life and Letters of Washington Irving*. New York: Putnam, 1862.

Irving, Washington. *A History of the Life and Voyages of Christopher Columbus*. New York: G. & C. Carvill, 1828.

Irving, Washington. *Astoria: Or Anecdotes of an Enterprize beyond the Rocky Mountains*. In *Three Western Novels*, edited by James P. Ronda. New York: Library of America, 2004.

Irving, Washington. "The Empire of the West (1840)." In *Miscellaneous Writings, 1803–1859, Vol. 2: Prose Writings, 1829–1855*, edited by Wayne R. Kime. Boston: Twayne, 1981.

Irving, Washington. *Voyages and Discoveries of the Companions of Columbus*. Philadelphia, PA: Carey & Lea, 1831.

Jackson, David T. "Poe's Knowledge of Law During the Messenger Period: Some Comments on Chapter II of Margaret Alterton's Origins of Poe's Critical Theory." *American Literature* 10, no. 3 (1938): 331–39.

Jackson, Holly. *American Radicals: How Nineteenth-Century Protest Shaped the Nation*. New York: Crown, 2019.

Jacobs, Harriet. *Incidents in the Life of a Slave Girl: Written by Herself*. Edited by Nell Irvin Painter. East Rutherford, NJ: Penguin Classics, 2000.

Jefferson, Thomas. *The Writings of Thomas Jefferson*. Edited by Paul Leicester Ford. New York: Putnam, 1892.

Jefferson, Thomas. *Notes on the State of Virginia*. Edited by William Harwood Peden. Chapel Hill, NC: University of North Carolina Press, 1995.

Johnson, Barbara. *Persons and Things*. Cambridge, MA: Harvard University Press, 2010.

Johnson, Eldon L. "The Dartmouth College Case: The Neglected Educational Meaning." *Journal of the Early Republic* 3, no. 1 (1983): 45–67.

Johnson, Walter. *River of Dark Dreams: Slavery and Empire in the Cotton Kingdom*. Cambridge, MA: Harvard University Press, 2013.

Jones, Gavin. "Poor Poe: On the Literature of Revulsion." *American Literary History* 23, no. 1 (2011): 1–18.

Jones, Samuel. *A Treatise on the Right of Suffrage, with an Appendix*. Boston: Otis, Broaders, and Company, 1842.

Kamuf, Peggy. *The Division of Literature: Or the University in Deconstruction*. Chicago: University of Chicago Press, 1997.

Kantorowicz, Ernst H. *The King's Two Bodies*. Princeton, NJ: Princeton University Press, 1997.

Kaplan, Amy. *The Anarchy of Empire in the Making of U.S. Culture*. Cambridge, MA: Harvard University Press, 2002.

Kaplan, Amy, and Donald E. Pease, eds. *Cultures of United States Imperialism*. Durham, NC: Duke University Press, 1993.

Kaser, David. *Messrs. Carey and Lea of Philadelphia: A Study in the History of the Booktrade*. Philadelphia, PA: University of Pennsylvania Press, 1957.

Kaufman-Osborn, Timothy V. *The Autocratic Academy: Reenvisioning Rule within America's Universities*. Durham, NC: Duke University Press, 2023.

Kennedy, J. Gerald, and Lilliane Weissberg. *Romancing the Shadow: Poe and Race*. Oxford: Oxford University Press, 2001.

Kennedy, John Pendleton. *Strictures on the Letter of Charles J. Ingersoll, Esq. Touching the Right of a Legislature to Repeal a Charter. With an Appendix, Containing the Letters of Mr. Ingersoll, of Mrs. Dallas, of Mr. Forward, and of Mr. Biddle, in Illustration of the Subject Discussed. By a Citizen of Maryland*. Baltimore, MD: Joseph Neal, 1836.

Kent, James. *Commentaries on American Law*. New York: O. Halsted, 1826.

Kime, Wayne R. "The Author as Professional: Washington Irving's 'Rambling Anecdotes' of the West." In *Critical Essays on Washington Irving*, edited by Ralph M. Aderman. Boston: G. K. Hall, 1990.

Kime, Wayne R. "Washington Irving's Revision of the *Tonquin* Episode in *Astoria*." *Western American Literature* 4, no. 1 (1969): 51–59.

Kornbluh, Anna. *Realizing Capital: Financial and Psychic Economies in Victorian Form*. New York: Fordham University Press, 2014.

Kornbluh, Anna. *The Order of Forms: Realism, Formalism, and Social Space*. Chicago: University of Chicago Press, 2019.

Kornhauser, Lewis A. "The Nexus of Contracts Approach to Corporations: A Comment on Easterbrook and Fischel." *Columbia Law Review* 89 (1989): 1449–60.

Kramnick, Jonathan, and Anahid Nersessian. "Form and Explanation." *Critical Inquiry* 43, no. 3 (March 2017): 650–69. https://doi.org/10.1086/691017.

Kutler, Stanley I. *Privilege and Creative Destruction: The Charles River Bridge Case*. Baltimore, MD: Johns Hopkins University Press, 1989.

Kyd, Stewart. *A Treatise on the Law of Corporations*. London: Printed for J. Butterworth, 1793.

Lamoreaux, Naomi R., and William J. Novak, eds. *Corporations and American Democracy*. Cambridge, MA: Harvard University Press, 2017.

Lamoreaux, Naomi R., and Novak, William J. "Corporations and American Democracy: An Introduction." In *Corporations and American Democracy*, edited by Naomi R. Lamoreaux and William J. Novak. Cambridge, MA: Harvard University Press, 2017.

Lang, Hans-Joachim, and Benjamin Lease. "Melville's Cosmopolitan: Bayard Taylor in The Confidence-Man." *Amerikastudien/American Studies*, 1977. https://doi.org/10.1007/978-3-476-99996-2_5.

Laski, Harold J. "The Personality of Associations." *Harvard Law Review* 29 (1916): 404–26.

Latour, Bruno. *Reassembling the Social: An Introduction to Actor-Network Theory*. Oxford: Oxford University Press, 2005.

"Law of Corporations." *United States Law Journal* 1 (1822): 294–95.

LeMenager, Stephanie. *Living Oil: Petroleum Culture in the American Century*. New York: Oxford University Press, 2014.

LeMenager, Stephanie. "Trading Stories: Washington Irving and the Global West." *American Literary History* 15, no. 4 (2003): 683–708.

Lepore, Jill. "The Humbug: Edgar Allan Poe and the Economy of Horror." *The New Yorker*, April 27, 2009. http://www.newyorker.com/arts/critics/atlarge/2009/04/27/090427crat_atlarge_lepore.
Levin, David. *History as Romantic Art: Bancroft, Prescott, Motley, and Parkman*. Stanford, CA: Stanford University Press, 1959.
Levine, Caroline. *Forms: Whole, Rhythm, Hierarchy, Network*. Princeton, NJ: Princeton University Press, 2015.
Lieber, Francis. "A Reminiscence." *Southern Literary Messenger* 2, no. 9 (August 1836): 535–38.
[Lieber, Francis]. "Corporation." In *Encyclopaedia Americana*, edited by Francis Lieber and Edward Wigglesworth. Philadelphia, PA: Carey & Lea, 1830.
[Lieber, Francis]. *Legal and Political Hermeneutics*. Boston: Little, Brown, 1839.
[Lieber, Francis]. *Letters to a Gentleman in Germany: Written After a Trip from Philadelphia to Niagara*. Ann Arbor, MN and Philadelphia, PA: With University of Michigan. Carey, Lea & Blanchard, 1834. http://archive.org/details/letterstoagentl00liebgoog.
[Lieber, Francis]. Review of *A Treatise on Gymnastics, Taken Chiefly from the German of F. L. Jahn*. *American Quarterly Review* 3 (1828): 126–50.
Lieber, Francis. *A Constitution and Plan of Education for Girard College for Orphans, with an Introductory Report, Laid before the Board of Trustees*. Philadelphia, PA: Carey, Lea and Blanchard, 1834.
Lieber, Francis. *Manual of Political Ethics: Designed Chiefly for the Use of Colleges and Students at Law*. Boston: Little, Brown, 1838.
Lieber, Francis. *The Life and Letters of Francis Lieber*. Edited by Thomas Sergeant Perry. Boston: J.R. Osgood and Co., 1882.
Lieber, Francis. *The Miscellaneous Writings of Francis Lieber*. Edited by Daniel C. Gilman. Philadelphia, PA: Lippincott, 1881.
Lieber, Francis, and Edward Wigglesworth. eds. *Encyclopaedia Americana*. Philadelphia, PA: Carey & Lea, 1829–33.
"Lieber's Political Ethics." *Boston Quarterly Review* 2 (1839).
Lilley, James D. *Common Things: Romance and the Aesthetics of Belonging in Atlantic Modernity*. New York: Fordham University Press, 2014.
Lipartito, Kenneth. "The Utopian Corporation." In *Constructing Corporate America: History, Politics, Culture*, edited by Kenneth Lipartito and David B. Sicilia. Oxford: Oxford University Press, 2004.
Locke, John. *An Essay Concerning Human Understanding* (1689). Edited by Roger Woolhouse. London: Penguin, 1997.
Locke, John. *Second Treatise of Government*. Edited by Richard H. Cox. Arlington Heights, IL: Harlan Davidson, 1982.
Luther, Seth. *An Address on the Origin and Progress of Avarice, and Its Deleterious Effects on Human Happiness, with a Proposed Remedy for the Countless Evils Resulting from an Inordinate Desire for Wealth. Delivered before the Union Association of Working Men, in the Town Hall, Charlestown, Mass., January 30, 1834*. Boston: Published by the Author, 1834.
Luther, Seth. *An Address to the Working Men of New England, on the State of Education, and on the Condition of the Producing Classes in Europe and America. With Particular Reference to the Effect of Manufacturing (as Now Conducted) on the Health and Happiness of the Poor, and on the Safety of Our Republic. Delivered in Boston, Charlestown, Cambridgeport, Waltham, Dorchester, Mass., Portland, Saco, Me., and Dover, N.H.* 2nd ed. New York: Published at the Office of the Working Man's Advocate, by George H. Evans, 1833.
Lutz, Rolland Ray. "The German Revolutionary Student Movement, 1819–1833." *Central European History* 4 (1971): 215–41.
Lutz, Rolland Ray. "'Turnvater' Jahn and His Teacher-Revolutionaries from the German Student Movement." *Journal of Modern History* 48, no. 2 (On-Demand Supplement) (1976): 7–8.
Machen, Arthur W. "Corporate Personality." *Harvard Law Review* 24, no. 4 (1911): 253–67. https://doi.org/10.2307/1324056.
Mack, Charles R., and Henry H. Lesesne, eds. *Francis Lieber and The Culture of the Mind*. Columbia, SC: University of South Carolina Press, 2005.

MacLaren, I. S. "Washington Irving's Problems with History and Romance in Astoria." *Canadian Review of American Studies* 21, no. 1 (1990).

Maine: Legislature. Committee on Capital Punishment. *Fifteenth Legislature. No. 25. House. Report of the Committee to Whom Was Referred the Several Memorials and Petitions for the Abolition of Capital Punishment.* [Augusta, ME]: Wm. J. Condon, 1835.

Maitland, Frederic William. *State, Trust, and Corporation.* Edited by David Runciman and Magnus Ryan. Cambridge: Cambridge University Press, 2003.

Majewski, John. *A House Dividing: Economic Development in Pennsylvania and Virginia Before the Civil War.* Cambridge: Cambridge University Press, 2000.

Majewski, John. "Toward a Social History of the Corporation: Shareholding in Pennsylvania, 1800-1840." In *The Economy of Early America: Historical Perspectives and New Directions*, edited by Cathy Matson. University Park, PA: Pennsylvania State University Press, 2006.

Malone, Christopher. *Between Freedom and Bondage: Race, Party, and Voting Rights in the Antebellum North.* New York: Routledge, 2008.

Mantell, Gideon. *The Wonders of Geology: Or, A Familiar Exposition of Geological Phenomena.* London: Relfe and Fletcher, 1838.

"Manufacturing Corporations." *American Jurist and Law Magazine* 2 (1829): 92–118.

Mark, Gregory. "The Personification of the Business Corporation in American Law." *University of Chicago Law Review* 54, no. 4 (September 1987). https://chicagounbound.uchicago.edu/uclrev/vol54/iss4/9.

Matthiessen, Francis Otto. *American Renaissance: Art and Expression in the Age of Emerson and Whitman.* Oxford: Oxford University Press, 1941.

McGann, Jerome. "Washington Irving, A History of New York, and American History." *Early American Literature* 47, no. 2 (2012): 349–76.

McGill, Meredith L. *American Literature and the Culture of Reprinting, 1834–1853.* Philadelphia, PA: University of Pennsylvania Press, 2013.

McLaughlin, Kevin. *Paperwork: Fiction and Mass Mediacy in the Paper Age.* Philadelphia, PA: University of Pennsylvania Press, 2005.

McManus, Edgar J. *Black Bondage in the North.* Syracuse, NY: Syracuse University Press, 1973.

Melville, Herman. *Moby-Dick* (1851). Edited by Hershel Parker and Harrison Hayford. New York: Norton, 2002.

Melville, Herman. *The Confidence-Man: His Masquerade* (1857). Edited by Harrison Hayford, Hershel Parker, and G. Thomas Tanselle. Evanston, IL: Northwestern University Press, 1984.

Memorial of the Free Citizens of Color in Pittsburg and Its Vicinity Relative to the Right of Suffrage: Read in Convention July 8, 1837. Harrisburg, PA: Thompson and Clark, 1837.

Merk, Frederick. *The Oregon Question: Essays in Anglo-American Diplomacy and Politics.* Cambridge, MA: Harvard University Press, 1967.

Michaels, Walter Benn. *The Gold Standard and the Logic of Naturalism: American Literature at the Turn of the Century.* Berkeley, CA: University of California Press, 1987.

Milton, John. *Complete Poems and Major Prose.* Edited by Merritt Yerkes Hughes. Upper Saddle River, NJ: Prentice Hall, 1957.

Modern, John Lardas. *Secularism in Antebellum America.* Chicago: University of Chicago Press, 2011.

Moore, Thomas. *Irish Melodies.* Philadelphia, PA: Carey, 1815.

Morawetz, Victor. *A Treatise on the Law of Private Corporations Other than Charitable.* Boston: Little, Brown, 1882.

Mueller, Stefanie. *The Corporation in the Nineteenth-Century American Imagination.* Edinburgh: Edinburgh University Press, 2024.

Muñoz, José Esteban. *Cruising Utopia: The Then and There of Queer Futurity.* New York: New York University Press, 2009.

Murison, Justine S. *The Politics of Anxiety in Nineteenth-Century American Literature.* Cambridge: Cambridge University Press, 2011.

Mussawir, Edward, and Connal and Parsley. "The Law of Persons Today: At the Margins of Jurisprudence." *Law and Humanities* 11, no. 1 (January 2017): 44–63. https://doi.org/10.1080/17521483.2017.1320041.

Nancy, Jean-Luc. "Of Being-in-Common," In *Community at Loose Ends*, translated by James Creech and the Miami Theory Collective. Minneapolis, MA: University Of Minnesota Press, 1991.

Nancy, Jean-Luc. *The Inoperative Community*. Edited by Peter Connor. Translated by Peter Connor, Lisa Garbus, Michael Holland, and Simona Sawhney. Minneapolis, MN: University Of Minnesota Press, 1991.

Newfield, Christopher. *The Emerson Effect: Individualism and Submission in America*. Chicago: University of Chicago Press, 1996.

Newmyer, R. Kent. *John Marshall and the Heroic Age of the Supreme Court*. Southern Biography Series. Baton Rouge, LA: Louisiana State University Press, 2001.

Newmyer, R. Kent. *Supreme Court Justice Joseph Story: Statesman of the Old Republic*. Chapel Hill, NC: University of North Carolina Press, 2010.

New Zealand Legislation. Te Awa Tupua (Whanganui River Claims Settlement) Act (2017).

Ngai, Sianne. *Ugly Feelings*. Cambridge, MA: Harvard University Press, 2007.

Nietzsche, Friedrich. *Untimely Meditations* (1873–76). Translated by R. J. Hollingdale. Cambridge: Cambridge University Press, 1997.

Noble, Mark. "Reading Melville Reading Character." *J19: The Journal of Nineteenth-Century Americanists* 4, no. 2 (2016): 237–47.

Nord, David Paul. "Benevolent Books: Printing, Religion, and Reform." In *The History of the Book in America. Volume 2: An Extensive Republic: Print, Culture, and Society in the New Nation, 1790–1840*, edited by Robert A. Gross and Mary Kelley. Chapel Hill, NC: University of North Carolina Press, 2010.

Nord, David Paul. *Faith in Reading: Religious Publishing and the Birth of Mass Media in America*. New York and Oxford: Oxford University Press, 2004.

Novick, Peter. *That Noble Dream: The "Objectivity Question" and the American Historical Profession*. Cambridge: Cambridge University Press, 1988.

Nys, Ernest. "Francis Lieber: His Life and His Works, Part 1." *The American Journal of International Law* 5, no. 1 (1911): 84–117.

O'Brien, Jean M. *Firsting and Lasting: Writing Indians out of Existence in New England*. Minneapolis, MN: University of Minnesota Press, 2010.

O'Brien, John. *Literature Incorporated: The Cultural Unconscious of the Business Corporation, 1650–1850*. Chicago: University of Chicago Press, 2015.

Oergel, Maike. "Constitutionalism and Cultural Identity as Radical Concepts in German Political Radicalism 1806–1819: The Case of Karl Follen." *Comparative Critical Studies* 15, no. 2 (2018): 183–205.

Ogborn, Miles. *Indian Ink: Script and Print in the Making of the English East India Company*. Chicago: University of Chicago Press, 2007.

Osman, Jena. *Corporate Relations*. Providence, RI: Burning Deck/Aynart, 2014.

Otter, Samuel. *Philadelphia Stories: America's Literature of Race and Freedom*. Oxford: Oxford University Press, 2010.

Padfield, Stefan. "Killing Corporations to Save Humans: How Corporate Personhood, Human Rights, and the Corporate Death Penalty Intersect." In *Human Rights after Corporate Personhood: An Uneasy Merger*, edited by Jody Greene and Sharif Youssef. Toronto: University of Toronto Press, 2020.

Paley, William. *Treatise on the Law of Principal and Agent*. Exeter, NH, 1822.

Parker, Ashley. "'Corporations Are People,' Romney Tells Iowa Hecklers Angry Over His Tax Policy." *The New York Times*, August 12, 2011. https://www.nytimes.com/2011/08/12/us/politics/12romney.html.

Paxson, James J. *The Poetics of Personification*. Cambridge: Cambridge University Press, 1994.

"Personal Responsibility of the Members of an Incorporated Company for the Debts of the Company." *United States Law Intelligencer and Review* 2 (1830): 212.

Phan, Hoang Gia. *Bonds of Citizenship: Law and the Labors of Emancipation*. New York: New York University Press, 2013.

Phillips, Michael J. "Reappraising the Real Entity Theory of the Corporation." *Florida State University Law Review* 21 (1994): 1061.

Poe, Edgar Allan. *Collected Works of Edgar Allan Poe*. Edited by Thomas Ollive Mabbott. Cambridge, MA: Harvard University Press, 1969.

Poe, Edgar Allan. "Peter Pendulum, the Business Man." *Burton's Gentleman's Magazine* 6, no. 2 (1840): 87–89.

Poe, Edgar Allan. "Silence. A Sonnet." *Burton's Gentleman's Magazine* 6, no. 4 (1840): 166.

Poovey, Mary. *Genres of the Credit Economy: Mediating Value in Eighteenth- and Nineteenth-Century Britain*. Chicago: University of Chicago Press, 2008.

Porter, James Madison. *Speech of James Madison Porter, of Northampton, in the Convention of Pennsylvania, on the Subject of the Right to Annul Charters of Incorporation. Delivered November 20, 1837*. Philadelphia, PA: Peter Hay & Co., 1837.

Porter, Kenneth Wiggins. *John Jacob Astor: Business Man*. Cambridge, MA: Harvard University Press, 1931.

Porteus, Beilby. *An Address to Christians, Recommending the Distribution of Cheap Religious Tracts: With an Extract from a Sermon by Bishop Porteus...* Charlestown, MA: Samuel Etheridge, 1802.

Posner, Richard A. *The Problems of Jurisprudence*. Cambridge, MA: Harvard University Press, 1993.

Poynder, John. *Literary Extracts from English and Other Works; Collected during Half a Century: Together with Some Original Matter*. London: J. Hatchard, 1844.

Pratt, Mary Louise. "Language and the Afterlives of Empire." *PMLA* 130, no. 2 (2015): 348–57.

Proceedings and Debates of the Convention of the Commonwealth of Pennsylvania to Propose Amendments to the Constitution, Commenced and Held at Harrisburg on the Second Day of May, 1837. Reported by John Agg, Stenographer to the Convention, Assisted by Messrs. Wheeler, Kingman, Drake, and M'Kinley. Harrisburg, PA: Packer, Barrett, and Parke, 1837–38.

Purrington, T. *Report on Capital Punishment, Made to the Maine Legislature in 1836, by Hon. T. Purrington*. 3rd ed. Washington, WA: Gideon & Co., 1852.

Purvis, Robert. *Appeal of Forty Thousand Citizens, Threatened with Disenfranchisement, to the People of Pennsylvania*. Philadelphia, PA: Printed by Merihew and Gunn, 1838.

Ratcliffe, Susan, ed. *Oxford Essential Quotations*. Oxford: Oxford University Press, 2016. https://www.oxfordreference.com/display/10.1093/acref/9780191826719.001.0001/acref-9780191826719.

Rattner, Ashley. "'No Such Faery Land, So Like the Real World': Miles Coverdale's Performance of the Utopian Spectacle." *Nathaniel Hawthorne Review* 47, no. 2 (2021): 231–49.

"Review of Astoria; or an [sic] Enterprise beyond the Rocky Mountains by Washington Irving (London: Bentley, 1837)." *London and Westminster Review* 26 (1837).

Ricardo, David. *Minor Papers on the Currency Question, 1809–1823*. Baltimore, |MD: Johns Hopkins University Press, 1932.

Ripken, Susanna Kim. *Corporate Personhood*. Cambridge: Cambridge University Press, 2019.

Robins, Nick. *The Corporation That Changed the World: How the East India Company Shaped the Modern Multinational*. London: Pluto Press, 2012.

Rogin, Michael. *Subversive Genealogy: The Politics and Art of Herman Melville*. Berkeley, CA: University of California Press, 1985.

Romano, Roberta, ed. *Foundations of Corporate Law*. New York: Oxford University Press, 1993.

Ronda, James P. *Astoria and Empire*. Lincoln, NE: University of Nebraska Press, 1990.

Rosenheim, Shawn, and Stephen Rachman. *The American Face of Edgar Allan Poe*. Baltimore, MD: Johns Hopkins University Press, 1995.

Ross, Alexander. *Adventures of the First Setters on the Oregon or Columbia River: Being a Narrative of the Expedition Fitted out by John Jacob Astor, to Establish the "Pacific Fur Company;" with an Account of Some Indian Tribes on the Coast of the Pacific*. London: Smith, Elder and Co., 1849.

Rothbard, Murray N. *The Panic of 1819: Reactions and Policies*. Auburn: Ludwig von Mises Institute, 2007.

Rowe, John Carlos. "Edgar Allan Poe's Imperial Fantasy and the American Frontier." In *Romancing the Shadow: Poe and Race*, edited by J. Gerald Kennedy and Liliane Weissberg, 75–105. Oxford: Oxford University Press, 2001.

Roylance, Patricia Jane. *Eclipse of Empires: World History in Nineteenth-Century U.S. Literature and Culture*. Tuscaloosa, AL: University of Alabama Press, 2013.

Runciman, David. *Pluralism and the Personality of the State*. Cambridge: Cambridge University Press, 1997.

Samson, Steven Alan. "Francis Lieber: Transatlantic Cultural Missionary." In *Francis Lieber and the Culture of the Mind*, edited by Charles R. Mack and Henry H. Lesesne. Columbia, SC: University of South Carolina Press, 2005.

Sedgwick, Theodore. *What Is a Monopoly? Or, Some Considerations upon the Subject of Corporations and Currency*. New York: Printed by G. P. Scott, 1835.

Sellers, Charles. *The Market Revolution: Jacksonian America, 1815–1846*. New York: Oxford University Press, 1991.

Shakespeare, William. *The Norton Shakespeare: Based on the Oxford Edition*. Edited by Stephen Greenblatt, Walter Cohen, Jean E. Howard, and Katharine Eisaman Maus. New York: Norton, 1997.

Shell, Marc. *Money, Language, and Thought: Literary and Philosophic Economies from the Medieval to the Modern Era*. Baltimore, MD: Johns Hopkins University Press, 1993.

Siraganian, Lisa. *Modernism and the Meaning of Corporate Persons*. Oxford: Oxford University Press, 2020.

Sklansky, Jeffrey. "A Bank on Parnassus." *Common-Place* 6, no. 3 (2006). https://commonplace.online/article/sklansky/.

Soifer, Aviam. "Facts, Things, and the Orphans of Girard College: Francis Lieber, Protopragmatist." *Cardozo Law Review* 16 (1995): 2305–19.

Sokolow, Jayme A. *The North American Phalanx (1843–1855): A Nineteenth-Century Utopian Community*. Lewiston, NY: Edwin Mellen Press, 2009.

Spaulding, K. A. "A Note on *Astoria*: Irving's Use of the Robert Stuart Manuscript." *American Literature* 22, no. 2 (1950): 150–57.

Stein, Jordan Alexander. "The Whig Interpretation of Media: Sheppard Lee and Jacksonian Paperwork." *History of the Present* 3, no. 1 (2013): 29–56.

Stern, Philip J. *Empire, Incorporated: The Corporations That Built British Colonialism*. Cambridge, MA: Harvard University Press, 2025.

Stern, Philip J. *The Company-State: Corporate Sovereignty and the Early Modern Foundations of the British Empire in India*. Oxford: Oxford University Press, 2012.

Stern, Simon. "Legal and Literary Fictions." In *New Directions in Law and Literature*, edited by Elizabeth Anker and Bernadette Meyler. Oxford: Oxford University Press, 2017.

Story, Joseph. *Commentaries on the Law of Agency, as a Branch of Commercial and Maritime Jurisprudence, with Occasional Illustrations from the Civil and Foreign Law*. Boston: Little and Brown, 1839.

Story, Joseph. *Joseph Story And the Encyclopedia Americana*. Edited by Valerie L. Horowitz. Introduction by Morris L. Cohen. Clark, NJ The Lawbook Exchange, Ltd., 2006.

Story, Joseph. *Life and Letters of Joseph Story: Associate Justice of the Supreme Court of the United States, and Dane Professor of Law at Harvard University*. Edited by William Wetmore Story. Boston: Little and Brown, 1851.

Stout, Daniel M. *Corporate Romanticism: Liberalism, Justice, and the Novel*. New York: Fordham University Press, 2016.

Stuart, James, and Nicholas Revett. *The Antiquities of Athens*. London: Printed by John Haberkorn, 1762–1816.

Sundquist, Eric. J. "The Literature of Expansion and Race." In *The Cambridge History of American Literature*, edited by Sacvan Bercovitch, Vol. 2. Cambridge: Cambridge University Press, 1995.

Swenson, Brynnar. "'From the Prostitute to the King': The Corporate Form, Subsumption, and Periodization." *Cultural Critique* 89 (2015): 61–82.

Thomas, Yan. *Legal Artifices: Ten Essays on Roman Law in the Present Tense*. Edited by Thanos Zartaloudis and Cooper Francis. Translated by Chantal Jaquet, Anton Schütz, and Chantal Schütz. Introduction by Thanos Zartaloudis and Anton Schütz. Afterword by Alain Pottage. Edinburgh: Edinburgh University Press, 2021.

Thoreau, Henry David. *Walden and Civil Disobedience*. Edited by Michael Meyer. New York: Penguin, 1986.

Tocqueville, Alexis de. *Democracy in America and Two Essays on America*. Edited by Isaac Kramnick. Translated by Gerald Bevan. London: Penguin, 2003.
Trilling, Samara. "A Tale of Two Columbias: Francis Lieber, Columbia University, and Slavery" (2015). A Tale of Two Columbias: Francis Lieber, Columbia University and Slavery - Samara Trilling.
Turner, Henry S. *The Corporate Commonwealth: Pluralism and Political Fictions in England, 1516–1651*. Chicago: University of Chicago Press, 2016.
Wahrman, Dror. *The Making of the Modern Self: Identity and Culture in Eighteenth-Century England*. New Haven, CT: Yale University Press, 2004.
Watson, David. "Lawless Intervals: Washington Irving's Astoria and the Procession of Empire." *American Studies in Scandinavia* 42, no. 1 (2010): 5–24.
Weber, Samuel. *Benjamin's -Abilities*. Cambridge, MA: Harvard University Press, 2010.
Weisbrod, Carol. *The Boundaries of Utopia*. New York: Pantheon, 1980.
Weiss, Gerhard. "The Americanization of Franz Lieber." In *German Culture in Nineteenth-Century America: Reception, Adaptation, Transformation*, edited by Lynne Tatlock and Matt Erlin. Rochester, NY: Camden House, 2005.
Whalen, Terence. *Edgar Allan Poe and the Masses: The Political Economy of Literature in Antebellum America*. Princeton, NJ: Princeton University Press, 1999.
White, Craig. "A Utopia of 'Spheres and Sympathies': Science and Society in The Blithedale Romance and at Brook Farm." *Utopian Studies* 9, no. 2 (1998): 78–102.
White, Richard. *The Middle Ground: Indians, Empires, and Republics in the Great Lakes Region, 1650–1815*. Cambridge: Cambridge University Press, 2011.
Wilentz, Sean. *The Rise of American Democracy: Jefferson to Lincoln*. New York: Norton, 2005.
Williams, Raymond. *Keywords: A Vocabulary of Culture and Society*. New York: Oxford University Press, 1985.
Winkler, Adam. "Citizens United, Personhood, and the Corporation in Politics." In *Corporations and American Democracy*, edited by Naomi R. Lamoreaux and William J. Novak. Cambridge, MA: Harvard University Press, 2017.
Winkler, Adam. *We the Corporations: How American Businesses Won Their Civil Rights*. New York: Liveright, 2018.
Wordsworth, William. *Wordsworth's Poetry and Prose: A Norton Critical Edition*. Edited by Nicholas Halmi. New York: Norton, 2014.
Zourabichvili, Francois. *Deleuze: A Philosophy of the Event: Together with The Vocabulary of Deleuze*. Edited by Gregg Lambert and Daniel W. Smith. Translated by Kieran Aarons. Edinburgh: Edinburgh University Press, 2012.
Zwicker, Lisa Fetheringill. "The Burschenschaft and German Political Culture, 1890–1914." *Central European History* 42 (2009): 389–428.

Index

Note: Figures are indicated by an italic '*f*' following the page number.

For the benefit of digital users, indexed terms that span two pages (e.g., 52–53) may, on occasion, appear on only one of those pages.